Carmelite
Studies
VIII

CARMELITE STUDIES

CARMEL AND CONTEMPLATION

Transforming Human Consciousness

Kevin Culligan, O.C.D.
Regis Jordan, O.C.D.

Editors

ICS Publications
Institute of Carmelite Studies
Washington, DC
2000

ICS Publications
2131 Lincoln Road, Northeast
Washington, DC 20002-1199

© Washington Province of Discalced Carmelites, Inc., 2000

Typeset and produced in the United States of America

Library of Congress Cataloging-in-Publication Data

Carmel and contemplation: transforming human consciousness/ Kevin
Culligan and Regis Jordan, editors.
  p. cm.— (Carmelite Studies: 8)
  Includes bibliographical references.
  ISBN: 0-935216-63-4 (pbk.)

1. Carmelite–Spiritual Life–Congress. 2. Contemplation–History of
doctrines–Congress. I. Culligan, Kevin, 1935–; II. Jordan, Regis,
1936– Institute of Carmelite Studies (Washington, DC) III. Series.

BX3203 .C37 2000
255'.73–dc21   99-056939
                                                                 CIP

iv

Do not conform yourself to this age
but be transformed by the renewal of your mind,
that you may discern what is the will of God,
what is good and pleasing and perfect.
St. Paul
Romans 12:2

O my Sisters, what strength lies in this gift! It does nothing less, when accompanied by the necessary determination, than draw the Almighty so that He becomes one with our lowliness, transforms us into Himself, and effects a union of the Creator with the creature.
St. Teresa of Avila
The Way of Perfection 32:11

O guiding night!
O night more lovely than the dawn!
O night that has united
the Lover with his beloved,
transforming the beloved in her Lover.
St. John of the Cross
The Dark Night, stanza 5

Table of Contents

viii

Saint John of the Cross

Preface

The chapters in this volume of *Carmelite Studies* were written, with one exception, by members of the Carmelite Forum over the last ten years. A small group of men and women representing both the Ancient and Teresian observances of Carmel, the Forum came into being in 1983. Its purpose was to retrieve, through study and discussion, Carmel's rich spiritual heritage and to find avenues for sharing it with others. One such avenue has been its seminars in Carmelite history and spirituality held nearly every summer since 1984 at Saint Mary's College, Notre Dame, Indiana. Sponsored by the Center for Spirituality at Saint Mary's, and graciously hosted by the Sisters of the Holy Cross, these seminars explore the writings of major Carmelite authors as a resource for Christian life and ministry. In 1994, the topic of investigation was "Education for Contemplation." The presentations at that seminar by John Welch, Vilma Seelaus, Kevin Culligan, Ernest Larkin, Keith Egan, and Constance FitzGerald are now chapters in this book.

Although not present for the 1994 seminar at St. Mary's, Forum members Donald Buggert and Kieran Kavanaugh were active elsewhere. In 1990, Buggert presented "The Contemplative as Iconoclast" at Carmel 200, a bicentennial symposium sponsored by Baltimore Carmel examining "Contemplation and American Culture." In 1992, Kavanaugh spoke on "The Art of Prayer according to St. Teresa" at the regional congress of the Secular Order of Discalced Carmelites in Birmingham, Alabama. Both talks, touching on the nature and practice of contemplative prayer in Carmel, compliment the other papers in this volume.

The one contributor who is not a member of the Carmelite Forum is Bernard McGinn, Professor of Historical Theology and the History of Christianity at the Divinity School, University of Chicago. McGinn gave "The Role of the Carmelites in the History of Western Mysticism" as the keynote address at the inaugural meeting of the Carmelite Institute in April 1993, at Whitefriars Hall, Washington, DC. The Institute, another collaborative effort of Carmelite nuns, friars, and laity, has since become an effective vehicle for spreading Carmel's spiritual message throughout the English-speaking world. McGinn's lecture is included here because it provides an informed historical backdrop for the discussion of Carmel's distinctive approach to the contemplative life.

Originally, we intended to entitle this volume "Education for Contemplation," after the theme of the 1984 seminar at St. Mary's. However, the more we worked with the individual papers in preparing them for publication, the more we recognized human transformation as a consistent, unifying thread running throughout the pages. We thus organized the chapters around the transformation of human consciousness as a characteristic motif in the Carmelite understanding of contemplation. We then arranged them in four parts, providing first a historical overview of Carmel's spiritual journey, followed by two reflections on the nature of contemplation, and finally various studies on particular aspects of the teachings of Saint Teresa of Avila and Saint John of the Cross, Carmel's foremost expositors of the theory and practice of contemplation.

We have attempted throughout these chapters to honor the principles of inclusive language. We have, however, let many quotations from authors of earlier centuries stand as translated, believing our readers would understand that these authors were not as sensitive to inclusivity as we are today.

We give special thanks to Steven Payne, O.C.D. and Connie Fritsche for their expert editorial advice.

Finally, we thank all our contributors for allowing their talks to appear as chapters in this volume, as well as for their patience and understanding with the long delay in the publication of their contributions. We also thank the various groups that have participated in bringing these pages to print—the Carmelite Forum, the Carmelite Institute, the Institute of Carmelite Studies, and the Center for Spirituality at Saint Mary's College. This collaboration has produced an exceptional set of essays, which we believe underscores the need today for education for contemplation as we see its power to transform human consciousness.

The Editors

Acknowledgments

John Welch's two chapters in this volume appeared substantially the same as chapters in his *The Carmelite Way* published in 1996 by Paulist Press.

Donald Buggert's chapter appeared in a shorter version in the *New Theology Review* 8 (August 1995): 40-52.

The editors gratefully acknowledge extended excerpts from the following works. From *Violence Unveiled*, by Gil Bailie, 1995, Crossroad Publishing Co. From *Dream of the Earth*, by Thomas Berry. Copyright 1990 by Thomas Berry. From *Women Who Run with the Wolves*, by Clarissa Pinkola Estés. Copyright 1992 by Clarissa Pinkola Estés. From *Return to the Center*, by Bede Griffiths. Copyright 1976 by Bede Griffiths. From *The Making of a Mystic*, by Francis L. Gross and Toni Perrior Gross. Copyright 1993 by State University of New York. From *The Meaning of God in Human Experience*, by William Ernest Hocking. Copyright 1963 by Yale University Press. From C.G. *Jung: Word and Image*, ed. Aniela Jaffé, Bollingen Series XCVII:2. Copyright 1979 by Princeton University Press. From "Jesus, The Wisdom of God: A Biblical Basis for Non-Androcentric Christology," by Elizabeth A. Johnson, in *Ephemerides Theologicae Lovaniensis* 61 (1985). From *Woman, Earth, and Creator Spirit*, by Elizabeth A. Johnson. Copyright 1993 by Saint Mary's College, Notre Dame, IN. From "Redeeming the Name of Christ," by Elizabeth A. Johnson, in *Freeing Theology*, ed. Catherine Mowry LaCugna. Copyright 1993 by HarperCollins Publishers, Inc. From *Fire in the Belly*, by Sam Keen. Copyright 1991 by Sam Keen. From The *Book of Guys*, by Garrison Keillor. Copyright 1993 by Garrison Keillor. From God *for Us: The Trinity and Christian Life*, by Catherine Mowry LaCugna. Copyright 1991 by Catherine LaCugna. From *The Great Divorce*, by C. S. Lewis, 1956, The Macmillan Co. From *Thomas Berry and the New Cosmology*, ed. Anne Lonergan and Caroline Richards. Copyright 1987 by Twenty-Third Publications. From *Summa of the Christian Life*, by Louis of Granada, vol. 1, trans. Jordan Aumann. Copyright 1954 by B. Herder Book Co.

COVER

The cover depicts Teresa of Avila and John of the Cross's rapturous discussion of the mystery of the Holy Trinity in the speakroom of the Incarnation monastery in Avila, Trinity Sunday, 1573. The Italian artists Francesco Zucchi and Francesco Zugni created the woodcut for a book containing the life and writings of John of the Cross printed by Stefano Orlandini in Venice in 1748.

Introduction

Throughout its long history, Carmel's life has been contemplation. The small group of laymen in the crusader states of the Holy Land who gathered at the end of the twelfth century on Mount Carmel sought solitude as a more intense way of following Jesus Christ. They formed a community resembling that of the first Christians recorded in the early chapters of the Acts of the Apostles. Central to their way of life was contemplation—daily Eucharist, ceaseless reflection on Sacred Scripture, continual prayer, and a hunger for God. Probably without realizing it, these lay hermits were beginning a new contemplative tradition in the Church whose eventual defining features would include a longing for solitude and a desire for personal union with God.

When the continuing Saracen invasions of the Holy Land forced the hermits to leave Mount Carmel and reestablish themselves during the thirteenth century as mendicants in the cities and universities of Europe, they took their eremitical spirit with them. Survival now demanded their involvement with God's people as preachers, teachers, and ministers of the sacraments; yet, they could never forget that they were primarily contemplatives. For the next two centuries, they struggled to balance the pastoral challenges of mendicant life with their desert origins. They looked to Elijah, the Old Testament prophet, as a model of zeal for God's glory combined with a desire for solitude. They embraced Mary of Nazareth as the exemplar of a human being always responsive to God's spirit, yet ever sensitive to the needs of those around her.

Carmel's contemplative life reached a high point in the sixteenth century with Teresa of Avila and John of the Cross. Experience taught these Spaniards that, more than physical solitude and quiet reflection on divine truth, contemplation primarily involves meeting God in the depths of one's own being. Contemplation, they discovered, is really God's work, God's self-communication to one disposed through prayer and self-denial to receive an inflow of God's life. This divine inflow both purifies and transforms persons. It burns hardness and resistance to the Gospel out of the human heart. At the same time, rather than destroying human potential, contemplation elevates it to its greatest possible effectiveness. This profound psychological transformation of the entire personality, instead of leaving one oblivious to the surrounding world, radically prepares one for faithful and effective service to God's people. In effect, contemplation makes us a "new creation," alive with a new heart and a new spirit, attentive always to God's presence, fit to be God's instruments in remaking the world.

This dynamic, interpersonal understanding of contemplation has shaped Carmel to this day. Thanks to John and Teresa, Carmelites think of the contemplative life as a love affair with God that transforms their entire lives. As lovers, God and the human person become filled with each other, taking on each other's life. Contemplation enables us to see ourselves, others, and our world with God's eyes. Thus, we both luxuriate in the beauty of God's creation, while at the same time see human interaction without illusion. Contemplation attunes us to the unpredictable movements of the Holy Spirit, not only in our own personal lives, but also in the hidden, yet real evolutionary changes that are gradually shaping our universe and our social structures. Contemplation quietly, but surely, releases the powerful grip of cultural stereotypes, freeing us to live fully as men and women collaborating with one another for the best possible growth of our human family.

In the chapters that follow, our contributors develop this understanding of contemplation in greater depth. They discuss the historical, theoretical, and practical aspects of Carmel's distinctive approach to the contemplative life—a "prophetic eremitism" to use Thomas Merton's words. They attempt to bring this tradition out of the monasteries and convents where it has been developing for the past eight centuries and share it with the countless men and women who today desire a deeper experience of God, yet face the sometimes chaotic and overwhelming demands of life in contemporary society that seem to block the fulfillment of that longing. Above all, they portray contemplation as a path of individual and social transformation, a realistic program of renewal for church and society, thereby stating that education for contemplation is the most critical need in Christian education today.

These chapters are a fruit of Carmel's own centuries-long struggle to be faithful to God in the midst of a continually changing world. We believe they will nourish contemporary readers who similarly struggle for fidelity amid uncertain circumstances. By explaining in contemporary language the implications of Jesus' call for a change of mind and heart, these chapters also respond to Pope John Paul's insistent cry for a New Evangelization. And in demonstrating that contemplation answers the deeply felt need today for a transformation of human consciousness, these chapters offer hope for the emergence of new world in a new millennium.

The Editors

Abbreviations and Citations

Unless otherwise noted, all English quotations from Saint Teresa of Avila in this volume are taken from Kieran Kavanaugh and Otilio Rodriguez, trans., *The Collected Works of St. Teresa of Avila,* 3 vols. (Washington, DC: ICS Publications, 1976–85). The following abbreviations indicate Saint Teresa's writings:

L=*The Book of Her Life*   W=*The Way of Perfection*
F=*The Book of Her Foundations*   C=*The Interior Castle*
T=*Spiritual Testimonies*   P=*Poetry*

In *Life* and *The Way*, the first number in a citation refers to chapter, the second to paragraph. Thus, W.6.5 signifies *The Way of Perfection,* chapter 6, paragraph 5. In *The Interior Castle*, the first number refers to one of the seven dwelling places, followed by numbers for chapter and paragraph. Thus, C.7.1.2 is to the Seventh Dwelling Places, chapter 1, paragraph 2. Citations for *Spiritual Testimonies* give the number of the testimony, followed by the paragraph; for the *Poetry,* only the single number of the poem.

Similarly, unless noted otherwise, quotations in English from Saint John of the Cross are taken from Kieran Kavanaugh and Otilio Rodriguez, trans., *The Collected Works of Saint John of the Cross,* rev. ed. (Washington, DC: ICS Publications, 1991). The abbreviations for Saint John's writings cited in this volume are:

A=*The Ascent of Mount Carmel*   N=*The Dark Night*
C=*The Spiritual Canticle*   F=*The Living Flame of Love*
S=*Sayings of Light and Love*   L=*Letters*

For *The Ascent* and *Night*, the first number refers to the book, the second to the chapter, the third to the paragraph. Thus, A.1.2.3 indicates *The Ascent of Mount Carmel*, book 1, chapter 2, paragraph 3. In the *Canticle* and *Flame*, the first number refers to the stanza, the second to the paragraph. Thus, C.27.2 is to the 27th stanza (or chapter) of *The Spiritual Canticle*, paragraph 2. Quotation marks are used for both "The Spiritual Canticle" and "The Living Flame of Love" when only the poem is cited. CB indicates specific references to the second redaction of "The Spiritual Canticle." References to John's *Letters* and to the *Sayings of Light and Love* give the single number of the letter or the individual saying.

History

TO RENEW A TRADITION:
THE REFORMS OF CARMEL

John Welch, O.Carm.
Whitefriars Hall
Washington Theological Union
Washington, DC

It is one matter to have a vision of life's possibilities; it is another matter to give it concrete shape; and it is a third matter to sustain the vision. This process is necessary whether for an individual or a community. The longer the vision must be sustained, the greater the possibility of it becoming dimmed and, concomitantly, the greater the need to renew and reinvigorate the original vision.

The Christian community calling itself Carmelite has attempted to sustain a vision for almost eight hundred years. The fact that the vision still energizes and challenges people is testimony to its power. But it is a vision necessarily incarnated in human beings whose faithfulness to the vision suffers the vagaries of human existence. In other words, the Carmelites have frequently let themselves and others down and have had to remorsefully pick themselves up. The history of the Carmelites, from one perspective, is a lesson about the danger of human hubris and the consequences of neglecting essential values; it is also a testimony to the human spirit, which has the capability of going once more to the well of its imagination and drawing up an image of what once was and what still could be.

3

"Nor is it in any way good," wrote the Carmelite Teresa of Avila, "for persons to complain if they see their order in some decline; rather, they should strive to be the kind of rock on which the edifice may again be raised, for the Lord will help toward that." [1] The story of Carmel is the story of just such people stepping forward, time and again, to call others to a renewal of the original vision, at the same time reminding them of their own deepest desires.

The following is a brief account of the beginnings of this community, and succeeding efforts by Carmelite men and women to take responsibility for their Order and its vision.

The First Carmelites

The path of Carmel begins in a place of attentiveness to God, a mountainous ridge jutting out into the Mediterranean Sea. Here between heaven and earth, sea and land, people gathered in prayer. Almost all are unknown to history, but the prophets Elijah and Elisha were among them. They would be identified with the path that would be Carmel.

In the twelfth century, the original Carmelites gathered on the mountain and in its canyons in order to escape their former lives, to be free of the pressures and expectations that imprisoned them, and to set straight their priorities. Probably most all were from another country, choosing to begin again in an unknown land.

They were from the West, Latins living in a crusader-protected area called the Latin Kingdom. The Latin Kingdom was a thin strip on the west coast of Palestine won back from the Moslems in 1191, after it had been lost to Saladin in the battle of Hattin in 1187. Between those two dates, it is probable that no Christian hermits would have lived on Mount Carmel. The original Carmelites then would have started to arrive singly or in groups sometime after 1191. Perhaps some were from other eremitical locations in Palestine and Antioch, now untenable. [2]

They settled on Mount Carmel by a spring known as "the fountain of Elijah." The spring was at the opening of the wadi 'ain es-Siah, which

THE MYSTERIES OF LIGHT
Thursdays

1. The Baptism in the Jordan: Jesus descends into the water of the Jordan River and is baptized by John. The heavens open and the voice of the Father declares Him the beloved Son. The Spirit descends upon Jesus in the form of a dove and fills Him with God's mission to save humankind from sin.

Matthew 3:17

2. The Wedding at Cana: Jesus changes water into wine at the request of Mary, who was first among believers. The disciples witness this miracle, their hearts open to the faith, and they begin to believe in Him.

John 2:1-12

3. The Proclamation of the Kingdom of God: Jesus preaches the Gospel in Galilee. He proclaims that this is the time of fulfillment, for the Kingdom of God is at hand. He asks all to repent and forgives the sins of those who believe in Him.

Mark 1:15

4. The Transfiguration: On Mount Tabor, the Apostles see the glory of God shining forth from the face of Jesus. The voice of the Father, coming from a cloud, says "This is my chosen Son, listen to Him."

Luke 9:35

5. The Institution of the Eucharist: At the Last Supper, Jesus offers His body and blood, under the signs of bread and wine, and washes the feet of the Apostles. He knows that Judas has betrayed Him and His hour has come. Jesus testifies to His everlasting love for each one of us by sharing the Sacrament of the Eucharist.

John 13:1

The Rosary

The Mysteries of Light

 Marianist Mission

Mount Saint John
4435 East Patterson Road
Dayton, Ohio 45481-0001
1-800-348-4732
www.MarianistMission.org

was approximately two kilometers inland from the point of the promontory. The wadi ran about a thousand meters east and west, opening to the Mediterranean. Here Carmelites lived for the first one hundred years of their existence.

These men left almost nothing in the way of written records. When history first took notice of them they are already a functioning community. Early in the 1200s, sightings of the Carmelites begin to appear in reports of pilgrims on their way to Jerusalem. Pilgrims landed north of Mount Carmel at Acre and traveled south along the coast on the "via maris," passing the location of the fountain of Elijah. Even at this early date, the pilgrims were able to report that the church visible in the wadi was dedicated to the Virgin Mary.

The local bishop of Acre, Jacques de Vitry, also left a testimony to their existence. Identifying locations in Palestine where the eremitical life flourished, he observed: "others after the example and in imitation of holy solitary Elijah the prophet lived as hermits in the beehives of small cells on Mount Carmel . . . near the spring which is called the Spring of Elijah."[3]

The earliest recorded communication from the Carmelites themselves has been preserved in the opening lines of their constitutions of 1281. These lines, identified as the "Rubrica Prima," quite possibly date back to the 1230s when some of the Carmelites had begun migrating back to Europe and their identity was in question. This response was to be given by members of the Order when questioned about their heritage:

> We declare, bearing testimony to the truth, that from the time when the prophets Elijah and Elisha dwelt devoutly on Mount Carmel, holy Fathers both of the Old and the New Testament, whom the contemplation of heavenly things drew to the solitude of the same mountain, have without doubt led praiseworthy lives there by the fountain of Elijah in holy penitence unceasingly and successfully maintained.[4]

These first Carmelites were part of a lay movement in Europe that wanted to return to the Gospels as the first rule and to follow the apostles in preaching God's kingdom. They were men who had a conversion in their life, a serious change of lifestyle, and a reordering of their values. They were known as men of penance. As part of their conversion, they went apart in solitude, leaving traditional roles in society. And they were pilgrims, people whose conversion took them to the periphery of society and the church to live on the patrimony of Jesus Christ and there serve their liege Lord.

We do not know the names of these first Carmelites, but we do know their hearts.[5] From the beginning, this tradition rooted itself in the deep hungers of the human heart. These men could only have located themselves on this mountain and begun a life together in response to such hungers, such "deep caverns of feeling," later captured in the poetry of John of the Cross. Why else live where they lived?

We can assume they had tried to feed these hungers with the normal food that nourishes life: relationships, possessions, plans, titles, reputations. They probably found that their efforts and their control brought little peace to their lives. They had not found food sufficient to feed their hunger.

And so they laid their lives down and began again. Perhaps they were escaping more than simply restlessness. Perhaps their lives had come apart in deep disappointment; perhaps they experienced unbearable losses; perhaps they were chased from other places or, even, were escaping the law.

But it was more than escape that brought them to Mount Carmel. They assembled there because of a call. I would think they were people who were haunted in some ways and who found one another on a mountain that evoked their desires. People today come to this tradition because they, too, experience themselves as pilgrims on this earth, having deep hungers and being haunted by a call.

The conditions on Mount Carmel are inviting. The site slopes to the waters of the Mediterranean. Its breezes cool the canyon. Within its walls, the men lived in individual cells at slight distances from one another, spending time in reflection and prayer. They read Scripture and carried its lines in their hearts. They fasted, abstained from meat, and worked in silence. They gathered regularly: daily for Mass, weekly for discussions. They lived a life of poverty, and what they owned, they owned together. Their leader was elected, and he was to live at the entrance to the site. Life on Mount Carmel focused their scattered lives and settled their confused minds. It freed hearts that had been anxious about many things. The oratory in the midst of the cells invited them to find a center in the midst of their lives.

These elements were collected into a brief formula that became the Rule of the Carmelites. Albert, the bishop who composed the formula, concluded: "Here then are a few points I have written down to provide you with a standard of conduct to live up to. . . . See that the bond of common sense is the guide of the virtues."[6]

This common sense led them to abandon the site on Mount Carmel and return to Europe after an existence of less than one hundred years in the canyon. Moslem and Christian warfare made the mountain untenable. "The inroads of the pagans," wrote Pope Innocent IV, "have driven our beloved sons, the hermits of Mount Carmel, to betake themselves, not without great affliction of spirit, to parts across the sea."[7]

They traveled to Cyprus, Sicily, France, and England. Initially they intended to continue an eremitical existence, but very quickly they were transformed into one of the mendicant orders, taking their place with the Franciscans, Dominicans, and Augustinians. Their formula of life given by Albert changed into its final form in 1247 and became the official Rule of the Carmelites. The change strengthened their common life and allowed them to live where it was convenient for the service of their brothers and sisters.[8]

The development of the Order took place over a vast geographical panorama. By the end of the thirteenth century, sixty years after arriving in Europe, the Order had grown from a small band of men in a narrow valley in Palestine to about 150 houses, divided into twelve provinces throughout Europe and the Mediterranean. With practically no official documentation of its beginnings, except for its Rule and constitutions, with no founder, and with an anonymous first community, Carmel closed the thirteenth century with its first doctorate in theology from the University of Paris. Gerard of Bologna received the doctorate in 1295, and subsequently, in 1297, was elected Prior General of the Order.

The brief time on Mount Carmel forevermore shaped the ancient path of the Carmelite tradition. Each major figure on the path of Carmel returned to the mountain in memory and in heart to be renewed by the original impulses that gathered the group in cells and around the oratory. John of Hildesheim (d. 1375) evoked their memory: "The primitive dwellers on Mount Carmel were simple hermits, unlettered, poor, they possessed no parchments, nor were they writers. They were accustomed to pray rather than to write."[9] Later travelers of the ancient path continued to mine the mountain, going deeper into the themes and implications of that long-ago existence. When Teresa of Avila began her reformed convents of Carmelite nuns, she had as a blueprint in her mind the original Carmelite setting on Mount Carmel. Earlier reforms, as well, attempted to return to the original vision.

Decline, the Reform of Mantua, and John Soreth

The enthusiasm of the beginning began to wane in the fourteenth century, and the malaise grew worse in the fifteenth century. Religious life slowly entered a period of decline everywhere. The general population of Europe was decimated by a plague, the Black Death, in the years 1348 and 1349. It is not known how badly the disease affected the Order directly, but it is known that during a General Chapter in Metz in 1348, two hundred friars died either during the sessions or traveling to or from the sessions. The Hundred Years' War was another type of plague that affected religious life. During this warfare between England and France (1337–1453), about thirty of the ninety Carmelite houses in France were destroyed, either through fighting or for use in building defenses.

In 1432, Eugene IV modified the Rule of Carmel. This "second mitigation" allowed the friars, on suitable occasions, to remain and walk about in their churches and cloisters and their periphery, and to eat meat three times a week. Later legislation reduced abstinence days to Wednesday, Friday, and Saturday. Although not written into the official text of the Rule, this second mitigation concluded the process of the hermits on Mount Carmel gaining mendicant status.

Blessed John Soreth (c. 1395–1471), who had received a doctorate from the University of Paris in 1438, was elected Prior General of the Order in 1451. A reform-minded general, Soreth nonetheless defended the changes in the Rule. Movement about the churches and cloisters was a fact and a necessity and did not necessarily undermine the prescription to remain in or near one's cell. He wrote:

> To remove the scruples of the weak, this has been declared by Eugene IV to mean that it is permitted to remain and freely walk about in churches, cloisters and precincts of convents, meditating on the law of the Lord, or praying, and serving in proper occupations.

He also defended changes in the abstinence prescriptions:

> Our mendicant state does not possess streams nor sources whence fish for the nourishment of the brethren may be obtained. . . . Our Father Basil says in his rule that those foods must by all means be used that can be more easily and cheaply obtained; but in many places meat is of this kind. Therefore out of a sort of pressing need we poor friars are obliged sometimes to eat it, lest on account of abstinence we be found to seek after food of a more expensive kind and difficult to obtain. [10]

However, to many people, these changes were an indication of a gradual loss of Carmel's original vision and spirit. Later reformers, including Teresa of Avila, often rejected this mitigation. Joachim Smet's judgment is that this second mitigation has done more harm than good, since "it has been the source of every subsequent division in the Order." [11]

Although he defended the changes, John Soreth was well aware of the unhealthy state of the Order. "The Rule and institutions of the Order now lie everywhere neglected. Who keeps them, or who knows them?"[12] he complained. The decline of religious life was marked by an absence of a vital prayer life, serious lapses in the practice of poverty, and a general disregard for the common life.

A reform had already begun early in the fifteenth century when LaSelve, a community located between Florence and Pisa declared itself a "house of observance." It was joined by another community in Mantua. Soon these houses and others who joined them became a distinct entity in the Order, the Mantuan Reform, and were placed directly under the jurisdiction of the general.

The Mantuan Reform stressed silence and cloister, forbidding entrance to outsiders. The friars were not allowed to be aimlessly outside the convent. Money was distributed from a common chest, and the reformers rejected the mitigation of the Rule that allowed them to include meat in their diet three times a week.

A leading reform figure, Blessed Baptist of Mantua, explained, "The Mantua Congregation, rising at the inspiration of God from the sordid neglect into which practically the whole Order had fallen, strives to pattern its life and customs after the ancient Fathers."[13] The reform grew under the generalate of John Soreth. By the time of the death of Baptist of Mantua the congregation had thirty-one houses of friars and seven houses of nuns.

Carmelite Sisters

As part of the renewal of the Order, John Soreth encouraged the establishment of communities of Carmelite women. The Carmelites had been exempted from responsibility for women's communities in 1261.[14] But in 1452 a papal bull, *Cum Nulla,* gave Carmelites the authorization to affiliate women's communities with the Order. It was in Florence that the first community of Carmelite women was formally constituted. Another early example, initiated under Soreth, was the incorporation of a community of nuns established by Frances D'Amboise in 1460. D'Amboise, who received the habit from Soreth, reminds one of a later Carmelite nun, Teresa of Avila, when she says, "The rule is not longer for one than for another. . . . To consider and be concerned with who is the grandest lady and comes from the noblest and richest family is the doctrine of the devil." [15] The communities of nuns established by Soreth were cloistered.

John Soreth never visited Spain. Consequently, communities there developed differently, but most began after *Cum Nulla*. The Incarnation in Avila, founded in 1479, was the earliest women's community in Castile. The Carmelite provincial gave the habit to Doña Elvira Gonzalez who became the first superior. In 1513, the Incarnation moved to bigger quarters outside the city. In 1535, Teresa de Ahumada, to be known as St. Teresa of Avila, entered the Incarnation.

The Reform of Albi

Hearing of the Mantuan Reform, the bishop of Albi in Aquitaine, France, contacted members of the Reform in northern Italy and invited friars to come to his diocese and reform the Carmelites. He had previously reformed the Franciscans and Dominicans. When only one friar returned as a candidate for the reform, the bishop sought vocations at the University of Paris. Twenty-six candidates responded, twenty-two of whom would eventually enter the Order. They lived in the bishop's palace for a month, receiving instruction in the Carmelite life. The twenty-two received the habit of Carmel in the episcopal palace. The bishop then invited the local community of Carmelites to dinner. While the convent was deserted, the twenty-two novices and the novice master entered and took possession. The former community was compelled either to join the Reform of Albi or go to other communities.

Just as the Mantuan Congregation became a separate congregation within the Order under a vicar-general, so too the Congregation of Albi received special status. Baptist of Mantua, previously vicar of the Mantuan Congregation, had been elected general of the entire Order. He warmly welcomed this new reform effort. He wrote:

> As from the beginning, I recall, I favored your congregation, when at the request of the Lord Bishop of Albi, I sent Friar Eligius, said to be still living, so ever since I have with a view to your advantage always favored it, favor it now and will continue to favor it, as long as God grants me life. I praise, approve and commend the privileges which his Holiness, our Lord the Pope, has granted you and your congregation. I exhort you never to abandon your proposal of leading a holy life, but to adhere to it more strongly and constantly day by day. By so doing you will win salvation for yourselves; for those who have set out down the wide road you will provide an incentive for reconsideration and for recalling and pondering the meaning of their vows. [16]

As with the Mantuan Reform, the Reform of Albi produced many holy men. The Albi Congregation, because it eventually included the student house at the University of Paris, also counted a number of the scholars of the Order. Neither reform impacted the entire Order.

The principal area of renewal in the Order was north of the Alps where John Soreth had long labored. His renewal of Carmel included a restoration of the common life, a renunciation of possessions, a commitment to a contemplative life, and careful observance of the Rule, constitutions, and liturgies of the Order.

Soreth's reforms did not spread to Spain, nor did he or any other general visit Spain in the fifteenth century. An early sixteenth-century report on the Carmelite Castilian houses of Toledo, Avila, and San Pablo de la Moraleja judged them to be in deplorable condition, with a number of the friars giving public scandal. Matters were probably not much better in other Spanish Carmelite communities. The Crown became involved in religious life renewal, and after the Council of Trent, when reform was introduced into the entire church, the often difficult relationships among

Rome, the Crown, and Order authorities added to the difficulties of renewal.

Nicholas Audet and a Program of Renewal

In 1523, a major program for renewal of the Order was published by Nicholas Audet, former provincial of the Holy Land and now vicar general of the Order. Audet was one of the great generals of the Order who labored for thirty years to renew the spirit of Carmel. He was appointed by Pope Adrian VI and confirmed by Pope Clement VII with the authority to visit and reform communities in the Order. After consulting with princes and prelates and before taking up his task, Audet expressed concern at the situation of the Order:

> From frequent conversations with them we learned of what sordid conduct many of our brethren are guilty and what a great threat hangs over the good because of their bad example, unless all of us together quickly come to our senses and reform our conduct . . . . We are threatened unless we quickly confront and immediately provide a remedy for a number of wrong and wicked deeds committed in our Order. [17]

Audet's program for beginning a reform was titled *Isagogicon,* and it included a number of specific prescriptions, among them:

> Within three days of receipt of the prescriptions, each friar is to hand to the prior a list of all his possessions. It is emphasized that what they have is not their own but for their use.

Specific academic disciplines are recommended for the various levels of formation of candidates and further training is recommended, including university training, to raise the intellectual level of the Order.

> No one is to live outside a house of the Order; anyone outside the Order is to return.
>
> Sermons are to be given on all Sundays and feast days and each day in Lent.

> Superiors are to receive only legitimate income and must cease selling certain privileges such as the office of prior, academic degrees, and permissions to live outside the Order.
>
> Detailed prescriptions are to be followed for liturgical services and presence in choir.
>
> Friars are allowed to leave the house only twice a week, in pairs, and with white mantles. Few lay men are to be admitted into the house, and no women, except those of the nobility who cannot be refused entrance.
>
> Professed students are to follow detailed instructions regarding studies and behavior. When playing sports they must wear their habits.
>
> All are to eat in the refectory; silence is the norm and there is to be reading from the Bible or other suitable book. No bread and wine may be taken to one's room. [18]

With this program, additional reform decrees from the general chapter, and a revised version of Soreth's constitutions, Audet began a visitation of provinces, beginning in Italy, in an attempt to carry out the necessary reforms. The turmoil of the Protestant Reformation added to his difficulties, especially in countries where reform efforts might prove effective. Audet spent three years in France and Germany and managed to introduce reforms in over one hundred houses. A number of men left the Order under pressure to reform. In the Spanish province of Castile, over half the friars walked away.

In 1553, Pope Julius III ordered the development of a plan for the renewal of religious life. The text of the bull was submitted to certain superiors for comment, and Audet's comments have been preserved. His supportive, tactful, moderate suggestions show the wisdom gained in his years of struggle to call the Order to a faithful following of its original impetus. By the time he died in 1562, a movement had begun in Spain that, had he known about it, would have received his full support. As it was, his successor, John Rossi, gave quick encouragement to this burgeoning reform effort beginning in Castile.

The Reform of Teresa of Avila

In sixteeth-century Spain, at the age of forty-seven, and after living twenty-seven years in the Carmelite convent of the Incarnation in Avila, Teresa de Ahumada gave fresh impetus to the tradition of Carmel. Dissatisfied with the size and atmosphere of the Incarnation, she envisioned small communities of women whose prayer would further the work of the church. These groups of women were to be friends with God and friends with one another.

In her time in the Incarnation, the community had grown to over 140 solemnly professed nuns. During one period of time, more than fifty were living outside the convent, in part because of the difficulty in feeding so many. The Incarnation had a cloister, but it was easily entered by relatives, servants, and young girls for education. Many of the nuns had their own patrimony. Nuns who were of the nobility might have suites with kitchens, as did Teresa, who was a doña; poorer nuns lived in dormitories. Singing the divine office took up much of the day. All things considered, the Incarnation was an observant community, but crowded. In too many ways it was entangled with, and mirrored, the surrounding society.

Teresa had a high regard for many of the women in the Incarnation. Later, when others were complaining that Teresa's Reform was draining the Incarnation of its best members, she replied that there were more than forty left who could be foundresses themselves. [19]

Remembering the beginnings of the Order on Mount Carmel, Teresa wanted to reestablish the eremitical conditions that prevailed in the wadi 'ain es-Siah. She wanted her nuns to understand themselves as solitaries in community. They were to follow the primitive Rule of Carmel, meaning the Rule of 1247, which she understood was "without mitigation." [20]

The atmosphere of the houses of Teresa's Reform was to be conducive to an attentiveness to God. The quiet of the caves and huts on Mount Carmel permeated the rooms and corridors of the new Carmels. Teresa encouraged the women to speak trustingly with Christ, as though with a friend. They could imagine their friend beside them, or within them, especially in Gospel settings, where he is alone and might appreciate company. Hermitages were established within the convent gardens for times of greater solitude.

But they were also to take time to be present to one another and nurture loving relationships. If you want to know God, she wrote, know God's friends. Initially, Teresa allowed no more than thirteen women in each community, a number allowing for levels of relationships, with the possibility of each woman being known at some depth by every other woman. Teresa set a clear but challenging goal: "all must be friends, all must be loved, all must be held dear, all must be helped" (W.4.7). As friends they recreated and worked together, prayed the psalms in chapel, and attended celebrations of the Eucharist.

As with the men who were drawn to Mount Carmel, Teresa's women were looking for conditions that would provide a setting, a structure, a support for attending to the mystery that haunted their lives and made them restless and unsatisfied with other forms of living. Teresa herself said, "I wanted to live (for I well understood that I was not living but was struggling with a shadow of death), but I had no one to give me life, and I was unable to catch hold of it" (L.8.12). For many of the women, to enter such a community was like coming home. "It seemed to me," wrote Anne of St. Bartholomew, one of the first members, "that from my earliest childhood until this, I had lived this kind of a life and had dwelt among these saints."[21]

When Teresa made her first foundation in 1562, John Rossi was vicar general of the Order. The next year, the Council of Trent ended, and Rossi had the task of visiting, correcting, and reforming the houses of the Order. In 1564, Rossi was elected general, and the Counter Reformation and implementation of the decrees of Trent began. Rossi was appreciative and supportive of Teresa's efforts to renew the Order. When he died, Teresa expressed deep sorrow.

Teresa would eventually create an inner space to complement the outer space of her convents. In *The Interior Castle,* she imagined the soul as a castle, and life's journey was through the various rooms of the castle to a central room where the King lived. The King, almost imperceptibly at first, invites those wandering outside the castle walls to enter within and join him in a loving union. Teresa's new communities were to be the settings for this interior journey. But she needed allies in her Reform.

John of the Cross

Juan de Yepes was restless in his new life with the Carmelites. He had recently completed his novitiate in the Order and was now a student of theology at the University of Salamanca. But he wanted something more, or something else. He was considering joining the Carthusians. Obviously, whatever his dissatisfactions were, they had something to do with the deeper hungers of his heart and the conditions in which these would be nourished.

Just at that point in his life, he was introduced to Teresa of Avila. She was busy beginning the second house of her Reform in John's hometown of Medina del Campo. Teresa was older than John by twenty-seven years. She saw in this little friar the person she was seeking to begin her reform among the male Carmelites. John immediately resonated with Teresa's vision. He volunteered to join her movement after he completed his last year of studies, but only if she moved quickly on the project.

One year later, Teresa put John through a short, second novitiate with her, introducing him to the spirit of her reformed communities. He then began his own community with two other friars in an isolated place called Duruelo. Their seriousness could be seen in the skulls and crosses that decorated the house; their asceticism was evident as the snow came through the cracks of the building and as they walked barefoot about the house and the countryside. The blueprint of the first Carmelites on Mount Carmel guided a new expression in sixteenth-century Spain.

When Teresa was assigned back to reform her original convent of the Incarnation, she requested John of the Cross as chaplain for the nuns. And so, for a period of two years, until Teresa completed her term as prioress, these two extraordinary people ministered in the same community.

But tensions were growing within the Order as a result of the reform efforts. One night, John was taken prisoner by some of his brothers in religion and brought to a monastery prison cell in Toledo. There, in the dark of his nine-month confinement, John began to compose the mystical poetry that was an expression of his experience of God's love. Later, after he had escaped, John continued writing poetry and also prose commentaries on his poems.

John was a specialist in analyzing the desires of the human heart. He spoke of our desires always being restless and our hearts endlessly searching. John likened our desires to little children who only momentarily quiet down, but soon erupt again; or they are like the situation of a lover who waits expectantly for a day with a loved one, only to have the day be a great disappointment. "Where have you hidden, beloved?" he wrote. "I went out calling you, but you were gone."[22]

John's conclusion was that human beings have a desire or yearning that nothing in this world can ultimately satisfy. In John's experience, only that mysterious Presence dwelling at the center of each one's life is sufficient food for the hungers of the heart. John imaged this Mystery as a night, a flame, a lover. "The soul's center is God," he concluded (F.1.12).

The Reform of Touraine

The Reform inspired by Teresa and John eventually became an Order itself, the Discalced Carmelites. In the next century, in France, three men would converge whose spirit provided the impetus that would eventually contribute to the reform of the entire Carmelite Order. Peter Behourt had joined the Order in 1582, the year Teresa of Avila died. His intent was clear: "From the time I entered the Order, I have always chosen, desired, and hoped for the restoration to a better state of the whole province."[23] He continually attempted to recruit others to become a core of reform. His efforts in a series of offices in several communities resulted in mixed outcomes. His was not the personality to rally men for a sustained living of a more disciplined life.

But a similar movement in the house of studies in Paris, the Place Maubert, took on life. There, Philip Thibault stood out as a leader. He was acquainted with Pierre Bérulle and was influenced by the spiritual movements associated with the salon of Madame Acarie. Thibault and several students made a pilgrimage to Rome in 1600 to ask church and Order leaders to allow them a separate existence within the Order, or to join the Discalced. They were persuaded to remain in the Order and work for its reform.

Thibault joined Behourt and a small community at Rennes. He was to be subprior and novice master. The friars renewed their profession, bound themselves to an effort at reform, and mandated a second novitiate for all who joined them. The Observance of Rennes had begun. Eventually, Thibault became prior, and to the Reform he contributed the new forms of prayer current in French spirituality.

Joining the community in Rennes in 1612 was a lay brother, John of St. Samson. John was blind from the age of three, an orphan at ten, and a devout, prayerful, searching soul who had been living in Paris with a grocer near the Carmelite house in Place Maubert. He spent long hours of prayer in the church and eventually asked one of the friars if he could play the organ.[24] John eventually was given a room in the convent in recompense for playing the organ and giving lessons. He became part of a study group in the house and listened to spiritual texts read aloud.

John entered the Carmelite novitiate at Dol, just as the community fled because of a plague. John remained to nurse the other novice who had become ill. Eventually, John contracted the disease and had to recover at a sanatorium. At age forty-one, he entered the reform community of Rennes, joining Behourt and Thibault. John made the prescribed sec-

ond novitiate and remained at Rennes the rest of his life. He became unof-
ficial spiritual director for generations of novices and professed students.
He was also esteemed and visited by many well-known people of the day
who came to talk to the blind mystic of Carmel. [25]

The Observance of Rennes spread to other houses and became the
Reform of Touraine. It was a Reform that took inspiration from Teresa
and the Discalced Carmelites. The Italian Discalced Congregation's constitutions of 1611 were available to members of the Reform as a model of
legislation, which was also a spiritual document. The contemplative nature of Carmel was emphasized by the statutes of the Touraine Reform as
they encouraged "the practice of divine contemplation and the love of
holy solitude, formerly the only part of our sacred Order, now its principal part." Again, "for our Carmelite forefathers dwelling in deserts and
solitude one thing was necessary: to attend upon (*vacare*) God by the
continual exercise of contemplation." But since they were now also called
by the church to active ministry, "the nature of our institute requires that
to mystical theology, which is the best part for Carmelites, we should add
the assiduous study of letters and the sciences." [26] The Reform of Touraine
was part of an Order-wide movement of the stricter observance. Eventually Touraine's statutes were the basis for reform throughout the Order,
influencing legislation into the twentieth century.

The Carmelite Contribution

The renewal of a life begins deep down in the heart. Individuals are
often alone in pulling their lives together and beginning again. Often, the
reform of a community depends, similarly, on just one person's desire for
change. Their spark is joined quickly by similar embers in the hearts of
others.

Most efforts at reform die. Some are misguided; some lack the soil
to take root; some are concretized in structures which humanly are unsus-
tainable. Given the history of Carmel, it is remarkable that the fragile life

woven in a wadi on Mount Carmel has not been completely unraveled by the vicissitudes of history and human fickleness. That Carmel exists today could be interpreted as a result of the Spirit moving over chaotic waters; human inconsistency and sinfulness answered by divine faithfulness.

Carmel learned to tell the story of the human heart as a love story. Thinking they were searching for something missing in their lives, Carmelites discovered they were being pursued by a loving Presence whose desire for them gave them increased life, greater freedom, and a trustworthy relationship for their guidance.

The core value at all times in Carmelite history has been that mysterious Presence met deep within searching lives. Carmelites have left a trail of structures and literature born out of engagement with that Presence. The ways of organizing Carmel's life have been multiple: an orderly, eremitical life in a canyon on the mountainous ridge of Carmel; later, a community of men living in the midst of people and serving their needs; still later, communities of women, cloistered and active, in the service of the church; and always, individuals who go even farther apart in the solitude of hermitages.

The external structures are meant to assist an internal journey, which Carmel's literature has imaged in various ways: among them, a journey through a castle, traveling a hidden path, a passage through a dark night, a search for the beloved in mountain pastures—the last image recalling where it all began.

Notes

1. St. Teresa of Avila, *The Book of Her Foundations,* Kieran Kavanaugh, O.C.D., and Otilio Rodriguez, O. C.D., trans., *The Collected Works of St. Teresa of Avila,* vol. 3 (Washington, DC: ICS Publications, 1985), 116.

2. Joachim Smet, O.Carm., *The Carmelites*, vol. 1 (Darien, IL: Carmelite Spiritual Center, 1988), 5.

3. Carlo Cicconetti, O.Carm., *The Rule of Carmel*, trans. Gabriel Pausback,

O.Carm., ed. Paul Hoban, O.Carm. (Darien, IL: Carmelite Spiritual Center, 1984), 62.

4. Smet, 15–6. The original Latin text may be found in Adrianus Staring, O.Carm., *Medieval Carmelite Heritage* (Rome: Institutum Carmelitanum, 1989), 40–1.

5. See Elias Friedman, O.C.D., *The Latin Hermits of Mount Carmel* (Rome: Institutum Historicum Teresianum, 1979), 189–93. Of the first generation of Carmelites who actually lived on Mount Carmel, only three names are known for certain: Dominic and James, witnesses to a will in Acre in 1273, and William of Sanvico, who was definitor from the Holy Land at the general chapter of 1287.

6. See Michael Mulhall, O.Carm., ed. *Albert's Way* (Rome: Institutum Carmelitanum, 1989). The text of the Rule can be found on pages 2-21.

Albert was chosen patriarch of Jerusalem in 1205. Arriving in the Holy Land, he settled his see at Acre during the first months of 1206. Before his election as patriarch he was bishop of Bobbio in 1184 and of Vercelli from 1185 until 1205. During that time, he had been delegated by Pope Innocent III to develop a "form of life" for the Humiliati, a group of workers who had several conflicts with the hierarchy. It was a movement comprised of clerics and lay celibates, as well as some married people. Albert became both patriarch of Jerusalem and Papal Legate to the Holy Land. He was given the task of reintegrating the Holy Land.

7. Smet, 10.

8. The Rule of 1247 shows a strengthening of comunity life and a movement to towns as the Carmelites took on a mendicant status. It does not set up an opposition between a contemplative life and ministry since these new mendicants would have understood themselves as contemplatives as well.

9. Smet, 50.

10. Ibid., 73.

11. Ibid.

12. Ibid., 67.

13. Ibid., 76.

14. Lay women and men had been associated with the Order in one form or another from early times. Records show that in 1284 lay people affiliated with the Order through vows of some type. In 1304, a woman made a profession in Bologna. In 1343, a husband and wife made vows in Florence, vows which seem to be identical to the vows of the friars. Joan of Toulouse is an early fifteenth-century example of a woman associated with the Order living as an anchoress. See Smet, 88.

15. Smet, 95.

16. Ibid., 110–1.

17. Ibid., 155.

18. For further details, see Smet, 155–8.

19. For a description of the problems of the Incarnation, see Kieran Kavanaugh's introduction to St. Teresa of Avila's *Foundations* in *The Collected Works*, 3:19–20.

20. Knowledge of the Rule would have been part of Teresa's formation. But it

is not known if she had access to a copy of the Rule. A manuscript rather recently discovered seems to have belonged to the Incarnation. It has three versions of the Rule, but in poor Spanish.

Neither Albert's formula of life nor the final 1247 text of Innocent IV forbids owning property in common and having fixed income. But a papal decree in 1229 forbade the ownership of common property and possessions. When Teresa was informed of this understanding of the Rule, she decided to found her communities "in poverty," without endowment.

By the time of the first foundation of St. Joseph's in Avila, Teresa had a copy of the Rule, and it appears to have been, along with customs, the only legislation for the new foundation. The text of the Rule in St. Joseph's was identical to the text used at the Incarnation, since the mitigations after 1247 were not written into the text of the Rule. Insisting that the Rule and Constitutions be read together, Teresa was instrumental in having published the first printed edition of the Rule in Spanish. See *Saint Teresa and the Carmelite Rule* (Roma: Casa Generalizia Carmelitani Scalzi, 1994).

21. *Autobiography of the Blessed Mother Anne of Saint Bartholomew* (St. Louis: Translated from French by a religious of the Carmel of St. Louis, 1916), 17.

22. John of the Cross, "The Spiritual Canticle," Stanza 1, Kieran Kavanaugh, O.C.D., and Otilio Rodriguez, O.C.D., trans., *The Collected Works of St. John of the Cross*, (Washington, DC: ICS Publications, 1991), 44.

23. Smet, *The Carmelites,* vol. 3, pt. 1 (Darien, IL: Carmelite Spiritual Center), 36.

24. John of St. Samson's musical abilities were apparently highly developed. He is reported to have been able to play two types of keyboard instruments, four stringed instruments, and three woodwinds. For further details of his life and a study of his poetry, see Robert Stefanotti, *The Phoenix of Rennes* (New York: Peter Lang Publishers, 1994).

25. John of St. Samson left over 4,000 pages of dictated notes. A critical edition of his collected works has been prepared by Hein Blommestijn, O. Carm., of the Titus Brandsma Institute in Nijmegen.

25. Smet, 3:57.

THE ROLE OF THE CARMELITES IN THE HISTORY OF WESTERN MYSTICISM

Bernard McGinn
Divinity School
University of Chicago
Chicago, Illinois

"O great is the praise of the desert because the devil who conquered in paradise is conquered in turn in the wasteland!"[1] These words are from *The Praise of the Desert*, a treatise by the fifth-century ascetic Bishop Eucherius of Lyon, who sketched the whole of salvation history in terms of the desert theme. According to Eucherius, God prepared the desert for his saints as the place to repair the evil done by Adam in paradise, the "place of pleasure." The desert is the "uncircumscribed temple of our God." "In the desert Moses, with his face in glory, beheld God; in the desert Elijah, afraid lest he gaze on God, covered his face."[2] In the desert, Christ, the Divine Bridegroom, lays down at midday and "those desert-dwellers who are wounded by charity contemplate him saying, 'We have found him whom our soul loves, we will hold him and not let him go'(Sg. 6:3)."[3] The theme of the desert as the place of loving encounter with God, as well as Moses and Elijah as archetypal examples of such encounter, has played a significant part in Christian spiritual traditions from the earliest times.

I begin with the theme of the desert and the figure of Elijah because my purpose here is to reflect on the significance of Carmelite mysticism, especially of the mysticism of Teresa of Avila and John of the Cross, in the course of the Western tradition. Two archetypal figures have been essential to the Order of Carmel from the start—Elijah and Mary. Whatever the historical and theological weaknesses of some of the earlier uses of these models in the Carmelite tradition, the present meaning of Carmelite spirituality, insofar as it is in living connection with its sources, can never dispense with how devotion to Elijah and to Mary formed its particular identity. I concentrate here on Elijah and the desert theme, though this is at best half the story. Even in taking this path, I wish to underline that I cannot pretend to possess full knowledge, either academic or existential, of the whole tradition of Carmel. My own reading of Carmelite spirituality has concentrated on Teresa of Avila and John of the Cross, though I have also profited from a number of illuminating studies of the general Carmelite tradition.[4] What I try to provide here are only some broad perspectives— a view of the desert of Carmel from afar rather than from within its depths or upon its heights.

Carmelite Origins

The mysterious origin of the Carmelite order was part of an important return to the ideal of the desert in twelfth- and thirteenth-century Western Christianity. The movement out into "deserted places" (which could even be islands in the sea) to seek a more austere form of life, of course, had been a growing part of Western monasticism since about the year 1000.[5] What was new in the late twelfth century was the increasing concentration on the symbol of the desert and the growing stress on the interior desert, the *solitudo cordis,* as the place for meeting God.[6] Cistercian authors played a large role in furthering the theme of the interior desert. The identification of the *desertum* with the inaccessible vastness of the unknowable divine nature itself, briefly noted by John Scottus Eriugena in the ninth century, is also found in the Cistercian Isaac of Stella in the twelfth. It was to become an important symbol in Christian mysticism in the thirteenth century, largely among the German mystics, especially Meister Eckhart and his contemporaries and followers.

The rich variety of movements that constituted the "evangelical awakening" of the twelfth and thirteenth centuries contained diverse, even opposing, tendencies. The impetus to withdrawal, both physical and spiritual, implied in the desert motif and found in groups like the Carthusians, Cistercians, and the first Carmelites contrasted sharply with new forms of pastoral engagement with the world realized in diverse ways among the Mendicants and in the Beguines who grew so rapidly in the early decades of the thirteenth century. The latter movements provided the institutional and spiritual location for new tendencies in late medieval mysticism, especially what I have elsewhere referred to as the secularization and democratization of traditional monastic mysticism.[7] The medieval monastic tradition had tended to insist, though never exclusively, that true experience of the divine presence was possible only through separation from the world and was largely realized within special communities of religious virtuosi.[8] The Mendicants and the Beguines called this into question, so that by the end of the thirteenth century, we not only have major mystical texts produced by Beguines and laywomen within the penumbra of the Franciscan movement, such as Angela of Foligno, but also mystical preaching, such as Meister Eckhart's, that is directed to the whole Christian body and deliberately relativizes physical separation from the world, and indeed all special religious forms of life and practices.

The tension between pastoral engagement and withdrawal to solitude is more than evident in the early history of the Carmelites.[9] Founded (if we can call it that) as a lay movement of hermits in the crusader states, the earliest window we have on the Carmelite life, the Rule of Saint Albert, provides us evidence of a loosely organized form of life devoted to rigorous asceticism, solitude, and continual prayer, but without much interest in pastoral ministry. The movement back to Western Europe, already well underway by 1240, inevitably brought the hermits from Carmel into a new world in which the success of the learned pastoral ministry of the friars became an offer that could not be refused.[10] The "friarization" of the Carmelites (if I can be allowed the phrase) was well underway by 1247 when Innocent IV approved the modified Rule, and it was finally cemented by Boniface VIII in 1298 and John XXII in 1317. The transition was not made without protest, as the famous *Ignea Sagitta* of Nicholas of France indicates. The stark opposition between the cell and the city forms the main theme of Nicholas's polemic:

> Happily hidden away from the world's vanity in the cell of solitude we obtain the true delights of paradise which so recreate and refresh our inner person that appetite for them always both satisfies us and makes us thirst for more. But you, not in the cell but in the swell of the turbulent city, possess the vain riches of this world which bring disgust through satiety and cannot refresh your appetite.[11]

Nicholas was not a happy man. His insistence on the inadvisability of any compromise in the commitment to solitude was quite the opposite of what actually happened in the history of the Order, but without the witness of those who resist compromise, the more difficult side of any healthy tension is all too easy to forget. Despite the growing pastoral mission of the Carmelites, the ideal of contemplation was not forgotten. The General Chapter of Montpellier in 1287, which encouraged Carmelite entry into the universities, also proclaimed, "We have left the world for effective service of our Creator in the citadel of contemplation" [*arx contemplationis*].[12] Later Carmelites would point out that Elijah had not only retreated into the desert of Horeb to encounter God, but had also preached the Lord's message before King Ahab and had confronted the priests of Baal. We should remember too that the tension between engagement and retreat was not peculiar to the Carmelites. Francis of Assisi, who preached in towns and cities by word and by example, felt impelled to retire to "deserts" for prayer and reflection, and even wrote a "Rule for Hermitages." The importance of these hermitages in the history of both the Franciscans and the Carmelites is only today being recognized. [13]

Development of Mysticism

What is perhaps most surprising about the early history of the Carmelites in the development of mysticism from 1200 to 1600 is how late they came to the game. The Rule of Saint Albert, not unlike other rules of life, sets up the institutional context for the life of prayer and contemplation but says nothing explicit about the nature of the interior life. Even the early documents, such as the *Ignea Sagitta*, are not what we would call mystical texts. The closest thing we can find to mysticism is in the late fourteenth-century *Institution of the First Monks* of Philip Ribot, which emphasizes the necessity of withdrawal into solitude and inner purification as the necessary prelude to the experience of union with God. The influence of this text was important for the Spanish reform movement of the sixteenth century and the mysticism that flourished there. There were also a number of fifteenth- and early sixteenth-century Carmelites who might be described as mystical authors, such as Baptista Spagnoli and Francis Amelry, but without reducing the seriousness of their contribution, it would be hard to consider them as major figures in the evolution of late medieval mystical theology.

The early Carmelites, then, confront us with not only a typical late medieval tension between withdrawal and pastoral engagement, but also with the anomaly of a group pledged to solitude and contemplation who were not given much to mystical literature and the copying of spiritual texts. (In this, they contrast with another eremitical order, the Carthusians, whose cells served as the late medieval equivalent of "publishing houses" for the dissemination of mystical literature.) [14] Of course, we must always remember that the history of Christian mysticism, as distinct from its actual practice, is restricted to textual evidence—it can only speculate about what has not been recorded.

The reasons for the florescence of Carmelite mysticism (at least written records of Carmelite mysticism) in the sixteenth century are complex and mysterious. One major internal element in the background to this key era in Western mysticism lies in the issue of reform. The notion of *reformatio*, of course, has always been central to Christianity, but there is still good reason to see the period between the thirteenth and the end of the sixteenth centuries as the age of reform par excellence.[15] Ninety years ago, Ernst Troetsch argued that the Great Reformation of the sixteenth century, which split Western Christianity into two opposed camps down to living memory, was not so much a break with the previous three hundred years as the final act in a long drawn-out conflict over what kind of reform Christendom needed and how best to achieve it.[16] Reform, as we know, operated on many levels, from the most universal of the reform of church in head and members, down through the levels of the reform of religious orders, of individual houses, and the personal reform that is the calling of all Christians. "Be not conformed to this world," as Paul put it in Romans 12:2, "but reformed [Gk. *metamorphousthe*; Lat. *reformamini*] in the newness of our mind."

The story of Carmelite reform does not begin with Teresa in 1562, but extends back more than a century to the work of the Congregation of Mantua and the generalate of Blessed John Soreth. Soreth's greatest reform activity was not his effort to restore a spirit of recollection and solitude, admirable as this was, but his encouragement of the entry of women into the Carmelite order, a movement which received papal recognition only in 1452. Given the central role taken by women in the era of the flowering of vernacular mysticism between 1200 and 1600, it is difficult to think that Carmelite mysticism would have ever come to be without the participation of women in the ongoing debate over the true form of the Carmelite life. As Michel de Certeau has put it in his *The Mystic Fable,* in the creation of the mystical discourse of the reformed Carmelites, "the gender difference takes on from the outset a theoretical and practical relevance. It takes *two* (masculine and feminine) for the new language to be born."[17] The ongoing debate over reform demonstrates once again that disputes that seem to have a limited, even a largely internal, significance for a particular group, often have wider repercussions. "Mystical reform," if I may be permitted such a category, was an important part of both the Catholic reform movement and what came to be called the Counter Reformation.

The confluence of these two major debates deeply engrained in late medieval Christianity—the tension between solitude and engagement and the issue of reform—helps us to understand something of the context of the flowering of Carmelite mysticism in the last decades of the sixteenth century. They emphasize the importance of seeing Carmelite mysticism as the final chapter in the development of a new stage, or better, layer in the history of Christian mysticism, one whose basic chronological contours stretch from about 1200 to 1600.

Christian mysticism, which I understand broadly as the preparation for, the consciousness of, and the effects produced by the immediate presence of God, was first explicitly formulated in the writings of Origen and his followers, especially Evagrius Ponticus.[18] As a particular modality of living the Christian life, however, it found its institutional setting and support within the monastic life, although the fathers and mothers of mysticism, both in the East and the West, usually did not restrict the possibility of attaining this practice of the presence of God to any particular group or class. The monastic milieu, though, had profound effects on most of the forms of mysticism found in Western Christianity to the end of the twelfth century, and often effectively limited mystical practice to monastics, as mentioned above. This monastic mysticism did not cease to exist after 1200. Rather, it remained an essential foundation and repository for later mystical teaching, as any reflection on the role of Cistercian and Victorine thought will show. But the new forms of religious life, the power of what German medievalists have called the *Frauenbewegung* (that is, the movement of women), and the shift to the use of the vernacular—all this taking place within a time of profound social and cultural change—produced a new and complex layer in the history of Western mysticism whose real contours are not yet fully explored, especially because many vernacular texts have been insufficiently studied. This is not the forum in which to try to give an overview of this era I have called the "flowering of mysticism,"[19] but I would like to give an example of how seeing the great Carmelite mystics within this broad perspective both casts light on their significance and also may provide food for thought concerning the possible role of Carmelite mysticism in general in the contemporary revival of spirituality.

John and Teresa

It has sometimes been claimed that the special attention given to the study of inner states, both states of dereliction and emptiness on the part of John of the Cross, and those of prayer and visionary experience found in Teresa, mark a new departure, the triumph of a "psychological" approach to mysticism (a term that none of the Carmelite mystics would have recognized). This is to confuse intensification with change in direction. There can be no question that Teresa and John provide a more detailed and often more pyschologically astute analysis of a wide range of interior experiences in the mystical path, both in its negative and positive moments, than almost all earlier mystics. Even a cursory reading of Teresa will also reveal how often she appeals to her own experience in presenting her teaching, as well as how much she wished her sisters to experience what she taught.[20] Part of this, of course, was a reaction to necessity. It was only after the promulgation of the Valdez Index of 1559, which effectively forbade all devotional literature in the vernacular, that Teresa received a message from Christ promising her that she would be given a "living book" that would leave her with very little need of any other books (L.26.5).[21] Her efforts to share her understanding of this "living book" with her sisters produced one of the most glorious achievements of Christian mysticism—reason enough to be thankful to Valdez!

The depth of analysis of various forms of the experience of divine presence and absence found in Teresa and John is truly unsurpassed, but looked at from the longer perspective of the development of mysticism over several centuries, this attention to inner experience takes on new meaning. Showing why will demand another brief, though I hope not superficial, review of a key trajectory in the history of mysticism.

The use of the term *mystikos* as a significant aspect of Christian belief and practice goes back to the second century, and the conviction that "mystical theology" [*mystikē theologia*] is not the same way of knowing God found by those who explore the divine nature by human reason is as old as the sixth century. However, "mysticism" (or even "mystics") as a rational investigation of the claims made by mystics themselves was not created until the seventeenth century, the product of an increasingly ossified Scholasticism whose final moments were lived out in fear of the Enlightenment rationalism to which it had perhaps already succumbed without knowing. If we can allow the term mysticism to describe an important element in Christian life during the first millennium and more of the history of Christianity, as I believe we can, then we must admit that, in general, such mysticism did not find expression in autobiographical accounts of union with God involving detailed descriptions of interior states.[22] During this period, mysticism was primarily an exegetical phenomenon, a particular mode of appropriating the mystical, that is, "hidden," message of the biblical text to discover the presence of God.

Beginning in the twelfth century, an important shift becomes evident in the relation between the book of Scripture, as the essential guide to the Christian life, and the book of experience, the individual's appropriation of the message of salvation revealed in the Bible. Even in the twelfth century, it is in the exegetical commentaries of great Cistercians, especially on the Song of Songs, and in the Victorines, as in Hugh and Richard's commentaries on Genesis and Exodus, that the most distinctive contributions to mystical literature are found. But when Bernard of Clairvaux invites his reader to set himself, or herself, between the "book of Scripture" and the "book of experience" [*Hodie legimus in libro experientiae—Sermon on Song of Songs 3.1*] a new kind of situation is evident—the book of experience has been given a correlativity with Scripture that sets the stage for the shift to greater emphasis on the exegesis of inner states of the soul on the part of many late medieval mystics.

This shift also affected the various genres of mystical literature. Rather than commentary on Scripture, preference begins to be given to visionary accounts, mystical treatises, sermons, even autobiographies. This change should not, of course, be exaggerated. The greater emphasis on the book of experience found among so many thirteenth-century mystics, both men and women, was a shift, not a revolution, primarily because experience never became the norm for discerning the true consciousness of the divine presence, but only the evidence that was to be tested and ordered by its conformity to the teaching of the church formed upon the word of revelation. The same always remained the case with the Carmelite mystics. Rowan Williams has put this well in his book on Teresa when he notes that both for Teresa and John " 'mystical states' . . . have authority only within a frame of reference which is believed in on quite other grounds, and are therefore properly to be tested according to their consistency with this."[23] The mystic becomes the living exemplar of Christian teaching; Teresa's *Life* vindicates her authority by showing its perfect conformity to the church and its practices. Mystical experience is important for the Spanish Carmelites, but in their concern for the proper evaluation of experience in the light of doctrine, they are part of a wider interplay between experiential states and scriptural teaching characteristic of the whole era of the flowering of mysticism.

The Nature of Mystical Union

A second crucial element in the teaching of Teresa and John, one in which their positions became in many ways normative for later Catholic mysticism, concerns mystical union.[24] Again, this careful attention to discussion of the nature of mystical union might be thought of as largely a sixteenth- and seventeenth-century phenomenon. Although neither Teresa nor John, to the best of my knowledge, ever used the *terminus technicus* of *unio mystica*, it was in use in discussing mysticism by the 1540s (e.g., by Louis de Blois), and in the early 1600s, it was to become a major item in the new genre of manuals of mystical theology (e.g., that of the Jesuit Maximilian Sandaeus). But I would argue that the attention that Teresa, and especially John of the Cross, give to discussing the proper way of understanding mystical union situates them in an intense debate that had been developing since the latter part of the thirteenth century. Again, some brief historical comments will be helpful.

The traditional Western Christian view of union between God and the human, found in the Latin Origen, in Ambrose, in Gregory the Great and others, had emphasized the loving union of wills by which finite and infinite Spirit became one, as proclaimed in the Pauline text so often cited in this connection—1 Corinthians 6:17: *"Qui autem adhaeret Domino, unus spiritus est"* ["Who cleaves to the Lord is one spirit with him"]. An alternative understanding of union between God and the soul, based on dialectical Neoplatonic metaphysics, first appeared in Christian mysticism with Evagrius Ponticus and was conveyed to the Latin West through the writings of Dionysius as translated by John Scottus Eriugena in the ninth century. This theory of union stressed the indistinction between the soul and its divine source, often in striking metaphors that suggest total absorption into God, as when Evagrius says, "When minds flow back into him like torrents into the sea, he changes them all completely into his nature, color and taste."[25] The unity of indistinction model, however, was not really used in Western mysticism prior to the thirteenth century, when it received considerable development, first in some of the Beguine mystics, and especially in Meister Eckhart, who may be called its most profound exponent, though John Ruusbroec gives him a close run for the title.

This is not the place to discuss the variations and the implications of this view of mystical union, especially the way in which "indistinction" was always conceived of in a dialectical fashion, that is, as simultaneously and reciprocally involving both indistinction and distinction. But it is important to note that this understanding of union was more controversial than the traditional *unitas spiritus* tradition. Much of the suspicion of late medieval mystics had its source in opposition to any *unitas indistinctionis,* which seemed to imply to many that there was no real difference between God and the soul. Many inquisitors believed that such a view of mystical union encouraged forms of autotheistic antinomianism. Theological controversy, condemnations of false mysticism, and even burning at the stake for heresy, as in the case of the Beguine Marguerite Porete in 1310 ensued. The great debate over how to understand union with God that percolated through the late Middle Ages is reflected in how Teresa, and especially John of the Cross, deal with the issue.

In a nutshell, the extensive discussion of mystical union by the major Carmelites represented a victory for the older and more traditional view of mystical union as an *unitas spiritus,* and this victory confirmed subsequent suspicions and condemnations of views of union as a dialectical *unitas indistinctionis.* St. Teresa's teaching on union evolved between the early stage represented in the *Life* (1562–5) and *The Way of Perfection* (1566) and the later stage of *The Interior Castle* (1577). In the earlier works, union, especially the "prayer of union" described in chapter 20 of the *Life,* is inferior to rapture seen as the soul's seizure by God. *The Interior Castle,* however, presents a picture close to the main traditions of the *unitas spiritus* tradition found in the Cistercians, Victorines, Franciscans such as Bonaventure, and so many others.

Though there are a number of complexities that cannot be entered into here, the "prayer of quiet" described in the fifth dwelling place involves both human effort to be fully conformed to God's will and the "delightful union" given in infused prayer (see especially C.5.3.3–5). The higher sixth and seventh dwelling places are presented in the erotic language of the betrothal and spiritual marriage; but now rapture is equated with the penultimate stage, and marriage is a "secret union [that] takes place in the very interior center of the soul" (C.7.2.3). Teresa makes use of metaphors that sometimes were employed by others to suggest a form of indistinction, such as the stream entering the sea and light entering a room. She also insists that in this favor "the soul remains all the time with its God" (C.7.2.4), but the context of the discussion shows that she is talking about a union, permanent as it is, of two spirits, one created and one uncreated, in absolute mutual love (see C.7.2.7).

John of the Cross contains some of the most detailed considerations of the nature of union to be found in the whole literature of Christian mysticism, especially in *The Spiritual Canticle* (1579–85). Like Teresa, he is not averse to using metaphors or language that taken in isolation could suggest some kind of indistinction between God and the soul. For example, he speaks of a "substantial union of the soul with God [*unión sustancial entre el alma y Dios*]," avowing "it would not be a true and total transformation if the soul were not transformed in the three Persons of the Most Holy Trinity in a clearly revealed and manifest degree" (C.39.3 & 6).[26] But when we inquire what he means by this transformation, or deification, that takes place in the spiritual marriage, we learn that he understands it primarily as a perfect union of love. "This thread of love binds the two . . . with such firmness and so unites and transforms them and makes them one in love, that, although they differ in substance, yet in glory and appearance the soul *seems* to be God and God the soul" (C.31.1). John's use of metaphors has greater theological precision than those of Teresa in this area. For example, note how he uses the traditional language of merging of lights or of flames. "When a small light unites with another that is great, it is the greater that overwhelms the lesser and gives light, and the smaller is not lost but perfected" (C.26.16–7).[27] The teaching of the Carmelites on mystical union, then, is the summation of one tradition that takes a definite stance against another.

Acquired and Infused Contemplation

There are, of course, other elements in the mystical theory of Teresa and John that are tied more closely to issues predominant in the sixteenth century, though they may have preparatory moments in the mysticism of the prior centuries. Prominent among these is the concern for carefully discriminating those stages of the mystical itinerary that permit of cooperation between God and the human from those that are purely the work of the Divine Lover, the kinds of distinctions that were later to be framed in terms of the difference between acquired and infused contemplation.

Earlier mystics tended to be relatively unconcerned about making such careful distinctions, though since Dionysius the Areopagite, at least, they had insisted that the immediate consciousness of the divine presence was a theopathic state (see *Divine Names* 2.9) in which the soul was passive to God. Some late medieval mystics had been more precise in attempting to describe this, such as the anonymous author of the fourteenth-century *Cloud of Unknowing*, well-instructed in Thomistic theology of grace, who spoke of the higher stages of prayer as "the work of God alone brought about in a special way in whatever soul that pleases him, without any merit on its part" (chap. 34).

The great care with which Teresa investigated this issue of the relation of human and divine action can be seen in *The Interior Castle,* especially in her distinguishing between the three active dwellings and the four passive ones, and in her discussion of the differences between "consolations" and "spiritual delights" (e.g., C.4.1.4). John of the Cross makes this discrimination the organizing theme for the structure of his four-part mystical summa. The active nights, of the "sensual part" and then of the "spirit," in which the soul cooperates with God, are treated in *The Ascent of Mt. Carmel,* while the passive nights of sense and spirit, ". . . wherein the soul does nothing and God works in it, and it remains, as it were, patient" (A.1.13.1) is the concern of the *Dark Night.* The illuminative and unitive stages treated in *The Spiritual Canticle* and *The Living Flame of Love* are, by definition, pure infusions of grace.

It would be misleading to seek for any simple and direct relation between this concern and the great debates over the nature of grace and human freedom that characterized the sixteenth century, but it is also difficult to deny that there is a deep inner connection. Catholic mystical theology, which in many ways was used as a living challenge to Protestantism in the polemics of the age, needed to be clear and resolute in a new way on the issue of how its position on the role of divine activity could be, in a sense, *experimentally* demonstrated through the description of mystical states. This concern remained dominant in the theology of mysticism down to living memory.

Given the close association of Teresa and John personally and in the reform movement, it has always been easy to take them together as forming a Carmelite "school" of mysticism. Under the influence of the ideology of uniformity that triumphed in Neoscholasticism, this interpretation reached an acme in the first half of our own century, especially when their own supposed "uniform" teaching had to be squared with the dogmatic theology of St. Thomas Aquinas. Today we are more open to the admission of plurality of viewpoints as not always being a disadvantage. Certainly, as emphasized above, there are many key areas in which Teresa and John are in fundamental agreement, and not only with regard to the attempt to evaluate inner experience on the basis of correct doctrine and to present the proper understanding of union with God. But what seems to me to be particularly important today, especially for the current retrieval of Carmelite mysticism, is the recognition of the differences between the two great mystics. Just as the tension between withdrawal into the solitude of the desert and engagement in pastoral mission—at times a creative tension, at other times a destructive one—has marked the Carmelites almost from the beginning, Teresa and John exhibit some important divergences that suggest that there can be no single model for regaining their message today. Let me give two illustrations of these differences.

Cataphatic and Apophatic Mysticism

The categories of positive and negative, cataphatic and apophatic, both to describe the divine nature and the mystic's preparation for and experience of God, have been central in Christian mysticism since Clement of Alexandria in the second century. All Christian mystics are apophatic in the sense of admitting that God is unknowable and that the mystic needs to undergo a process of purification in order to attain consciousness of the divine presence; some mystics give much greater attention to the role of purgation than others, and some (not always the same ones) are more resolutely apophatic in the way in which they present the encounter between God and the human. John of the Cross stands with Dionysius and Meister Eckhart—though very much in his own way—as one of the pinnacles of the apophatic tradition in Christianity. Nothing [*nada*] is everything for him—the nothingness to which the soul must be reduced in the awesome process of the dark nights and the nothingness of the "God, who, equally is dark night to the soul in this life" (A.1.2.1), even though this Divine Nothing is really the excess of light and the superabundance of the flame of the Divine Love. Teresa and John share a common fund of erotic language, especially the use of the images of the wound of love, of the betrothal and the spiritual marriage, to characterize the mystery of the soul's encounter with God; but Teresa does not interweave erotic and apophatic language as does John.

This also may help explain why John employs the language of the desert in a way that is lacking in Teresa.[28] In *The Spiritual Canticle* 14/15.12–20, John exegetes the line *"El silbo de los aires amorosos"* ["The whistling of the lovesick winds that rove," in Roy Campbell's version] by appealing to the traditional Old and New Testament archetypes of mystics, especially Elijah, who had experienced the touch and sound of the communication of the Divine Spouse, namely the feeling of delight given by the infusion of divine virtues and graces and the "whistling" of substantial knowledge of God infused into the passive intellect.[29] Two powerful passages, one from *Dark Night* and another from the thirty-fifth stanza of *Canticle* make direct use of the desert motif that was so often tied to Moses and Elijah.

Dark Night 2.17 is a lengthy explanation of the secret character of dark contemplation that John identifies with Dionysian mystical theology. It is secret not only because the soul has difficulty revealing or explaining it, but also because it "has the property of hiding the soul within itself" (N.2.17.6), that is, removing it into a "secret abyss" far from all creatures. John continues:

> . . . it considers itself as having been placed in a most profound and vast retreat, to which no human creature can attain, such as an immense desert [*un inmenso desierto*], which nowhere has any boundary, a desert the more delectable, pleasant and lovely for its secrecy, vastness and solitude, wherein, the more the soul is raised up above all temporal creatures, the more deeply does it find itself hidden. (N.2.17.6) [30]

Unlike Meister Eckhart and his followers, John does not identify God directly with the desert (perhaps because this might have suggested a different understanding of mystical union). The desert of which he speaks, as the passage from *Canticle* 35.1–7 indicates, is the inner solitude of the soul, her "desire to be without all the things and blessings of the world for the sake of its Spouse" (C.35.4). But John comes close to some earlier uses of the desert motif by stressing that it implies a direct, nonmediated, and reciprocal encounter:

> And thus he would not leave her alone; but rather, wounded by her through the solitude wherein for his sake she lives, and, seeing that she is content with naught else, he alone guides her to himself, draws her to himself and absorbs her in himself; which he would not do in her had he not found her in spiritual solitude. (C.35.7) [31]

If John of the Cross emphasizes the apophatic side of mysticism more powerfully than Teresa, thus allowing him to make use of the traditional desert theme of interior solitude, I would suggest that Teresa's teaching, on the other hand, is in some ways more open to the world, more "engaged" than that of John. This is not to say that the foundress does not insist on the centrality of interiorization, the movement of the soul within to find God in its very depths, as we can see from a noted passage at the beginning of the discussion of the fifth dwelling place (C.5.1.2). *The Interior Castle* presents one of the most structured and sustained accounts of mystical interiorization in Christian literature. But, on two important themes in the history of mysticism, Teresa provides a more accessible and perhaps more universal teaching than does John: first, with regard to the call to contemplation; and second, concerning the relation of action and contemplation.

John of the Cross at times appears elitist in the model of many of the representatives of the ancient monastic teaching about mystical union. In discussing the passage from the night of sense to the night of spirit as the way to divine union in *Dark Night* 1.14.1, he says that "not all pass habitually to this, but only the smallest number." Teresa does not discuss the numbers of those who might be called to attain the "fourth water" of the *Life*, or the "Prayer of Quiet" of *The Way of Perfection*, though she admits in chapter 17 of that work that not all are called to contemplation because it is a gift of God. In *The Interior Castle* at the beginning of the fifth dwelling place, she says that few of her sisters will fail to enter this, but that only a few will experience "some of the things that I say are in this room" (C.5.1.2). But this does not mean that the two higher dwelling places were not accessible to many of the sisters for whom she spent so much time discussing them. Indeed, in talking about the sixth dwelling place, she even mentions conferring about the various kinds of rapture with "so many spiritual persons" (C.6.4.2). Therefore, although Teresa wrote primarily for her own sisters, pledged to the austere and withdrawn life of the Reform, and insisted that contemplation was not for everyone, I think that the combination of solitude of life along with pastoral concern present in her idea of reform, as well as the flavor of accessibility in her writings, is different from what we find in John. This is the note that can be found in the advice she gives the sisters toward the end of *The Way of Perfection:*

> Do not let your soul dwell in seclusion [*No dejéis arrinconar vuestra alma*], or, instead of acquiring holiness, you will develop many imperfections, . . . in which case, as I have said, you will not do the good that you might, either to yourselves or to others. (W.41.8) [Peers, 2:181]

Action and Contemplation

This claim about a difference in tone, admittedly somewhat subjective, is supported by another aspect of the teaching of the two Carmelites. Teresa's goal of the union of action and contemplation in the highest stages of spiritual marriage is different from John's usual insistence on the priority of the contemplative aspect. Teresa's view of the unity of action and contemplation in the highest mystical stage continues an ancient and honorable tradition in the history of Christian mysticism. This is most evident in her description of spiritual marriage in the seventh dwelling place, but it is also found in what she has to say about the "Prayer of Quiet" in chapter 31 of *The Way of Perfection*. The traditional appeal to the union of the lives of Mary and Martha has rarely been put with greater power: "This, my sisters, I should like us to strive to attain: we should desire and engage in prayer, not for our own enjoyment, but for the sake of acquiring this strength which fits us for service" (C.7.4.12; cf. C.7.4.6).

John of the Cross never thought that spiritual marriage frees one from the obligation to good works, but he is more ambiguous about the relation of action to contemplation, holding a position, I believe, closer to that found in texts like the *Cloud of Unknowing,* which teach that it is incorrect and possibly even harmful to distract the contemplative from the higher state down to the level of action. As he put it in the commentary on stanza 28 of *The Spiritual Canticle*:

> Therefore if any soul should have aught of this degree
> of solitary love [*solitario amor*], great wrong would be done
> to it, and to the church, if, even but for a brief space, one

> should endeavor to busy it in active or outward affairs, of
> however great moment . . . . After all, it was to reach this goal
> of love that we were created.[32]

John's teaching on the relation of action and contemplation, to be sure, is too complex to be restricted to a single passage; but such texts indicate a difference in emphasis from the engaged quality of the union of action and contemplation that dominates in Teresa.

These remarks about Teresa and John are not meant to present any kind of summary of their rich mystical teaching, but only to highlight how aspects of their writings look when viewed from broad perspectives of the history of Western mysticism. It is also important to insist that the history of the Carmelite contribution to mysticism should not be restricted to these two giants, no matter how central they are. In the modern retrieval of Carmelite mysticism, it is not only the followers and system-atizers of Teresa and John in the seventeeth and eighteenth centuries that deserve renewed attention, but also the special figure of Thérèse de Lisieux, as well as the great independents, such as the Italian Maria Maddalena de'Pazzi, the French Jean de Saint-Samson, and the Belgian Maria Petyt, to name but a few, who need to be given renewed attention. The work of the Carmelite Institute in Washington, DC, represents a creative attempt to recapture both the fullness and the complexity of the whole story of Carmelite spirituality, a task which itself will cast a new light on both Teresa and John.

Two generations ago, during the era of the triumph of Neoscholasticism, it would have seemed as otiose to inquire about the importance of the role of the Carmelites in the history of mysticism as it would have been to wonder how significant Thomas Aquinas was in theology. Thomas was not just *a* theologian, but *the* theologian: everything of worth led up to him in some way, or else was scarcely worth consideration. The validity of what came after him was easily determined on the basis of how closely it approached his thought—at least according to whatever happened to be the regnant view of true Thomism.

The historical and political roots for the triumph of Neo-Thomism, which, in all lasted only some eighty years, that is, a long human lifetime, have been well documented. Its rapid decline in the quarter century since Vatican II has been the subject of diverse reactions—anger and chagrin, regret and nostalgia, and even satisfaction and some degree of hope. I count myself in the last category, not because of any opposition to Thomas Aquinas, whom I count as one of the greatest of all theologians, but because of my conviction that no theologian and no mystic or school of mysticism can be well served by being made the measuring stick by which all others are to be judged. Thomas was convinced that good theology, not theologians, partook of the eternity that formed its subject matter.

A somewhat similar fate overtook the great Carmelite mystics. Thomas Aquinas was declared a Doctor of the church as early as 1567. It was not until 1926 that John received this honor, to be followed by Teresa's declaration as one of the first two female *doctores ecclesiae* in 1970. If one looks back at the history of modern Catholic study of mysticism over almost a century, it is clear that Teresa and John exercised a preponderant role in what Neoscholastic thought identified as mysticism, one similar to Thomas's position in dogmatic and speculative theology. I would argue that the consequences of identfying mysticism with what Teresa and John said it was were in many ways unfortunate, both for the study of mysticism and also for the true appreciation of their own special contribution to a long, complex, extremely varied tradition in Christian history.

You all know the story of the two inebriated gentlemen who wandering home one night found the half-empty bottle that one promptly decried as "almost-gone," while the other hailed as "not-dead-yet." Just as unreconstructed Thomists find it difficult to believe that seeing the great Dominican as *a* theologian rather than *the* theologian can do no more than encourage sloppy thinking or rampant historical relativism, there may still be some who believe that the solution to the current confusion surrounding the terms mysticism and spirituality would be easily solved if we could only return to the "authentic" mystical teaching of

Teresa and John. These views, while perhaps understandable expressions of the nostalgia that can affect all those who have become deeply immersed in any great system of thought and life, are among the most severe obstacles to true and fruitful retrieval in a historically conscious age. The challenge confronting a body like the Carmelite Institute is precisely that of avoiding the attempt to rebuild the recent past by returning to the deep and original sources of the long and complex Carmelite tradition.

Conclusion: Reform and the Desert

I would like to suggest in closing that the two themes I identified as helpful for evaluating the role of the Carmelites in the evolution of late medieval mysticism might also be worthy of thought for the contributions the Carmelite tradition could make to the contemporary situation. The problem of reform was not solved in the sixteenth century any more than it was in the thirteenth or in the first century. The necessity for reform is constant in the Christian tradition. One message of the reform initiated by Teresa is perhaps especially pertinent today, when we are so often tempted to think that everything has to be done on a large scale in order to have any real effect. Who could have predicted the effects that a movement of such modest beginnings was to have, not only on the structure and growth of the Order, but on the whole history of Christian spirituality? What is being initiated with the Carmelite Institute is relatively modest too, at least by contemporary standards, but the dynamics of reform allow for possibilities that only the Spirit knows.

The other theme that I would suggest for your consideration is that of the desert and the necessary tension between withdrawal and engagement that the desert has always presented in the history of Chrisitan spirituality.[33] The first monks withdrew, or in their own language, made an *anachōrēsis,* into the Egyptian wastes in order to find God in solitude and abnegation. Yet, paradoxically, the world sought them out, and those who had fled society became its saviors and sometimes, unfortunately, its masters as monasticism became a dominant institution in Eastern and Western Christianity.

The first Carmelites were a part of the great eremitical revival in Western Christianity, though they too found that they could not abandon a world in need of redemption. A large part of the secret of the Carmelite contribution seems to have been found in the ongoing tension between the desire for solitude—that is, withdrawal into the desert, especially the desert of the heart—and the need to be actively engaged in the work of spreading God's love in the world. There is no single model, either in the history of Christianity or in Carmelite history, for making this a creative and not a destructive tension. But I would hope that the work of the Institute would be attentive to this issue and especially to the demands for withdrawal into the desert and the diverse forms that this can take today. In an activist age and in a culture that tends to prize action above contemplation, this part of the Carmelite heritage is important both for the Carmelites themselves and for the witness they give to the rest of us.

There are doubtless those who think that withdrawal into the solitude of the inner desert can easily encourage self-absorption and allow for neglect of the love that is the fundamental value of our Christian calling. This is always possible, but only to those who forget the words of one of the early desert fathers, Evagrius Ponticus, with which I would like to close. In his *Sentences to Monks*, Evagrius says:

> *Anachōrēsis en agapē kathairei kardian,*
> *anachōrēsis de meta misous ektarassei autēn.*
> Anachōrēsis in love purifies the heart;
> anachōrēsis in hate agitates it.[34]

Notes

1. *De Laude Heremi* 23, in *Sancti Evcherii Lvdvnensis Opera Omnia*, ed. C. Wotke (*Corpus Scriptorum Ecclesiasticorum Latinum* [CSEL]), 31:185.16–8).
2. Ibid., 3 (CSEL 31:178.25–179.1).
3. Ibid., 39 (CSEL 31:191.3–7).

4. Among the helpful introductions to Carmelite spirituality, see "Carmes (Spiritualité de l'ordre des). I. En dehors de la reforme de Sainte Thérèse (Titus Brandsma), II. Ecole mystique théresienne (Carmes dechaussés) (Gabriel de Sainte-Marie-Madeleine)," *Dictionnaire de spiritualité* [DS] 2:156–209; "Carmelitani II. Spiritualità" (O. StegginK), *Dizionario degli Istituti di Perfezione* (Rome: Edizioni Paoline, 1975), 2:476–501; Keith J. Egan, "The Spirituality of the Carmelites," in *Christian Spirituality II: High Middle Ages and Reformation*, ed. Jill Raitt in collaboration with Bernard McGinn and John Meyendorff (New York: Crossroad, 1987), 50–62; and Kieran Kavanaugh, "Spanish Sixteenth Century: Carmel and Surrounding Movements," in *Christian Spirituality III: Post-Reformation and Modern*, eds. Louis Dupré and Don E. Saliers in collaboration with John Meyendorff (New York: Crossroad, 1989), 69–92.

5. For an introduction, see Henrietta Leyser, *Hermits and the New Monasticism* (London: Macmillan, 1984).

6. For some general remarks, see Giles Constable, "The Ideal of Inner Solitude in the Twelfth Century," in *Horizons marins, Itineraires spirituels (Mélanges, Michel Mollat)*, eds. Henri Dubois, Jean-Claude Hocquet, and André Vauchez (Paris: 1987), 1:27–34.

7. See B. McGinn, "Mysticism," *The Oxford Encyclopedia of the Reformation*, 4 vols., eds. Hans Hillerbrand et al. (New York: Oxford University Press, 1996), 3:119–24.

8. Among the "founding fathers" of Western mysticism, only John Cassian holds to a strong form of this position. Both Ambrose and Augustine preached the message of achieving the presence of God to the whole Christian community, as did Gregory the Great, who explicitly notes that even lay Christians can taste contemplation. But the power of monasticism as the cultural form of mysticism meant that by the twelfth century, the major mystical theorists, especially Cistercian and Victorines, wrote largely for their fellow monastics.

9. On this tension, see Egan, 52–3, 59–60.

10. For a sketch of the earliest stages of the Carmelite movement and a translation of the Rule of St. Albert, see Franz-Bernard Lickteig, "Medieval Roots of Carmelite Spirituality," *The Sword* 37 (1977): 20–37; and 38 (1978): 16–30.

11. Nicholas, *Ignea Sagitta,* chap. 9, in Adrianus Staring, "Nicolai Prioris Generalis Ordinis Carmelitarum Ignea Sagitta," *Carmelus* 9 (1962): 295.33–38.

12. Cited in Stegginк, "Carmelitani Spiritualità," c. 479.

13. The history of the deserts or hermitages in the Carmelite and Franciscan orders has been surveyed in the article, "Déserts (saints)," in DS 3:534–49. See also André Cirino and Josef Raischl, eds., *Franciscan Solitude* (St. Bonaventure, NY: The Franciscan Institute, 1995).

14. This is not to take away from the efforts of some English Carmelites in the translation of spiritual literature into the vernacular, on which see Stegginк, "Carmelitani Spiritualità," c. 483.

15. Two major summaries of the period, those of Jaroslav Pelikan and Steven

Ozment, both use reform as the central category. See Ozment, *The Age of Reform 1250–1550* (New Haven, CT: Yale University Press, 1980); and Pelikan, *The Christian Tradition 4: The Reformation of Church and Dogma (1300–1700)* (Chicago: University of Chicago Press, 1984).

16. Ernst Troeltsch, *Die Bedeutung der Protestantismus für die Entstehung der modernen Welt*, first published in 1906, and translated into English in 1912 as *Protestantism and Progress*. For a later translation, see *Protestantism and Progress: A Historical Study of the Relation of Protestantism to the Modern World*, trans. W. Montgomery (Boston: Beacon Press, 1958).

17. Michel de Certeau, *The Mystic Fable*, vol. 1, *The Sixteenth and Seventeenth Centuries* (Chicago: University of Chicago Press, 1992), 135.

18. For more on this interpretation of the meaning of mysticism, see Bernard McGinn, *The Foundations of Mysticism: Origins to the Fifth Century*, vol. 1 of *The Presence of God: A History of Western Christian Mysticism* (New York: Crossroad, 1991), especially the "General Introduction," xi–xx.

19. I have surveyed the early stages of this movement in Bernard McGinn, *The Flowering of Mysticism: Men and Women in the New Mysticism (1200–1350)*, vol. 3 of *The Presence of God: A History of Western Christian Mysticism* (New York: Crossroad Herder, 1998).

20. In speaking of the "fourth water" in the *Life* 18, e.g., Teresa says, "I shall say nothing of which I have not myself had abundant experience [*experimentado mucho*]." (I will cite Teresa according to the translation of E. Allison Peers, *Complete Works of St. Teresa*, 3 vols. [London: Sheed and Ward, 1957] 1:108.) Also note how in chap. 39 of *The Way of Perfection* she appeals to her own experience in discussing the temptations that come to contemplatives (Peers, 2:169,171). In chap. 40 she prays that her sisters may experience true love of God: "May his Majesty be pleased to grant us *to experience* this before he takes us from this life, for it will be a great thing at the hour of death, . . . to realize that we shall be judged by one whom we have loved above all things" (Peers, 2:175–6).

21. *Life* (Peers, 1:168).

22. There are, to be sure, exceptions to this general claim. Some mystics, like Symeon the New Theologian, do insist on the necessity for personal experience and say a good deal about it. Many major figures, such as Origen, Augustine, Gregory the Great, and Bernard of Clairvaux, mention their own experiences of God only on rare occasions.

23. Rowan Williams, *Teresa of Avila* (London: Geoffrey Chapman, 1991), 149.

24. For background here, see Bernard McGinn, "Love, Knowledge, and *Unio Mystica* in the Western Christian Tradition," in *Mystical Union in Judaism, Christianity and Islam: An Ecumenical Dialogue*, 2nd ed., eds. Moshe Idel and Bernard McGinn (New York: Continuum, 1996), 59–86.

25. Evagrius Ponticus, *Epistola ad Melaniam* 6. This text, however, was not available to the Latin West.

26. I will cite John of the Cross in the translations of E. Allison Peers as reprinted in the Image Books Series [Garden City, NY: Doubleday]—*Ascent of Mt. Carmel* (1958), *Dark Night of the Soul* (1959), *Spiritual Canticle* (1961), *Living Flame of Love* (1962).

27. Also compare John's use of the illustration of the ray of sunlight passing through a window as found in *Ascent* 2.5.6–7; 14.9; *Dark Night* 2.8.3–4; and *Canticle* 26.4, with Teresa's employment in *The Interior Castle* 7.2.4.

28. The term "desiertos" occurs in Teresa in generic fashion, mostly referring to saints who dwell in the desert and there experience demonic temptations; see the references in Fr. Luis de San José, *Concordancias de las obras y escritos de Santa Teresa de Jesús* (Burgos: Tipografía de "El Monte Carmelo," 1945), 295. Teresa uses "soledad" frequently (see the references on 879–82) but not as a synonym for the desert experience. For the use of "desierto" in John of the Cross, see Juan Luis Astigarraga, Agustí Borrell and F. Javier Martín de Lucas, eds., *Concordancias de los Escritos de San Juan de la Cruz* (Rome: Teresianum, 1990), 545; and 1731–2 for "soledad." On the desert motif in medieval mysticism, see Bernard McGinn, "Ocean and Desert as Symbols of Mystical Absorption in the Christian Tradition," *Journal of Religion* 74 (1994): 155–81.

29. *Canticle* 14/15.14: "Since this whisper signifies the said substantial knowledge, some theologians think that our father Elias saw God in that gentle whisper of the breeze which he felt on the mount at the mouth of the cave" (Peers, 324). There is a similar passage concerning Elijah's reception of the "delicate touch" of the Word in *The Living Flame of Love* 2.17.

30. *Dark Night* (Peers, 162).

31. *Canticle,* (Peers, 454).

32. *Canticle* 29.3. (Peers, 417. In the Peers translation, this passage is found in stanza 28.3 under "Annotation for the Stanza Following.") Admittedly, there are other passages that seem to qualify this and insist that love of God wishes to overflow in both interior and exterior fashion; see, e.g., *Canticle,* 36.4 (Peers, 457).

33. The importance of the desert motif has recently been studied by Andrew Louth, *The Wilderness of God* (Nashville: Abingdon, 1991); and Belden C. Lane, *The Solace of Fierce Landscapes: A Journey into Desert and Mountain Spirituality* (New York: Oxford University Press, 1998).

34. *Ad Monachos* 8, from Jeremy Driscoll, *The 'Ad Monachos' of Evagrius Ponticus: Its Structure and a Select Commentary,* (Rome: U. Detti, 1991. Studia Anselmiana 104), 46.

Contemplation

THE CONTEMPLATIVE AS ICONOCLAST: THE COUNTERCULTURAL NATURE OF CONTEMPLATION

Donald W. Buggert, O.Carm.
Whitefriars Hall
Washington Theological Union
Washington, DC

As an introductory comment, let me say that I am not a mystical theologian. I approach this topic as a systematic theologian, and so I present my position more as a question or a "perhaps" rather than as a statement of fact. I ask the reader to receive it as such. Having said that, I am not too sure that what I have to say is all that startling or new. Perhaps I am like the scribe in Matthew 13:52 who brings forth from the storeroom of tradition both the old *and* the new.

Let me begin by stating my underlying thesis. As goes our understanding of God, so goes our understanding of contemplation and the contemplative. But our understanding of God is culturally and linguistically determined. Hence, if our understanding of God changes, so also our understanding of contemplation and of the contemplative will change.

This chapter has five sections: (1) reasons for my thesis; (2) a few words about the understanding of God that emerges in Christianity in the second century and which for the most part has dominated Western Christianity since Augustine; (3) the understanding of contemplation and the contemplative which corresponds to this "classical theism"; (4) a contemporary and more biblically inspired understanding of God; and (5) the implications of this contemporary understanding of God for our understanding of contemplation and the contemplative. Here I will conclude that *one* dimension of a contemporary understanding of contemplation is that contemplation of its very nature is countercultural and hence the contemplative is an iconoclast.

Understanding God and Contemplation

Let me first substantiate my thesis that as goes our understanding of God, so goes our understanding of contemplation; that our understanding of God is culturally and linguistically determined, and that, therefore, if our understanding of God changes, so also will change our understanding of contemplation.

Prior to Immanuel Kant (d. 1804), most philosophers held that human experience is totally derived from the "object," "the out there." The human knower or subject is merely a passive receiver. In no way is the human knower creative or constructive in knowing. Kant showed that the human knower is active in knowing, that is, that the knower himself/herself contributes something to experience. Today we call this insight of Kant "the turn to the subject." Hegel, and even more so Marx, further developed Kant's basic insight regarding the role of the subject in knowing. Both held that consciousness or experience is very much determined by one's particular place in history. In other words, consciousness or experience is always historically conditioned or circumscribed.

Applying this position to the question of experiencing God, Karl Rahner holds that all experience of the divine is mediated by one's historical experience. We are not pure spirits who have direct, unmediated access to the divine. In experiencing the divine, we never leave the world or our history. We are always "*in the world* spirits" or embodied spirits,

spirits whose embodiment places us in this particular history, in this particular culture, at this particular time, and hence spirits who have access to the divine only through our particular worldly experience. Transcendence is always historically mediated.[1]

Contemporary philosophers of language, such as Paul Ricoeur have further developed this turn toward the subject to understand experience, including the experience of the divine. These philosophers tell us that precisely because experience, including the experience of the divine, is culturally conditioned or constituted, it is also therefore conditioned or constituted by the language of any given culture. If Marx says (and he does) that "life determines consciousness" or experience, today we must also say that language determines experience, including, therefore, one's experience of the divine. There is no language-free experience of the divine.[2]

Since there is no language-free experience of the divine, one's experience of the divine (contemplation) is always very much determined by one's religious tradition, or, to put it in more contemporary rhetoric, by one's inherited religious story and its understanding of the divine. The contemplative experiences of the likes of Meister Eckhart, Teresa of Avila, and John of the Cross did not just appear on the scene from nowhere. That experience was itself already to a great extent (though I do not say *totally*) programmed by their religious tradition or story, by their understanding of the divine. Another way to say this: There is no universal, raw, acultural contemplative experience, because the contemplative experience is very much determined by the God contemplated. And the God contemplated is very much determined by one's religious story. Hence, if the story (understanding of God) changes, the contemplative experience changes.[3]

Early Christian Understanding of God

As Christianity moved into the Hellenistic world, its faith came to be articulated in Greek categories and hence influenced by Greek philosophy or the Greek story. This is merely another instance of the influence of culture and language on thought. There are two areas in which Hellenistic philosophy influenced Christian thought that are of interest to us: (1) our understanding of God and (2) our understanding of the human subject. I shall briefly address the Hellenistic understanding of the human subject, because it also influences somewhat our understanding of contemplation. But my main concern is the understanding of God.

First, the understanding of God.[4] Under the influence of various strains of Platonic thinking, the God of Judeo-Christianity came to be conceived along the lines of the "Absolute One" of Hellenistic philosophy and thus quickly came to be understood in very apophatic or world-negating terms (e.g., immutable, infinite, indivisible, ineffable, incomprehensible). This Hellenistic view of God itself presupposes the absolute abyss between the divine and the creaturely (the world of "being" and the world of "becoming" posited by Plato).[5] The otherness of the divine is so stressed that God is no longer truly related to the world and history. God's creative activity is understood as merely a past act of God through which God established the created world as a completed given in which nothing truly new happens and which needs only to be sustained by God's governance and directed by his providence. In this Hellenistic view of God, God has nothing new to do. Hence, God has no history. God exists in the timeless and simultaneous perfect self-possession of his infinite being.

Perhaps nowhere is this view of God more clearly seen than in its understanding of God as absolutely immutable or unchangeable in every respect. Because God is perfect and infinite in his being, he lacks nothing and hence cannot change. No wonder this God appears as unrelated to an ever-changing history and himself has no history, has nothing new to do. No wonder this God appears so static and timeless.[6] Pannenberg notes clearly the implications of an immutable God: ". . . the concept of the immutability of God necessarily leads to the consequence that the transition to every innovation in the relationship between God and man has to be sought as much as possible on the side of man."[7]

In fairness to the past, this ahistorical, static view of God did not totally dominate the patristic or later Christian tradition. Pannenberg correctly states: "On the whole, one ought not to speak of an uncritical acceptance of the philosophical idea of God."[8] However, this view of God definitely exercised its influence and coexisted in an uneasy tension with the biblical view of God, which I will take up later. In Pannenberg's words, "The ideas of God as world principle and as the free Lord of history remained for the most part inharmoniously alongside each other."[9] Thus, the Christian appropriation of the philosophical notion of God has yet to be critically completed.[10] There is still need for dialogue between Jerusalem and Athens, the God of the Scriptures and the God of philosophy.

The second area of interest to us in which Hellenistic philosophy influenced Christian thinking is in its view of the human subject. Here I see two influences. Briefly, the first is the Greek ideal of the human subject as "the knower."[11] Knowledge or contemplation of that which is eternal, of the world of the divine, is the highest and most noble perfection. Hence, in Plato's *Republic,* primacy of place is given to the philosophers, those who know the world of the divine, the world of being. Lowest on the social ladder are the "doers," the artisans, who live only in the world of "becoming." The view of "knowing" here is understood in that quite passive sense, which I mentioned above. Vis-à-vis its already constituted object or truth, with which it becomes one, the knower is purely receptive and passive. Here we are dealing with the Greek ideal of contemplation: the passive union in knowing with the divine. Also, this primacy of knowing over doing is itself related in Platonic thinking to the primacy of spirit over matter, a primacy that at times could lead to the denigration of and flight from matter and, hence, history.

The second influence of Hellenistic thinking upon the understanding of the human subject is its highly individualistic or substantival view of the human subject as a being whose existence, meaning, and intelligibility are self-contained. This view is quite different from both a Marxian and process philosophy view, which sees the human subject not as an isolated island, but as a political or organic subject constituted in its very being by its various relations (e.g., political, social, economic). I will point out below how I believe this highly individualistic view of the human person has affected our understanding of contemplation and the contemplative.

Classical Theism, Contemplation, and the Contemplative

If the God of your story is a God who is infinitely removed from history, who is timeless, who himself has no history, one would anticipate that contemplation is going to be understood in somewhat ahistorical terms. This, I believe, is to a great extent the case. If you read Evelyn Underhill's *Mysticism,*[12] for example, you will see that again and again she talks about contemplation as a loving knowing, an altered state of consciousness, in which one transcends this world and becomes one with or rests in the divine.[13] And she clearly distinguishes the contemplative or mystic from the artist who, unlike the mystic, must *do* something, must *act*.[14] Citing Eckhart, Underhill says, "The Soul is created in a place between Time and Eternity: with its highest powers it touches Eternity, with its lower (powers) Time." [15] She then goes on to say, "These, the world of Being and Becoming, are the two 'stages of reality' which meet in the spirit of man. By cutting us off from the temporal plane, the lower kind of reality, contemplation gives the eternal plane, and the powers which can communicate with that plane, their chance," that is, their opportunity.[16]

This is the world of Greek philosophy with its infinite abyss between the divine and the creaturely, with God understood as timeless and beyond history. Contemplation takes us out of the world of the creaturely and puts us into the world of the divine, which Underhill, just as Plato, calls "the real world." [17] Notice here the emphasis upon knowing, albeit a loving knowing, in speaking about contemplation. Nothing is said about a possible action or praxis dimension of contemplation. This same understanding of contemplation appears in the six definitions which Harvey

Egan presents in his book *Christian Mysticism.*[18] In all six cases, including the definitions of Teresa of Avila and John of the Cross, contemplation is conceived as loving knowledge that results in union with God, a union that in its highest form involves transformative union resulting in mystical marriage.[19]

The critique of Segundo Galilea and others of this traditional understanding of contemplation is that (1) the God contemplated is the timeless, immutable God, who has no history, who has nothing new to do; (2) contemplation is the loving awareness of and union with that God, which on the one hand results in a tranquil resting in God (in its highest form, mystical marriage) and on the other hand is opposed to action.[20] This understanding of contemplation as tranquil resting in the Lord should come as no surprise, given that the God contemplated is quite tranquil, that is, ahistorical and immutable, a God who has no future. No wonder that contemplation and the contemplative tend here to be understood as aworldly, as indifferent to history, since in contemplation, one transcends the world and history into the quite distinct and unrelated realm of the divine. The contemplative becomes more and more transformed into and one with a God who is beyond history, change, and action.

Galilea and others formulate their critique in another way. This understanding of contemplation and of the contemplative is overly privatized, spiritualized, and eschatologized. It is focused too much upon the subject as an isolated individual, upon the otherworldly and the hereafter. Lacking is the importance of salvation or the reign of God for the social, the worldly, and the here and now.[21]

A Biblical Understanding of God

In my opinion, Georg Hegel (d. 1831) inspired the rediscovery of a biblical view of God.[22] I want to say a few words about this biblical understanding.[23]

The Hebrews did not understand their God as a static essence that was both removed from history and himself had no history. God for them was not the *actus purus* of Thomas, which admitted neither of change nor relation outside of God. Rather, the Jews had a much more dynamic view of God. God is not pure act but pure *action*, and more specifically, pure *saving* action. Furthermore, beginning with Abraham 1750 B.C., God is not conceived so much as a God who acts only or even primarily in the past or the present, but rather a God who acts from the future, a God of the future, a God of the promises, a God who from the future calls us into the future and empowers us to create that future. This is the God of "salvation history." For Israel, God is the big "saving doing," the God who in the history of his people more and more manifests himself as and in fact *becomes* their savior, the God who becomes more and more God-for-us.[24] With and after Isaiah, Israel believes that this God, Yahweh, will only be fully God when he is fully savior, when he is fully manifested and victorious over his creation. And that is the end of time as we know it, the eschaton.

This eschatological view of God, is captured in the symbol "the reign of God," the *malkuth Yahweh,* which I translate as the reigning God. The reigning God is God himself/herself precisely as the God of the absolute future, the God of the End, the God who will be fully victorious over his creation.[25] For the Jew, God is a God who has a history, because he/she is not yet fully our God, the saving God, the reigning God. And this history of God comes to its completion only in the End, when God fully reigns. The Jews have a much more futuristic and hence also historical understanding of God than we have. God for them is the God of the Future, who has always yet new and surprising things to do on our behalf until he/she fully reigns.

This also was the God of Jesus. The twist that Jesus gave to his understanding of this reigning God is that this God of the Future is *now* beginning to break into history through him. He is the agent of the reigning God. The followers of Jesus after his death and resurrection, for reasons too involved to go into here, will confess that this reigning God had indeed fully occurred in advance of the Absolute End (the Eschaton) in

Jesus himself, especially in his resurrection. Moreover, they will confess that the reigning God of the End-time has now, in raising Jesus, filled this Jesus with his own creative presence and power, that is, his own Spirit, the Holy Spirit. And so Jesus in his Resurrection has become the life-giving, powerfully creative Spirit of God, who now sends forth that Spirit into the world to continue God's work of creating and saving, until God reigns fully over all (1 Cor 15:28).

Given this view of God as the God of the absolute future, it is no surprise that Jesus in his preaching of the reigning God used parables.[26] Parables are iconoclastic, for they bring together two aspects of experience or reality that do not belong together (e.g., Samaritan and good). In doing so, they shatter the past and bring about a whole new experience of reality, in fact a whole new reality, namely, the reality of the God of the Future, who in bringing about the absolute future must shatter every past and present. The reigning God, present in Jesus, is the new wine that shatters every old wine skin. No wonder then that Jesus' parables, and in fact his whole ministry, were perceived, rightly, by the leaders of Israel as such a challenge. The reigning God present in Jesus was challenging Israel to shatter and transcend its past and present into the ever new future. Jesus and his parables were iconoclastic because Jesus' God is iconoclastic, the God who demands that we shatter and transcend every past and present until she fully reigns.

We need, therefore, to formulate a new understanding of God that is more compatible with the biblical experience and the experience of Jesus. We need a theology of God that does justice to God's own history of becoming God for us not only in Christ but also in the Holy Spirit, for the Spirit is God as a God who is still creating and reconciling his creation and will do so until the Eschaton, until God fully reigns, until God is all in all (1 Cor 15:28).

A Contemporary Understanding of Contemplation and the Contemplative

I have presented a new and biblically inspired dynamic view of God. If this God were to become once again the God of our story, how would that affect our understanding of contemplation and the contemplative? This is an important question, for as Jon Sobrino points out, the issue is not whether one believes in God or prays to God, or contemplates God. The issue is which God? In which God do you believe, to which God do you pray, and which God do you contemplate?[27] The God of the Christian story as influenced by Hellenistic philosophy or the God of the Judeo-Christian Scriptures, the God of Athens or the God of Jerusalem?

So what is contemplation, or what does contemplation involve if the God contemplated is the historical God of the Judeo-Christian Scriptures? If contemplation involves the loving experience of God, union with and transformation into the divine, then I question whether it can be only a "tranquil dwelling of the person in the presence of God"[28] or a "resting" in God. For the God contemplated here is the reigning God, the God opposed to all suffering and injustice, to all that dehumanizes, the God who continually sends forth her Spirit to complete her reign. This God is a restless God, a God whose history of creating-reconciling-saving is not yet finished. This is a God who is still sending forth her mighty spirit to empower us as prophets to denounce the world of dis-grace and announce the world of grace.[29] This is a God whose spirit summons us to be iconoclastic and parabolic, that is, to build the reign and to challenge every idol of our culture that is opposed to that reign, every false god that dehumanizes and enslaves human beings. In the words of, Moltmann, "peace with God means conflict with the world, for the goad of the promised future stabs inexorably into the flesh of every unfulfilled present."[30]

With this God, the prophetic and the mystical cannot be opposed as Friedrich Heiler maintained.[31] One can be a prophet only because one first tastes the divine. Prophets experience the divine absence or dis-grace in history only because they first experience the divine presence or grace. This experience of the divine presence compels the prophet to denounce its absence, the reign of Satan, and to announce a new future, the reign of God. Because prophets first stand in the sight of the living God, they are filled with zeal for the Lord God of Hosts. One cannot rest tranquilly in the God of Israel, the God of Jesus, because this God himself is doing anything but resting tranquilly. And so with this God, one can only be a contemplative prophet, not a contemplative or a prophet.[32] We must beware of a "contemplative Docetism," an ahistorical contemplation. As Gustavo Gutiérrez cautions, we must not set a "praxis of heaven" against a "praxis of earth" and vice versa.[33] Along similar lines, Rahner says:

> The Christian cannot simply dismiss politics as a "dirty business" and expect God to give this "dirty business" to others to carry out and not to him, so that he himself can pursue his own quiet devotions in the comfort of the petit-bourgeois.[34]

William Ernest Hocking nicely articulates this intrinsic relationship between the prophet and the mystic. He writes:

> The prophet is but the mystic in control of the forces of history, declaring their necessary outcome; the mystic in action is the prophet. In the prophet, the cognitive certainty of the mystic becomes historic and particular, and this is the necessary destiny of that certainty: mystic experience must complete itself in the prophetic consciousness.[35]

Carmelite Implications

Now what are some implications from what I am proposing? How are we to be contemplative prophets? I am a systematic theologian, and systematicians are theoreticians, not "how-to-do-it" persons. But I do hazard a few practical "how-to-do-it" suggestions. In the long run, the "how-to-do-it" is a question that all Carmelites today must address.

First, the rather obvious "how-to-do-it" is direct and immediate involvement in the socio-political-economic sectors of our world. Some examples here are Oscar Romero, Raymond Hunthausen, Daniel Berrigan, Gustavo Gutiérrez, Mother Teresa, Titus Brandsma, Carlos Meesters, Canisius Hinde, Alban Quinn, and Julio Labayan. Each of us could add many other names to to this of rather extraordinary contemplative prophets, extraordinary iconoclasts.

But, besides these extraordinary mystical prophets, there are the ordinary mystical prophets such as ourselves. Rahner speaks about ordinary, everyday mysticism.[36] And so I also speak about an ordinary, everyday prophetic mysticism or iconoclastic mysticism. Perhaps there is a more ordinary way of being countercultural. I have in mind not so much what we do by way of *ministerial activity,* but what we say and witness to by the way we live.

I have said that true contemplatives are iconoclastic and countercultural. They shatter and transcend all false and oppressive idols in our culture. The Jesuit philosopher, John Kavanaugh, in his book *Following Christ in a Consumer Society: The Spirituality of Cultural Resistance,*[37] has exposed in a challenging way *the* number one false idol of our Western culture. He calls it the "commodity form." The commodity form is a way of perceiving ourselves and others as things or commodities. Things replace persons; material relations displace human relations. The commodity becomes an idol that drives us to worship things and relate to them as if they were persons and to relate to persons as if they were things. The result is that persons are possessed by their possessions and produced by their products.[38] The commodity form with its values of marketability and consumption becomes a pathology against which we evaluate ourselves and others in terms of productivity and usefulness, with the result that there is no intrinsic human value.[39] Likewise, the commodity form gives rise to a commodity ethics of rugged individualism, which results in violence, domination, manipulation, racism, sexism, abortion, euthanasia, ecological plunder, and excessive consumption.[40]

Opposed to this commodity form is the "personal form." This is a "mode of perceiving and valuing men and women as irreplaceable persons whose fundamental identities are fulfilled in covenantal relationship."[41] The personal form promotes the intrinsic worth of persons, promotes respect, freedom, detachment, self-donation, justice, peace, forgiveness, healing, compassion, and the empowerment of those who are least.[42] The personal form is most fully revealed in Jesus of Nazareth.

To contemplate the God of Jesus and to walk in the footsteps of Jesus (*in obsequio Jesu Christi*) demands, I believe, living according to the personal form, and to live according to the personal form is to be countercultural and iconoclastic. It is to denounce the commodity form, which leads to death, and to announce the reign of God, which leads to life. The idol of the commodity form is the new Baal, the new Satan, the new adversary who prowls around like the roaring lion in chapter 14 of the Carmelite Rule seeking those whom he can devour. To contemplate the God of Jesus, the reigning God, is to enter into battle with this roaring lion of the commodity form.

I return now to my question: How can we Carmelites be iconoclastic or countercultural? Over and beyond any direct ministerial involvement in the socio-political-economic spheres, we can be iconoclastic and enter into spiritual combat with the roaring lion of the commodity form in three ways, which have to do with lifestyle, the way we live.

The first form of spiritual combat is the life of the vows, especially today the vow of poverty. The vows are quite countercultural and opposed to the commodity form. Their purpose is humanization and liberation—liberation *from* the powers that drive us to the commodity values of power, domination, and possession; liberation *to* empowering others as human beings. The vows are a direct denunciation of the commodity form whose god is mammon and whose goal is productivity. The vows after all are really quite useless for our commodity world and its concern for productivity.[43]

Through the vow of poverty, we can enter into combat with the commodity form of our culture. In our day, I would define the vow of poverty as material, emotional, and spiritual identification with the materially poor. This identification is often called the "preferential option for the poor," for those who are *most* victimized, *most* enslaved, and *most* dehumanized by the rapacious greed of the commodity form. But we cannot prophetically denounce, we cannot be iconoclastic, we cannot shatter the idols of the commodity form if we ourselves are nothing but a celibate echo, a mirror of our materialistic society, of the commodity form, if we ourselves have become enslaved to the commodity. In that case, we are neither contemplatives nor prophets, for we are merely helping to legitimate dis-grace, the absence of the divine in our society.

The second way in which we can do battle with the commodity form and hence be countercultural is through our Carmelite life of silence, solitude, and prayer, which also are utterly useless in the commodity world. Silence and solitude force upon us the journey within where we encounter our radical poverty and need, where there is revealed to us the demons that drive us to control and manipulate and which deceive us with the dizzying illusion of autonomy. Prayer arising from this silence and solitude puts us in touch with the God of the reign, reveals to us our true identity as persons, and liberates us from the illusions and the lies of the roles demanded by the commodity form. Authentic prayer is a decommodification of our lives and a reappropriation of our personhood.[44]

The third form of countercultural spiritual combat is community life. The hermits on Carmel contextualized their walking in the footsteps of Jesus Christ by embracing the ideal vision of the Jerusalem community. As Sr. Constance FitzGerald, O.C.D., has pointed out, our Rule spells out this communitarian vision in terms of a sharing of goods and life, an egalitarian style of life, communal-dialogical discernment, and a respect for the individual.[45]

This communitarian life, signaled in our Carmelite Rule, is itself a countercultural protest against the commodity form with its objectifying of the person through dominative and dehumanizing relationships, its lack of care and respect, its enslavement of freedom, and its idolizing of competition, achievement, and control. In turn, such a communitarian life witnesses to the values of the personal form: the intrinsic worth of persons, freedom, detachment, generosity, justice, peace, forgiveness, healing, compassion, and the empowering of those who are least.

Our Carmelite lifestyle, therefore, with or without active ministry (as that term is usually understood)—our lifestyle of the vows, of silence, solitude, and prayer, of community—can be a prophetic denunciation of the commodity values of our society and a prophetic annunciation of a new way of living. Kavanaugh calls it the "personal form." I would suggest a different word, a word from Eckhart, *"Gelassenheit,"* letting-be.[46] Letting-be is a way of living according to which we no longer view things, persons, or events in terms of their usefulness but accept them in their autonomy. We no longer wish to possess or subvert things to our own projects; we wish only to restore things to themselves and persons to their own freedom.[47] In our lives as Carmelites, we should be witnesses of "letting-be." To the extent that we are, we are truly countercultural, for letting-be attacks the very roots of a culture hell-bent on possession, productivity, and domination.

In view of the God of Israel, the God of Jesus, we Carmelites must challenge ourselves in many ways. (1) We must ask ourselves to what extent we take seriously our contemplative vocation to live in the sight of the living God. (2) We must ask ourselves to what extent we take seriously our prophetic vocation to be zealous for the Lord God of Hosts, that is, to what extent our contemplative life leads to a truly prophetic life, for not to be prophetic, not to be iconoclastic and countercultural is to reinforce the status quo. If in our contemplation we evanesce from history, then we leave history in its state of dis-grace. (3) Likewise, if in our ministry we do not truly challenge the Baals of our society, the oppressors, the dehumanizers, those who deal out death, sometimes even in the name of God, then again we merely reinforce the status quo, the reign of Satan. We are making the "haves"—the rich and the powerful—more comfortable with a pseudo-God, for the God of Jesus is certainly not the God to whom the rich and the powerful pray. Again, the question is: In *which* God do you believe, to *which* God do you pray? Not any old God will do! Some gods end up reinforcing the status quo of oppression and injustice and hence also become a defense of social privilege and ruthless power.[48] Contemplatives who have no commitment to history and its transformation into the reign of God send out the message that what happens here and now is of no consequence, that salvation is strictly "pie in the sky." We must be careful not to be in league with the powerful and rich, even if only by default, by saying and doing nothing.

Carmelite Nuns

Before I close, I would like to say a special word to my contemplative sisters in Carmel. I hesitate to use the word "cloistered," because I fear that term might be understood in such a way as to indicate precisely the view of God, of contemplation and the contemplative that I am questioning.

First, almost all that I have said above applies to you. Second, there are many who question your life of silence, solitude, and prayer. They believe that you are foolish. I do not. To those who do, I respond with the words of St. Paul: "Brothers and sisters, you are among those called . . . . Not many of you are wise, as people account wisdom; not many are influential; and surely not many are wellborn. But God chose those whom the world considers foolish to shame the wise; he singled out the weak of this world to shame the strong. He chose the world's lowborn and despised, those who count for nothing, to reduce to nothing those who were something; so that humankind can do no boasting before God" (1 Cor 1:26–29).

You, especially, through your somewhat hidden life, can and do shout out to all of us and to our commodity society that in the end only God can heal, *only God* can save, that in God alone do we find our salvation. Your silent life of solitude and prayer is a scathing prophetic denunciation of those who peddle the ersatz salvation of oppressive power, enslaving possessions, and naked autonomy. In turn, you also prophetically announce a new way of living, a new way of being human, an annunciation of authentic salvation, which is found only in God. Through your parabolic lives, you too, and perhaps I should say "especially you," are iconoclastic and countercultural.

Conclusion

I began by saying that perhaps I am like the scribe who brings forth from the storehouse things old and new. To say that the contemplative is iconoclastic is nothing really new. Apophatic mystics have always shown us that all idols, all finitudes, even our images and concepts of God must be transcended. The mystics of old have always reminded us that God is no-thing, that God is always yet greater. I have merely recast this teaching by calling this God the God of the Absolute Future, the God of the reign who remains always yet ahead of us. In using the biblical symbol of the reigning God, I have tried to bring out the historical-social-political or prophetic dimension of contemplation and of the contemplative.

True contemplatives are thus, by their very nature, iconoclasts, image breakers, those in search of that one fine pearl, the reigning God. The images that the contemplative shatters are not only the images and concepts of God but all those idols that enslave society and prevent the reign of God from becoming a reality within it. The true contemplative, in shattering and transcending all images of God, likewise shatters all the ersatz gods within the church itself that surreptitiously attempt to displace God and to enthrone themselves as the true God, the reigning God, the God who is always yet ahead of us, the God who remains "not-yet." The true contemplative prophetically challenges not only society but also the church to absolutize nothing, least of all herself, to move beyond every past so that the reigning God may be ultimately victorious in her creation.

In doing this the true contemplative provides both society and the church with the much needed "eschatological proviso,"[49] with the message: "Let God be God," with the message that the reign is "not-yet," that no-thing alone is God, that not even the church with all of her church-men and all of her church-women, with all of her creeds and doctrines, with all of her sacraments and liturgy is the reigning God. Indeed, we Carmelites must recall today the subversive memory of our mystics.[50] But we must also listen attentively to Marx's well-known eleventh thesis against

Feuerbach. Marx said: "The philosophers have only interpreted the world in various ways; the point is to change it."[51]

Perhaps contemplatives at times have left the world to itself to rest tranquilly in a tranquil Lord. I am proposing that, with a biblical understanding of God and contemplation, contemplatives are those who are passionately in love with a God who herself is passionately about the business of bringing her reign to completion. And hence their passionate love for God turns them not from the world or history but radically commits them to a world and a history for which our God in Christ has died and to which he through Christ still sends forth his Spirit until he is all in all.

Notes

1. See, e.g., Karl Rahner, *Foundations of Christian Faith: An Introduction to the Idea of Christianity,* trans. William Dych, (New York: Seabury Press, 1978), 81–9, 140–2, 151–2.

2. Hence, for Ricoeur, language is the new "transcendental," i.e., a universal or a prior structure of the human subject, which accounts for experience. See Paul Ricoeur, "The Question of the Subject: The Challenge of Semiology," in *The Conflict of Interpretations* (Evanston, IL: Northwestern University Press, 1974), 258. A key writing of Ricoeur dealing with the relationship between language and religious experience is "Biblical Hermeneutics," *Semeia* 4 (1975): 29–148. Regarding the relation of language and experience in the thought of Paul Ricoeur, see John W. Van Den Hengel, S.C.J., *The Home of Meaning: The Hermeneutics of the Subject of Paul Ricouer* (Lanham, MD: University Press of America, 1982), 10–22, 117-27. In chapters eight and nine of this same work, Van Den Hengel discusses the role of language for religious experience. Many contemporary systematic theologians in their methodology have taken what might be called "the linguistic turn," and hence reflect this sensitivity to the importance of language, tradition, and narrative for experience, including therefore religious experience. Best known perhaps is David Tracy, *The Analogical Imagination: Christian Theology and the Culture of Pluralism* (New York: Crossroad, 1981), esp. 47–98, 99–153, 154–229, 405–45. Similar to Tracy is Claude Geffré, *The Risk of Interpretation: On Being Faithful to the Christian Tradition in a Non-Christian Age,* trans. David Smith (New York: Paulist Press, 1987), 21–45, 46–64. See also George A. Lindbeck, *The Nature of Doctrine: Religion and Theology in a Postliberal Age* (Philadelphia: Westminster Press, 1984), 30–45. Lindbeck critiques the "experiential-expressive model" for understanding the relationship between experience and language, according to which language is nothing but an expression of a previously exist-

ing, prelinguistic experience. In place of this experiential-expressive model, Lindbeck suggests "a cultural-linguistic alternative."

3. Harvey Egan notes: "Many contemporary commentators emphasize . . . that the contemplative's total formative milieu is an intrinsic part of his mystical experience. The person's entire conceptual, social, historical, and linguistic matrix enters into the contemplative consciousness and experience" ; see Harvey D. Egan, S.J., *Christian Mysticism: the Future of a Tradition* (New York: Pueblo Publishing Company, 1984), 107; see also 153–4. The same point is made by Jure Kristo, "The Interpretation of Religious Experience: What Do Mystics Intend When They Talk about Their Experiences?" *The Journal of Religion* 62 (1982): 21–38.

4. Among other sources, I am dependent here especially upon the following: Wolfhart Pannenberg, "The Appropriation of the Philosophical Concept of God as a Dogmatic Problem of Early Christian Theology," in *Basic Questions in Theology,* vol. 2, trans. George H. Kehm (Philadelphia: Fortress Press, 1971), 119–83; Hans Küng, *The Incarnation of God,* trans. J. R. Stephenson (New York: Crossroad, 1987), 430–59, 509–58; Piet Schoonenberg, "God as Relating and (Be)coming: A Meta-Thomistic Consideration," *Listening* 14 (1979): 265–79; "Process or History in God?" *Louvain Studies* 4 (1973): 303–19; "Denken über Chalkedon," *Theologische Quartalschrift* 160 (1980), 295–305; William M. Thompson, *Jesus, Lord and Savior: A Theopathic Christology and Soteriology* (New York: Paulist Press, 1980), 113–61; Walter Kasper, *The God of Jesus Christ,* trans. Matthew J. O'Connell (New York: Crossroad, 1984), 147–57; John Macquarrie, *In Search of Deity: An Essay in Dialectical Theism* (New York: Crossroad, 1985), 3–56.

5. Thus for example in the *Phaedo* 79a, the following dialogue between Socrates and Cebes: "So you think that we should assume two classes of things, one visible and the other invisible? Yes, we should. The invisible being invariable, and the visible never being the same." Socrates continues in 80b: "Now, Cebes, . . . see whether this is our conclusion from all that we have said. The soul is most like that which is divine, immortal, intelligible, uniform, indissoluble, and ever self-consistent and invariable, whereas body is most like that which is human, mortal, multiform, unintelligible, dissoluble and never self-consistent." See also among other dialogues Plato's *Republic*, books 6 and 7, and *Timaeus*, esp. 28–9.

6. In the words of Jaroslav Pelikan, himself citing Whitehead's *Process and Reality:* "Whether theologians found Platonic speculation compatible with the gospel or incompatible with it, they were agreed that the Christian understanding of the relation between Creator and creature required 'the concept of an entirely static God, with eminent reality, in relation to an entirely fluent world, with deficient reality'—a concept that came into Christian doctrine from Greek philosophy." See Jaroslav Pelikan, *The Emergence of the Catholic Tradition (100–600)* (Chicago: University of Chicago Press, 1971), 53.

7. Pannenberg, "The Appropriation of the Philosophical Concept of God," 162.

8. Ibid., 178. See Macquarrie, 59–167 for his treatment of an alternative, more

dialectical tradition within Christianity regarding God and God's relation to the world.

9. Pannenburg, "The Appropriation of the Philosophical Concept of God," 179.

10. Ibid., 182–3.

11. For more detailed development and bibliography, see my "Liberation Theology: Praxis and Contemplation," *Carmelus* 34 (1987): 3–58, especially 21–32 where I discuss Karl Marx's critique of the Western philosophical tradition.

12. New York: Meridian Books, 1955. For an extended treatment of this "classical" view of contemplation, see R. Garrigou-Lagrange, O.P., *Christian Perfection and Contemplation According to St. Thomas Aquinas and St. John of the Cross*, trans. Sr. M. Timothea Doyle, O.P. (St. Louis: B. Herder Book Co., 1945), esp. 221–60.

13. See, e.g., Underhill, 71–4 .

14. Ibid., 75.

15. Ibid., 65.

16. Ibid.

17. Ibid., 67; see also 54, 55–6.

18. Egan, 4–5.

19. Ibid., 193–97.

20. See, e.g., Segundo Galilea, "Liberation as an Encounter with Politics and Contemplation," in *The Mystical and Political Dimension of the Christian Faith*, ed. Claude Geffré and Gustavo Gutiérrez (New York: Herder & Herder, 1974), 19–33; Gustavo Gutiérrez, "Liberation Praxis and Christian Faith," in *Frontiers of Theology in Latin America*, ed. Rosino Gibelleni (Maryknoll, NY: Orbis, 1979): 1–33; Jon Sobrino, "Christian Prayer and New Testament Theology: A Basis for Social Justice and Spirituality," in *Western Spirituality, Historical Roots, Ecumenical Routes,* ed. Matthew Fox (Sante Fe, NM: Bear Company, Inc., 1981), 76–114.

21. See my "Liberation Theology: Praxis and Contemplation," esp. 6–7.

22. For the importance of Hegel for a contemporary and yet very biblically inspired understanding of God, see Küng, 430–60, 509–58, and Peter C. Hodgson, *God in History: Shapes of Freedom* (Nashville: Abingdon Press, 1989).

23. For this biblical view of God, I am influenced by, among others, Piet Schoonenberg, John Macquarrie, and the eschatologically oriented theologies of Jürgen Moltmann and Wolfhart Pannenberg, both of whom are influenced by Hegel. For Schoonenberg, see the sources mentioned in n. 4 above as well as *The Christ,* trans. Della Couling (New York: Herder & Herder, 1971), n. 16 on 83–6. For Macquarrie, see his *In Search of Deity* and his earlier work *Thinking About God* (New York: Harper & Row, 1975), esp. chaps. 8–11. For Moltmann, see among other works, *Theology of Hope*, trans. James W. Leitch (New York: Harper & Row, 1967), 37–229; "Theology as Eschatology," in *The Future of Hope: Theology as Eschatology,* ed. Frederick Herzog (New York: Herder & Herder, 1970), 1–50; *The Crucified God*, trans. R. A. Wilson and John Bowden (New York: Harper & Row, 1974), esp. 249–90; for Pannenberg, see among other works "Dogmatic Theses on the Doctrine of Revelation," in *Revelation as History,* trans. David Granskou, ed. W. Pannenberg (London: The Macmillan Com-

pany, 1968), 123–58; "Theology and the Kingdom of God," in *Theology and the Kingdom of God,* ed. Richard John Neuhaus (Philadelphia: Westminster Press, 1969), 51–71; "Appearance as the Arrival of the Future," in *Theology and the Kingdom of God,* 127–43; "The Appropriation of the Philosophical Concept of God," 119–83; "Historical and Theological Hermeneutics," in *Basic Questions,* vol. 1; "What is Truth?" in *Basic Questions,* vol. 2, 1–27; "The God of Hope," in *Basic Questions,* vol. 2, 234–49; "The Revelation of God in Jesus of Nazareth," in *Theology as History,* vol. 3 of *New Frontiers in Theology,* eds. James M. Robinson and John B. Cobb, Jr. (New York: Harper & Row, 1967), 101–33; "Response to the Discussion," in *Theology as History,* 221–76; "Father, Son, Spirit: Problems of a Trinitarian Doctrine of God," *Dialog* 26 (1987): 250–57; *Jesus God and Man,* trans. Lewis L. Wilkins and Duane A. Priebe, (Philadelphia: Westminster Press, 1977), 53–114; 127–32; 225–35; 365–97. Other influential sources are: Abraham Heschel, *The Prophets* (New York: Harper & Row, 1962), esp. 218–20; 221–31; 232–35; Thompson, 113–61; Eberhard Jüngel, *The Doctrine of the Trinity: God's Being Is in Becoming* (Grand Rapids, MI: William B. Eerdmans Publishing Co., 1976).

24. Not available at the time at which I wrote this paper was Catherine LaCugna's masterful work *God For Us: The Trinity and Christian Life* (San Francisco: Harper, 1991). I believe that I accurately state LaCugna's position in saying that it is precisely in becoming Trinitarian in history that God realizes God's being as a God-for-us. Thus God does have a history, and this history is the history of God's becoming in our history Father, Son, and Spirit.

25. See Norman Perrin, *Rediscovering the Teaching of Jesus* (New York: Harper & Row, 1967), 56.

26. For Jesus' use of parables, see Norman Perrin, *Jesus and the Language of the Kingdom: Symbol and Metaphor in New Testament Interpretation* (Philadelphia: Fortress Press, 1976), 32–56, 194–205; and John Dominic Crossan, *In Parables: The Challenge of the Historical Jesus* (New York: Harper & Row, 1973).

27. See Jon Sobrino, "Christian Prayer and New Testament Theology: A Basis for Social Justice and Spirituality," 80–1, 93–102, 110, and *Spirituality of Liberation: Towards Political Holiness,* trans. Robert R. Barr (Maryknoll, NY: Orbis, 1988), 117–24. See also Segundo Galilea, *The Way of Living Faith: A Spirituality of Liberation,* trans. John W. Diercksmeier (San Francisco: Harper & Row, 1989) 23–5; and Edward Schillebeeckx, *On Christian Faith: The Spiritual, Ethical, and Political Dimensions,* trans. John Bowden (New York: Crossroad, 1987), 54–6.

28. See Karl Rahner and Herbert Vorgrimler, *Theological Dictionary* (New York: Herder & Herder, 1965), s.v. "contemplation."

29. For the themes of prophetic denunciation and annunciation, see Gustavo Gutiérrez, *A Theology of Liberation,* trans. Caridad Inda and John Eagleson (Maryknoll, NY: Orbis, 1973), 265–72; Segundo Galilea, "Liberation as an Encounter with Politics and Contemplation," passim, and Rosemary Haughton, "Prophetic Spirituality," *Spiritual Life* 35 (1989): 3–12. For the themes of grace and dis-grace, see Leonardo

Boff, *Liberating Grace*, trans. John Drury (Maryknoll, NY: Orbis, 1979), 4, 60–3, 84–7.

30. *Theology of Hope*, 21.

31. Friedrich Heiler, *Prayer* (New York: Oxford University Press, 1958), 136. Concerning the essentially biblical nature of authentic Christian mysticism, see Richard Woods, *Mysterion: An Approach to Mystical Spirituality* (Chicago: Thomas More Press, 1981), 25–39.

32. For the relationship between the prophetic and contemplative or mystical, see my "Liberation Theology: Praxis and Contemplation," 50–8, as well as Schillebeeckx, 65–75 and Woods, *Mysterion*, chap. 10, "Mysticism and Social Action," 159–73. For Rahner's resolution of the mystical-prophetic dialectic, see Karl Rahner, "The Ignatian Mysticism of Joy in the World," *Theological Investigations*, vol. 3, trans. Karl-H. and Boniface Kruger (Baltimore: Helicon Press, 1967), 277–93. For an excellent treatment of the "iconoclastic" role of the prophet, see Walter Brueggemann, *The Prophetic Imagination* (Philadelphia: Fortress Press, 1978), esp. 44–79.

33. Gustavo Gutiérrez, "Liberation, Theology, and Proclamation," in *The Mystical and Political Dimension of Christian Faith,* eds. Claude Geffré and Gustavo Gutiérrez (New York: Herder & Herder, 1974), 63. Latin American liberation theologians are more and more constructing a synthesis between spirituality and life, prayer and action, the contemplative and the prophetic. As recent examples of this synthesis, see, besides the references already made to Gutiérrez and Galilea, Jon Sobrino, *Spirituality of Liberation*, esp. 23–45, 80–6.

34. Karl Rahner, "Christian Living Formerly and Today," *Theological Investigations,* vol. 7, trans. David Bourke (New York: Seabury Press, 1977), 19.

35. William Ernest Hocking, *The Meaning of God in Human Experience* (New Haven, CT: Yale University Press, 1963), 511.

36. See, e.g., "The Ignatian Mysticism of Joy in the World," "Christian Living Formerly and Today," "Everyday Mysticism," in *The Practice of Faith: A Handbook of Contemporary Spirituality* eds. Karl Lehmann and Albert Raffert (New York: Crossroad, 1983), 69–70, and in the same work, "The Theology of Mysticism," 70–7. For a very lucid presentation of Rahner's everyday mysticism, see Harvey D. Egan, "The Mysticism of Everyday Life," *Studies in Formative Spirituality* 10 (1989): 7–26.

37. Maryknoll, NY: Orbis Books, 1983.

38. Ibid., xviii, 3–5, 26.

39. Ibid., 21, 26.

40. Ibid., xviii, 9, 30–40.

41. Ibid., 51.

42. Ibid., 96–7.

43. Ibid., 48, 137–8.

44. Ibid., 121–2.

45. "How to Read the Rule: An Interpretation," in *Albert's Way,* ed. Michael Mulhall, O. Carm. (Rome: Institutum Carmelitanum, 1989), 61–2.

46. Eckhart himself proposes *Gelassenheit* as an alternative and response to what he calls "the merchant mentality," which has points of similarity to Kavanaugh's "the commodity form." See Matthew Fox, O.P., "Meister Eckhart and Karl Marx: The Mystic as Political Theologian," in *Understanding Mysticism* ed. Richard Woods, O.P. (Garden City, NY: Doubleday, 1980), 544–50.

47. See Reiner Schürmann, *Meister Eckhart: Mystic and Philosopher* (Bloomington: Indiana University Press, 1978), 16.

48. One of my major difficulties with a God who is absolutely immutable, who does not change, who has no history, is that such a God too easily ends up reinforcing the status quo.

49. Johannes B. Metz has given this term common currency, although he did not "coin" it. See his *Theology of the World*, trans. William Glen-Doepel (New York: Herder & Herder, 1969), 114. Regarding the iconoclastic significance of the Carmelite tradition as witnessed by Teresa of Avila and John of the Cross, see Segundo Galilea, *The Future of Our Past: The Spanish Mystics Speak to Contemporary Spirituality* (Notre Dame, IN: Ave Maria Press, 1985), esp. 25–43.

50. Again it is Metz who has given common currency to this notion of "dangerous and subversive memory." See his *Faith in History and Society*, trans. David Smith (New York: Seabury, 1980), 184–99, 200–4.

51. See Karl Marx, "Theses on Feuerbach," in *The Portable Karl Marx*, ed. Eugene Kamenka (New York: Penguin Books, 1983), 158.

CONTEMPLATION AND THE RECOVERY
OF THE MASCULINE

John Welch, O.Carm.
Whitefriars Hall
Washington Theological Union
Washington, DC

It is tempting to say the Carmelite Order was begun by a group of "wild men" gathered in a wadi on a mountainous ridge jutting out into the Mediterranean. It is hard to imagine a more primitive setting, and it is certainly one that would warm the heart of anyone today seeking to recover the masculine. The mountain constellated myths about it, particularly the stories of that original "wild man," Elijah the Tishbite.

These men embraced the feminine quickly, but welcoming actual women took a little longer. They identified themselves as brothers of the Virgin Mary and named their chapel in her honor. In their sensitivity to the feminine and honoring "the lady of the place," these spiritual warriors were true to their medieval heritage.

But they were not as quick to accept women into the Order. Unlike other mendicant groups that developed both men and women's communities, the Carmelites successfully fended off responsibility for a women's branch for over two hundred years. Almost from the beginning some women were affiliated with local communities but not officially as Carmelite women religious. John Soreth, a fifteenth-century general of the Order, established the first communities of Carmelite women. Today, especially because of the impact made on the church and the wider society by the Teresian communities of women, large segments of the church are unaware of the existence of Carmelite men.

Anonymity of Carmelite men is, perhaps, a minor issue, but it calls to mind the paucity of attention given to the situation of men in the Church today. Without denying the need to further explore the role of women in society and Church, some additional thought needs to be given to the complicated situation of men. Undoubtedly the feminine has blessings to bestow upon humankind, and we read about them regularly, but what is, if any, the masculine contribution today?

Men, the Problem

Consideration of this topic at least gave me a chance to read some of the current material, especially the authoritative source, *The Book of Guys* by Garrison Keillor. One of the themes from *The Book of Guys* holds that the masculine has been going downhill for quite some time. Keillor writes:

> Years ago, manhood was an opportunity for achievement, and now it is a problem to be overcome. Plato, St. Francis, Michelangelo, Mozart, Leonardo da Vinci, Vince Lombardi, Van Gogh—you don't find guys of that caliber today, and if there are any, they are not painting the ceiling of the Sistine Chapel or composing "Don Giovanni." [1]

In listening to talks and reading texts in the areas of spirituality and theology, a man cannot help but be slightly overwhelmed by the emphasis on the feminine in church discourse today, often with an accompanying critique of the masculine. In many discussions, masculine domination is viewed as the culprit—control of the church, control of theological sources, control or domination of dialogue within the church. The 1994 letter by Pope John Paul II regarding women's ordination, *Ordinatio Sacerdotalis,* could be offered as further evidence.

Men, too, see many of the problems. We see the overwhelmingly masculine leadership in the church. We realize theology may be used inappropriately to prop up such structures. We too are embarrassed about the weight given to nonissues such as altar girls.

We see many of the problems, but we hear in many spoken and unspoken ways that *men are the problem!* Often discussion seems to imply that men, by their nature, just by being men, are responsible for many of today's problems.

I remember a discussion I had with two women religious who were quite upset with the masculine church. I said, while I realize that most of the positions of authority in the church are held by men, as a man I experience the church as quite feminine. The two women could not imagine how I could say the church seems feminine.

Women are often the chief nurturers of a young boy's faith. Women, certainly in the past, strongly encouraged a young man to enter church ministry. But if it is necessary for a young man to pull away from home and family in order to find his own identity and adulthood, entering ordained ministry, at least at an early age, may be experienced as simply an extension of the control of home life. The boy has simply moved from his own mother to Mother Church without a pause in between to find himself. He goes from one situation where he was being named by others and told how to behave, to another more powerful situation where he is again named by others and shaped in his behaviors.

The young man may have had to fight as hard for his identity in the church as he did at home. The persona of priesthood is quite strong, and keeping in touch with oneself within that persona may be difficult. The experience of the church for a man can be one of a controlling, smothering womblike existence. Furthermore, the restriction on women priests diminishes not only women but men as well. One theologian observed that being a priest today is like being a member of an exclusive club that excludes Jews and blacks.

Vasalisa's Doll

In a class on spirituality and human development at the Washington
Theological Union, we were studying feminine and masculine psychology
and spirituality. For women's psychology, we read a story from Clarissa
Pinkola Estés's book, *Women Who Run with the Wolves*.[2] Two of the women
in class summarized the material, presented their reactions to it, and led the
discussions. The story we discussed from Estés's book was about a young
girl named Vasalisa.

Vasalisa is given a doll by her dying mother. After the mother's death,
the doll becomes a sure guide for the young girl. The father remarries, and
Vasalisa now has a stepmother and stepsisters. Her new family does not
like the girl. They want to get rid of her, so they tell her that the flame in the
house has gone out and that she will have to go into the woods to Baba
Yaga's house to fetch a new fire. They hope she will never return.

Naturally, there are dangers on the journey, but the doll in her
pocket keeps giving her good advice. She safely arrives at Baba Yaga's
house. Estés describes Baba Yaga:

> Now the Baba Yaga was a very fearsome creature. She
> traveled, not in a chariot, not in a coach, but in a cauldron shaped
> like a mortar which flew along all by itself. She rowed this
> vehicle with an oar shaped like a pestle, and all the while she
> swept out the tracks of where she'd been with a broom made of
> long-dead persons' hair.
>
> And the cauldron flew through the sky with Baba Yaga's
> own greasy hair flying behind. Her long chin curved up and
> her long nose curved down, and they met in the middle. She
> had a tiny white goatee and warts on her skin from her trade in
> toads. Her brown-stained fingernails were thick and ridged like
> roofs, and so curled over she could not make a fist.
>
> Even more strange was the Baba Yaga's house. It sat
> atop huge, scaly yellow chicken legs, and walked about all by
> itself and sometimes twirled around and around like an ecstatic
> dancer. The bolts on the doors and shutters were made of human

fingers and toes and the lock on the front door was a snout with many pointed teeth.[3]

Vasalisa bravely asks for fire. Baba Yaga replies that she must perform many tasks before getting the fire. The tasks turn out to be impossible, but the doll in Vasalisa's pocket accomplishes the tasks for her.

Baba Yaga finally gives her the flame. It is in a skull, and it shines out the eyes. Vasalisa returns home with the fiery skull, and the flame streaming from the eyes burns the stepmother and stepsisters to cinders.

An Interpretation

Estés interprets the story of Vasalisa as a story about a woman finding her true feminine nature. The doll given her by her mother is her matrilineal heritage, which can be a true guide. The frightening hag, Baba Yaga, is an image of the woman's instinctual self, her primal core. In Baba Yaga's house, she gets in tune with her true nature, finds her own voice, and is able to return with her own fire. With that wisdom, she is able to detect and defeat inauthentic, controlling voices around her, as well as the ones she has internalized.

Estés stories continually amplify her theme that woman must find the wild woman inside. Drawing on her hispanic heritage, she calls this deep layer of identity the *río abajo del río* (the river below the river), or the *canto hondo* (the deep song).

The young girl has several developmental tasks before receiving the fire: letting the too-good mother die, both outside of her and inside her; coming to know her own shadow side as she lets go of the overly positive mother; learning to trust and follow—and feed—her intuition; learning to rely on her inner sense; facing the Wild Hag, Baba Yaga, her inner feminine nature without wavering (Estés comments that not only men are afraid of women's power!); serving the nonrational, acclimating herself to the "great wildish powers of the feminine psyche"; separating this from that, learning to make fine distinctions in judgment; eventually taking on new, immense power to see and affect others, looking at one's life situations in a new light.

It is Estés's conviction that women have a soul hunger. She encourages recovering the "wild woman." The name evokes the archetypal, the intuitive, the sexual and cyclical, the ages of women, a woman's way, a woman's knowing, her creative fire. To quote Estés, this wild woman has become "ghostly from neglect, buried by overdomestication, outlawed by surrounding culture, no longer understood anymore."[4] Estés's analysis is that when a woman is cut away form her basic source, when her instincts and natural life cycles are lost, subsumed by the culture, or by the intellect or the ego (one's own or those belonging to others), then it is time to recover the innate spiritual being at the center of feminine psychology.

Estés points to fleeting tastes of the wild; they come through beauty as well as loss: during pregnancy, while nursing a child, during the change in oneself in raising a child, during a love relationship tended like a garden. They come while seeing sights of great beauty, sunsets, fishermen coming up from the lake at dusk with lanterns lit. They come in the sound of music that vibrates the sternum, excites the heart—the drum, the whistle, the call. All may be tastes of the wild and remind us that "one has given scant time to the mystic cookfire or to the dreamtime, too little time to one's own creative life, one's life work, one's true loves."[5]

Men, Meanwhile

The discussion about women recovering their "wild woman" found a receptive audience among the men in the class. As we heard about the woman's journey and special tasks, many of the men recognized the need for a similar process in their own lives. And so we discussed the need for the recovery of the "wild man." Although, as one of our Irish Carmelites said, "You don't have to tell me about the wild man; I've been trying to keep him under control for years!"

With all the talk of the dominance of the masculine and the problems men generate, one would think the last thing the world needs is more masculine, let alone more wild men. But some authors today say there is not enough of the right kind of masculine. They write about another, more mature masculine that needs to be attended to.

In this analysis, men too have trouble finding *their* inner voice, their innate masculinity. Some of the blame is placed on the patriarchy itself, that form of the masculine often associated with control, power, domination, manipulation, competition, aggressiveness, abuse, and so forth. If this is the only kind of masculinity offered a man, then patriarchy is not only an attack on the feminine, but it also is an attack on the truly masculine. The structures and dynamics of patriarchy can trap a man in his fears of both women and other men.

Part of the blame is placed on absent fathers, physically or emotionally absent. No one is available to mentor the young man into other dimensions of the masculine.

Some of the blame is also placed on the lack of rituals that could initiate a man into a responsible adulthood. Victor Turner observed we no longer have rituals, but "mere ceremonials." They do not have real power to achieve genuine transformation.

The result of a confining patriarchy, the lack of caring father figures, and the absence of transforming rituals is a type of masculine that certain authors call "boy psychology." Robert Moore and Douglas Gillette in their book on masculine psychology, *King, Warrior, Magician, Lover,* argue the marks of boy psychology are easy to see around us:

> abusive and violent acting-out behaviors against others, both men and women; passivity and weakness, the inability to act effectively and creatively in one's own life and to engender life and creativity in others (both men and women); and, often, an oscillation between the two—abuse/weakness, abuse/weakness.[6]

Boy Psychology

As a boy grows up, there are several stages of development leading to adolescence, all of them belonging to what could be called the immature masculine, or boy psychology. The presence of loving adults greatly helps the boy's development: he develops a basic trust in himself and in life; a secure and competent ego emerges; he adjusts to society's norms and values.

What damages a boy's development is a lack of response to his attachment needs, the use of threats of abandonment, inducing guilt in the boy, or parental clinging to the child. Potentially, the most disastrous occurrence for a developing child is the loss of parents or the loss of caring adults.

From the first efforts to play with toys and crawl in exploration of the world, the boy is finding transitional objects and behaviors that will assist him in moving away from the parents and into his own identity and adult life. It is the archetypal journey of the hero.

Joseph Campbell identified stages of the hero's quest. The hero receives a call to adventure and sets out from his home. After he has crossed some kind of threshold, he is subjected to a series of trials and ordeals. Eventually, he undergoes the supreme ordeal, which is the fight with the monster. When, finally, he defeats the monster, he is rewarded with the treasure hard to attain, that is, the throne of the kingdom and the beautiful princess as his bride.

In adolescence the boy/hero has certain developmental tasks: a loosening of the bonds to the parents (who no longer shimmer as gods), a sense of identity, confidence as an adult member of one's sex, a competent social role, sexual maturity, a readiness to marry, and so forth. While the young girl has similar tasks, there is some thought that a boy may have to make a more radical break from parents, especially the mother, in order to find his identity.

Because spiritual writers in the Carmelite tradition are adults addressing adults, their message may need careful interpretation for a young person in this first part of life. Certainly, without interpretation, their warnings to avoid attachments could be interpreted as a warning against any involvement in life at all. They could be interpreted as advising avoidance of commitments, responsibilities, relationships, care for this world. They could be understood as saying that the young person will have a more direct route to God if he or she can avoid life's entanglements.

To the young person, the mystics' call for detachment is not an excuse for avoiding life but an encouragement to leave the womb of the unconscious, to fight the inertia of collectivity, to step forward into one's life and become someone. The liberation called for in the first half of life is a freedom from the enslavement of the dark forces that undermine personhood and stifle the development of values and competency. Psychologically, sin is a refusal to come to consciousness, wrote Carl Jung. A contemplative stance at this time in life should assist one in hearing more clearly and responding to the archetypal forces that come on-line within the personality. And an important early archetypal story telling itself within the individual and moving him or her more fully into a unique life is the story of the hero.

In reality, the Carmelite mystics are addressing men and women who have entered into life fully, have been committed to it, passionate about it, and who find themselves fragmented and still hungering for a fulfillment that continually escapes them. At this point in life, the mystics' call for detachment and liberation of the heart is not a call to disengage but to let die what has taken God's place and is now a source of death, not life. It is a call to hear within the debris of one's life the offer of a love that has not disappeared and will not disappoint.

Man Psychology

The analysis of some writers is that the hero story is about this transition from adolescence to adulthood, not about the man's growth into a deeper masculinity. The hero story represents the culmination of boy psychology. The reason we never hear about the hero and the princess after he wins her is that he does not know what to do with her.

These authors argue that further development, development beyond the hero's adventure, is required so that a man may attain a more mature masculinity. This "man psychology," as distinct from a "boy psychology," is not attained through greater integration of the feminine, as important as that may be. At this point, what is needed is less feminine. Men often feel overwhelmed by the feminine. What is needed is more masculine, a masculine connected to the deep and instinctual masculine energies, the potentials of the mature masculine.

Although our culture no longer provides rites of initiation, there persists in all of us, regardless of gender, an archetypal need to be initiated. Attainment of a new stage of life, a more mature masculine stage, for example, seems to demand that symbols of initiation, appropriate to that stage, must be experienced. The masculine principle, in particular, seems to demand culturally sanctioned trials and ordeals if it is to achieve full actualization in maturity. Therapists report that there is an *initiation hunger* in many people going into analysis. If society fails to provide a suitable initiation, then there must be a self-initiation. The rites of initiation today often must be self-administered. The man must enter into a deeper relationship with himself, become an authority in the nuances of his own experience, define manhood for himself.

Sam Keen in *Fire in the Belly*[7] identifies two stages in the development of a more mature masculine. The first stage of the journey, the "Soulful Quest," is a pilgrimage into the depths of the self. "Homecoming," the second stage, is a return to the everyday world with a new sense of self, new virtues, and a new understanding of virility. It may be understood as the journey of the hero once more, but into neglected regions of the masculine psyche.

It is not a stretch to say that this process is best done contemplatively, with a listening attitude and a faith that one is being addressed in the depths of one's being by a transcendent source of identity. So used to wording his reality, a man is asked to listen and endure what he hears.

It is a listening to one's depths, a psychological task but also a religious pilgrimage. The self-knowledge encouraged by Teresa of Avila, for example, certainly includes psychological discovery where appropriate, but such knowledge is more fruitfully gained in an encounter with the Mystery met within the psyche yet from beyond it. If the psychological experiences and insights become more interesting and absorbing than the transcendent source of identity, then one is heading back out the door of the castle.

The beginning of a journey that is both psychological and spiritual is usually not the result of an unpressured decision. Often, something invites our attention. For example, Clarissa Pinkola Estés, in talking about the woman's point of departure, identifies many things that may be a door opening to this process. She says if you have a deep scar, that is the door to begin the journey; if you have an old, old story, that is a door; if you love the sky and the water so much you almost cannot bear it, that is a door; if you yearn for a deeper life, a full life, a sane life, that is a door. Remember Teresa writing, "I wanted to live . . . but I had no one to give me life."

Sam Keen says it can begin with the death of a parent, a spouse, a friend. It may happen through boredom and the urge to run away. Perhaps it begins when we are overwhelmed by the plight of the world's starving and poor or when we age and feel vulnerable. He writes: "Call it mid-life crisis, depression, alienation, the dark night of the soul, the opening of a new path. Honor it. Listen. Respond . . .Good-by to the stereotyped roles—of rich man, poor man, doctor, lawyer, merchant, chief—of warrior and conquistador."[8]

John of the Cross says it may begin when you find your normal thought processes are not able to sort out your world. When John identifies an inability to meditate, he is saying we can no longer word our life as before. The normal strategies are not working. And this sense of powerlessness is probably not helped by being thrown into prison by one's brothers in religion. Being mute within and voiceless without must certainly plunge one into an intense silence.

Teresa might say it happens when your carefully controlled life starts to come apart. Your tidy rooms in the castle are no longer enough. She identifies times when God can break through even a good, virtuous life.

A dying process is beginning. Something is being sloughed off. For any new life to happen, old life has to give way. Estés speaks about letting the too-good mother die. There is much more to the woman than she has been allowed thus far to claim. Jung wrote about the woman carrying man's feminine dimension for him, thereby excusing him from knowing himself more deeply and keeping the woman from finding her own feminine reality. Sebastian Moore refers to this situation as "Seeing your life through somebody else's eyes."

In speaking about men, Sam Keen argues that, at some point, "we must kick dad and mother, priest, pope and president out of our psyche and seize the authority for our own lives. We must become responsible for our own values and visions . . . . Growing into the fullness of our humanity means that we become co-authors of the rules by which we will agree to have our lives judged."[9]

The contemplative would argue that this process happens most authentically when the personality is reoriented around a center that is experienced as Otherness. From this center comes a new identity. A man is learning to shift from a stance of being his own ground to trusting an unknown Ground. As John of the Cross writes, a man has to take off his shoes and walk reverently because his journey is on sacred ground. He does not know the way; he does not have the provisions. He is learning to be led and fed.

The mystics warn this contemplative journey, this "loving attentiveness," can be quite difficult and confusing along the way, especially initially, as hard-earned identities are set aside and one begins to walk a less clear, less sure path. It may be so disconcerting that John was able to write: "everything seems to be functioning in reverse."

John of the Cross describes this night as a loving experience of God. Nothing in the love is confusing, dark, or painful, but it is because of who we are that this love initially darkens us. Before, we knew by knowing; now, we know by an unknowing. It is poverty of spirit; it is contemplation, an openness to God's transforming love as it approaches us in a dark way.

A psychological agenda may surface in this contemplative process. Keen describes what it might mean for a man:

> We leave the sunlit world of easy roles and prefabricated tokens of masculinity, penetrate the character armor, get beneath the personality, and plunge into the chaos and pain of the old "masculine" self. This isn't the fun part of the trip. It's spelunking in Plato's cave, feeling our way through the illusions we have mistaken for reality, crawling through the drain sewers where the forbidden "unmanly" feelings dwell, confronting the demons and dark shadows that have held us captive from their underground haunts. In this stage of the journey we must make use of the warrior's fierceness, courage, and aggression to break through the rigidities of old structures of manhood, and explore the dark and taboo negative emotions that make up the shadow of modern manhood.[10]

John of the Cross encourages entering the dark of the experience with patience, trust, and perseverance. It is a time for going quiet, a time for listening, for being a "watch in the night." There are different ways of describing what is going on: a crucifixion, losing ego, descending into hell, battling dragons, encountering demons. Keen warns that we lose a spiritual dimension to this experience if we simply name it stress, depression, or burnout. It may be difficult for a man to believe that anything of value is happening unless he is in control. To man's impatience, John of the Cross says, be patient. To man's deep mistrust of the universe, John says enter this dark time with trust. A graciousness is at work that will not fail us.

Homecoming

But there does come a turning point. Somehow, where there apparently had been death, life is reborn. Keen comments that the experience is like a traveler laying a burden down, a falsely accused man recovering his innocence, the prodigal son returning home, a bone slipping back into its socket. John of the Cross writes about the night that slowly becomes a guide, a flame which begins to heal, an absence that gives way to Presence. The path of the soulful quest begins to turn upward.

Keen tries to identify times when this graciousness becomes apparent:

> Such moments of grace may overtake you while you are dancing, eating cold cereal, watching a commercial on TV, making love, sitting still and thinking about nothing in particular. After years of being constipated and compulsive it occurred to him that his life was of ultimate worth not because of any work he accomplished, but because he was accepted by God even as he remained a constipated sinner. No sooner did it occur to him that "I live by the grace of God," than his bowls opened, his anal compulsive personality underwent a conversion, and the Protestant Reformation began.[11]

While the Christian has a goal of self-forgetfulness, it cannot be done until we have a self-remembrance. Until we remember ourselves, we remain a problem to ourselves. We can be self-absorbed, compulsively introspective, and narcissistic. We do not really have self-love. It is when we are able to grow into a deep sense of self-acceptance that we can forget the self.

What will a man look like today as he emerges from a heroic journey in which he has had to jettison old identities, confront his shadow, face hidden fears, and renew links with life forces deep within him? As I read about the potential for a renewal or recovery of a different kind of masculine, I kept thinking about two characters I have been following in several historical novels written by Patrick O'Brian. O'Brian has created a remarkable series of stories involving a British naval captain during the Napoleonic Wars and his friend who is the ship's surgeon. Some aspects of the new masculine, it seems to me, may involve a combination of qualities exemplified in these two figures.

Jack Aubrey, the British naval officer, is an old-fashioned hero. He strides the quarterdeck of his sailing vessels in complete command. His ships are usually not the best nor largest in the fleet, but his crews are well trained and dedicated. Aubrey overcomes the odds by his uncommon navigational ability and meticulous preparation. His loyalties are to the British Crown and the naval service. He is fearless and fierce in battle, compassionate in victory. Life on his ships reaches a dramatic high point on Sundays when the ship is rigged for church. The men are arranged according to ship's divisions, Episcopal prayer services are followed, and Jack Aubrey reads the Articles of War. His men generally appreciate this orderly and disciplined world. Almost every evening they are called to general quarters and practice firing the great guns with speed and accuracy.

Steven Maturin, his longtime friend, is usually the ship's surgeon on Aubrey's voyages. Maturin lives below decks, working to heal those who have become ill during the long voyages or wounded in intense battles. His loyalties are not to the Crown. He is Irish and Papist, and part of his youth was spent living in Spain. He does not have a thirst for action, but as a naturalist, he appreciates the opportunity to visit strange lands and observe new species. He often reports back to scientific societies. Frequently, however, he suffers disappointments as the ship sails past a particularly promising island. His friend Aubrey has orders to follow and a mission to accomplish, and, as usual, "there is not a moment to lose!"

The two men are quite dissimilar. The tall, imposing Aubrey went to sea at an early age, and consequently, his education focused on sciences that allowed for accurate navigation and all that goes into commanding a man-of-war. He speaks only English. On land, he is out of his element. Marriage, family, property, investments are welcome and respected realities, but he is awkward around them. He is truly comfortable only when land is fading astern, sails are beginning to billow, deep waters beckon, and a regular routine of life at sea commences.

The short, nondescript Maturin is broadly educated and a polyglot, often speaking in Latin when he wants to consult with another medical man in privacy. He is clumsy at sea, usually falling between ships when transferring from one to another. His clothing is generally an afterthought, his wig unkempt and crooked. He pretends interest in his friend's explanations of ship matters and battle sequences, just as Aubrey feigns interest when Stephen begins to describe a rare species or becomes enthusiastic about something discovered while dissecting a specimen. They gladly put up with one another's passionate interests because of their friendship.

Jack Aubrey and Stephen Maturin appreciate, and perhaps call forth, the best in one another. And when one is not his best, the other stands as a reminder of forgotten virtue. Their friendship, as a whole, forms a collage of masculine qualities. The strengths of each man tend toward an extreme but are tempered by the other. Would a mature masculine be, in some way, a composite of such men?

The New Hero

Sam Keen believes the new heroic man will not look like the traditional hero; perhaps he will look the opposite of a traditional hero. He perhaps will have more modesty and humility. He may not be as visible because he has given up the conceit that any man is "larger than life." He will be marked by a new willingness to fit in, to be a part of the whole. He will not need the spotlight as much. His life may have great dignity but lack the kind of dramatic largeness of the traditional hero. Keen names some of the virtues or characteristics which may be part of the new hero.

Wonder. The new hero will pause to wonder and to see the world as wonderful. Through contemplation, John of the Cross describes the world becoming a symphony. Without wonder, men remain compulsively active, perhaps becoming experts and efficient professionals, but also possibly becoming puppets and functionaries of institutions. Wonder opens up greater possibilities in life.

Stephen Maturin becomes absorbed in watching a school of dolphins playfully accompanying the ship. The seas grow rougher, the waves higher, the troughs deeper. Suddenly, as the ship descends deeply into a trough, the dolphins rise in a wave and appear before Stephen; he is looking directly at them through a translucent wall of water. Then the moment passes; the ship rises and the dolphins subside with the water.

Empathy. The new hero, after remembering himself, now can forget himself and be available to others. He is an "available" person. He flows out to others with a natural empathy. Keen observes: "Empathic men have stepped out of the hierarchical way of viewing relationships where you are either one up or one down, and have become co-beings." [12] My father never liked to talk about someone working for him; they always worked *with* him.

Men with this empathic virtue do not talk at people, they do not interrupt, they do not give advice. They listen and stand beside you, and in their presence, you have the feeling that you are allowed, even encouraged, to be yourself.

After sorting through observations about men's behavior, perhaps the most pointed, practical advice one could give men is to *listen,* especially to women. By listening, men learn what they have been missing, and by being listened to, women are helped to find their voice. Such advice may seem patronizing to both men and women, but it is worth the risk.

Heartfelt Mind. Howard Thurman, formerly dean of the chapel at Howard Divinity School in Washington, DC, talked about listening to the rhythm of one's own time, life, body. He advised learning to "simmer" in the morning and evening. Apparently he meant to take time to know not only what I truly think, but also how life is affecting me at depth. A heartfelt mind seems best done by cultivating a discipline of solitude and the habit of recollection and autobiographical thinking.

Both Aubrey and Maturin, alone in their respective cabins, in long letters to their wives, written over thousands of miles of sailing, sort through their actions and motives. The letters may never reach their wives; they may never actually be sent. But in these lines, the two men sort through their moods and word what is often only dimly perceived. They take their own pulse, as well as the pulse of the ship. In this activity, they catch up with themselves, bring themselves up to date, and find their bearings.

Moral Outrage. Writers affirm the need to maintain a warrior dimension in men. These contemporary warriors are men who are alive with moral outrage and who are willing to wrestle with the mystery of evil in one of its many disguises. They become warriors in defense of the sacred—not able to save every single suffering child, but reducing the number of suffering children. The contemplative tradition is actually the deepest source of compassion for the world. It is not inimical to social justice concerns.

Besides being the ship's surgeon, a naturalist, and a man who is decidedly nonmilitary, Stephen Maturin is also an intelligence agent for Britain. While Jack Aubrey pursues the tasks his orders demand of him, Maturin often has his own secret orders that involve coded messages and clandestine meetings. Aubrey is only slightly aware of the intelligence activities of his friend, but out of respect for their friendship, he asks no questions. He supports Stephen's endeavors as best he can. Stephen undertakes these missions not out of loyalty to Britain, but out of determined opposition to Bonaparte and in support of Catalan independence.

When ashore and carrying out a secret mission, Stephen is as determined as Jack Aubrey is in a naval engagement. Shipmates who see

Stephen coming down a street in the seaport are mistaken when they assume they know him well, throw their arms about him, and invite him to come with them for a drink. Stephen shrugs off their gestures and passes through their midst with a fierce look in his eye.

Right Livelihood. What to do in life? Joseph Campbell says, "Follow your bliss!" Keen asks: What are your gifts? What gives you the greatest joy? What have you to offer?

Many people, perhaps most, have an occupation that differs from their vocation. We may find such a situation tolerable if our occupation does not do violence to our vocation. But it is crucial to find a way to incarnate our care. It is equally important to look for the transcendent in our ordinary life of work.

Enjoyment. The one spiritual disease of men Keen would identify above others is the *lack of joy.* He maintains that a cure lies in reviving atrophying senses: bird-watching, walking, visiting, working a garden, playing ball in the streets, playing music, reading, doing nothing.

After the sails have been trimmed for night sailing, the watch has been set, and the ship settles down for the night, Aubrey and Maturin will sometimes sit down in the Captain's cabin with their violin and cello and follow one another through their favorite classical music. The sound leaks through the timbers and carries out over the dark waters.

Friendship. Friendship with other men offers a type of validation and acceptance that can only be received from someone of the same gender. Such friendships may help counter the alienation that often occurs in corporate and professional styles of life.

The core of Patrick O'Brian's stories of the sea is the friendship between two men. Fortunes wax and wane, battles are won and lost, relationships with others fray and heal; but there is a constancy in their affection and appreciation for one another. No matter how stormy the night or difficult the situation, no matter how tired or out of sorts, they are always genuinely pleased to see one another, and their greetings and observations are gentle, respectful, and heartfelt. When a sharp or impatient word does occur between them, it is almost a shock to the reader.

Community/Communion. We have ignored the fundamental truth of interdependence, the inescapable call to community. Twelve-step groups have reestablished that truth. The second part of the heroic journey, homecoming, takes place within the bonds of community.

The Carmelite mystics emphasized that the quality of one's community life was an indication of the authenticity of one's prayer. Through his contemplative prayer, John of the Cross learned to esteem his sisters and brothers and not judge them. Such a result leads to the conclusion that true community is formed from the relationship each has, not only with the others, but with God at the center of the community.

Husbanding. A husbandman takes care of the place with which he has been entrusted. Psychologically, the husbandman is one who makes commitments, puts down roots, and incarnates his compassion and empathy in actions of caring. He may have been on the road a long time, but he now has the courage to come home again and tend a single spot with the wisdom gained during his pilgrimage.

Wildness. Here Keen returns to the idea that both men and women may be overdomesticated and kept from being in touch with the life-giving forces at the core of their identity. I imagine that the church's acceptance of an Order's original charisms, and the Order's gradual institutionalization, would tend to domesticate the men and women attempting to live that tradition.

Does the contemplative impulse within the tradition provide a means for recovering our "wildish" powers? If contemplation means the openness to God's transforming love, no matter how it is approaching us, then it makes some sense that the new life within us will have gender related characteristics.

For twenty years Keen, has been giving workshops helping men identify their personal myths. When he asks them to draw their ideal living environment, almost all draw an isolated setting near a lake, a sea, or in mountains or a desert. It reminds one of the "wild men" on Mount Carmel!

Notes

1. Garrison Keillor, *The Book of Guys* (New York: Viking, 1993), 11.
2. Clarissa Pinkola Estés, *Women Who Run with the Wolves* (New York: Ballantine Books, 1992), 75–80.
3. Ibid., 77.
4. Ibid., 7.
5. Ibid.
6. Robert Moore and Douglas Gillette, *King, Warrior, Magician, Lover* (San Francisco: HarperSan Francisco, 1990), xvi.
7. Sam Keen, *Fire in the Belly* (New York: Bantam Books, 1991).
8. Ibid., 130.
9. Ibid., 144–5.
10. Ibid., 127–8.
11. Ibid., 150.
12. Ibid., 157.

Saint Teresa of Avila

BLUEBEARD'S PALACE AND THE INTERIOR CASTLE:CONTEMPLATION AS LIFE

Vilma Seelaus, O.C.D.
Carmelite Monastery
Barrington, Rhode Island

I grew up in a large family with all of us close in age. As children, one of our favorite pastimes in winter was to gather under the baby grand piano in the living room and tell stories. We often made up our own, but we also told fairy tales. A favorite was *Bluebeard's Palace.* Sometimes we would act it out in mock opera with my parents as captive audience.

These memories come back to me as I attempt to interface three significant stories, one with the other. They are about *Bluebeard's Palace*, Teresa of Avila's *Interior Castle,* and the Story of the Universe. In conversation with each other, these stories open doors to hidden realities in the soul. They also expand the mind's contemplative vision to see the interconnectedness of all of reality.

Bluebeard's Palace is well-known among lovers of the fairy tale. Like the beginning of a fairy tale, "once upon a time" could well be the beginning of Teresa's masterpiece, *The Interior Castle*. From her gifted imagination flow images as varied as diamond castles to worms and butterflies. Crystal clear fountains contrast with muddy earth and light from heaven intensifies darkness. These images tell of a journey to hidden treasure in the center room of the castle.

101

We do not know if Teresa ever read fairy tales. We do know that as an adolescent she enjoyed reading books of romantic chivalry. She and her brother actually wrote such a book themselves. "Much could be said for it," according to Ribera, her early Jesuit biographer.[1] From early childhood, faith and fantasy worked together in Teresa. Imaginings of heroic deeds and eternal glory stirred her youthful heart. At her instigation, she and her brother Rodrigo ran off together to have their heads cut off by the Moors for the sake of Christ. This heroic venture was aborted by an uncle, so Teresa and her friends settle for playing hermits.

Years and many struggles later, Teresa read the *Letters* of St. Jerome, which rekindled her religious imagination. Again she went off; this time to the Carmelite Monastery in Avila to give her life to God as a nun. Here, her contemplative eye and creative mind continued to see wider worlds and hidden meaning beneath the surface of her limited environment.

Urged by her confessors to put her religious experience in writing, Teresa lamented her lack of knowledge about the properties of things. Intuitively she knew that the boundaries of their disclosure were limitless, coming as they do from the creative heart of God. Everything in creation has symbolic meaning. Teresa's sixteenth-century world of Old Castile, with its castles and kings, possibly provided her with a language to tell her story about the journey of the human spirit as it seeks itself in God. So effective was she that she took her place among the world's great storytellers.

Teresa's writings quickly became classics in spiritual literature. Her gift is to engagingly typography the world of the spirit. We resonate with her because she captures in symbolic language what is wordless, yet true, in the human search for God and God's outreach to the human. God's desire to communicate with Teresa **is** the human story. We recognize our own experience of God in Teresa's efforts to describe hers. Like all classics, her writings continue to speak through the ages. In the process, they take on a life of their own and a meaning beyond Teresa's envisioning.

The fairy tale is another classic literary form whose meaning has a continued unfolding. Today, Jungian writers in particular find that in the fairy tale, as in a mirror, can be seen the basic patterns of the psyche. In their variety and antiquity, they present in symbolic language a broad motif of the human condition. Enclosed within the plot of the fairy tale is psychological meaning that is expressed in a series of symbolical pictures and events.

Events that happened "once upon a time" arouse a sense of mystery. Fairy tales touch preconscious fears, longings, and aspirations. They confront us with the basic human predicaments, the existential dilemmas of life. As is true of the spiritual classic, their richness, depth, and effectiveness can easily be lost as we attempt to express what they mean.

At the same time, in conversation with spiritual classics, fairy tales bring out the continuity of the inner journey as both a psychological and spiritual reality. Psychologists begin to recognize that psychological wholeness finds its center in spiritual realities. Healthy ego development is not the ultimate of human endeavor. Spirituality charts a path beyond ego to the soul's center where one's true identity is found within the mystery of human-God relatedness. The soul's center is in God. The symbolic meaning of fairy tales connects with the spiritual journey as these tales lead us, sometimes to hidden treasure, sometimes to places of terror.

Bluebeard's Palace

A shortened version of the Bluebeard story goes like this. Once upon a time, Bluebeard, a giant of a man with an eye for women, courted three sisters at once. They were frightened of his beard, but his congeniality convinced them to accept an invitation to a day of frolic in the forest. He so regaled them with stories and dainty treats that the sisters began to think, "Well perhaps this man Bluebeard is not so bad after all." But when they returned home, the two older sisters' suspicion and fears returned. The younger sister, however, found him charming, and the more she talked to herself the less awful he seemed. So when Bluebeard asked for her hand in marriage, she accepted, and together they rode off to his palace in the woods.

One day Bluebeard told her that he must go on a journey. She was free to do anything her heart desired, and he gave her the keys to all the rooms of the palace. She was free to use any key except the tiny key with the scroll work on top.

In his absence, her sisters came for a visit. For amusement, they decided to make a game of finding which key fit which door. The palace was large with many rooms on each floor, so they went from room to room having an immensely good time opening each door and finding immeasurably good things. At last, they came to the cellar and to a blank wall. They puzzled over the last tiny key, the one with the scroll work. A noise alerted them to a door around the corner just closing shut. They tried to open it, but it was firmly locked, so without a thought, they tried the remaining tiny key.

The door groaned and swung open. They lit a candle to penetrate the darkness within. All three sisters screamed at once. In the room was a mire of blood and the blackened bones of corpses with skulls stacked like a pyramid in each corner of the dreadful place. They slammed the door shut, and shook the key from the lock, only to find it stained with blood. No effort on the part of the wife would stop the key from bleeding drop after drop of pure red blood. So she hid the little key in the wardrobe, convincing herself it was all a bad dream.

Next morning, her husband came home and demanded his keys. With a glance, he saw a key was missing. "You infidel," he snarled and threw her to the floor. "You've been into the room, haven't you? Now it is your turn, my lady." He screamed and dragged her into the cellar before the awful door where lay the skeletons of all his previous wives. "Please, please," she pleaded, "allow me a quarter-hour so I can prepare for my death and make my peace with God." "All right", he growled, "but be ready."

The wife raced up the stairs to her chamber and posted her sisters on the castle ramparts. "Sisters, sisters," she called from her prayer, "do you see our brothers coming?" At first they saw nothing, but at her second cry, they replied, "We see a whirlwind of dust in the distance." Meanwhile, Bluebeard roared for his wife as he prepared to behead her. With impatience, he began to clomp up the stone steps toward his wife's chamber. As he came nearer, her sisters cried out, "Our brothers are here." With that, her brothers on horseback galloped down the palace hallways and charged into her room. There they routed Bluebeard as he was about to seize his wife. Then and there, they advanced upon him with swords, striking him and killing him at last.

Clarisa Pinkola Estés, in her book, *Women Who Run with the Wolves*,[2] does an insightful Jungian interpretation of the Bluebeard story as it affects women's psyche, although she admits that Bluebeard is the foe of both genders—men as well as women. According to Estés, "Bluebeard represents that part of ourselves that desires superiority and power over others—a kind of psychological inflation which wishes to be loftier than, as big as, and equal to the Ineffable."

The power urge in us goes back to our primordial beginnings. Man and woman ate of the forbidden tree because the tempter assured them that they would be like God. This deed inevitably forced them from their garden home, the place of inner truth, into exile. Our progenitors were the first to succumb to Bluebeard's charm. Since then, his victim is all of us. If the lure of ego inflation fails, he tries inverse inflation. We begin to put ourselves down; we inflate what we consider to be negative, either within ourselves, in other persons, or in the life situation. Consistent negative attitudes toward oneself or others is a kind of inverse ego inflation. According to Estés, "Bluebeard is also the internal representative of the myth of the outcast, of that deep and inexplicable loneliness which at times washes over us as we experience our exile from redemption (from our true home in God). Bluebeard represents that malignant inner force which acts in opposition to what is most true within."

Merton says that every one of us is shadowed by an illusory person, a false self. Speaking of himself, Merton writes:

> This is the man I want myself to be but who cannot exist, because God does not know anything about him, and to be unknown to God is altogether too much privacy. My false and private self is the one who wants to exist outside the reach of God's will and God's love—outside of reality and outside of life. And such a self cannot help but be an illusion. . . . A life devoted to the cult of this shadow is what is called a life of sin.[3]

Our first step, then, is to recognize this Bluebeard dimension of ourselves, to protect ourselves from its devastations, and to let God deprive it of its murderous energy. Bluebeard, the younger sister who yields to Bluebeard's seductions, the two older sisters who on the one hand resist his charm and on the other seek amusement opening doors in his palace, and the brothers who come to the rescue represent in symbol the soul's inner dynamic. The drama of Bluebeard personifies soul energies—the pull toward divine realities and the pull toward satisfactions which, in the end, fail to satisfy. Bluebeard would keep us from opening the eyes of our heart to the soul's need for deeper self-knowledge, healing, conversion, and freedom for a fuller life in God. Contemporary psychology offers invaluable assistance in this awakening, but in the end, true freedom and transformation are gift, the fruit of our journey into God.

The Interior Castle

Bluebeard's Palace is a story about the inner destructive energies of the human, but this is only one facet of the human reality. Teresa of Avila rounds out the human story with her own tale about an interior castle. Bluebeard marries for the pleasure of killing. In Teresa's castle, a king, in fact, the King of kings, invites both women and men into the castle, not to trick them to destruction, but to bring them into fullness of life in God. These stories are not separate to each other; in them, as in a prism, we recognize the conflicting pulls of daily living.

This castle—a beautiful diamond castle—represents the totality of ourselves in relationship to God. Its outer wall, like the setting of a diamond, is our body. Prayer opens the door to the castle. From the outer regions, we travel through many rooms to a special one in the center. Here secret exchanges take place between the soul and God (C.1.1.3).[4] God desires to communicate with us. *The Interior Castle* is about the many ways in which Teresa experienced this reality. Bluebeard is a destructively possessive predator. Dead bones are in the center room of his palace. In Teresa's center room is hidden treasure: fullness of life, union with God (C. 5.1.2). Christ, the *divine predator,* would also take us as prey. God entices the human heart to life, to intimacy, to union in spiritual marriage. If God wishes our all, it is not that we be destroyed. For, as Teresa says in the seventh dwelling place, it is very certain that in emptying ourselves of all that is creature and detaching ourselves from it for the love of God, the same Lord will fill us with himself (C. 7.2.7).

Bluebeard is God's competitor. Writes Estés:

> While he captures the heart of the younger sister, men are not spared. They too have an inner predator who seduces them in their psychic center. Destructive choices and patterns of behavior shout warnings that we are mesmerized by Bluebeard's charm. He forbids his wife the use of the one key that would bring her to consciousness. He forbids her to open the door of self-knowledge where she would see the inner destruction toward which she is heading.

Bluebeard's Palace and *The Interior Castle* each have a secret room of self-knowledge. Finding the inner room is important. God invites us in. Bluebeard forbids entrance lest we become free of his influence. For fullness of life in God, we need to find out what is in *both* rooms—the room of the psyche and the room of one's deeper spirit. Bluebeard's inner room reveals our dark side, which he would keep hidden from us to our own disadvantage.

For Teresa, self-knowledge is so important for entering the center room of her castle that, in fact, each of Teresa's dwelling places has a room of self-knowledge. Estés says that questions are the keys that cause the secret doors of the psyche to swing open. In the Bluebeard story, the sisters ask the question, "Where do you think the door is and what might lie beyond it?" What is behind the visible that casts such a large shadow? Such questions sincerely pursued often lead through a path of pain but always to greater freedom.

Prayer opens doors in *The Interior Castle*. When Teresa puts her questions to the door of prayer, it opens gradually to reveal not only God but also all the shocking carnage in the secret room of her spirit. So terrible is the experience, it seems everything is lost. In chapter 1 of the sixth dwelling place, Teresa describes in detail her sufferings. No consolation is allowed her in the midst of internal and external trials. She experiences contempt from others, bodily ailments, self-doubt, and such darkness in the understanding that she is incapable of seeing the truth, thus believing whatever the imagination wants to represent to her.

> The Lord, it seems, gives the devil license so that the soul might be tried and even be made to think it is rejected by God. (C. 6.1.9)

> And thus however much it forces itself not to do so, the soul goes about with a gloomy and ill-tempered mien that is externally very noticeable. (C. 6.1.13)

Hardly our image of a saint! It might seem that Bluebeard has the upper hand here, but God is not malevolent. Teresa learns that such experiences have profound meaning.

> Our great God wants us to know our own misery and that God is sovereign; and this is very important for what lies ahead. (C. 6.1.12)

Through this time of suffering, Teresa is led to an inner door that only God can open. Christ Crucified is the key to this room. The door opens to an astounding sight.

> In this vision it is revealed how all things are seen in God and how God has them all in God's very self. . . . The evil of offending God is seen more clearly, because while being in God (I mean being within God) we commit great evils. (C. 6.10.2)

As in a hologram, Teresa sees all things in God—even her destructive Bluebeard energies. Bluebeard's palace and Teresa's castle are one reality. The dynamics of both are the human story. God calls to conversion the dead bones of our sinfulness and enfleshes them with new life in Christ.

Until now, the castle symbol has been the human soul, but here in chapter 10 of the sixth dwelling place the image shifts.

> Let us suppose that *God* is like an immense and beautiful dwelling or palace and that this palace, as I say, is God's very self. Could the sinner, perhaps so as to engage in his evil deeds leave this palace? No, certainly not; rather, within the palace itself, *that is, within God,* . . . the abominations, indecent actions and evil deeds committed by us sinners take place. The greatest evil of the world is that God, our Creator, suffers so many evil things from His creatures within God's very self. (C.6.10.3)

In the sixth dwelling place, Bluebeard is no longer the enemy because, as Teresa says, the soul knows clearly its wretchedness, and the very little it can do of itself if God abandons it (C. 6.1.10). In this dwelling place a remarkable transformation occurs. One's Bluebeard energy is transformed into soul-fire. Here, says Teresa, the soul acquires a special and tender love for its persecutors (C. 6.1.5).

When we can acknowledge in true humility that within us is a cellar room full of bones, *God* dismantles the predator. God both strips Bluebeard of his power and then unlocks the inner wine cellar where lover and beloved are united in an embrace of love. All dualism gives way to a unified vision of life. Near the journey's end, Teresa sees all existence to be within God. Even her struggles with seductive Bluebeard—with the dev-

ils who tempt and plague her—she now sees as mysteriously happening
within God. She no longer fears the devil, who has little capacity for harm
at this level, and in humility she prays never to leave this path of self-
knowledge (C.6.10.7–8). From the depth of her being, Teresa knows her
need for God.

Human activity and the life of the spirit, the struggles of the psyche,
and our prayer-relationship with God are inseparable to each other. In the
seventh dwelling place, Martha and Mary join together (C.7.4.12). Teresa
willingly becomes the slave of the Crucified (C. 7.4.8). She insists:

> If there were no other gain in this way of prayer except to under-
> stand the particular care God has in communicating with us and
> beseeching us to remain with Him, . . . it seems to me that all the
> trials endured for the sake of enjoying these touches of God's love,
> so gentle and penetrating, would be well worthwhile. (C. 7.3.9)

Catherine LaCugna, in a significant work entitled *God for Us*, shows
the relationship between the castle that is God and the castle that is ourselves. She writes:

> The perfection of God is the perfection of love, of communion, of
> personhood. Divine perfection is the antithesis of self-sufficiency,
> rather it is the absolute capacity to be who and what one is by
> being for and from another. The living God is the God who is alive
> in relationship, alive in communion with the creature, alive with
> desire for union with every creature. God is so thoroughly in-
> volved in every last detail of creation that if we could truly grasp
> this it would altogether change how we approach each moment of
> our lives. For everything that exists—insects, agate, galaxy—
> manifests the mystery of the living God. While divine simplicity
> means that God is not composed of parts, everything points to the
> absolutely diverse relatedness of God who is alive as communion,
> who is constantly seeking to touch the creature, even if our senses
> are numbed by sin.[5]

The Story of the Universe

We are more significant than we realize—so are our lives. Our efforts as women and as men to relate to each other in mutuality and respect, without cowardice or domination, have more meaning than we realize. They take place within God, and they reflect the life of communion that is God. Everything in the universe reflects the life of God. In his fascinating book, *The Holographic Universe,* Michael Talbot challenges our almost universal tendency to fragment the world. He writes:

> We believe that we can extract the valuable parts of the earth without affecting the whole. We believe it is possible to treat parts of our body and not be concerned with the whole . . . that we can deal with various problems in our society, such as crime, poverty and drug addiction, without addressing the problems in our society as a whole . . . . Our current way of fragmenting the world into parts not only doesn't work, but may even lead to our extinction.[6]

In his general theory of relativity, Einstein astounded the world when he said that space and time are not separate entities, but are smoothly linked and part of a larger whole he called the space-time continuum. David Bohm, one of the world's most respected quantum physicists, takes the idea a giant step further. He says that everything in the universe is part of a continuum. Despite the apparent separateness of things at the explicate (manifest) level, everything is a seamless extension of everything else, and ultimately even the implicate (hidden) and explicate (manifest) orders blend into each other.[7]

Like fairy tales and like the writings of the mystics, the universe has its own story to tell. *The Universe Story*, coauthored by Thomas Berry and Brian Swimme, reminds us that the Earth is so integral in the unity of its functioning that every aspect of the Earth is affected by what happens to any component member of the community. A desolate Earth will be reflected in the depths of the human.[8]

Already we have moved from such evils as suicide, homicide, and genocide, to biocide and geocide, the killing of the life systems of the planet, and the severe degradation—if not the killing—of the planet itself. Bluebeard has grown in size and destructiveness. Our moment in history demands that we open the hidden room full of dead bones of destroyed species, polluted air and water, and all the many ways human overconsumption kills the Earth-bride of God.

We face massive problems within the human-earth community. If we are to move from what Thomas Berry calls the Technozoic to an Ecozoic age, then we must learn to reverence the earth as integral to reverencing one another regardless of differences. We are at an exciting, challenging, and, literally, deadly serious moment in human history. Our future lies in seeing one another and our incredible planet earth, truly—perhaps for the first time—as held within the embrace of God.

Talbot asks the question: Is it possible that what Bohm has called the implicate level of reality is actually the realm of the spirit, the source of the spiritual radiance that has transfigured the mystics of all ages? [9] Teresa, in a moment of prayer, sees the entire castle journey—her encounters with God and her encounters with Bluebeard—all taking place within an immense and beautiful dwelling or palace that is God.

We, too, need a deeply contemplative vision to see today's human misery and our planet's devastation happening within God. Without the realization that *nothing* is outside of God's redeeming love, we will lose heart. Teresa reminds us that "God does not cease to love us even though we have offended God very much" (C. 6.10.4). The terrifying room full of dead bones contains within itself the promise of resurrection. Our struggles with our own and others' inner destructive forces, our struggles to reverence the earth, take place within God. Our destructive tendencies will not have the last word if only we open ourselves to the embrace of God. God will reawaken within us reverence for the sacredness of the earth and for one another.

We can go forward in hope, "since," says Teresa, "it was God in Christ, who paid the highest price, His majesty wants to join our little labors with the great ones he suffered so that all the work may become one" (C.5.2.5). Contemplation and spiritual marriage are toward the birth of good works, says Teresa (C.7.4.6), that all of our stories, human-divine, be experienced in God as one reality.

The story of Bluebeard, the story of the *Interior Castle*, and the Story of the Universe together carry on through time and space in the lives of the countless humans who inhabit planet earth, the mystery of Christ, God's Beloved, enfleshed in the human. The dead bones of the human struggle have the potential for new life in the Risen Christ.

Notes

1. See Kieran Kavanaugh O.C.D., and Otilio Rodriguez, O.C.D., trans., *Collected The Works of St. Teresa of Avila,* 2d rev. ed., vol. 1 (Washington DC: ICS Publications, 1987), 17.

2. Clarissa Pinkola Estés, *Women Who Run with the Wolves* (New York: Ballantine Books, 1992), 39–73.

3. Thomas Merton, *New Seeds of Contemplation* (New York: New Directions, 1961), 34.

4. All references to *The Interior Castle* are taken from Kieran Kavanaugh, O.C.D., and Otilio Rodriguez, O.C.D., trans., *The Collected Works of St. Teresa of Avila*, vol. 2 (Washington DC: ICS Publications, 1980).

5. Catherine Mowry LaCugna, *God for Us: The Trinity and Christian Life* (San Francisco: Harper, 1991), 304.

6. Michael Talbot, *The Holographic Universe* (New York: Harper Perennial, 1992), 49.

7. Ibid., 48.

8. Thomas Berry and Brian Swimme, *The Universe Story* (San Francisco: Harper, 1992). A chapter from this book entitled "The Ecozoic Era" is reprinted in *Anima:The Journal of Human Experience* 20 (Spring 1994).

9. Talbot, 271.

HOW TO PRAY: FROM THE LIFE AND TEACHINGS OF SAINT TERESA

Kieran Kavanaugh, O.C.D.
Institute of Carmelite Studies
Washington, DC

What does St. Teresa of Avila teach us about how to pray? So many articles and books have discussed her teaching that it would seem redundant to take up this topic again. However, new methods and techniques of prayer taught today prompt a return to Teresa and another look at her doctrine. Notorious for her digressions and incapable of speaking about prayer without speaking of her own experiences as well, Teresa did not bother to restrict herself to some kind of order in presenting her thought. Yet her works are never devoid of a certain order. Her writings, in fact, reflect her inability to practice discursive meditation, where one proceeds in logical form from point to point. Syllogisms were not her cup of tea. Important assertions about prayer are apt to appear anywhere in her writings.

A surprising logic and consistency, nonetheless, underlies what at first sight seems to be a mound of scattered thoughts. Through experience and questioning, she got to understand more about prayer probably than all the great theologians of her day. With an astounding wealth of experience providing her with resources far beyond the average author of a book on prayer,

115

Teresa advises us not to be surprised "that the Lord makes a little old woman wiser in this science of prayer than the theologians" (L.34.12).[1]

Prayer, like so many other endeavors, can get caught up in faddism. How to pray is a subject requiring some knowledge, first, about what prayer is; more specifically, if we are Christians, about what Christian prayer is.

At the core of an understanding of Teresa's teaching about prayer must lie some knowledge of her own experience. She developed her teaching out of that rich field. The great lengths she went to with learned, and not-so-learned, men to gain some enlightenment about what was happening to her and receive confirmation of her experience from Sacred Scripture are well-known. In her *Life,* she explains that her teaching will come "from what the Lord has taught me through experience and through discussions with very learned men" (L.10.9).

Clearly delineated in the history of Teresa's own prayer, especially as it is described in her *Life,* are two main periods: a long ponderous period in which prayer was taxing; another one, also long, but permeated with ardor, an influx of light and love almost as though imposed from above, which led to the summit of prayer.

Efforts and Instruments

Before we search into the characteristics of these two periods, some events from Teresa's childhood invoke our attention. Once, she and her brother—the one she liked most—in order to get to heaven quickly and cheaply by having their heads cut off decided to steal away to the land of the Moors. It does not take much reading between the lines to see Teresa as the instigator of this enterprise. This was only the beginning incident in the life of a woman who was never truly at home anywhere on this earth. "Longing to see you, death I desire," she wrote later in one of her poems (P.7).

In another fascinating tale about her childhood, Teresa shows us the depth of her sense of transcendence when still so young. After stating that she and her brother spent a lot of time talking about the glory that was to last forever, she says they "took delight in often repeating: 'forever and ever and ever'" (L.1.4). The repetition of these words, like the repetition of a mantra, or other prayer words, became an instrument of grace. "As I said this over and over," she writes, "the Lord was pleased to impress on me in childhood the way of truth" (L.1.4).

At the age of twenty, Teresa entered surreptitiously a Carmelite monastery of nuns in Avila. Contrary to what anyone might expect today, she seems to have received no instruction in her novitiate about mental prayer. The thrust of her training apparently centered around the Divine Office sung daily by the nuns in choir. Learning to follow the many complicated rubrics did not come easily to Teresa, but the nun's major task at that time, in the eyes of many, was to satisfy the republic's obligation to praise God by singing the Divine Office.

Only after her novitiate, once her uncle had given her Francisco de Osuna's *Third Spiritual Alphabet,*[2] did Teresa begin on her own initiative the practice of interior prayer. Enthralled with this book, which taught her how to proceed in prayer and how to practice recollection, she took it for her teacher and resolved to follow the path it taught (cf. L.4.7).

This new discovery does not mean that Teresa had not previously practiced a kind of meditation, which she had done indeed from her childhood. Before going to bed at night, she tells us, she would spend a little while pondering the scene of our Lord's prayer in the garden. That there were many indulgences attached to this devotion prompted her to make this effort. Luther's protest against indulgences a couple of years before Teresa's birth hardly fazed Spain, and Teresa was the beneficiary of a number of indulgenced prayers and practices: "I believe my soul gained a great deal through this custom because I began to practice prayer without knowing what it was; and the custom became so habitual that I did not abandon it" (L. 9.4).

The impact of Osuna's book on Teresa was so forceful that she resolved to spend two hours every day in the prayer of recollection, as was recommended by the author, in addition to the liturgical prayer required by the Carmelite timetable. She considered the hours set aside for this recollection as time for solitude, for being with God. In the beginning, Teresa's practice met with immediate and surprising success. The Lord began to favor her with infused prayer, what she would later term the prayer of quiet and the prayer of union, although at the time she did not understand the nature of her experience or how highly prized it should be.

Teresa had been staying at her sister's house because of a severe undiagnosed illness. The illness later increased in severity to the point of making it impossible for her to continue her practice of prayer. Recovering from her illness after three years of patient endurance in a body racked with pain, she took up again the practice she had so much esteemed, but it was no longer the same. What had been easy was now laborious; what had been sweet was now bitter.

She encountered three major problems in her hours for solitude. First, she was unable to meditate or cope with a mind running wild with distractions. Second, she felt that the way she was living was incompatible with the divine intimacy she sought in prayer. Finally, the hour seemed to drag on forever.

For the first and the third problems, she had recourse to a book. The book served as a shield to protect her from her thoughts and drive away dryness. Despite this help, she still had to confess that she often found herself wishing the hour were over, or sad at the thought of having to enter the oratory for another period of prayer (L.8.7).

One book Teresa used for prayer was *The Life of Christ* by Ludolph of Saxony (or "the Carthusian," as Teresa calls him). The meditations in the book followed in orderly arrangement the mysteries of the life of Christ. It offered the devout a simple way of meditating through the imaginative exercise of the senses upon some mystery of our Lord's life. The goal was to move the heart to pious affections and the will to good resolutions conformable with Christ's example. Meditators were to imitate the divine exemplar and restore in themselves the divine image that was effaced through sin.

This presented the second problem. Reform of one's life made Teresa anxious. It was a responsibility that made her unhappy either when with the world or when with God. "When I was experiencing the enjoyments of the world, I felt sorrow when I recalled what I owed to God. When I was with God, my attachments to the world disturbed me" (L.8.2).

One cannot help but recall St. John of the Cross's three classic signs of initial, purgative contemplation: inability to meditate, dryness in the things of God, weariness with the things of the world.[3] But Teresa did not have at this time a spiritual director like John of the Cross to explain how God works with us. She reasoned that she was trying for something far beyond her and that to continue under such circumstances was not a humble thing to do. So she quit; but fortunately not for long—a year or so. A good Dominican confessor chided that her understanding of humility was strange indeed and insisted she should never give up.

In her difficulties, the barrier for Teresa was never God's transcendence or inapproachability. God was not a problem for Teresa. For her, Christ was right at hand. Her problem welled up out of her own humanity.

She confesses that she spent most of her prayer reading a book "for God didn't give me talent for discursive thought or for a profitable use of the imagination" (L.4.7). Often overlooked is Teresa's candid admission that she could never picture in her mind the humanity of Christ.

In her dire need of something, Teresa turned to her book, where she found the means to reign in the uncontrollable comings and goings of her thoughts and allow her soul to be drawn to recollection. Yet sometimes, she did not have to do any more than open the book. Though she speaks of the entire eighteen-year period as a struggle, there were, nonetheless, experiences of recollection and times when the prayer was much less difficult than at other times.

Another instrument of inspiration and recollection for Teresa was images of Christ. Unfruitful in her attempts to picture Christ with her imagination, she grew to love images of the Lord and commissioned artists to do paintings of Jesus for her. Those were the times when the Reformers in the North were smashing statues and burning images.

Beyond these two means, though, was her whole person crying out for relationship. The book and the picture became transparent, revealing the presence of Christ. They helped her become present to Jesus as teacher and friend. They fueled her communion with him. "I tried as hard as I could to keep Jesus Christ, our God and our Lord, present within me, and that was my way of prayer" (L.4.7).

This personal approach inspired her to find in the gospel characters a wide variety of ways of relating to Christ. She would note their conversation with him and then enter into that same relationship herself, reliving what went on in the gospel narrative. The Samaritan woman and Mary Magdalene (whom she identified with Mary of Bethany and Luke's repentant woman along with the understanding of the times) fascinated her and could easily stir her devotion to Jesus.

But for the most part, this was hard going. Only after God began to reveal again the divine presence to her in mystical prayer was she able to enter without struggle into these relationships, or others such as those of Our Lady at the foot of the cross (W.26.8), St. Paul at the moment of his conversion (W.40.3), or St. Peter in tears (C.7.4.5; 6.7.4; L.19.10).

Always at the center of Teresa's prayer stood Jesus Christ, her indispensable focal point. She wanted to keep before her eyes an image of him since "I was unable to keep him as engraved in my soul as I desired" (L.22.4).

As time went on, Teresa grew to understand that to approach prayer was to approach Christ. The biblical figures and images were the means by which she drew near to him and kept her prayer moored in reality.

The psychoanalysts Ann and Barry Ulanov in their book *The Healing Imagination* [4] explain that we can live vicariously the falsifications of the TV series, or we can live the reality of the gospels. Now someone is sure to object that nobody takes those inconsequential TV soap operas seriously. But the Ulanovs answer, "Our imagination is always with us. If we fill it with silly little entertainments, which millions, let it be said, take very seriously, we move it far from its moorings in being." On the other hand, in the gospel narrative, "nothing we are told is aimless, without substance, without value. It covers all the possible purposes to which a life may be put."

Using biblical figures and narratives as a means of approaching Christ, Teresa developed her own method of prayer. She says that since she could not practice discursive meditation, she endeavored to represent Christ within herself, particularly in those gospel scenes where he was most alone. We can easily misunderstand what Teresa wants to say when she uses the term "represent." It is not always the equivalent of picturing with the imagination, or working at the highly regarded composition of place. "I could only think about Christ as He was as man, but never in such a way that I could picture Him within myself" (L.9.6). In this regard, she felt blind, or as though she were with someone in a dark room; you do not see the other despite their presence.

When she speaks of representing Christ within her, she is referring to a kind of activity in which she would bring into her awareness the presence of Christ, the person to whom she was about to relate in friendship. A detailed picture in her imagination was unnecessary for her communion with the Lord.

On the basis of these simple and humble means, she was able to recollect herself and come to the point in which only a short step remained between the effort to represent Christ as present and the gift of experiencing his presence without effort. As she tells the story of God's mercies, she moves through the account of the "life she lived" to a second and longer account of the "life God lived in her." Describing the moment in which the transition occurs, she mentions her usual way of beginning prayer, pointing out that she represented Christ within her in order to place herself in his presence. But then a feeling of the presence of God would come over her unexpectedly so that she could not doubt the divine presence within her or that she was totally immersed in God. She muses that such an experience must be what they are talking about when they use the term "mystical theology" (L.10.1).

When this passive or infused or, as Teresa calls it, supernatural prayer began, the long, arduous period of nearly twenty years ended, seemingly almost abruptly. Teresa's struggles were no longer with prayer itself. The mental anguish and the many humiliations that awaited her came from ignorant confessors and others who understood little about Teresa's prayer or were even suspicious of it. But the remainder of the story of Teresa's life of prayer–the degrees of contemplation and other favors–adds up to no more than an intensification of the divine presence. Jesus Christ present within her gradually appeared as the prominent object of her contemplation. He led her further into an awareness of the three Persons in the trinitarian mystery of the one God.

General Notions

Books about prayer, especially older ones, invariably present an account of the stages of prayer. Adolphe Tanquerey, whose thorough treatise on the spiritual life was surely the most widely read and used in the first part of the twentieth century, divided prayer, to begin with, into vocal and mental. He then divided mental prayer into discursive meditation and affective prayer, the former being more suited, he thought, to beginners. He discussed meditation under the general category of the purgative way and affective prayer as belonging to the illuminative way. Finally, in the unitive way, he speaks of the prayer of simplicity. In this unitive way, he also deals with the various stages of contemplation and other mystical phenomena. Although he allows for an amount of overlapping, Tanquerey leaves the reader with a conception of steps something like this: vocal prayer, discursive meditation, affective prayer, prayer of simplicity, and infused contemplation (prayer of quiet, arid or sweet; prayer of full union; ecstatic union, sweet or arid; and transforming union or spiritual marriage).[5] Treatises on the ascetical and mystical life by other authors followed similar outlines. Teresian Carmelite authors generally accepted this pattern as well. However, they used Teresa's term "recollection" (the prayer of recollection) instead of the prayer of simplicity and concentrated on her specific teaching about this method of prayer, making it clear that Teresa speaks of both an active recollection and a passive recollection.[6]

The general understanding was that beginners must start with discursive meditation. Some of the better-known methods of this kind of meditation were the Ignatian and Sulpician; also well known were the methods taught by St. Francis de Sales and Luis de Granada. Beginners were to follow one of these methods and heed Tanquerey's warnings against semiquietism: "Beginners do not generally arrive at the prayer of simplicity except through discursive meditation. . . . There are many stages to be traversed before we can attain to the passive state and to union with God."[7]

As interest in the meditation practices found in other world religions grew, new nondiscursive methods of prayer suitable for beginners, as much as for the more advanced, were suggested. The use of the mantra or prayer word together with certain bodily techniques aid concentration and calm. The West has also seen a surge of interest in the Jesus prayer as practiced in Byzantine spirituality, as well as a return to the *lectio divina* as a method of prayer once used by monks in the middle ages.[8]

The new *Catechism of the Catholic Church* divides the expressions of prayer into vocal prayer, meditation, and contemplation. It is content to say that "there are as many and varied methods of meditation as there are spiritual masters." And the *Catechism* defines contemplative prayer with St. Teresa's definition of mental prayer, suggesting that contemplation is for everyone. According to the *Catechism,* contemplative prayer does not even have to exclude meditation: "Contemplative prayer seeks him 'whom my soul loves.' It is Jesus, and in him, the Father. We seek him, because to desire him is always the beginning of love, and we seek him in that pure faith which causes us to be born of him and to live in him. In this inner prayer we can still meditate, but our attention is fixed on the Lord himself."[9]

Teresian Notions

When Teresa spoke of contemplation (or contemplative prayer) she always had in mind passive (infused) prayer, insisting that contemplation is a gift from God. When she was young and just beginning, she received the gift of contemplation, the prayer of quiet and even of union for short periods, without first having to pass through any standard stages. But if we consider her life from another horizon, that in which her contemplative prayer had become habitual and perceptible to her, we note her assertion that what the Lord gave her after twenty-seven years, he gave to others only after thirty-seven or forty-seven years. The many years delay, however, could never become a rule. Contemplation "is given by God when he desires and how he desires," Teresa used to say. And she goes so far in her assertions as to state that "Often the contemplation the Lord doesn't give to one in twenty years he gives to another in one" (L.34.11). Speaking of some young girls entering her new community in Avila, she reminds spiritual directors that God did with them in three months—some even in three days—what it took a great number of years for him to do with her. Teresa fears that directors may urge such gifted persons to turn back and walk at a pace more like their own. She concludes with engaging wit: "nor would I want to make those who fly like eagles with the favors God grants them to advance like fettered chickens" (L.39.12).

The question that comes to the fore is, Do beginners generally need to practice discursive meditation before arriving at the prayer of simplicity, or recollection? Must they traverse many stages before attaining to the passive state and to union with God, as people used to think, following authorities like Tanquerey? The query may be phrased in another more practical way: Must the beginner of necessity use a method different from one who is advanced in contemplative prayer? And, more specifically for our purposes here, does Teresa provide us with an answer to this question?

Fortunately, Teresa, indirectly, does answer this doubt. Discussing the first, tedious way of obtaining water for the garden in chapter 12 of her *Life,* in which she is expounding her little treatise on prayer by means of an analogy on four ways of getting water for a garden, she deftly describes what we can do through our own efforts. The soul "can place itself in the presence of Christ." One who remains in his precious company is already advanced, having found therein the key to spiritual progress. Teresa at this point makes a major statement critical to an understanding of her teaching: "This method of keeping Christ present with us is beneficial in all stages and is a very safe means of advancing in the first degree of prayer, or reaching in a short time the second degree, and of walking secure against the dangers the devil can set up in the last degrees. Keeping Christ present is what we ourselves can do" (L.12. 3–4). To come right to the fundamentals, this is what we do in Christian prayer. In faith, we direct our awareness to the presence of Christ. With the deepening of prayer, Christ intervenes making his presence known independently of our efforts. This is what Teresa means by "supernatural" prayer—Christ's presence experienced passively as a gift. But whether it comes as the result of our human efforts influenced by grace or passively in contemplation, we carry in our awareness the presence of Christ as the One whom we believe in and love.

Putting this in different words, Teresa speaks of keeping Christ present as looking at him with the eyes of the soul. Helpful for such a practice is an important prior understanding that Christ is a friend, a good companion who is always with us and never takes his eyes off us. He is always present to us first. With this in mind, Teresa pleads, "Is it too much to ask you to turn your eyes from these exterior things in order to look at him sometimes?" In our pausing to turn and look at Christ, she characteristically perceives the beginning of a desire for him. Not stopping there, she goes on to assert encouragingly that he "esteems our turning to look at him" (W.26.3).

Teresian Mental Prayer and Its Forms

By considering Teresa's often-quoted definition of mental prayer, we discover some other notions connected with being present to Christ. "For mental prayer, in my opinion, is nothing else than an intimate sharing between friends; it means taking time frequently to be alone with Him who we know loves us" (L.8.5).

The note of friendship and intimacy appearing in these words tells us that we are working here with something deeper than a mere "friendly conversation" as her words are often rendered. The Spanish *tratar de amistad* in the context of the whole passage speaks of actualizing a friendship that exists between intimate friends who love each other. In their friendship, each shares and communicates deeply with the other.

Time is a requisite for anyone desiring to cultivate a friendship. Friends must give their time to each other. Without communication, the friendship grows cold. Teresa laments the mockery of our refusal to give the Lord the little bit of time we devote to him in prayer. The time will easily be spent on ourselves or on someone else who would not even thank us for it. After reading Osuna's *Third Spiritual Alphabet* and at its urging, Teresa began generously to dedicate two hours daily to this mental prayer.

The two other notions found in her definition assert that we are alone and that we know that he loves us. The point in the first is not that we are alone, but that we are alone "with" him. Being "with him" is another expression for "being present to him." "Being alone with him" is not so much a matter of physical isolation as it is one of having the mind and heart set on him, looking at him who is always looking at us, as was said, like the biblical face-to-face communion.[10] You can go to many lengths to find physical solitude and then fail to be alone "with him." "Being alone" alludes mostly to being free of other superfluous thoughts and desires. Candidly confessing that in the beginning she was not really with Christ during the time of prayer, Teresa then uses the word "with" in reference to something else, "with a thousand disturbances from worldly cares and thoughts" (L.8.6).

That we are alone "with him who we know loves us" highlights God's presence through grace, as a friend inviting us into intimacy, a friend we know loves us, whose fidelity we need never doubt but can always trust. Through faith, we know these truths, that the friend is good and true and beautiful, and, in fact, constitutes the source of all good, truth, and beauty. As Teresa persevered, what she knew through faith she began to know more deeply and powerfully through experience, an experiential penetration into the abyssal depths of faith.

If we take the word "mental" to involve the mind alone, we will assuredly misunderstand the reality of mental prayer. In Teresa's thought, both the mind and the heart should be attentive to the one with whom we are in communication. In this realization, Teresa was able to defend mental prayer against those who pressed that the unlettered restrict themselves to their vocal prayers (cf. W.21.10; 22.2–3).

Recollection. At the persistent urging of her nuns to write something about prayer for them, Teresa wrote *The Way of Perfection,* openly confessing in it that she had nothing to say about discursive meditation since there were excellent books on the matter for those "who can form the habit of following this method of prayer" (W.19.1). She planned to present a method for those who could not recollect their minds through discursive thought (W.21.3; 24.1), to teach them how to pray by using words, vocal prayer, particularly the *Our Father* (W.24.2), directing her teaching more specifically to those whose minds are as scattered as wild horses. These minds are now "running here, now there, always restless" (W.19.2). If they are going to recite the *Our Father,* they should first of all "remain at the side of the Master who taught this prayer" to us (W.24.5). Focusing the mind on the one to whom the words are addressed is the best remedy for keeping our thoughts away from a thousand irrelevant topics.

How do you remain at the side of the Master? Teresa answers this question by turning again to her notion of representing Christ. "Represent the Lord Himself as close to you and behold how lovingly and humbly He is teaching you." She says it is like being with a friend. You get accustomed to having him present at your side. After a while, you will not be able to get away from him; you will find him everywhere, never failing you, helping in your trials. "O Sisters, those of you who cannot engage in much discursive reflection with the intellect or keep your mind from distraction, get used to this practice!" (W.26.1 & 2).

In a further step, she suggests that the mood we may be experiencing at a given time can assist us in looking at him, so that when joyful we look at him as risen, when sad, or experiencing trials, we look at him in his Passion (W.26.5). And we can also relate to him in different ways, as to a father, brother, lord, or spouse (W.28.3).

Explaining this whole art, Teresa moves almost unnoticeably from our being present to the Master at our side—outside of us then—to finding him within. Turning within to be with the Master within is what Teresa calls the prayer of recollection. "This prayer is called recollection, because the soul collects its faculties together and enters within itself to be with its God" (W.28.4).

The truth that God is within us, not so generally known in her time, for which Teresa found confirmation in St. Augustine, gave her joy in many ways, but particularly because of her sense of his nearness. We do not have to shout in order to be heard by God; "however softly we speak, he is near enough to hear us" (W.28.2).

Appearing, perhaps, to some as approaching the naive, Teresa, we must remember, was not well instructed in the doctrines of the faith and did not in the beginning know many truths that she later experienced. Groping for an image to illustrate her thought, she suggests that we think of ourselves as a palace made of gold and precious stones and that a King who has been gracious enough to adopt us as his children is seated in the palace on an extremely valuable throne (W.28.9). Thoughts like these assisted Teresa to persevere and grow in this practice of recollection. She confesses that "if I had understood as I do now that in this little palace of my soul dwelt so great King, I would not have left him alone so often" (W.28.11).

This prayer of recollection may accompany either discursive meditation-when associated with the above-mentioned presence to Christ– or vocal prayer in that the loving attention to Christ is directed to him as dwelling within us. Teresa holds out the promise to us that if we practice this method of enclosing ourselves within ourselves, "in this little heaven of our soul" where the Master is present, and grow accustomed to refusing to look in the direction of the exterior senses and their distractions, we will not fail to drink water from the fount (W.28.4 & 5). Since drinking water from the fount is for Teresa the equivalent of contemplation, this method of recollection admirably disposes a person for the gift of contemplation. "And its divine Master comes more quickly to teach it and give it the prayer of quiet than He would through any other method it might use" (W.28.4). She is utterly amazed that the Lord would enclose himself in something so small, God "who would fill a thousand worlds and many more with His grandeur" (W.28.11).

Meditation. Beginners in mental prayer usually need to employ more efforts of their own, for which reason Teresa recommends meditation as a practice that could be helpful to some. In chapter 13 of her *Life* she describes the procedure of meditation as she sees it:

> Let us begin to think about an episode of the Passion, let's say of when our Lord was bound to the pillar. The intellect goes in search of reasons for better understanding the great sorrows and pain His Majesty suffered in that solitude and many other things that the intellect, if it works hard, can herein deduce. How much more if it is the intellect of a learned man! This is the method of prayer with which all must begin, continue, and finish; and it is a very excellent and safe path until the Lord leads one to other supernatural things. (L.13.12)

As she continues, she explains that we may use other topics for our meditation as long as we often reflect on the Passion and life of Christ "from which has come and continues to come every good" (L.13.13). Our meditations can produce in us feelings of devotion and even result in tears of sorrow and compassion or feelings of joy and delight. All of these tend to result in resolutions to render God more service (L.12.2).

What may well go unnoticed in Teresa's words about meditation is her insistence that within the activity of meditation one must not lose sight of the essential and more personalist element of prayer, that is, being present to Christ:

> But one should not always weary oneself in seeking these reflections but just remain there in His presence with the intellect quiet. And if we are able we should occupy ourselves in looking at Christ who is looking at us, and we should speak, and petition, and humble ourselves, and delight in the Lord's presence. (L.13.22)

Looking at Christ in the awareness that he is looking at us, speaking and listening to him—these were what Teresa found most attractive and helpful in meditative prayer. Subtly instructing some of her theologian friends, it seems, she says they should take some time just to delight in the presence of Christ and not wear themselves out composing syllogisms (L.13.11).

Although Teresa presents this kind of discursive meditation as the work of beginners, she knew perfectly well from experience that there were many beginners who were unable to practice mental prayer in this way; moreover she counted herself among them, frankly admitting that she could not reflect discursively with the intellect (L.9.4; 13.11).

Discursive meditation calls for the use of imagination as well, imagination in the sense of picturing scenes from Christ's life to oneself. Here, too, Teresa fumbled helplessly and simply admitted that she could never picture things in her imagination (L.9.6).

Vocal Prayer. Vocal prayer, the recitation of a prayer formula such as the *Our Father*, when accompanied by the prayer of recollection, presents no obstacle to contemplation. It is perfectly compatible with mental prayer, recollection, and contemplation. "I tell you that it is very possible that while you are reciting the Our Father or some other vocal prayer, the Lord may raise you to perfect contemplation" (W.25.1).

From Teresa's teachings, then, we can conclude that mental prayer, the presence to Christ, embraces a wider field than does the prayer of recollection. The method of mental prayer Teresa teaches is the prayer of recollection. Vocal prayer was always to be accompanied by mental prayer, and she urged the practice of recollection in vocal prayer; certainly vocal prayer does not represent a stage of prayer preceding meditation. In contemplation, vocal prayer slows down into silence, and recollection deepens. Discursive meditation was for Teresa, generally, a means to mental prayer and recollection, although the meditation could incorporate some of the elements of the two. In contemplation, meditation reaches its goal and must cease.

Bodily Posture. Teresa left little in the way of instructions about bodily posture. Following the custom of her times, where chairs were often not in use, she sat back in a kneeling position on her heels as a posture for prayer. Such a posture resembles the one employed in the use of a small prayer bench. It has been recommended for relaxing the body, lowering the center of gravity, and fostering an attitude of hope, listening, and receptivity. The posture favors a bodily calm. What Teresa does recommend is to close one's eyes as a means of turning the gaze away from the persons or material things around us. She found that as the habit of recollection grows, no effort is needed to keep the eyes closed; indeed, a greater effort would be needed to open them (W.28.6). Bodily illnesses can make prayer difficult. Her advice in such cases is to avoid any effort to force prayer (L.11.15). To the sick she offers this hope: "And even in sickness itself . . . the prayer is genuine when it comes from a soul that loves to offer the sickness up and accept what is happening and be conformed to it" (L.7.12).

External Means. Two outside helps esteemed and used by Teresa to assist us to recollect our thoughts and "keep from thinking of a thousand other vanities" (W.29.5) are images and books, especially those about our Lord's life and sufferings. Since people in sixteenth-century Spain were allowed to read the Scriptures only in Latin, Teresa searched out books that quoted copiously from the Gospels in the vernacular and that preferably dealt with the life of Christ. Words from Scripture impressed her deeply. Speaking with irony in a situation where many spiritual books had been placed on the Index, she tells her nuns in *The Way of Perfection* that no one will be able to take from them the book of the *Our Father* (W.21.3). The words of our Lord recorded in Scripture bore for her a special force: "I have always . . . found more recollection in them than in very cleverly written books" (W.21.3). The repetition of some words, or a word, from the Gospel, could serve for one's mental prayer just as well as the *Our Father* or other vocal prayer formulas.

For Teresa, then, being present to Christ by means of the prayer of recollection, whether in meditation or in the repetition of words from Scripture, amounts to what we ourselves can do. With this, all that is necessary is to persevere (L.8.5). Her classic text on the determination to persevere lies at the heart of all Teresa has to say on prayer:

> They must have a great and very determined determina-
> tion to persevere until reaching the end, come what may,
> happen what may, whatever work is involved, whatever
> criticism arises, whether they arrive or whether they die
> on the road, or even if they don't have courage for the
> trials that are met, or if the whole world collapses.
> (W.21.2)

Persevering in the effort to practice this prayer of recollection, a person will find that the recollection gradually deepens (W.28.7). With this deepening, the practice becomes easier. While the soul is in this recollection, the Lord begins to grant it the prayer of quiet, in which he "puts it at peace by His presence" (W.31.2).

Theological Reflections

What can one say theologically of Teresa's understanding of prayer as a being present to Christ in these different ways? Briefly, Christians know through revelation that the initiator of our relationship with God is God. God spoke to us and invited us to communion, going out to meet us at a more profound level than that of Creator and creature. All our life of prayer is no more than a response to God's call to communion. "In this is love: not that we have loved God, but that he loved us" (1 Jn 4:10). Our first assertion should not be that we must pray but that we can pray. God has given us the possibility of entering into intimacy with him and called us to share the divine life.

In many ways, with gestures and words, God entered into dialogue with human beings throughout history. Yet, in Christ, God spoke to us the most that could be said, revealing himself totally and inviting us to enter into a new relationship (cf. Heb 1:14; Eph 1:3–14). Since Christ is the unique mediator in our relationship with the Father, every call that God actually makes to us to live in communion with him comes addressed to us through Christ.

The Aramaic word *Abba*, which Jesus uses in his prayer, reveals the intimacy and affection of his relationship with God. In making those who believe in him his brothers and sisters, Christ enables them to have a relationship with the Father like his, and so a prayer like his.

The mediation of Christ is central, but Christ is also an object of our prayer. That he is the unique means through which our prayer touches the Father does not exclude his being also the direct object of our prayer.

Finally, the Holy Spirit is sent into our hearts to aid us in our weakness in prayer, in our not knowing how to pray, in our world bursting with worries, distractions, and busy activities. The secret of prayer well done is letting ourselves be "led by the Spirit" (Gal 5:18).

Through her persevering efforts to be present to Christ in her prayer, Teresa advanced beyond the need, generally, for such efforts. Christ gave her in contemplation an awareness of his presence that continued to influence her until she could hardly be distracted from him. But even in the seventh dwelling place, the Lord is still the initiator of the dialogue through his touches of love deep within the center of her soul (C.7.3.7). In this mystical touch, he continues to call her to remain with him in prayer. These gentle and penetrating touches demonstrate in Teresa's words "the particular care God has in communicating with us and beseeching us to remain with Him" (C.7.3.9).

Not only the presence of Christ but the presence of the other persons of the Trinity ultimately became manifest to Teresa. The three Persons, although One, really communicate with her soul, "speak to it, and explain those words of the Lord in the gospel: that he and the Father and the Holy Spirit will come to dwell with the soul that loves him and keeps his commandments" (C.7.1.6). Each day Teresa grew more amazed that these Persons never seem to leave her, although this profound awareness did not subtract from her other work. She declared that she is more occupied than ever before with all that pertains to the Lord's service. When the soul's "duties are over it remains with that enjoyable company" (C.7.1.8). This company brings with it bounteous and indescribable blessings, especially the blessing that "there is no need to go in search of reflections in order to know that God is there" (T.65.9).

Notes

1. For an excellent study in Spanish on this topic, see T. Alvarez and Jesús Castellano, *Teresa de Jesús, enseñanos a orar* (Burgos: Editorial Monte Carmelo, 1981). All quotations from St. Teresa will be taken from Kieran Kavanaugh, O.C.D., and Otilio Rodriguez, O.C.D., trans., *The Collected Works of St. Teresa of Avila*, 3 vols. (Washington, DC: ICS Publications, 1976–85).

2. For an English translation, see Francisco de Osuna, *The Third Spiritual Alphabet*, trans. Mary E. Giles (New York: Paulist Press, 1981).

3. See Kieran Kavanaugh, O.C.D., and Otilio Rodriguez, O.C.D., trans., *The*

Collected Works of St. John of the Cross, rev. ed. (Washington, DC: ICS Publications,1991), 377–80.

4. Ann and Barry Ulanov, *The Healing Imagination: The Meeting of Psyche and Soul* (New York: Paulist Press, 1991), 99–100.

5. Herman Branderis, trans.,*The Spiritual Life: A Treatise on Ascetical and Mystical Theology*, 2d rev. ed., (Tournai: Desclée & Co., 1930).

6. Cf., e.g., P. Marie-Eugène, O.C.D., *I Want to See God: A Practical Synthesis of Carmelite Spirituality*, trans. Sister M. Verda Clare, C.S.C. (Notre Dame, IN: Fides Publishers, 1953); *St. Teresa of Avila: Studies in Her Life, Doctrine and Times*, eds., Father Thomas, O.D.C. and Father Gabriel, O.D.C. (Westminster, MD: Newman Press, 1963).

7. Branderis, 699. Tomás de Jesús, who made his profession as a Discalced Carmelite in Spain five years after Teresa's death taught that discursive meditation evolves into a form of contemplation that becomes a habit, which he called acquired contemplation. During the first half of the twentieth century, a debate arose about this term that had its roots in another debate occasioned by a treatise on mystical theology by the Jesuit A. Poulain entitled *The Graces of Interior Prayer*. Poulain asserted that an essential distinction lay between the ascetical and mystical life. The two do not constitute parts of one and the same way leading to perfection. Those who opposed him taught that anyone journeying on the path to perfection would have to pass through both the ascetical and mystical life as two steps along one path. Many Carmelites sided with Poulain and held that acquired contemplation was the term of the prayer of one following the ascetical path and that perfection or union with God was reached when individuals had attained to complete conformity of their wills with God's will. Those journeying on the mystical path would experience the gift of infused contemplation in preparation for the mystical union of the spiritual marriage. Attempts to use Teresa to support theories about the essential distinction between the ascetical and mystical paths have been abandoned. Current literature approaches questions on prayer and spirituality from broader perspectives; see, e.g., Lawrence S. Cunningham and Keith J. Egan, *Christian Spirituality: Themes from the Tradition* (New York: Paulist Press, 1996); William Johnston, *Mystical Theology: The Science of Love* (London: Harper Collins, 1995); John Welch, O.Carm., *The Carmelite Way: An Ancient Path for Today's Pilgrim* (New York: Paulist Press, 1996).

8. See Sam Anthony Morello, O.C.D., *Lectio Divina and the Practice of Teresian Prayer* (Washington, DC: ICS Publications, 1995).

9. *Catechism of the Catholic Church* (Vatican City: Libreria Editrice Vaticana, 1994), 648–53.

10. "Thus the Lord used to speak to Moses face to face, as one speaks to a friend" (Ex 33:11).

TERESA, SUFFERING, AND THE FACE OF GOD

Vilma Seelaus, O.C.D.
Carmelite Monastery
Barrington, Rhode Island

1. Teresa's *Way of Perfection*

How we envision God really matters, because our experience of God and how we see ourselves are related. Our perception of God also signals the degree of freedom or unfreedom with which we relate to the events of life, especially those which occasion pain and suffering. Karl Rahner claims that while the experience of God and the experience of self are not identical, both exist within a unity. Apart from this unity, it is quite impossible for there to be any such experience at all. For Rahner, the experience of God and the experience of self is ultimate and all-embracing.[1]

Human Suffering and the Experience of God

Teresa of Avila finds in her experience of Christ an interpretative model both for self-understanding and for finding meaning in her sufferings. Her *Way of Perfection* connects the acceptance of suffering and the experience of God. With the certitude of experience, she assures us that

137

we shall never lack crosses in this life if we are in the ranks of The Crucified. Her words ring true today.

> It is useless, Sisters, to think that while we live we can be free of many temptations and imperfections and even sins, for it is said that whoever thinks he is without sin, deceives himself—and this is true. Now, if we turn to bodily ailments and hardships, who is without very many and in many ways? Nor is it good that we ask to be without them. (W.4.2.2) [2]

Suffering is a fact of life. Confronted by suffering, persons often feel victimized and ask, "Why me?" Suffering, its meaning and place in human life, is difficult to understand and even more difficult to accept. Most persons understandably resist and avoid what is painful. Teresa's *Way of Perfection* is a way of friendship with Christ who suffered, died, and rose for us. To walk with Teresa through her way of perfection is to see how intimacy with Christ removes the constraints of suffering and releases its transformative power. Through her relationship with Christ, Teresa reveals suffering's potential for life and growth, even in the midst of diminishment. Her contemplative soul sees suffering through the eyes of God who answers suffering with compassionate love. In the end, Teresa is transformed, not destroyed by it.

God, the absolute future of all history, responds to human suffering by suffering, and by rising, in the historical Jesus. According to Rahner, Jesus' resurrection completes and makes effective the very thing that happened in his death. The incomprehensibile God finally accepts human suffering as redeemed, precisely because Jesus surrendered it unreservedly into the incomprehensibility of God. In the historical event of his resurrection, Jesus raises this historical world of becoming into the eternity of God. [3] The risen Christ, therefore, stands before us as a model for making sense of human suffering. In Christ, the God of incomprehensible mystery is seen as in solidarity with those who suffer.

Teresa and the Suffering Christ

Teresa of Avila finds in the suffering Christ a container, a holding environment, a safe place to sort things out and find meaning in her many trials.[4] The God of Teresa is present and involved in her struggles. *The Way of Perfection* shows how intimate her relationship is with Christ. Through a gospel path of humility, detachment, and love, Teresa finds the peace her soul longs for even in the midst of trials. Humility, detachment, and love become the inner dynamic of her relationship with God, with herself, and with her world.

Francisco de Osuna's *Third Spiritual Alphabet* had great influence on Teresa's mysticism. Osuna titles the first chapter of his Seventeenth Treatise: "Our Body Must Follow Our Lord in His Sufferings." Those who follow Christ, says Osuna, run in the sweetness of love; he went first to make the way easier.[5] Such thoughts flow through Teresa's many prayers to Christ found in *The Way*. These outpourings of her heart reveal the God of Teresa. Here one finds multiple names for God and for Christ. These express reverence, strength, intimacy, and love. From this relationship, she finds meaning and courage in her trials.

As Osuna's translator points out, the copy of his work used by Teresa is preserved in the convent of Avila. Its yellow pages bear the traces of constant study. Whole passages are heavily scored and underlined, while on the margins a cross, a heart, and a hand pointing (her favorite marks) indicate the thoughts that seemed to her most worthy of notice. "I was very happy with this book and resolved to follow that path with all my strength."[6] Teresa internalizes what she reads. We find evidence of this in strikingly similar passages to those of Osuna in her own writings. At the same time, Teresa's experience in prayer takes her beyond what Osuna describes.

Is it possible that today's spiritual awakening, with its postmodern consciousness, holds an invitation to go beyond even mystics like Teresa of Avila? More than ever, we realize our connectedness to each other, to the earth, and to the unfolding universe. Thomas Berry reminds us that we bear the universe in our beings just as the universe bears us in its being. The two have a total presence to each other and to that deeper mystery out of which both the universe and ourselves have emerged.[7] A sixty-two-year-old business man describes this reality after cardiac arrest and a near-death experience:

> One thing I learned was that we are all part of one big, living universe. If we think we can hurt another person or another living thing without hurting ourselves we are sadly mistaken. I look at a forest or a flower or a bird now, and say, "That is me, part of me." We are connected with all things and if we send love along those connections, then we are happy.[8]

Suffering and the Face of God

Such cosmic connectedness is both an awesome and a harsh reality. It opens the heart to the immensity of God as cosmic presence; while at the same time, it exposes deeper levels of potential suffering. Bede Griffith reminds us:

> Conflict and suffering are part of the pattern of things evolving in space and time. They belong to the world of becoming, of change and decay. The misery of human suffering lies in the fact that our consciousness is divided. We experience the world and ourselves in their dispersion in time and space, in the flux of becoming. But if we could see with an undivided consciousness, we should know the world and ourselves not in the process of becoming but in the achievement of being, not as separate parts but as an organic whole. When Christ was hanging on the cross he experienced the pain of the whole world from the beginning to the end of time, because he experienced it in the Word, which is before all things and in all things and above all things. By this suffering the pain of the world was reconciled with God, brought into the unity of the divine life.[9]

As humans, each one of us is integral to the evolving universe. We live its reality in the moment-by-moment events of our daily lives. As members of Christ, through our sufferings, the pain of today's world can find a home in God.[10] This can only happen if God is a welcoming presence. If, instead, we perceive God as wrathful and condemning, guilt and anxiety exacerbate pain. Suffering is not the action of a punitive god. Instead, suffering evokes the compassion of God who knows suffering in the sufferings of Christ.[11] Catherine Mowry LaCugna, in developing her understanding of the Trinity as *God for Us,* dismisses the notion of an uninvolved, punitive God.

> The God too hidden for us to know, or too powerful to evoke anything but fear, does not exist . . . . The God who keeps a ledger of our sins and failings, the divine policeman, does not exist. These are all false gods, fantasies of the imagination that has allowed itself to become detached from the rule of God's life disclosed in Jesus Christ. What we believe about God must match what is revealed of God in Scripture: God watches over the widow and the poor, God makes the rains fall on just and unjust alike, God welcomes the stranger and embraces the enemy.[12]

Perhaps the most painful of human suffering is accepting the invitation to let go of false notions of God. Like the passing of clouds, which allows the sun to shine, the God of compassion can then shine forth. With this experience comes a truer sense of self as mirrored in the divine presence.

The difficulty is that the initial experience of seeing oneself in God can be shocking and painful. As the divine light within illumines the dark corners of the soul, we see the stark reality of our undeveloped potential as well as sin and all that we hold separate from God. One's image both of God and of the self undergo a gradual revisioning and transformation. As she herself goes through this process, Teresa develops a deep sense of what her contemporary, the theologian Louis of Granada, calls the "Grandeur of Divine Justice." Teresa abhors what God abhors, and she suffers deeply her own sins and infidelities as well as the evils of her time.[13] Teresa stands in respectful fear before divine justice, especially after her vision of hell.[14] Paradoxically, this vision strengthened rather than strained her experience of God as friend and lover. Christ, the compassionate one, is the ground of her hope. God ordains all things toward her good.

Brokeness and sin are everywhere. The reality of the human as *imago dei* exists both as a present reality and as a future hope. Sin, our oppression of ourselves, others, and, in a sense, God, obscures the divine image in the human. Our likeness to God is in process. Self-acceptance means that we embrace the fragile, yet strong, sinful, yet holy, human/divine being that is ourselves. To acknowledge sin dispels the clouds of untruth and clears the soul's inner vision. Such self-acceptance awakens the heart's deepest desires. John of the Cross, in his *Spiritual Canticle,* describes eloquently such awakened desire. Like music, this lyric poem sings of lover in search of her beloved. Stanza 12 reads:

> O spring like crystal!
> If only, on your silvered-over faces,
> you would suddenly form
> the eyes I have desired,
> which I bear sketched deep within my heart.

John's comments make the sketch that of both lover and beloved in a single drawing.[15] The eyes of God the Beloved are always upon us. In the face of Christ, we find both forgiveness and the fullness of God's self-communicating love. God companions the human journey. We are never alone in our struggles; Christ walks with us as he did with the disappointed, sorrowing disciples on the road to Emmaus. As we break the bread of our pain and loss with him, our eyes will be opened to see the Risen One in whom suffering surrenders to glory. Before the mystery of pain, like the apostle Thomas, we need to place the fingers of our doubt into the wounded Christ. He will implant within our struggle the seed of faith.

Prayer and Pain

Indeed, how we envision God really matters. God is not over against the human race. Instead, God transforms human suffering in the sufferings of Christ. Teresa's *Way of Perfection* integrates within a single vision the trials of life and the experience of God. She guides us as we walk this *way*. The journey is not easy, but the rewards are great. With practical wisdom, Teresa shows "how one reaches this fount of living water, what the soul feels there, how God satisfies it, takes away thirst for earthly things, and makes it grow in the things pertaining to the service of God" (W.42.6).

Teresa directs us "toward the complete gift of ourselves to the Creator, the surrender of our wills to God's, and detachment from creatures" (W.32.9). She shows how to gain from life's trials and, through them, come to a closer union with God. She writes this book amidst much suffering and turmoil in her own life. Confessors judge fraudulent her spiritual experiences. Endless business matters, lawsuits, and other problems regarding her new monasteries claim attention. She suffers from poor health. Through all of this, Christ is there as friend and companion. The outpourings of her soul in prayer reveal not only the intimacy of her relationship with Christ, but also her process in dealing with pain. The depth of her mysticism never obscures her struggling humanity. Teresa is no stoic. Two contrasting texts show the extent of her inner struggle. In chapter 32 of *The Way of Perfection,* love overflows in ardent self-surrender.

> Your will, Lord, be done in me in every way and manner that You, my Lord, want. If You want it to be done with trials, strengthen me and let them come; if with persecutions, illnesses, dishonors, and a lack of life's necessities, here I am; I will not turn away, my Father, nor is it right that I turn my back on You. Since Your Son gave you this will of mine in the name of all, there's no reason for any lack on my part. (W.32.10)

However, ten chapters later, Teresa prays in a different voice. Her patience is at an end. She concludes her reflections on the *Our Father* with a prayer for deliverance, not only from suffering, but from life itself. Overwhelmed with trials of every kind, she cries out in her pain:

> Deliver me, Lord, from this shadow of death, deliver me from so many trials, deliver me from so many sufferings, deliver me from so many changes, from so many compliments that we are forced to receive while still living, from so many, many, many things that tire and weary me, that would tire anyone reading this if I mentioned them all. There's no longer anyone who can bear to live. This weariness must come to me because I have lived so badly, and from seeing that the way I live now is still not the way I should live since I owe so much. (W.42.2)

Suffering wears thin Teresa's strong determination. She longs for death. In her weakness, she speaks most meaningfully to our own experience. We learn about prayer within the context of fragile human life. Union with God is not absence of suffering.

Teresa ends *The Book of Her Life* appearing very much at home with God. She enjoys frequent visions of the glorious Christ, of His Mother, and of the saints, and she seems to live more in heaven than on earth. Just to eat is a chore, and she longs to die and be united with Christ forever. In the first chapter of *The Way of Perfection,* however, Teresa appears very much back on earth. Her own problems afflict her and so do those of the whole suffering church. Mystical graces have expanded her vision. Her soul is not confined by the walls of Avila. Her life is now inseparably one with Christ in His suffering members.

Today, the suffering face of Christ surrounds us. Christ suffers in the person with AIDS, in the homeless, and in the abused. The face of Christ is in the sufferings of families and nations. Christ suffers in the oppression of women, in the neglect of children, and in the forgotten elderly. Suffering stirs the compassionate heart of God and invites a renewed humanity. According to the Latin American liberation theologian,

Gustavo Gutiérrez, salvation and liberation, God and humanity, grace and freedom are always related through the nature of history as the continual quest for new ways of being human.[16]

Self-Transcendence through Everyday Trials

The documents of Vatican II remind the church of the universal call to holiness. Teresa's *Way of Perfection* is for everyone. Our greatest dignity as persons is in union with God and with each other in this earth community. Our significance is in ourselves as images of God. Each person uniquely reflects God. Our heritage for others is not money or achievement. Rather, what truly lasts is the radiance of human love transformed in God. Such love creates an enduring energy field which revisions and revitalizes both the earth and its human inhabitants.

John Navone writes:

> Through the mystery of the cross, Jesus has created a new perspective which frees us from the domination of the world as the ultimate source of human happiness. This new perspective is that of a love which sees all things as grace [Rom 8,28] enabling us to accept the limitations of the human condition good-naturedly with the broader vision of a love which even now transcends them. The mystery of the cross reveals that there is no self-transcendence without suffering and that the freedom, love and decision of Jesus can and must be shared in the attainment of that self-transcendence through which men become sons of God [*sic*].[17]

Suffering can shrivel a person, or it can open one to depths of divine intimacy. Pain can shrink one's world so that nothing exists beyond one's pain, or it can open a person to see the world through the eyes of the suffering Christ.

The perspective of sixteenth-century Spain increasingly narrowed to protect its own interests, while Teresa's increasingly expanded. Rumors of religious wars in France fired, her to pray for the preachers and theologians whose task is to defend the faith. Accounts from missionaries in the New World further expand the ardor of her heart's embrace. Her sufferings also increase. She faces separation from her brothers who, lured by rumors of fortune and adventure, leave for the Americas.

Teresa bore the challenge of her own historical reality. Suffering was inescapable as she began to establish communities of prayer in the midst of ecclesial and even societal distrust of prayer. She gathered a small group of women whose life was one of continuous prayer for the church. They would be good friends of Christ and would serve Christ and the church through prayer and contemplation. In an age with a flair for mysticism, with false mystics gaining renown, concerned church and civil leaders understandably looked upon Teresa's foundations with caution and distrust. Men's attitude toward women intensified the problem—prayer put women in danger of error and foolish sentimentalism. Just to be a woman, Teresa once lamented, was enough to make one's wings fall off.

Women were seen as a mistake of nature, a kind of unfinished man. Kavanaugh, in his introduction to *The Way of Perfection,* gives a shocking example of the culture's antifeminism. He quotes from the writings of Osuna:

> Since you see your wife going about visiting many churches, practicing many devotions, and pretending to be a saint, lock the door; and if that isn't sufficient, break her leg if she is young, for she can go to heaven lame from her own house without going around in search of these suspect forms of holiness. It is enough for a woman to hear a sermon and then put it into practice. If she desires more, let a book be read to her while she spins, seated at her husband's side.[18]

In this context, we can understand Teresa's clear and forceful defense of women. We can also understand her struggles with self-doubt. As if this were not enough, Teresa lived in a society obsessed with honor, wealth, and purity of blood. Persons with Jewish or Moorish blood suffered discrimination, if not banishment. Teresa hid well the fact that her grand-father was a *converso,* a Christianized Jew. Class distinction was ingrained in the psyche of her nuns. In *The Way of Perfection,* Teresa regularly challenges them to a Gospel life of sisterly love where all are equal. In this they will find the peace necessary for a life of prayer.[19]

Teresa faced societal issues not unlike those that daily confront us in our own lives. As Kavanaugh points out in his introduction:

> Remarkably, Teresa avoids any claim that nuns have a greater occa-sion for the practice of detachment or that their life is harder; rather, at times, she observes that married people are forced to practice greater self-discipline because of their obligations and that people living in the world have difficult trials from which the nuns are freed.[20]

Spontaneous outpourings to Christ bring clarity to troubling issues for Teresa. From her prayers, we learn the relationship between prayer and life; we also learn about the God to whom Teresa prays. In chapter 3 of *The Way* there is a lengthy prayer-conversation with Christ and his Father (W.3.7–9). Teresa is at ease to be herself; she shares with Christ the concerns and desires of her heart. In this lengthy passage, worth looking up, Teresa bargains with God and makes a pointed polemic concerning men's attitude toward women, so different from the way Christ treats her. With theological astuteness, she holds the sufferings of Christ before God in her own defense, and she intercedes for suffering humankind.

Prayer is an outpouring of the heart, but stillness and the silence of God soon take over; Teresa's heart comes to rest in God. She simply opens the mouth of her ardent desires and lets herself be filled at the foun-tain of living water.

> In this contemplation, as I have already written, we don't do anything ourselves. Neither do we labor, nor do we bargain, nor is anything else necessary—because everything else is an

> impediment and hindrance—than to say *fiat voluntas tua:* Your
> will, Lord, be done in me in every way and manner that You, my
> Lord, want. (W.32.10)

Human effort gives way to surrender. Contemplation absorbs words into silence before Christ who suffered so much for Teresa. Within each of her prayers, Teresa uses multiple names for God. To cite but two examples: In chapter 3, God is Creator, Lord, His Majesty, just Judge, eternal Father, loving Lamb, Emperor, sovereign Judge, and God of mercy (W.3.7–9). In chapter 22, God is emperor, supreme Power, supreme Goodness, and Wisdom itself (W.22.6). Teresa tends to use strong masculine images for God but always within a context of God as caring and nurturing life. Metaphors for God reflect the culture in which Teresa lives. Along with Scripture, the language of chivalry provides Teresa with titles and names for God.

Women Today and Naming God

Today, women are acutely conscious of their exclusion in the naming of God. Liturgical worship urgently needs the corrective of a language and symbol that include both genders in the naming of God who yet ever remains Incomprehensible Mystery. The whole of women's reality, created and blessed in the divine image and likeness, offers suitable, even excellent metaphors for speaking about divine mystery. There remains the ultimate inadequacy of human naming of God; yet the importance of speech about God in female symbols cannot be underestimated.[21]

Despite the sexist connotations of Jungian archetypal imagery, the words of Clarissa Pinkola Estés are worthy of note. In the interest of truly empowering women, she offers thought-provoking words for women whose experience leads them to name God *only* in the feminine. She writes:

> So living as we do in a world that requires both meditative
> and outward action, I find it very useful to utilize the concept of a

masculine nature or animus in woman. In proper balance animus acts as helper, helpmate, lover, brother, father, king. This does *not* mean animus is king of the woman's psyche, as an injured patriarchal point of view might have it. It means there is a kingly aspect existent in the woman's psyche, a king who is in loving service to the wild nature (woman's basic nature), who is meant to work in a woman's behalf and for her well-being, governing what she assigns to him, ruling over whatever psychic lands she grants to him.[22]

Such names as King, Lord, and Majesty are favorite titles of God for Teresa. They empower her to stand strong in defense of women. She does so with both secure determination and gracious charm. She writes:

Is it not enough, Lord, that the world has intimidated us . . . so that we may not do anything worthwhile for You in public or dare speak some truths that we lament over in secret, without Your also failing to hear so just a petition? I do not believe, Lord, that this could be true of Your goodness and justice, for You are a just judge and not like those of the world. Since the world's judges are sons of Adam and all of them men, there is no virtue in women that they do not hold suspect. Yes, indeed, the day will come, my King, when everyone will be known for what he is. I do not speak for myself, because the world already knows my wickedness— but because I see that these are times in which it would be wrong to undervalue virtuous and strong souls, even though they are women. (W.3.7)

Teresa has a determined sense of what women can and should contribute to the world, and she holds this before God with confidence and trust. She reminds God that the nuns have left all and desire nothing else than to please God. She concludes in her own favor: "Since You, my Creator, are not ungrateful, I think You will not fail to do what they beg of you" (W.3.7). The remainder of this extensive prayer is strongly persuasive. Teresa shores up arguments as to why God must hear her since it pertained to the honor of God's Son. After holding forth the sufferings of Christ, Teresa challenges God: "Let Your Majesty be at once appeased!

Do not look at our sins but behold that Your most Blessed Son redeemed us, and behold His merits and those of His glorious Mother and of so many saints and martyrs who died for You!" (W.3.8).

Weak woman that she often calls herself, Teresa's prayers reflect a person of great inner strength.[23] Consistently throughout *The Way*, Teresa sees God as sympathetic to her prayer and as passionately involved in her concerns and in her suffering. Teresa shares what Rosemary Haughton understands as "the instinct that God's love is essentially, and not merely accidentally, 'passionate.' "[24]

The God of Teresa is never a detached observer of human life. Instead, God is always present. Teresa easily identifies the events in Christ's life with her own. Her sufferings, the sufferings of her church, of Christians, is Christ's suffering. In her own sufferings and in the sufferings of others, the God of Teresa is present and passionately involved. Today, as physicists offer the challenge of cosmic connectedness, we need a contemplative vision to see anew the significance of our lives for each other and for the earth.[25] The deeper Teresa's journey into God, the more she becomes God's welcome to the world.

2. Humility

Teresa is God's welcoming presence to the world; she is also God's critique of much of what her world holds dear. The yearnings of the heart are easily led astray by disordered affectivity. Within the human heart is both an attraction toward God and a resistance to letting go of that which displaces God's centrality in our life. As desire for God intensifies in Teresa, to that extent does her perception of reality undergo transformation. She comes to view all of life from the prism of her relationship with Christ.

Contemplative Prayer and Expanded Consciousness

Growth in consciousness is Teresa's primary concern for those dedicated to a life of prayer. Those who pray vocally must understand what they are saying and be mindful of the one to whom they pray (W. 24.2–3). The prayer of recollection (chap. 28) and the prayer of quiet (chap. 31) describe a process of interiority. Contemplation issues in a whole new way of knowing, understanding, and judging. Contemplative consciousness finds its actuality in love through union with God. As Teresa puts it, "The soul understands in another way, very foreign to the way it understands through the exterior senses, that it is now close to its God and that not much more would be required for it to be one with Him in union" (W.31.2).[26] Everything that Teresa writes about is, as she says, directed toward the complete gift of ourselves to the Creator, the surrender of our will to God (W.32.9).

Surrender as an abiding attitude is the fruit of transformed consciousness. One cannot exist without the other since the process of such transformation takes place in actual acts of surrender. Surrender is both an act and a gift. It does not come easy because each act of surrender is the response to an invitation to an ever deeper conversion of heart. Surrender is not a disclaimer or abdication of the human, but the means through which we most truly become ourselves. The whole impetus of the human spirit is toward surrender to the embrace of God ever present as abiding offer.

According to Teresa, surrender happens through a dynamic of love, detachment, and humility. Together they bring about inner harmony and peace which allows the fountain of living water to flow freely. Love, detachment, and humility as Teresa describes them, often in practical detail, are the insights of contemplative wisdom. These offer explicit means toward a contemplative methodology that can uncover the deeper meaning of the sufferings and hurts of life. Says Teresa: "The practice of these three virtues helps us to possess inwardly and outwardly the peace Our Lord recommended so highly to us" (W.4.4). Difficult circumstances may remain, but the heart finds peace and clarity of vision in surrender.

Theologian Bernard Lonergan locates the experience of God within the emergence of consciousness. The movement of the psyche proceeds from simple experience to an attempt to understand what has been experienced, to a judgment about the accuracy or truthfulness of the understanding, to choices for living based on the meaning derived in the process. Psychic life appears to operate according to certain transcendental precepts: be attentive, be intelligent, be reasonable, be responsible.

According to Lonergan, our questions for intelligence, for reflection, and for deliberation constitute our capacity for self-transcendence. That capacity becomes an actuality when one falls in love. One's "being becomes being-in-love." The final precept, then, is "be in love" or "be loving." Lonergan describes the different kinds of being in love: the intimacy between husband and wife, of parents and children, and so on. From a faith perspective, the self-transcending process toward "be loving" is meant ultimately to involve a relationship with God.

All love is self-surrender, but being in love with God is being in love without limits or qualifications or conditions or reservations. Being in love with God "dismantles and abolishes the horizon in which our knowing and choosing went on and it sets up a new horizon in which the love of God will transvalue our values and the eyes of that love will transform our knowing."[27]

True Humility

For Teresa, this transformation is the fruit of contemplative prayer supported by love and detachment with humility as the foundation. "Even though I speak of it last, it is the main practice and embraces all the others" (W.4.4). Humility is "not acquired by the intellect," but is the fruit of intimate friendship with Christ. Humility gives "a clear perception that comprehends in a moment the truth one would be unable to grasp in a long time through the work of the imagination about what a trifle we are and how very great God is" (W.32.13).

Humility situates persons within the realm of right relationships. They are in a place of truth before themselves and before God. Humility is never self-depreciation; rather, the self is within its center of truth. In the sixth dwelling place of her *Interior Castle,* Teresa describes what came to her, not as a result of reflection, but suddenly, that humility is truth. "God is supreme truth; and to be humble is to walk in truth, for it is a very deep truth that of ourselves we have nothing good but only misery and nothingness" (C.6.10.7). Lonergan points out that while the love of God is the utmost in self-transcendence, human self-transcendence is ever precarious. Aware of this, Teresa insists: "However sublime the contemplation, let your prayer always begin and end with self-knowledge" (W.39.5). She prays: "Instruct us, Lord, so that we may understand ourselves and be secure" (W.39.6). Humility, grounded in the truth "that of ourselves we have nothing good but only misery and nothingness," does not "disturb or disquiet or agitate; . . . it comes with peace, delight, and calm" (W.39.2).

To experience oneself in God is to experience the reality that of ourselves we are indeed nothingness and misery. At the same time, as Teresa writes in the *Interior Castle,* "Our Lord grants these favors of self-knowledge to the soul because, as to one to whom He is truly betrothed, one who is already determined to do His will in everything, He desires to give it some knowledge of how to do His will and of His grandeurs" (C.6.10.8).

True humility is the reflection of the self within the mirror of God's abiding presence.[28] From the perspective of her nothingness, from a profound sense of finitude before the all of God, Teresa instructs her daughters. Humility, as consciousness transformed in truth, establishes right relationships with God, with oneself, and with others. Such "clear perception . . . about what a trifle we are and how very great God is" (W.32.13) invites continual conversion of heart.

Conversion brings one's life and behaviors into conformity with new insights and perspectives. It need not imply guilt or moral wrongdoing, but a need for the clarity of truth to be realized in life. What was previously acceptable is no longer so; new insights need integration into daily living.

Reflections on humility weave themselves in and out of the text of *The Way*. Teresa desires to imitate the humility of Christ.[29] From her contemplative experience, she knows what everything is truly worth (W.36.9). Her own worth before God was concretized for Teresa in the experience of the angel who pierced her heart with a fiery dart, leaving her aflame with great love. "When he drew it out, I thought he was carrying off with him the deepest part of me" (L.29.13). The heart of Teresa is one with the heart of God. From this vantage, she can speak of the trifle that is herself and of the greatness of God.

The Lessons of Humility

Teresa begins to particularize humility with a lengthy precaution:

> Once we have detached ourselves from the world and from relatives and have enclosed ourselves here under the conditions that were mentioned, it seems that we have done all there is to do and that we don't have to struggle with anything. Oh, my Sisters, do not feel secure or let yourselves go to sleep! By feeling secure you would resemble someone who very tranquilly lies down after having locked his doors for fear of thieves while allowing the thieves to remain inside the house. And you already know that there is no worse thief than we ourselves. For if you do not walk very carefully and if each Sister is not alert in going against her own will as though doing so were more important than all else, there are many things that will take away this holy freedom of spirit by which you can fly to your Maker without being held down by clay or leaden feet. (W.10.1)

The Inevitability of Suffering. This passage overflows with insight and wisdom. First, we see that no human situation secures us from struggle and suffering. Teresa's Discalced Nuns are not exempt, even though they live in strict enclosure, detached from the world and from relatives. As humans, we are all vulnerable to suffering and pain; nothing protects us from this. To be humble is to accept the reality that we cannot earn the right not to suffer. We are vulnerable to it from varied and unexpected sources. Humility surrenders to the fragility of human life. The heart may cry out: "No fair!" or "Why me?" But if such sentiments harden into a consistent attitude, we lose touch with truth and unwittingly inflict on ourselves added suffering through our own wilfulness before the human condition.

We Suffer from Ourselves. "We may bolt the door but the thief is already inside." The source of our suffering is often our critical, judgmental heart or a heart too filled with self-doubt to take its rightful place in life. Like a thief, we steal from ourselves when the heart is not grounded in humility. An attached, wilful, controlling heart creates inevitable suffering for oneself and for others. In *The Ascent of Mount Carmel,* John of the Cross describes the harm and even torment that voluntary habitual faults inflict on the soul.[30] These are like dark ego zones not open to conversion. A habitual, negative, complaining, self-centered attitude is a thief that steals inner peace. Teresa advises:

> Be determined, Sisters, that you came to die for Christ, not to live comfortably for Christ. The devil suggests that you indulge yourselves so that you can keep the observance of the order; and a nun will so eagerly want to strive to care for and preserve her health for the sake of keeping the observance of the order that she dies without ever having kept this observance entirely for so much as a month, nor perhaps for even a day. (W.10.5)

Teresa addresses overconcern about oneself with ironic examples from daily living in the monastery. She describes the nun who stops going to choir because of a headache, which, she says, "won't kill us either. We stay away one day because our head ached, another because it was just now aching, and three more so that it won't ache again." (W.10.6).

Regarding the prioress, Teresa continues:

> Since you tell her about your need and there is no want of a doctor to
> side with you about the advisability of such permission, or a friend or
> relative to weep at your side, what can she do? She has a scruple
> that she might fail in charity. . . . Oh, God help me, this complaining
> among nuns! (W.10.7)

Teresa devotes an entire chapter to the habit of complaining. "It
wears everyone out" (W.11.1). The poor usually have no one to complain
to, and married women of her day had to suffer in silence.

> Recall as well many women who are married. I know of some
> who are persons of high station and who have serious illnesses
> and heavy trials but for fear of annoying their husbands dare not
> complain. . . . If a woman in an unhappy marriage suffers much
> adversity without being able to receive comfort from anyone lest
> her husband know that she speaks and complains about it, shouldn't
> we suffer just between ourselves and God some of the illnesses
> He gives us because of our sins? And even more so because by
> our complaining the sickness is not alleviated. (W.11.3)

Teresa accepts responsibility for the inner thief. Her example points
to its many faces in contemporary life. Today, advertising is ever ready to
advise us about the pleasure and comfort we owe ourselves. Persons who
internalize pain like a silent suffering martyr inevitably give it release in
acts of passive or active aggression or in codependent behavior. The inner
thief might convince a woman to stay in an abusive relationship rather
than take responsible action. Like the husband in Teresa's example, women
and men can be insensitive or indifferent toward the sufferings of others.
The inner thief creates both personal and societal dysfunction through
disruption of right relationships. We harm ourselves and others, through
food, substance, or sex abuse. We harm the environment with poisons
and pollutants, by litter, by misuse, and by overuse of our natural resources. Teresa's intent is not to judge or condemn, but to open up to

the sufferer the compassionate face of Christ who is always present to human pain, regardless of its source. To be present to another's pain is difficult because it mirrors our own fragile hold on life. The inner thief would have us deny feelings of fear and fragility in the face of suffering.

From Willfulness to Willingness. The third lesson Teresa teaches in this text is that going against one's own will is integral to humility. To go against one's will is willingness to surrender to a deeper reality for a greater good. This is not easily understood in our immediate-gratification culture. The message is if you want it, take it; if it feels good, go for it, regardless of its impact on others. Today's myth is one of constant happiness. To feel bad means we need to get back in control. Gerald May says it well:

> A growth mentality exists which is a highly creative, forward-look-ing and fundamentally optimistic attitude that harks back to the very roots of the American dream. At its best, it holds out the hope that if people can just find themselves and work through their blocks and inhibitions, they will be able to free their inner potential and achieve both individual happiness and a better world. The growth mentality however tends to fall prey to the idea that one can learn, earn, or otherwise achieve fulfillment by virtue of personal will. Compare this to the "let-go" of Buddhism or the self-surrender of Christian mysticism.[31]

In this chapter, entitled "Willingness and Willfulness," May points out that the growth movement has been psychologically helpful for a large number of people. For some, it has enabled a deeper, clearer sense of the mystery of self and facilitated a degree of psychological freedom that has helped in later spiritual surrender. Problems arise, however, when one remains attached to the growth-mentality's false promise of ultimate sal-vation, or when one continues to cling to the notion that final liberation is a thing to be personally accomplished.

Such willfulness is the antithesis of humility because it takes away freedom of spirit needed for surrender to mystery. Willfulness fosters self-importance, narcissism, or a happiness-minded spirituality that judges success or failure by one's mood. To feel sad is to feel rejected by God. When we feel happy, all is right with God. As May points out, mystery threatens our willfulness; there is nothing for us to do with it. Being in the presence of mystery tends to make us feel very vulnerable and out of control.[32] The ability to transcend self-possession to self-surrender is integral to humility as Teresa presents it. Transcendence, or the giving up of one's own will, leads to "holy freedom of spirit by which you can fly to your Maker without being held down by clay or leaden feet" (W.10.1).

The Gift of Inner Freedom. St. Teresa's fourth lesson is that we can possess, and in fact, already do possess, this holy freedom of spirit by which we can fly to our Maker. It is ours to claim. Going against one's own will means resisting a kind of self-love that keeps us unfree, centered in ourselves, and unable to truly love God and others. In *The Way of Perfection* Teresa insists: "The first thing we must strive for is to rid ourselves of our love for our bodies, for some of us are by nature such lovers of comfort that there is no small amount of work in this area" (W.10.5). The term "couch potato" says it all. It is hard to dislodge oneself from a place of comfort. Teresa observes:

> A fault this body has is that the more comfort we try to give it the more needs it discovers. It's amazing how much comfort it wants; and since in the case of health the need presents itself under the color of some good, however small it may be, the poor soul is deceived and doesn't grow. (W.11.2)

Teresa would have us get rid of love for our bodies. Perhaps today, integral to humility's freedom, is learning truly to love this body of ours. It companions our journey through life. More than ever, information is available regarding good health habits. We know what is good and what is not good for maintaining health. To abuse the body by poor eating habits, by lack of exercise, or by inadequate rest can be as destructive as excessive indulgence.

Cognitive behaviorists suggest practical training steps toward free-dom from compulsions. Teresa also has practical advice to offer:

> Bear in mind continually how all is vanity and how quickly everything comes to an end. This helps to remove our attachment to trivia and center it on what will never end. Even though this practice seems to be a weak means, it will strengthen the soul greatly, and the soul will be most careful in very little things. When we begin to become attached to something, we should strive to turn our thoughts from it and bring them back to God—and His Majesty helps. (W.10.2)

Success is not the issue, but an ever deeper desire for such inner freedom. For as Teresa says in the conclusion of her *Interior Castle:*

> The Lord doesn't look so much at the greatness of our works as at the love with which they are done. And if we do what we can, His Majesty will enable us each day to do more and more, provided that we do not quickly tire. But during the little while this life lasts—and perhaps it will last a shorter time than each one thinks—let us offer the Lord interiorly and exteriorly the sacrifice we can. His majesty will join it with that which He offered on the cross to the Father for us. Thus even though our works are small they will have the value our love for Him would have merited had they been great. (C.7.4.15)

Discovering "Dust thou art splendor." These thoughts bring us to Teresa's fifth and final point, which is that our clay or leaden feet do not have the last word. We are not determined by fragile humanity. A good part of the work of humility and detachment has already been done. For her nuns, this happens through the limitations of their lifestyle. But God also does much of the work for all of us. Circumstances, often painful, provide a framework for letting go. Serious heart disease dictates that we stop smoking; a close friend and confidant of many years moves away; illness drains one's finances so that desirable things are no longer possible; an only child is killed by a drunken driver; separation or divorce shatters dreams for happiness in marriage. Life asks for much letting go, often through painful circumstances.

Many things, says Teresa, will take away this holy freedom of spirit by which we can fly to our Maker. At the same time, life itself and our fragile hold on it present many opportunities to realize this inner freedom of spirit as we surrender to life's demands. Our clay or leaden feet need not have the last word. With humility, our fragile humanity touches deeper levels of resource for surrender and a deeper union with God.

The dictionary of symbol offers interesting insights into Teresa's image of the human with clay and leaden feet. Clay is a common symbolic synonym for flesh. The goddesses of ancient Mesopotamia and Assyria were potters who formed human beings from their own clay and infused humans with the breath of heaven and so brought them to life. A version of this story found its way into the Judeo-Christian Bible where God forms humans from the clay of the earth and breathes into them the breath of life.[33]

The specific symbolism of lead is the transference of the idea of weight and density onto the spiritual plane. The alchemists employed the image of a white dove contained in lead to express their central idea that matter was the receptacle of the spirit.[34] This "leaden dove" gives a sense of the complexity of the human as spirit and matter. As Thomas Berry points out, we live in a relationship of mutual presence not only to one another and to God, but to every species on planet earth.

> Empirical inquiry into the universe reveals that from its beginning in the galactic system to its earthly expression in human consciousness the universe carries within itself a psychic-spiritual as well as a physical-material dimension. . . . Humans emerge in the evolutionary process not only as an earthling but also as a worldling. We are of earth, but we are also part of the wider world of the universe. This means that we bear the universe in our being as the universe bears us in its being. The two have a total presence to each other and to that deeper mystery out of which both the universe and ourselves have emerged.[35]

Physicists explain the human body as just one more level of density in the human energy field. The Eastern Church speaks of God as Divine Energy. Today, the truth of humility is an expanded consciousness that our lives are more important than we realize. Decisions that we make at work, at home, and for pleasure and leisure require such consciousness, lest we contribute to the oppression of earth, our matrix. We can ask the question: Does our pleasure seeking violate planet earth through needless pollution? Do we mindlessly litter? So much in life is throwaway; does that include people?

Humility tells us that we cannot hurt another person or another living thing without hurting ourselves. We too can look at a forest or a flower or a bird and say in truth "this is part of me," even as we are a part of the body of Christ. We are members one of another. God invites *all* persons to drink of the fountain of living water. Teresa insists: "The pain of genuine humility doesn't agitate or afflict the soul; rather, this humility expands it and enables it to serve God more" (W.39.2).

Suffering and Transformation

In summary, Teresa experiences inner peace in spite of the suffering she attributes to her sinfulness. Such peace is the gift of a heart expanded through humility: a true and clear perception of herself before God. Through the eyes of God, Teresa sees herself as finite, fragile, and sinful, yet passionately loved by God. Humility keeps her on the alert for the thief within who would drag her down into sadness and self-pity. Teresa reclaims the purpose of suffering: her duty is to suffer as Christ did and to hold high the banner of the cross so that her life be life-giving for others (W.18.1–7). There is no transformation of person or society without suffering. The suffering and exalted Christ is our model.

The recent death of a community friend and his response to suffering illustrates the power of humility in the life of an ordinary person. He was a lawyer, a tall, well-built, impressive man who lived close by and who came to daily Mass at the monastery. Though he seemed to be in good health, he was diagnosed with cancer. Treatment proved ineffective; death loomed close. A person of deep faith, he retained his sense of humor, remained interested in others, and did his best to handle often intense pain with the least amount of fuss. We watched this powerful six-foot man waste away. We felt compassion, but we could not feel pity; he was too impressive as someone in touch with a source of inner strength.

He requested to be buried in a plain wooden coffin. One of his lawyer sons did carpentry. He made the coffin, but the whole family of six grown children each helped in some way in its construction. They watched their father both fight the disease and then surrender his strong will to live before the inevitability of death. The face of God for him was an inviting presence. His funeral was as much a celebration as it was a time of grief. The whole family participated. In various presentations, they recalled with humor and tears both the shortcomings and the holiness of his life. In spite of a life-threatening illness, this man did not let the inner thief drag him down to self-pity; at least not for long. Neither his wife nor family do so in the face of their loss. Like the fire that is contemplative prayer, his courage in suffering enkindles hope in others (W.40.4).

3. Detachment

Humility enables us to see the truth of ourselves in relation to God, to others, and to the universe. We are born of human parents as children of earth; we are also born of God. Our parents, the world of nature, and the presence of God provide the ambience for human unfolding. Humility helps us to see ourselves within the vast network of God and creation. Ours is a relationship of interconnectedness and mutuality with all that exists. To consider oneself superior to anything or anyone fosters mindless suffering for the earth and for other people.

Humility, however, always needs the corrective of detachment. As Teresa insists, humility and detachment go together; one cannot exist without the other. Detachment, like humility, issues from contemplative prayer, which brings our entire being and life experience into the presence of God. From the depth of prayer, we most clearly sees things in their uniqueness. Just as humility connects a person with the truth of mutual relatedness and interconnectedness, detachment ensures that persons and things retain their own unique identity as reflections of God.

Detachment and the Experience of God.

True to her style, Teresa weaves words about detachment throughout the entire text of *The Way*. Two short chapters address it specifically. Chapter 8 begins:

> Now let us talk about the detachment we ought to have, for detachment, if it is practiced with perfection, includes everything. I say it includes everything because if we embrace the Creator and care not at all for the whole of creation, His Majesty will infuse the virtues. Doing little by little what we can, we will have hardly anything else to fight against; it is the Lord who in our defense takes up the battle against the demons and against the world. (W.8.1)

This text disarms us. Detachment is not about fighting to be free, but about embracing the Creator who struggles on our behalf. The dynamic of detachment happens insofar as we let ourselves be embraced by God. To be embraced by God is a movement of love through which God becomes our ultimate good. This embrace, like a sunrise, warms and colors all that is otherwise dear to us. Enfolded in God's brilliance, we relax our hold on things, which, seen from a divine perspective, become of secondary importance. Our grasp on life loosens. Detachment necessarily includes everything because all things are in God. To cling to anything separate from God is to grasp an illusion. God alone can satisfy the heart's deepest longings. Letting go, then, is not a matter of force—"we will have hardly anything to fight against." Instead, the enemy is no more.

Teresa disclaims not the world, but the illusion that a world exists outside of God. Her appreciation of the world shows in her life story. Teresa is comfortable in her suite of rooms at the monastery of the Incarnation. Misgivings afflict her at the thought of founding a monastery in greater austerity (see L.32.12;36.7). Teresa appreciates the wonders of nature. Taken-for-granted things like water, earth, and fire offer symbolic language to speak about God and the meaning of detachment. Detachment opens the eyes of the heart to see all things as reflections of the divine creativity. When we become attached, we elevate what is finite to the level of the absolute. Created reality cannot meet such expectations.

As Teresa's love for the world becomes increasingly rooted in the love of God, she gains insight into love.

> Now it seems to me that those whom God brings to a certain clear knowledge love very differently than do those who have not reached it. This clear knowledge is about the nature of the world, that there is another world, about the difference between the one and the other, that the one is eternal and the other a dream; or about the nature of loving the Creator and loving the creature. (W.6.3)

To experience ultimate Love, the embrace of God, gives clarity of vision. When we become attached to things or entangled in situations, we distort and even destroy their uniqueness. They are no longer free to be themselves. We have invaded their space. My experience as a gardener provides a striking example.

The grounds of the Barrington Monastery include wooded areas where bittersweet and wild rose vines thrive. Flowering bushes border these wooded areas. The roots of these vines make their way underground and, with uncanny precision, grow shoots just at the base of these beautiful flowering bushes. Imperceptibly at first, the vine encircles the bush. Without constant uprooting and pruning, the vine will choke life from the bush. What then remains is an abundant entwining of bittersweet or wild rose.

Bittersweet is beautiful, especially in autumn with its colorful orange berry. The wild rose has a delicate white flower in spring. Both have their own unique beauty; so too do the flowering bushes. Separate from each other, they each have a unique life of their own with a place to be and grow. Bittersweet images attachment in that it does not seem to know its place. It takes over and controls the environment. Even large trees die because of its tenacious entwining. It needs constant pruning to remain in place and in right relationship with surrounding plant life.

The Dynamics of Detachment

Like the vine, our inner being needs the careful pruning of detachment if we are to grow and, at the same time, remain in *our place*, the embrace of God. Teresa's title, *The Way of Perfection,* suggests a dynamic of both place and journey; stability and movement. "Perfection" implies fullness of being. We humans find our fullness in God. Jesus extends the invitation: Live on in my love. Make your home in me as I make mine in you. I am the vine, you the branches (Jn 15). To be in God is to be connected with all that is. God is *the place* of infinite connectedness. At the same time, our *place* in God identifies us in our uniqueness, separate from the rest of creation.

Paradoxically, *place* in the mystical life is not a static reality. It is "the still point of the turning world."[36] To live from one's center is to be in a place both of quiet rest and responsive movement. Here the tension between distinct uniqueness and interrelatedness works itself out at the deepest level of being. Detachment insures that one's personal identity, and that of others, remains true to itself and, at the same time, that we remain free to journey together with others in compassionate mutuality. Detachment, if practiced with perfection, does indeed include everything (W.8.1). It has both a "within" and a "without" dimension. When we let external, created realities—persons, things, situations—entangle us, or when we entangle them through our attachments, we are unfaithful to

God and to our deepest inner self as centered in God. That we are in the embrace of God, and that all things—from pebble to star—also exist within the embrace of God is life's true perspective. From the heart of God mysteriously come both uniqueness and communion.

Teresa says that if we embrace the Creator, we will care not at all for the whole of creation, that is, the world as disconnected from God, and if so, His Majesty will infuse the virtues (W.8.1). This means that God will give us, moment by moment, whatever we need in order to relate—without entanglement—to people and things amidst the ups and downs of every day. Virtue comes from the Latin *virtus,* which means strength. From the divine embrace issues strength, courage, and insight either to endure or to resist what is painful. Teresa assures us: "Doing little by little what we can, we will have hardly anything else to fight against; it is the Lord who in our defense takes up the battle against the demons and against the world" (W.8.1).

The spirituality of Teresa's time followed the tradition of the Christian life as a constant warfare. Louis of Granada writes:

> Just as the defenders of a besieged city put all their strength and resistance at the weakest point, where the enemies are trying to make a breach in order to enter, so the true servant of God should understand that the Christian life is a perpetual battle and constant warfare. . . . As a soldier constantly under siege, he will protect and defend this weakest point of his passions so that he will not be overcome.[37]

Teresa's contemplative soul readily realized that the battle was beyond her. Christ would fight on her behalf. In contemplative prayer, her entire being and life experience comes into the presence of God; nothing remains hidden. Christ knows the demons in Teresa's life and willingly comes to her defense. "Doing little by little what we can, we will have hardly anything left to fight against." For Teresa this "little" means being honest with the areas of conflict in her life in order to grow in self-knowledge.[38] She prays: "Let public enemies come, for by Your favor we will be more easily freed. But these other treacheries; who will understand them, my God? . . . Instruct us, Lord, so that we may understand ourselves and be secure" (W.39.6). Life's difficulties, along with inner turmoil, occasion for Teresa an ever truer self-knowledge. From her own experience, she can point out pitfalls for her nuns. Teresa identifies attachment to relatives (W.9.1), overconcern about health (W.10.5), complaints about honor, and stirrings of privileges and rank (W.12.4) as especially harmful to contemplative living. Regard for honor was deeply embedded in the collective psyche of Teresa's Spain. This demon she regularly confronts both in herself and in others; in fact, says Teresa: "Ambition, or concern about some little point of honor . . . is the main evil in monasteries" (W.7.10).

We have our own demons. As we deal with our inner darkness, our neurotic complexes, and the split-off, unintegrated parts of the self, God fights on our behalf. Walter Wink maintains: "traditional Christian pietism has done little to help embrace these inner demons. It has either denied their reality and projected the evil out on others, whom it has then 'demonized' (communists, adulterers, homosexuals), or it has demonized the very emotions themselves, naming and 'casting out' a Spirit of Anger, a Spirit of Envy, or a Spirit of Lust."[39] Neither solution acknowledges this evil as our own. Wink does not deny the existence of something more virulently evil than the personal shadow, but he does suggest that most of what is terrible in our own souls is, in its deepest being, something helpless that wants help from us. It takes faith to trust that the massive evils of our day are twisted and contorted "goods" that want to be redeemed. "Unquestionably we experience the demonic; but if it arises from the personal unconscious it must be accepted, owned, loved and integrated. Otherwise exorcism becomes the amputation of a part of the self, not a healing. Only if the 'demon' is genuinely collective, outer, alien, should it be 'cast' out.' "[40]

The Voice of Our Attachments

What we fear as evil may be our attachments making themselves known. The disturbance they create may be their cry for freedom, redemption, and transformation. Without self-knowledge, we protect and defend what longs to be free of our grasp. Strong emotional reactions, as well as persistent distractions in prayer, might well be the voice of an inner demon pleading release. The "little" that we can do is to be honest about areas of conflict in our lives and to use available means to grow in self-knowledge and inner freedom. We do this, however, realizing that our part in the journey toward inner freedom is not the compulsion of frenzied activity but openness to the gift of surrender. It is God who frees us from activity's compulsive demands. With the gift of surrender, the heart understands that human activity, however necessary, does not have the last word. God is "our defense" (W.8.1). Christ companions our journey and works through our efforts. These may fall short, and we may fail by human standards; God does not insure success as humans see it. What God does, through detachment and humility, is to free us from our compulsions and the paralyzing fear of failure. The seeming failure of Christ in death through his resurrection holds before us the mystery of self-transcendence through suffering.[41]

A specific area for Teresa, which occasioned suffering, and which issued in self-transcendence, was her fondness for her relatives and friends. In chapters 8 and 9, Teresa stresses detachment from relatives in words that come from personal experience. At the Incarnation, the popular and charming Teresa was a frequent visitor to the parlor. Nuns depended on gifts from relatives for survival in a monastery too poor to provide adequately for such a large community as existed in Teresa's time. Benefactors were cultivated and entertained. In *The Book of Her Life,* Teresa describes the deleterious effects on her prayer of frivolous conversations with relatives, friends, and community benefactors. Having gained insight and freedom in this regard, Teresa consequently took a strong stand for detachment from relatives at her new monastery of St. Joseph's. As from a rude awakening, she writes:

> I have been much loved by my relatives—according to what they have said—and I loved them so much that I didn't let them forget me. But I know through my own experience as well as that of others that in time of trial my relatives helped me least. It was the servants of God who helped me. (W.9.3)

Teresa concludes:

> All that the saints counsel us about fleeing the world is clearly good. Well, believe me, our relatives are what clings to us most from the world, as I have said, and the most difficult to detach ourselves from. Consequently, those who flee from their own countries do well—if it helps them, I say, for I don't think it helps to flee bodily; rather what helps is that the soul embrace the good Jesus our Lord with determination, for since in Him everything is found, in Him everything is forgotten. (W.9.5)

Teresa's personality, as well as her writings, are full of seeming contradictions. Her advice to flee the country, if necessary, in order to avoid relatives, looks like self-centered indifference. And yet her letters reveal the warmth and concern, the depth and quality of her human relationships. Detachment does not mean lack of care. Teresa remains devoted to her sisters and brothers throughout her life. She asks God continually to make them holy, she assists them with their many problems, she desires their mutual support for the journey to heaven, and she receives their help in her Reform.[42]

Teresa had many close friends, including lay persons, as well as nuns and friars of the Reform. A discerning judge of character, usually her gift for friendship did not blind her to the faults of her friends. One exception was Nicholas Doria. Teresa was so taken by his competence that she failed to perceive his relentless, determined will to power. Eventually, she suffered much over his control of the reformed monasteries of both friars and nuns. A will to power and control needs the deterrent of detachment. Detachment channels such energies away from destructive patterns and reconnects them to the creative energies of God. Physicists, for example, now claim that a single energy field connects matter and consciousness. Our body, and even our consciousness, according to the neurophysiologist, Karl Pribram, is a powerful energy field that immerses us into the energy field that is the universe.[43] A developed sensitivity to the human energy field is a way of growing in self-knowledge. The interaction of energy, its loss or gain, can alert us to our attachments and to the power/control dynamic. Our need for power and control is a like a powerful, invasive energy field. Encounter with behavior that is aggressive and controlling can leave one feeling drained of energy. Such persons take over our energy space. Our loss of energy suggests that we have not remained detached, separate from them. The strength of their feelings, like the bittersweet, has entangled itself around us and choked out life, draining us of inner strength. Such situations offer a challenge to remain separate, yet in relationship. To the extent that humility has exposed our own, perhaps latent, power/control needs, will we be able to center ourselves in God during such an encounter. From this center, the strength of God's energy, which is love, will direct our energies away from defensiveness toward compassionate understanding. If we need to take a stand, we do so with respect and humility.

Here self-knowledge is key. As we become increasingly aware of our own strengths and limitations, we are able to constructively channel the energy of our feelings and emotions. These have their own energy patterns. Sadness, fear, and anxiety tend to drain us of energy, while other emotions exhilarate.[44] A sudden energy drain can alert us to our attachments. Is there something we fear to lose that we need to hold with a lighter grasp? Likewise, a sudden burst of energy can do the same. How intensely do we want the things which energize us? Would we compromise our values to obtain them? How do we respond to frustrated desire?

The Root of Attachments Are Within

Where do we find our sense of inner well-being? Is it in God? The roots of our attachments are not in other persons or in the material objects that we cling to. They are within ourselves. We reach out toward that which supports our preferred self-image. In sixteenth-century Spain, one's self-image was based on prestige, rank, wealth, and purity of blood. Teresa gives sound advice against such a false sense of self:

> Take careful note of interior stirrings, especially if they have to do with privileges of rank. God, by His passion, deliver us from dwelling on such words or thoughts as, "I have seniority," "I am older," "I have done more work," "the other is treated better than I." (W.12.4)

Such inner stirrings are gift in that they help us to identify where we find our sense of worth. At the same time, the freedom of detachment does not mean that we passively accept unjust treatment. Persons in oppressive work situations need to take a stand for justice. Teresa is not one to encourage pusillanimity and fearfulness. She does not let herself be manipulated by those who live by power and control. In 1570, she writes to her brother Lorenzo: "My experiences with these houses of God and the order have made me so good at bargains and business deals that I am well up in everything."[45] *The Book of Her Foundations* shows the courage of Teresa in the face of injustice as she successfully negotiates multiple lawsuits and all the other troubles of founding her monasteries.

At the same time, assertive as she is, Teresa has little patience with vain esteem for honor and wealth or self-pity over false or imagined injuries. In *The Way of Perfection* (12.8–9), Teresa develops in detail the temptation to self-pity with keen insight. She observes that something small happens to one of the nuns. Then the devil stirs another nun to think it is something big. This nun says things like: "How do you put up with it?"

> The devil puts such malicious talk on the other Sister's tongue
> that though you barely overcome the offense, you are still tempted
> to vainglory, when in reality you did not suffer with the perfec-
> tion with which you should have suffered. (W.12.8)

Feeling sorry for oneself is like falling into a black hole. Life looks
darker and darker. Self-pity drains energy and clouds understanding needed
for revisioning of the experience and for constructive action. In Teresa's
time, it was a point of honor to be in the right. She gives strong advice in
this regard:

> You should run a thousand miles from such expressions as "I was
> right." "They had no reason for doing this to me." "The one who
> did this to me was wrong." God deliver us from this poor way of
> reasoning. (W.13.1)

Teresa reasons from a heart held in the embrace of God. "Does it
seem to have been right that our good Jesus suffered so many insults and
was made to undergo so much injustice? I don't know why the nun who
doesn't want to carry the cross, except the one that seems to her reasonable, is in the monastery. Let her return to the world, although even there
they will not respect such reasonings" (W.13.1).

Teresa's standard for judging is Christ, her friend. Christ frees
Teresa from the temptation to self-pity and opens her to love in God,
both herself and others. Her attitude toward people is perhaps best
expressed in one of her letters to Jerónimo Gracian whom she loved
above all others: "May his Majesty give us love, and Himself too."
Teresa receives both in abundance: God and friends. "I keep on making new friends," she writes to Ambrosio Mariano in 1576.

While a pattern of making friends continues to the end of her
days, humility keeps her realistic before the shortcomings of others.
We see this in a letter to her young cousin, María Bautista, prioress of
Valladolid. María complains to Teresa that she feels neglected by their
mutual friend, the famous Dominican theologian, Domingo Báñez.

Drawing on her own experience with a man she highly reveres, Teresa writes:

> I can assure you the friend [Báñez] will continue being attentive to you till he meets someone else he likes, and then, never fear, however much you may reckon on his friendship, he will lose interest in you . . . . I know he is God's servant, and for that reason he ought to be loved, and deserves to be, like all God's servants who live on this earth. We shall be very foolish if we expect to get more from them, but that is no reason why we should be like him, though we must always be grateful to him for the kindnesses he has done us. So your Reverence must stop being so persnickety, and not give up writing to him but try gradually to gain freedom of spirit. For myself, glory be to God, I have plenty of this, though not as much as you say. Blessed be God, Who, when we seek God's friendship, is always our true Friend.[46]

Teresa does not let neglect fester into self-pity. Detachment frees her from emotional entanglement, while humility enables Teresa to be grateful for the kindness Báñez has shown her. She remains in relationship without attachment. To live in the embrace of God is to remain connected not only with those dear to us, but also with those who hurt us. It also keeps us connected with our matrix, the universe, who is both an enjoyable, life-giving friend, and at times, a stormy, destructive foe. With the balance of detachment and humility, we more easily weather the ups and downs of life. The heart's eye gains a more comprehensive perspective on life and our expectations become less self-centered. Detachment frees one from the urge toward always having more so that others, less fortunate, might at least have some. Today, seductive advertising makes it difficult for us to restrain our wants and to think of others. And yet if we do not grow in detachment and freedom of spirit, the consequences exceed what Teresa could imagine in her day.

Today's Need for Detachment

Thomas Berry in his paper, "Economics: Its Effect on the Life Systems of the World," holds this reality before us:

> The mythic drive [for more] continues to control our world even though so much is known about the earth: its limited resources, the interdependence of life systems, the delicate balance of its ecosystems, the consequences of disturbing the atmospheric conditions, of contaminating the air, the soil, the waterways and the seas, the limited quantity of fossil fuels in the earth, the inherent danger of chemicals discharged into natural surroundings.[47]

Detachment is not something we can take or leave. Unless we come to freedom of spirit in regard to our wants, the by-products of technologies that supply wants will destroy the very life system that sustains us. This is not an idle threat. The effects of pollution are all around us. Beautiful Narragansett Bay, a stone's throw from my monastery, is frequently closed to shellfishing—and at times to swimming—because of high levels of pollution.

A contemplative attitude toward life fosters detachment from excessive need for things. Integral to inner peace is freedom to love without attachment. Without this freedom, says Teresa, love is not healthy. Such a person needs a doctor (W.8.3). We obtain freedom through prayer and embracing the good Jesus with determination. "In Him everything is found, in Him everything is forgotten" (W. 9.5). Our wants and attachments no longer have the final word. Within the embrace of God, we remain in profound interconnectedness while becoming ever more uniquely ourselves as images of God. In the process, the universe achieves its own God-relatedness through the human. In us, as it were, the universe drinks of the fountain of living water. It realizes the fullness of its spiritual dimension through the holiness of our lives. As we grow in union with God, the universe advances in its own self-transcendence.

4. Love

In her reformed Carmels, Teresa creates a tapestry of life designed for unceasing prayer. Her followers live in the spirit of the early hermits on Mount Carmel. These hermits of old stayed in their hermitage meditating day and night on the law of the Lord and watching in prayer. Intimacy with God and walking in the footsteps of Jesus shaped their way of life as they witnessed to God's abiding presence.

Human and Divine Intimacy

Teresa invites others to follow in this tradition. God, the horizon of human consciousness, always present as abiding offer, companions her journey.[48] Such is the God of Teresa's experience. God is not a distant God who sustains the universe from afar. Rather, God's loving presence is the heart of her life experience; prayer is her response to God. Discourse about love in *The Way of Perfection* is about God's desire to commune with the soul in intimate friendship. For Teresa, prayer is a love affair that finds expression in intimate conversation, in ardent groanings of the heart, as well as in profound silence. Prayer unites Teresa with the divine source of all love. God's indwelling Spirit stirs Teresa to love with the compassionate self-giving of God. Christ communes with her soul in so intimate a friendship that He not only gives her back her own will but gives her His. "For in so great a friendship the Lord takes joy in putting the soul in command, as they say, and He does what it asks since it does His will" (W.32.12).

Teresa also learns, sometimes through bitter experience, the shortcomings of love that seeks a life separate from God. While God's passionate love in Teresa at times transports her into rapture and ecstasy, God also furrows the ground of displaced desire and awakens Teresa to conversion of heart. From her own experience, she understands that prayer and comfortable living are incompatible (W.4.2). The fasts and disciplines of Carmel may be difficult, but these are not her greatest challenge. Not because of self-inflicted penances are prayer and comfortable living incompatible; rather, Teresa's discomfort is over fragile love's subtle deviations. Prayer discloses her attachments even as it guides her toward humility and freedom. Humility, detachment, and love are like emanations of God's inner life in Teresa, a life intimate to her deepest self. Within God's embrace, Teresa can embrace herself as fragile, limited, and imperfect; within the chaos of her sometimes weak and divided heart does Christ lure Teresa to the complete gift of her fragile self to her Creator, and to the surrender of her will to God. Held in God's loving embrace, she learns through humility and detachment a stewardship of self-limitation that, paradoxically, quickly brings her to human fullness at the overflowing fount of living water (W.32.9). Peace "inwardly and outwardly" comes through the practice of love, detachment, and humility (W.4.4). Within the divine Trinity, "Each divine person is irresistibly drawn to the other, taking his/her existence from the other, containing the other in him/herself, while at the same time pouring self out to the other."[49] God patterns human persons in communion with one another. Humility, detachment, and love are God's enablers toward human inclusiveness, community, and freedom. These virtues not only facilitate the human community as true icon of God's relational life, but they also reflect the mystery of one communion of all persons, divine as well as human. The mystery of communion includes God and humanity as beloved partners in the dance of life.[50]

For all of us, prayer unites us with God even as it exposes deficiencies in our love. God, ourselves, and others share a mutual urge toward communion in the one Holy Spirit. Because the divine is both the necessary supporting ground of the human and because God allows us to participate with God in a single communion of life, the holy Mystery that is God refuses to allow itself to be domesticated by our attachments to created realities. The enthronement of human values by our attachment and the complete handing over of ourselves to God are incompatible. Even small attachments can keep us unattuned and insensitive to the lure of God. At the extreme is the demonic when we elevate created realities to the position of the absolute and make them the center of our loyalties. Perhaps the ultimate cause of human bondage is the inability to trust in a divine source of meaning and love. Humility makes this possible. It centers us in the truth that our worth as persons comes from God. Rooted in this reality, we can disentangle ourselves from wealth, position, success and even persons we love as the final word about who we are. These may all be important to us, but they cannot be the source of our self-definition.

As we center in God, and increasingly open ourselves to God's embrace, love for others, for creation, and for the good things it offers actually grows. Such love is not harmful when we see all things within the embrace of God and as a single flow of human/divine communion that encompasses all that is. For those who love in this way,

> There is nothing annoying that is not suffered easily. . . . A thing would have to be extremely annoying before causing any displeasure. And if this commandment were observed in the world as it should be, I think such love would be very helpful for the observance of the other commandments. (W.4.5)

Love is a way of life that brings persons and things into harmony with each other. "But, because of either excess or defect," continues Teresa, "we never reach the point of observing this commandment perfectly" (W.4.5). Much of life's disharmony and suffering comes from loving too little or too much. Excessive love first claims Teresa's attention as she begins her chapters on love. Her experience of God present in a communion of loving friendship provides a perspective for viewing love's deviations:

> It may seem that having excessive love among ourselves could not be evil, but such excess carries with it so much evil and so many imperfections that I don't think anyone will believe this save the one who has been an eyewitness. The devil lays many snares here, for this excess is hardly noticed by persons having consciences that deal only roughly with pleasing God, and the excess even seems to them virtuous; but those who are interested in per-

fection have a deep understanding of this excessive love, because little by little it takes away the strength of will to be totally occupied in loving God. (W.4.5)

The Deformation of Love

From Teresa's experience, excessive love results in failing to love all equally; feeling sorry about any affront to a friend; desiring possessions so as to give her gifts; looking for time to speak with her, and often so as to tell her that you hold her dear and other trifling things rather than about your love for God (W.4.6). Teresa's concern is "having strength of will to be totally occupied in loving God." While persons in relation are the building blocks of every society, not every configuration of persons in relation images God. Indeed, many do not. Such "trifling things" concern Teresa because they are antithetical to divine life flowing freely in her communities. Exclusive relationships are but a microcosm of polarization between rich and poor, between differing nationalities, races, and religions. In a climate where an all pervasive system of "honor" sharply divides people of "pure and impure blood," Teresa well could insist that "all must be friends, all must be loved, all must be held dear, all must be helped" (W.4.7).

Teresa recognizes that seemingly insignificant examples of excessive love are on a continuum with the violence of religious wars and the greed of New World conquest. Chapter 3 of *The Way of Perfection* is an impassioned plea that the nuns see their life of prayer in relation to church and world events. Everything in life has a broader significance than the immediate. Love in community that excludes others is a spark of the same destructive fire that on a larger scale leads to conflict, oppression, and war. Teresa would have her nuns be such that their lives and their prayer "merit from God" what was needed for the church and world. Teresa turns to Christ and to "His glorious Mother and the many saints and martyrs" who suffered and died for Him. From a profound sense of interconnectedness, and with artless spiritual insight, Teresa not only directs the gaze of God toward Christ and His redeeming love, she also dares herself to act as intermediary for the church (W.3.7–9). Christ is always her focal point. From Christ, her soul's center of gravity, she reflects on love's excesses and defects.

Her description of excessive, or what today, from a psychological perspective, we might call immature love, can be seen as analogous to the early stages of erotic love where two persons become centered on each other to the exclusion of all else. When intense erotic desire or possessive affection in friendship *dominates* a relationship, particularly over a long period of time, it drains energy needed for realizing the self in God. "Little by little it takes away the strength of will to be totally occupied in loving God. . . . When love is in the service of His Majesty, the will does not proceed with passion but proceeds by seeking help to conquer other passions" (W.4.5–6).

Warm and affectionate herself, Teresa does not intend that we be cold or indifferent toward others, but rather that our love grow in maturity, that it be less self-centered and more within the flow of God's all-embracing love. Excessive love is like an addiction—persons lack self possession and name themselves in relation to another and so look to each other for energy to sustain the "high" of being in love. Love that is not both self-possessed and other-oriented inevitably reaches the end of its energy level. As feelings of love wear thin, the once "beloved" now appears with all the irritating qualities of the human. Now is the time not to separate, but for lover and beloved to discover one another on a level deeper than feelings that come and go. This "dark night" in human relationships is toward true love with its all-inclusive mutuality. Erotic love, while particular and exclusive, opens out to a love that has universal dimensions. Teresa gives sound advice against privatizing love:

> Let us not condescend, oh daughters, to allow our will to be slaves to anyone, save to the One who bought it with his blood. Be aware that, without understanding how, you will find yourselves so attached that you will be unable to manage the attachment. (W.4.8)

Excessive love is destructive because it does just that: it privatizes love. It is self-serving rather than within the flow of Trinitarian love. Personhood requires the balance of self-love and self-gift. Within such a balance, erotic love becomes an expression of universal communion. M. Scott Peck defines love as the will to extend oneself in furthering one's own and another's spiritual growth. Gerald May enlarges this definition: "love springs from spirit and spirit springs from love so that spiritual growth is the willingness to further another's love."[51]

May names the traditional faces of love: narcissistic or self-love, erotic or romantic love, filial or compassionate love, and agape—divine, unconditional love. With narcissism, the investment of attention and concern is toward oneself. In erotic or romantic love, fusion occurs in which the external world simply "falls away." (Popular music tends to voice the longings and the disappointments of romantic love.) Filial or compassionate love, also called charity, is that firm, committed, giving of time, energy, attention, and monies to further the welfare and improve the lives of other human beings, especially within the family and among friends. It is the love of parents, brothers, and sisters, as well as the love that embraces others as neighbor and friend. Such love gives the realization that within the human community, we are all connected, one to the another. Agape is ultimate, unconditional love poured into our hearts as God's abiding presence to human life. We cannot enhance or destroy it, we can only recognize and accept it as that which alone satisfies our spiritual longing.[52]

The Inner Freedom of Spiritual Love

Love for Teresa is always toward agape: God's passionate love awaiting our response. Within the context of agape, Teresa reflects on the difference between spiritual love and love that is spiritual but mixed with sensuality and weakness. She says it is good love, for it seems to be licit, as is love for our relatives and friends (W.4.12). At the same time, Teresa knows by experience that strong emotions can blind one to truth. "Where passion is present the good order is thrown into complete disorder" (W.4.13).

Imagine yourself on a committee discussing an issue. As the discussion begins, you are open to hearing both sides. However, as someone you strongly dislike argues persuasively for a particular position, you react to the person and instinctively defend, without personal conviction, the opposing position. You may also find yourself arguing the position of a friend, even though it is not truly yours. The aversion/attraction dynamic, always present in such situations, has thrown good order into complete disorder. "And this is what wears you down: you realize you have let your affection become involved like children in their games" (W.41.1). Learning to love others with inner freedom and in truth is the life task of each of us.

In chapter 4 of *The Way of Perfection*, Teresa stresses the importance of choosing wisely our friends and especially the persons we confide in. These must share our values (W.4.16). A true friend or advisor will be both a healing and a challenging presence (W.4.16). Teresa's advice is pertinent today both in selecting a spiritual director and in choosing a psychotherapist or counselor. It is even more important in choosing a life partner in marriage.

While she questions her own understanding of the matter, Teresa continues to discuss love that is purely spiritual in chapters 6 and 7:

> Now it seems to me that those whom God brings to a certain clear knowledge love very differently than do those who have not reached it. This clear knowledge is about the nature of the world, that there is another world, about the difference between one and the other, that the one is eternal and the other a dream; or about the nature of loving the Creator and loving the creature (and this seen through experience, which is entirely different from merely thinking about it or believing it); or this knowledge comes from seeing and feeling what is gained by the one love and lost by the other, and what the Creator is and what the creature is, and from many other things that the Lord teaches to anyone who wants to be taught by Him in prayer, or whom His Majesty desires to teach. (W.6.3)

In this significant text, Teresa would have us understand that all true human loving is, in fact, a contemplative experience. A certain clear knowledge, that is, consciousness enlightened by God, gives perspective to our life. We no longer look for ultimate satisfaction where it cannot be found. The limitations of human love no longer have the same power to distress us. Such clear knowledge places us in the center of truth. Love becomes humble and compassionate as we increasingly accept the fragility of our own and others' human capacity for love.

Love Flowing from Contemplation

Prayer is the foundation for right relationships (W.4.9). When we relate to another person, we stand at the threshold of mystery: God present in the human. Each relationship potentials a fuller participation within the sphere of infinite relatedness that is God. Within such a faith vision, attachments lose hold; hurts and annoyances that might otherwise end a relationship no longer have the last word. Not without reason is Christ Crucified the symbol of true love for Teresa. Love is the living out of the Christian paschal mystery: Christ dying and rising in each of us for a fuller life in God. Teresa encourages us along this path. "Such persons," she says, "are not content with loving something as wretched as these bodies, however beautiful they may be, however attractive." She admits that she feels pleasure before someone who is beautiful and attractive— Teresa herself is a beautiful woman—but she also realizes that to stop at physical beauty is to love a shadow, something of no substance (W.6.4). She knows from experience the limitations of a love not rooted in God.

While Teresa encourages us toward the ideal of spiritual love, she realizes that we often fall short "since we are the way we are: inclined to base things and with so little love and courage that it was necessary for us to see His love and courage in order to be awakened, not just once, but every day" (W.33.2). The distortions and inadequacies of love, untrue as they are, have yet a divine spark and potential flame. God is love's seed as well as its flowering. Because of deformations in a person's life, narcissistic love may be the only love available. While primitive, it may be a person's best effort toward being a loving person. The Gospels show Jesus accepting people in their brokenness even as he calls them to a fuller life. The risk of love is worth taking. In its developmental stages, it may look inadequate, but the potential for a fuller, truer love is always present as divine invitation. As Teresa matures in love, she continues to feel pleasure at being loved, but if it is not within the context of God's love, in the end it wearies her (W.6.5). Seeing those she loves through the eyes of God frees Teresa from love's entanglements. Her words about true love are the fruit of much struggle:

> They leave it to His Majesty to repay those who love them, and they beg Him to do so. In this way they remain free, for it seems to them that repaying the love is not their business. (W.6.5)

Teresa likes to repay love. As her letters attest, she herself could be won over by a sardine.[53] For someone who ardently longs for heaven, Teresa is equally committed to loving people here on earth. She finds no contradiction in this since God's love and her own are one love. Love for others that is centered in God endures forever, so Teresa loves freely. Speaking of perfect love, she writes:

> If a person loves, there is the passion to make the other soul worthy of being loved. . . . It is a love that costs dearly. This person does everything he can for the other's benefit; he would lose a thousand lives that a little good might come to the other soul. O precious love that imitates the Commander-in-chief of love, Jesus, our Good! (W.6.9)

Here again, the detachment Teresa insists upon is not detachment from loving, however imperfectly, but rather detachment from that which blocks God's love from freely flowing through our human efforts so that love ultimately becomes one with the infinite communion of love that is God. Love from this divine source is never cold nor indifferent toward the neighbor. Instead, Teresa says:

It's strange how *impassioned* this love is, the tears it costs, the penances and prayer; what concern to ask prayers for the one loved from all who it thinks can help that person toward God; what constant desire that others recommend him to God. It is not happy unless it sees that person make progress. If, on the other hand, it sees him improving and then sees him turning back somewhat, there doesn't seem to be any pleasure for it in life. . . . It is, as I said, a love with no self-interest at all. (W.7.1, italics mine)

Spiritual love, having its source in God, "seems to be imitating that love which the good lover Jesus had for us. Hence these lovers advance so far because they embrace all trials, and the others, without trial, receive benefit from those who love" (W.7.4). To love well is to suffer much; trials are inevitable. Teresa says that such persons bear a truly heavy cross. She gives the example of Monica's care for her son Augustine. True love does not flatter or hide anything from the other. To be so loved is a precious gift. If in the beginning love is not perfect, God will gradually perfect it (W.7.4). With God as source of all love, persons become less judgmental and grow in compassion and humility. To avoid being judgmental, Teresa advises her nuns

to feel [the sufferings of others], even though these may be small. For at times it happens that some trifle will cause as much suffering to one as a great trial will to another; little things can bring much distress to persons who have sensitive natures. . . . If you are not like them, do not fail to be compassionate. And perhaps our Lord desires to exempt us from these sufferings, whereas in other matters we will suffer. And those sufferings that for us are heavy—even if in themselves they truly are—may be light for another. (W.7.5)

If we do not remember that our strength comes from God, the devil will make charity toward one's neighbor grow cold (W.7.6). With profound wisdom, Teresa rephrases for her nuns the Gospel admonition to take the beam from one's own eye before being concerned about the speck in another's eye. Says Teresa: "Strive yourself to practice with great perfection the virtue opposite the fault that appears in her" (W.7.7). Practiced with humility, this leads to great inner freedom, but not without struggle. We need always to remember that even a little love, with all its imperfection, is the stuff of complete transformation.

Imperfect Love Transformed

A powerful example of transformation, seemingly aborted, is Par Lagerkvist's prize winning novel *Barabbas*.[54] Barabbas, a thief and murderer, is set free in exchange for the death of Jesus. Jesus is crucified in his stead. Barabbas stumbles onto the scene of Jesus' crucifixion; he hears his dying words, and experiences the earth sink into darkness at his death. The novel unfolds with the memory of Jesus haunting, attracting, and repelling Barabbas. By chance, Barabbas meets Peter who speaks of his own betrayal and a promise of resurrection. Barabbas also sees the empty tomb, and he listens to the tale of a woman who claims she saw an angel with a shaft of light break its seal.

The story continues, and Barabbas hears snatches of what it means to be a Christian: words about love, about setting the world on fire, and about giving one's life for Christ. Stealthfully he enters side rooms filled with furtive Christians at prayer. The image of the crucified rabbi is always with Barabbas, even though he struggles with doubt and can never get himself to join the followers of Jesus.

Toward the end of the story, Barabbas is in Rome. Christians are being hunted down and killed under any pretext. One day Barabbas comes upon a burning house. He is fired within. This must be the moment. Christians are setting the world on fire, and Barabbas wants to be part of it. With limited understanding and misguided zeal, Barabbas, with abandon, starts throwing burning torches into buildings. Inevitably, he is caught and imprisoned. Christians everywhere are being accused of the crime, thrown into prison, then crucified. Barabbas is with them—a man who

cannot pray, who cannot believe—who can only want to believe. Crucified, with the death which he had always been so afraid of upon him, he
cries out to the darkness: "To thee I deliver up my soul." And then he
dies.

This powerful story is about that part of our soul that never quite
makes it to faith and to love. Barabbas follows his distorted, narrow vision of the crucified/risen rabbi to the limit, even though it means his own
death. He delivers up his soul to darkness, but in the darkness, one sees
the face of Christ welcoming Barabbas.

Like Barabbas, some of our best efforts to be loving are often inadequate. All of us struggle within a tension of sin and grace as we move
from total self-reference to universal communion. Love in process embraces the pain and accepts one's own and others' limited vision of God
and therefore one's own and others' limited ability to love. The good
news is that Christ's love has been poured into our hearts by the Holy
Spirit who has been given to us. In the end, it is God who loves in and
through our feeble loving. As Teresa says of Christ, "He doesn't make
any difference between Himself and us" (W.33.5). Like Barabbas, we
need only say moment by moment, in loving surrender, "To you I deliver
up my soul." As the Gospels affirm, Jesus seems to enjoy the company
of inadequate lovers. Teresa assures us that He unites the pain and suffering of our efforts to love with his own sufferings for love of us. Sparks of
love, tiny as they may be, are yet sparks of the divine flame.

Humility, detachment, and love reflect our participation in the divine
communion of love that is God. Humility illumines the truth both of human fragile finitude and of God interpenetrating our humanity in Jesus
Christ. We are all one, connected one to the other, within a single flow of
human/divine life. We exist as persons in relation called to communion.
We need one another to mirror each other's value and worth.[55] At the
same time, persons in themselves are not the absolute source of our identity. Detachment assures that we be true to our deepest self in God. As we
drink from this divine source of living water, we become fertile ground

for love to grow so that the mystery of communion that is God, and the Gospel imperative to love one another, become one mystery of human/ divine communion. As we increasingly open ourselves to love with God's own love regardless of the cost, and as the Spirit of God, the Spirit of Jesus, becomes the Spirit of the Christian Community, the mystery who is God increasingly becomes a reality in our world. Our lives and our effort to love well are that significant.

5. Friendship with Christ

In part 1, as we began our walk with Teresa along *The Way of Perfection* we glimpsed the God of Teresa who shines through her spontaneous prayers to Christ. As she grows and matures, her life story and the life of Christ in her become a single reality. She experiences both the joy and even the ecstasy of Christ's abiding presence, as well as the pain and struggle inevitable to the human condition and to her times. The remarkable giftedness of her person increases both joy and pain. As her perception of reality is increasingly God-directed, contemplative consciousness becomes a lens for viewing her life story. Her joys and suffering become interpretative qualities that make her question her basic assumptions about life and about her culture as she experiences it. Christ's intimate and also challenging presence increasingly impels her to live differently and to understand life differently.[56] Her writings are the fruit of this prayerful, reflective, and often painful process of revisioning events and circumstances of her past life in the light of an ever-deepening intimacy with Christ. Everything that happened to her now has meaning in Christ.

As a child, Teresa is venturesome and self-willed. Her trust in God leads her to muse on the "foreverness" of eternity. The words "forever, forever, forever" resonate in the soul of this precocious child. They also spark her aborted flight toward martyrdom in the land of the Moors. Everything in her story is of a piece. The mature nun of forty-seven, who with remarkable courage reforms the Carmelite Order, is on a continuum with Teresa, the determined child.

Michael Hubner, in an article entitled "Pain and Potential Space," claims that pain is ultimately the experience of being ripped away from something else, of being separated, of being alone. We are most alone when we are in the grip of pain. At the same time, pain is the common experience of the human condition. We all know pain in one form or another. It connects us with others. Within the experience of separateness, we search for connection, for something of value to link ourselves to. Ultimately, we seek to transcend our limitations of space and time. We all look for something that holds meaning from which we derive a sense of connection with God and with all that is other than ourselves.

Hubner believes that within the question of meaning arises the pain of loss and separation. The beginnings of separation, or first space between self and object (other), is what Winnicott calls potential space or that widening field that is the natural maturational process—like the space between child and parent as children reach out to the wider world and grow to be separate adult individuals. We need space, "somewhere to put what we find" of meaning, namely, one's individual and unique created response to the question of "what life is about." From this process comes an enduring sense of self that can survive the endless cycles of separation and reunion that define the human condition from cradle to grave.[57]

Teresa's Early Relationships

Teresa knew loss and separation early in life. Beside the normal process of child/parent separation, her mother died when she was in her early teens. She was close to her mother. Teresa recalls their reading novels of chivalry together, but secretly because of her father's disapproval. When her mother died, Teresa probably felt in some way responsible for her death as children tend to do. Feeling alone and in the grip of pain, Teresa began her search for meaning. Normal to her age, she reached for it in the girlhood romances, which we read about in chapter 2 of the

Life. When his oldest daughter married, Teresa's concerned father sent Teresa off at age sixteen to live in a convent school. Here the influence of a friendly nun rekindled Teresa's piety and she began an intense inner struggle with the idea of being a nun. So intense was the struggle, that it affected her health and Teresa returned to her father's house. At age twenty, against the wishes of her beloved father, she secretly entered the monastery of the Incarnation.[58] She writes in the *Life:*

> I remember, clearly and truly, that when I left my father's house I felt that separation so keenly that the feeling will not be greater, I think, when I die. For it seemed to me that every bone in my body was being sundered. (L.4.1)

Teresa, not prone to exaggeration, reveals here the depth of her suffering. She had distanced herself from her father, she carried the burden of her mother's death, and so again, she felt separated and alone. She had as yet to find a secure "holding environment," somewhere to put what she found of meaning. She had yet to find her own individual and uniquely created response to the question of "what life is about." [59] To add to her burden, Teresa lived in the monastery determined to be an obedient and perfect nun. She says in the *Life:* "I forgot to tell how in the novitiate year I suffered great uneasiness over things that in themselves were of little consequence" (L.5.1).

Through these early years, Teresa's need to please led to many compromising friendships, which resulted in continued inner conflict. Small wonder that within two years Teresa became extremely ill. At one point, she was taken for dead. Teresa slowly recovered and at age twenty-eight was able to care for her father during his last illness. He died in her arms. She writes: "When I saw him coming to the end of his life, it seemed my soul was being wrenched from me, for I loved him dearly" (L.7.14).

Fortunately for Teresa, the religious environment of her home and her experience in the convent school had already opened her to God's persistent pursuit. God had always been a part of her immediate world.

Donald Winnicott, the English pediatrician and psychoanalyst who worked extensively with children, stresses the delicate balance between the environment and the evolving self. He endows the ordinary, everyday appearance of the child's first object—the teddy bear or blanket—with rich symbolic meaning. Winnicott calls them "transitional objects," since they give a sense of connectedness to the child as it reaches out in its growth process. As maturation takes place, the teddy bear is replaced with things like the consolation of friendship, the joy of music, or the enjoyment of nature. These give a sense of stability in the midst of change. Certain transitional objects can reflect later personality disorders, like the child whose little wagon is always running out of gas.[60]

We might consider early transitional objects for Teresa to be her romantic affection for her cousins (L.2.2), the nun she befriends at the convent (L.2.10; 3.1), and then at the Incarnation admirers who visit her in the parlor. These relationships are like containers within which Teresa's affectionate soul searched for meaning but with conflicting results. She attempted both "to practice prayer and to live for my own pleasure" (L.13.6). Only with Christ's persistent pursuit (L.7–9) did she begin a committed prayer journey of friendship with Christ. Through prayer, Christ became a reference point, a safe "holding environment" where Teresa could sort out her experience. With God's grace pursuing her, she let go of attachments to sensory joys, pleasures, and pastimes. Instead, the person of Jesus and the symbol of his cross became for Teresa the "transitional objects" that gave her an enduring sense of self in the midst of the unique cycle of separation and change that ever defined her life story. After her father's death, she embraced prayer with a new earnestness. What was immediate to her lived experience was the content of her spontaneous prayers in *The Way of Perfection*. Her sufferings and trials became the stuff of her prayer by way of complaint or of surrender to the One whom she knew loved her so much. As Gross puts it:

It was prayer that brought Teresa out of the terrible decade of her twenties. Prayer was a central means whereby she overcame the paralysis of her own guilt and its accompanying compulsive perfectionism. It was prayer that was the chief means by which she learned to love her friends rather than just being in love with the feelings that accompany friendship. Prayer allowed the great trust sown in her infancy to blossom in a new way. It gave her a framework and a goal for her deep set wilfulness.[61]

Teresa and Christ

In her developing prayer relationship with Christ, Teresa found a carrier of meaning which sustained her through incredible physical and mental sufferings. Like all of us, Teresa needed something of value to hold on to.

If Teresa, along with her complaints about suffering, was able also to rejoice in it, it was because of the intimate presence of Christ, her Beloved. Within all of her relationships was the desire to imitate "that love which the good lover Jesus had for us." She loved what her Beloved loves and as He loves. Christ's love for Teresa is the model for her reflections in *The Way of Perfection* on spiritual love between friends. If she insisted on the challenge to truth and fidelity within such friendships, it was because it was rooted in Christ who was such a true friend to Teresa (W.7.4). In her combat with the devils, Christ came to her defense. Her prayer shows embarrassement that her divine friend needs to be involved in such struggles.

> What shame we Christians ought to have for making Christ wrestle arm to arm . . . with so foul a beast. It was truly necessary, Lord, that you have such strong arms. But how is it that they didn't weaken by the many torments You suffered on the cross? [Thinking of Christ's resurrection, she exclaims] Oh, how everything that is suffered with love is healed again! . . . O my God, grant that I might put medicine like this in everything that causes me pain and trial! How eagerly I would

desire these if I could be sure that I'd be healed with so sooth-
ing a balm! (W.16.7)

That suffering borne with love has healing qualities is key to understanding Teresa and her relationship to suffering. Suffering united her
with Christ Crucified, the symbol par excellence of suffering humanity. It
also united her with the power of Christ's resurrection. St. Paul assures
the Roman Christians that the same power that raised Jesus from the dead
is at work in them to raise their mortal bodies from death to life (Rom
8:11). Within human suffering is the seed of resurrection. For Teresa, this
seed flowered in contemplative awareness of Christ's abiding presence.
Like favored children,

> [Christ] would not want them [those who would be contempla-
> tive] to leave His side, nor does He leave them, for they no longer
> want to leave Him. He seats them at His table, He shares with
> them His food even to the point of taking a portion from His own
> mouth to give them. (W.16.9)

At the Vedanta Center in Cohasset, Massachusetts, the spiritual leader
takes food from her own plate and puts it on that of honored guests as a
token of esteem. Continues Teresa:

> Well why, my Sisters, shouldn't we show our love for Him as
> much as we can? . . . Oh Lord, how true that all harm comes to us
> from not keeping our eyes fixed on You; if we were to look at
> nothing else but the way [Christ], we would soon arrive. (W.16.10–11)

The Experience of Vision

Teresa's experience of Christ in contemplative prayer became a har-
monizing, even mysterious fusion of opposites. The fire of God's love
became a blaze as she drank from the fountain of living water. This living
water paradoxically allowed Teresa to communicate the fire of love to

others as Her Beloved invites all persons to drink of this living water (W.19.15). So clearly did Teresa hear the invitation that she said:

> I hold as certain that all those who do not falter on the way will drink this living water. May the Lord, because of who He is, give us the grace to seek this living water as it should be sought, for He promises it (W.19.15). . . . And if that person should do no more than take one step, the step will contain in itself so much power that he will not have to fear losing it, nor will he fail to be very well paid. (W.20.3)

Christ excludes no one. Friendship with Christ is a rewarding experience.

Teresa defended her insistence on mindfulness in mental prayer— being aware of the One with whom we speak—by an example from married life. "Oh, God help me," she said, exasperated at the arguments of those who opposed her, "here below before getting married a person will know the other party, who he is and what he possesses. . . . Here below they don't try to make those who are betrothed renounce such thoughts." "Well, my Spouse, must they in everything pay less attention to You than to men?" (W.22.7–8)

Her companion Christ is very sensitive to human weakness. God is a consoling presence:

> Let the intention be firm; God is not at all touchy; God doesn't bother about trifling things. . . . In taking account of us, God is not at all petty, but generous. However great our debt may be, God finds it easy to pardon; but when there is a question of God repaying us, God is so careful that you need have no fear. Just the raising of our eyes in remembrance of God will have its reward. (W.23.3)

Teresa reiterates:

> I have already said this and would like to say it many times, for the devil intimidates persons who don't yet fully know the goodness

> of the Lord through experience, even though they know it through
> faith. But it is a great thing to have experienced the friendship and
> favor Christ shows toward those who journey on this road and
> how He takes care of almost all the expenses. (W.23.5)

Teresa recalls her many years of suffering in not being able to quiet her mind in prayer. In the misdt of her struggle, Christ became increasingly intimate with Teresa. She offers words of encouragement: "Your spouse never takes His eyes off you. . . . In the measure you desire Him, you will find Him" (W.26.3). Teresa turned to the Scriptures to find strength in her times of sadness and suffering. Scriptural prayer gave her perspective:

> If it's true, Lord, that You want to endure everything for me, what
> is this that I suffer for you? Of what am I complaining? . . . I desire
> to suffer, Lord, all the trials that come to me and esteem them as a
> great good enabling me to imitate You in something. Let us walk
> together, Lord. Wherever You go, I will go, whatever you suffer,
> I will suffer. (W.26.6)

Suffering put Teresa in solidarity with Christ. Teresa repeatedly insists that we draw near "to this good Master with strong determination to learn what He teaches you, and His Majesty will so provide that you will turn out to be good disciples. He will not abandon you if you do not abandon Him" (W.26.10).

The Transforming Energy of Friendship with Christ

Teresa's reflection on the *Our Father* demonstrates her tenderness toward Christ. She also uses Christ's relationship with his Father to work out her own guilt feelings. Not mere pious sentiment but vision for life comes from her relationship with Christ. Contrary to the culture where people dispute over lineage, and where purity of blood, honor, and wealth determine one's place in society, Christ puts Teresa on an equal par with himself. Teresa applied this to life in her monasteries. All the nuns are to be equal regardless of their worldly rank. The only honor they are to concern themselves with is the honor of God and their Beloved Christ who invites all to intimacy (W.27.6).

Teresa insists on the nearness of Christ (W.29.4). Her words gain momentum as again and again she reiterates the reality of Christ's loving presence to all of life. Regarding prayer: "It isn't necessary to shout in order to speak to Him for His Majesty will give the experience that He is present." Such Christ awareness bears fruit in everyday life. Christ begins "to give His kingdom here below so that we may truly praise and hallow His name and strive that all persons do so" (W.31.1). "The soul enters into peace or, better, the Lord puts it at peace by His presence, . . . so that all the faculties are calmed." As the child Jesus did to the just Simeon in the Gospel, Christ gives a new understanding. While the soul fails to understand how it understands, "it sees it is in the kingdom, as least near the King who will give the kingdom to the soul" (W.31.2).

From the depth of contemplative understanding, Teresa invites both women and men to give Christ, her faithful friend, a try. Negative experiences of God, of church, of persons, or of life in general need not become what one author calls negative negativity. Teresa's way of friendship with Christ insures against this. According to this author, negative negativity germinates in the comments, interpretations, and judgments we place upon negative experiences. Then we decide that these judgments are justified in being there. Something tragic happens and we ask: "Why me? It isn't fair!" This is the beginning of negative negativity. Negative thoughts and interpretations start to germinate, and then they grow. The tragic happening becomes wildly embellished by personal negativity. Negative negativity is usually self-justifying and self-contained and allows nothing to pierce its protective shell. It is a self-righteous way of trying to pretend that things (church, religious or parish community, husband, wife, children) are what we would like them to be—an idyllic world—instead of what they are.

Teresa reminds us that pure negativity, in contrast to the negative interpretations of the mind, breeds positive energy. When clearly seen, this energy becomes true intelligence (a free space for God-Sophia-Wisdom to enlighten and enliven us) rather than speculation or concoctions of the mind. We simply name the negative experience without interpretation. When we leave the energies as they are with their natural qualities, they are living rather than conceptualized. They remain energy in the body and so can strengthen us to be constructive in our sufferings.[62]

Teresa's outpourings in prayer, her complaints to Christ about difficult situations, short-circuit negative negativity. In her prayer, she clearly names the problem, she touches the energy, but instead of reinforcing the negative, she uses the energy to do something about it. In chapter 36 of *The Way,* Teresa uses the example of the academic world with its over-concern for academic rank—one who teaches theology can not descend to teach philosophy. That would be an affront. Someone is always at hand to reinforce such negative feelings. Teresa makes sure that in her monasteries, the prioress, after leaving office, takes her place among the other sisters without distinction. Christ, her companion, model, and master, gives Teresa the courage to take a remarkable countercultural position about rank in community. Through her union with Christ, her sufferings and the wrongs she endures, instead of generating negativity, become constructive energy through the gifts of humility and forgiveness.[63] Christ does not hold Teresa's sins against her, so neither can she hold others' against them (W.36.8–12).

Teresa learns from experience that love is the measure of being able to bear a large or small cross. It enables acceptance of what can not be changed. As she says: "Strive to suffer what His Majesty desires you to suffer. For, otherwise, when you give your will, it would be like showing a jewel to another, . . . and asking that he take it; but when he extends his hand to accept it, you pull yours back and hold on tightly to the jewel" (W.32.7).

Attachments, the things we cling to, can become seedbeds of negative negativity. The comfort of nursing our hurts and indulging in self-pity is not easily relinquished. Such negative negativity drains energy necessary for constructive action. Self-pity does not easily give way to the freedom of surrender. The way of Christ is a way of surrender:

> Everything I have advised you about in this book is directed toward the complete gift of ourselves to the Creator, the surrender of our wills to God, and detachment from creatures. . . . We are preparing ourselves that we may quickly reach the end of our journey and drink the living water from the fount. (W.32.9)

Contemplation, Global Mysticism, and Transforming the Ordinary

Teresa is ever concerned to educate for contemplation. She would have us drink from God, the source of living water who loves us, and who frees us to love. Contemplation is a journey to freedom; not freedom from suffering, but freedom from the added suffering caused by our inner constraints and attachments. Only with such freedom can we find meaning in the sufferings inevitable to the complexity of a creature that is finite yet with an infinite capacity for God. To be a contemplative is to humbly accept the reality of finitude, of limits. Jung maintains that:

> This feeling for the infinite . . . can be attained only if we are bounded to the utmost. In knowing ourselves to be unique . . . that is, ultimately limited . . . we possess also the capacity for becoming conscious of the infinite. But only then![64]

Contemplation, intimacy with Christ, enables Teresa to break through personal limits as well as prevailing cultural systems. The Gospel of Jesus offers her alternatives to dominator/dominated structures and modes of relating. Jesus offers a vision of equality and freedom to both women and men. Today, the issues are the same. Their resolution is not in competition or hostility, but in a cooperative, mutual effort of women and men together toward societal transformation. As the human community is increasingly able to name dominator societies in which men must keep conquering—be it nature through mindless technology, women, or other men—will women, minorities, and the underprivileged be able to let go of their own destructive ways of compensating.

As tales of religious wars in France reach Teresa, as she hears about the plight of the native peoples of the New World and of the courage of the conquistadors, her soul expands to embrace her known world and her sufferings take on new meaning. Insignificant as she is in herself, Teresa dares to believe that united with Christ, the energies of her prayer carry the infinitude of God.

In our time, physicists like Bohr, then Bohm, building on Einstein, dare to claim that at the subquantum level, the level in which the quantum potential operates, location does not exist. All points in space become equal to all other points in space, and it is meaningless to speak of anything as being separate from anything else.[65] Thomas Berry needs to be heard again in reminder: we humans bear the universe in our being as the universe bears us in its being—the two have a total presence to each other and to that deeper mystery out of which both the universe and ourselves have emerged.[66] The earth suffers and so do we as we progressively destroy its delicate ecosystem through our attachments and greed. Smog and pollution, the effects of mindless technology, do not make for healthy living. Nature herself, although unwillingly, nails us to the cross of suffering.

Riane Eisler tells us that the symbol of the cross in prehistoric times as it appears on figurines of the goddess appears to have been her identification with the birth and growth of plant, animal, and human life. In Egyptian hieroglyphics, the cross stands for life and living, forming part of such words as health and happiness. Only later, in Assryian and Roman androcratic art, does the cross become a symbol of death as a common way of execution. With Jesus, the cross on which He was executed becomes a symbol of rebirth and of such "feminine" concepts as gentleness, compassion, and peace. She notes that during the Crusades and the Inquisition, the cross again became associated with killing and torturing. A grisly modern use of the cross as a symbol of death and oppression is its use by the Ku Klux Klan.[67]

The contemplative challenge is to find in the cross what is life-giving—its potential for transformation. External circumstances may not change, but we will be changed. Francis Gross concludes his book about Teresa with this reminder:

> Prayer doesn't get you out of the ordinary things of living. It doesn't get you out of having difficult relatives or children who are some-times horrible beasts. It doesn't mean you'll never be sick or get depressed. It certainly doesn't mean you'll be rich. Horrible to say, it doesn't guarantee a good marriage. It is, in sum, not an escape. Its meaning lies more in being willing to be nobody but yourself and being willing to face what comes to you with joy, acceptance, and love.[68]

Love's unlimited potential is hard to realize. The least of what we do or bear with love has an infinite radiation. Our lives are more important than we realize. What contemplation teaches us is precisely how significant we are, how significant is suffering borne with love for human, even global transformation. C. S. Lewis, in his short, amusing, but profoundly insightful book, *The Great Divorce,* offers a striking example on which to conclude.

The book is about the yearly bus ride of hell's inhabitants to the outskirts of heaven where they are given a second chance to let go of their attachments. At one point, the narrator is startled at the sight of a magnificent procession with flowers, lights, and singing with splendid, heavenly music. The woman whom the procession honors shines with the unbearable beauty of her face. He supposed it was the mother of God. But no, it is Sarah Smith from Golders Green—not famous on earth but now one of the great ones in heaven. The crowd of people in the procession are her children, for everyone on earth was a son or daughter to her. Every beast and bird that came near her had its place in her love. These now are present among the rejoicers as they too share in the abundance of life she has in Christ.

I looked at my teacher in amazement. "Yes," he said, "It is like when you throw a stone into a pool, and the concentric waves spread out further and further. Who knows where it will end? Redeemed humanity is still young, it has hardly come to its full strength. But already there is joy enough in the little finger of a great saint such as yonder lady to waken all the dead things of the universe into life."[69]

Says Teresa: "Don't be frightened. . . . A great treasure is gained by traveling this road; . . . The time will come when you will understand how trifling everything is next to so precious a reward" (W.21.1). In a world of suffering, what is at stake is loss of hope, loss of God as self-giving love, loss of human significance. Teresa's *Way,* which is the way of Christ, reveals God's face in the face of human suffering. Like Teresa's, our lives too provide an interpretive framework for the ongoing narrative of God's love redeeming creation through the cross and resurrection of Christ.

Notes

1. Karl Rahner, "Experience of Self and Experience of God," *Theological Investigations*, vol. 13 (New York: Crossroad, 1983), 125.

2. References to Teresa of Avila are taken from Kieran Kavanaugh,O.C.D., and Otilio Rodriguez, O.C.D., trans., *The Collected Works of St. Teresa of Avila,* 3 vols. (Washington, DC: ICS Publications, 1976–85).

3. Karl Rahner, "Following the Crucified," *Theological Investigations*, vol. 18, 166–70.

4. Michael St. Clair, *Object Relations and Self Psychology* (Belmont, CA: Brooks/Cole Publishing, 1986). This book is an overview of significant theorists in this field. D. W. Winnicott maintains that a safe "holding environment," or "good enough mothering," is integral to infant development. The mother is "good enough" when she provides an environment that holds and facilitates; that is, the environment adapts to the needs of the infant's emerging self and fosters a True rather than a False Self. Throughout life, we continue to need a container or holding environment, a safe place to work through difficult issues. See pp. 68–86. To understand the self in postmodern thought, see books such as Daniel Kolak and Raymond Martin, *Self and Identity: Contemporary Philosophical Issues* (New York: Macmillan, 1991); Walter Truett Anderson, *The Future of the Self: Inventing the Postmodern Person* (New York: Jeremy P. Tarcher/Penguin Putnam, 1997); Paul Lakeland, *Postmodernity: Christian Identity in a*

Fragmented Age (Minneapolis: Fortress Press, 1997).

5. Francisco de Osuna, *The Third Spiritual Alphabet*, trans. a Benedictine of Stanbrook (Westminster, MD: Newman Bookshop, 1948). See esp. his "Seventeenth Treatise."

6. In *The Book of Her Life* 4.7, Teresa tells of Osuna's profound influence on her prayer. She then describes how she herself prays. See *Collected Works of St. Teresa*, 1:43–4.

7. Thomas Berry, *The Dream of the Earth* (San Francisco: Sierra Club Books, 1990), 132.

8. Michael Talbot, *The Holographic Universe* (New York: Harper Perennial, 1992), 255.

9. Bede Griffiths, *Return to the Center* (Springfield, IL: Templegate, 1977), 50.

10. For an interesting theological development of the world as God's body, see Sallie McFague, *Models of God: Theology for an Ecological, Nuclear Age* (Philadelphia: Fortress Press, 1987).

11. Raymond E. Brown, *The Death of the Messiah: From Gethsemane to the Grave*, vol. 1 (New York: Doubleday, 1994). On pages 227–32, Brown's reflections on Heb 5:7–10 present the passage as plausibly reflecting an early Christian hymn. As a mosaic of psalm motifs, it identifies Jesus with the struggle of the psalmist and therefore with the human struggle.

12. Catherine Mowry LaCugna, *God For Us: The Trinity and Christian Life* (San Francisco: Harper, 1991), 397.

13. Louis of Granada, O.P., *Summa of the Christian Life*, trans. Jordan Aumann, O.P., vol. 1, (St. Louis: B. Herder Book Co., 1954), 71–8.

14. See *Life*, chap. 32, 1:213-30.

15. See Kieran Kavanaugh, O.C.D., and Otilio Rodriguez, O.C.D., trans. *The Collected Works of St. John of the Cross* (Washington, DC: ICS Publications, 1991), 515–9. At the end of st. 11, the soul desires the completion of the sketch of love which is the image of her Bridegroom. In st. 12, the soul knows that *she* is like a sketch, and she calls for the one who did this sketch to finish the painting and image.

16. Gustavo Gutiérrez, "A Theology for Historical Amnesia," in *The Praxis of Suffering*, ed. Rebecca S. Chopp (Maryknoll, NY: Orbis Books, 1986), 46–63.

17. John Navone, *A Theology of Failure* (New York: Paulist Press, 1974), 15.

18. *Collected Works of St. Teresa*, 2:23.

19. Vilma Seelaus, O.C.D., *Teresa's Way of Peacemaking in a Nuclear Age*, 4 audiocassettes (Canfield, OH: Alba House Communications TAH, 1987).

20. *Collected Works of St. Teresa*, 2:30.

21. Elizabeth A. Johnson, *She Who Is: The Mystery of God in Feminist Theological Discourse* (New York: Crossroad, 1992), 54. As Johnson points out, "speech about God in female metaphors does not mean that God has a feminine dimension, revealed by Mary . . . or a masculine dimension revealed by Jesus. . . Images and names of God do not aim to identify merely "part" of the divine mystery, were that

even possible. Rather, they intend to evoke the whole."

22. Clarissa Pinkola Estés, *Women Who Run with the Wolves: Myths and Stories of the Wild Woman Archetype* (New York: Ballantine Books, 1992), 312.

23. Alison Weber, *Teresa of Avila and the Rhetoric of Femininity* (Princeton, NJ: Princeton University Press, 1990). The author shows how Teresa embraces ironically the stereotypes of female ignorance, timidity, or physical weakness to her own advantage.

24. Rosemary Haughton, *The Passionate God* (New York: Paulist Press, 1981), 90.

25. David Bohm, *Wholeness and the Implicate Order* (London: Routledge & Kegan Paul, 1980), 205.

26. For an interesting development of the origins of human consciousness, which undergird mystical experience, see John Welch, "From Lucy to John of the Cross," in *The Land of Carmel: Essays in Honor of Joachim Smet, O.Carm.*, ed. Paul Chandler and Keith J. Egan (Rome: Institutum Carmelitanum, 1991), 347–60.

27. Bernard Lonergan, *Method in Theology* (New York: Seabury Press, 1979), 101–24.

28. For Teresa's developed understanding of humility in *The Interior Castle*, see Vilma Seelaus, "Teresa Revisions Humility: A Matter of Justice," in *The Land of Carmel*, 337–46.

29. See *The Way* 13.3; 15.2; 16.2.

30. *Collected Works of St. John.* See *The Ascent of Mt. Carmel*, bk 1, chaps 6–12, 6–12, 130–47.

31. Gerald G. May, *Will and Spirit: A Contemplative Psychology* (San Francisco: Harper and Row, 1982), 18.

32. Ibid., 18–32.

33. Barbara Walker, *The Woman's Dictionary of Symbols and Sacred Objects* (San Francisco: Harper & Row, 1988), 337.

34. J. E. Cirlot, *A Dictionary of Symbols* (New York: Philosophical Library, 1971), 181.

35. Berry, 131–2.

36. T. S. Eliot, "Burnt Norton," from *Four Quartets* (New York: Harcourt, Brace & World, 1943), 5.

37. Louis of Granada, 1:205. While Teresa begins *The Way* using strong battle imagery (see chap. 3), her intent is that her nuns "possess inwardly and outwardly the *peace* our Lord recommended so highly to us" (W.4.4). Hers is not a strident spirituality.

38. The theme of self-knowledge is present in all of Teresa's writings. We can never be without it. "However sublime the contemplation, let your prayer always begin and end with self-knowledge" (W.39.5).

39. Walter Wink, *Unmasking the Powers: The Invisible Forces That Determine Human Existence* (Philadelphia: Fortress Press, 1986). See chap. 2, "The Demons," 56.

40. Ibid., 60.

41. Navone, 15.

42. Kevin Culligan, "Teresa of Jesus: A Personality Profile," *Spiritual Life* 29 (Fall 1983): 146–54.

43. Talbot, *The Holographic Universe.* This book shows how David Bohm, one of the world's most respected physicists, and Karl Pribram, one of the architects of our modern understanding of the brain, together suggest a concept of the universe as a giant hologram containing both matter and consciousness as a single field of energy.

44. See *The Ascent of Mount Carmel*, bk. 3, chaps. 16 and following, where John treats the four emotions or passions: joy, hope, sorrow, and fear. "When these emotions go unbridled they are the source of all vices and imperfections, but when they are put in order and calmed they give rise to all the virtues" (A.3.16.5).

45. E. Allison Peers, trans. and ed., *The Letters of St. Teresa of Jesus*, 2 vols., (Westminster, MD: Newman Press, 1950), 72.

46. Ibid., 326; see also pp. 376 and 903 for Teresa's letters to Gracían and Mariano.

47. Anne Lonergan and Caroline Richards, eds., *Thomas Berry and the New Cosmology* (Mystic, CT: Twenty-Third Publications, 1987), 11.

48. Karl Rahner, *Theological Investigations*, vol. 13:124–5. Rahner has made a major contribution toward understanding the presence of God to human life.

49. LaCugna, 271.

50. Ibid., 270–8. LaCugna suggests a remarkable shift in the traditional understanding of *perichoresis* used in the eighth century by the Greek theologian John Damascene to highlight the dynamic and vital character of each divine person, as well as the coinherence and immanence of each divine person in the other two within the Trinitarian Mystery. LaCugna believes that the central claim of feminist theology—that a human community structured by relationships of equality and mutuality rather than hierarchy is a true icon of God's relational life—could be more trenchantly and more convincingly made by side stepping the methodological starting point—and ending point—of Latin theology *in divinis,* and returning to the economy of salvation and the revelation of the concrete forms of human community proclaimed by Jesus as characteristic of the reign of God. Through God's election from all eternity (Eph 1:3–14), humanity has been made a partner in the divine dance. There are not two sets of communion—one among divine persons, and the other among human persons with the latter supposed to replicate the former. The one mystery of communion includes God and humanity as beloved partners in the dance. This is what Jesus prayed for in the high-priestly prayer in John's gospel (Jn 17:20-1). LaCugna's insight stands well against Teresa's mystical experience and in particular the dynamics of her relationship with Christ particularly as found in *The Interior Castle* but also as suggested in *The Way of Perfection.*

51. May, 129.

52. Ibid.,129–41.

53. Letter to María de San José, in *Letters of St. Teresa,* 602.

54. Par Lagerkvist, *Barabbas,* trans. Alan Blair (New York: Vintage Books, 1951).

55. D. W. Winnicott, W. R. Fairbairn, Heinz Kohut, and others who have developed the Self-Object Relations Theory show the effects of parental empathetic mirroring and a facilitating environment on personal development. See Vilma Seelaus, "The Self: Mirror of God," *The Way* [England] 32 (1992): 225–36.

56. A powerful example of this is the revisioning of Teresa's obsession with honor. Her struggle to integrate the demands of her sixteenth-century honor-bound society with life in Christ is evident throughout her writings. In the end, as we find in *The Interior Castle,* "how little it [the soul] cares for its own honor" (C.7.4.6). At the same time, through the intimacy of her relationship with Christ, "the soul draws honor for His Majesty out of everything (C.6.4.16; see also C.7.3.2). Most remarkable is *Spiritual Testimonies* 31, where Christ tells her, "from now on not only will you look after My honor as being the honor of your Creator, King, and God, but you will look after it as My true bride. My honor is yours, and yours Mine" (*Collected Works of St. Teresa,* 1:336).

57. Michael K. Hubner, "Pain and Potential Space: Toward a Clinical Theory of Meaning," *Bulletin of the Menninger Clinic* 48 (1984): 443–54.

58. See the insightful book by Francis L. Gross, Jr., with Toni Perior Gross, *The Making of a Mystic: Seasons in the Life of Teresa of Avila* (Albany: State University of New York Press, 1993), 16. The authors believe that the feeling of guilt at her mother's death, coupled with her terrible sense of loss, along with identification with her mother, are keys to Teresa's revolt against her father's authority and her girlhood romances. They are key as well to her later emotional and physical troubles, first as a young boarding school student and later as a young Carmelite nun.

59. D. W. Winnicott, "The Location of Cultural Experience," *International Journal of Psychoanalysis* (1967): 370.

60. Hubner, "Pain and Potential Space," 450.

61. Gross and Perior, 26.

62. Chogyan Trungpa, "Working with Negativity," in *The Myth of Freedom and The Way of Meditation,* ed. John Bakon and Marvin Casper (Berkeley, CA: Shambhala, 1976), 73–80.

63. A sad example of inability to forgive is found in Sigred Undset's stirring novel, *Gunner's Daughter.* Gunner's daughter, Vigdis, cannot let go of the hurt and anger she feels toward the man who raped her in her youth. Negative negativity eventually kills the true and passionate love she has for him in spite of the hurt. As the story unfolds, unknown to her, and at the risk of his own life, he saves the life of her son (also his, which he does not know at the time). He returns looking for forgiveness and the hope of a life together. In the end, the fruit of unforgiveness is profound aloneness, separation, and death.

64. Bollingen Series XCV11:2, *Word and Image,* ed. Aniela Jaffé (Princeton, NJ: Princeton University Press, 1979), 214.

65. Talbot, 35.

66. Berry, 132.

67. Riane Eisler, *The Chalice and the Blade* (San Francisco: Harper, 1987), 187.

68. Gross and Perior, 210. For a delightful development of the sacredness of the ordinary, see Kathleen Norris, *The Quotidian Mysteries: Laundry, Liturgy, and "Women's Work,"* The 1998 Madeleva Lecture in Spirituality (New York: Paulist Press, 1998).

69. C. S. Lewis, *The Great Divorce* (New York: Macmillan, 1946), 108.

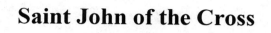

Saint John of the Cross

FROM IMPRISONMENT TO TRANSFORNMATION: JOHN OF THE CROSS IN TOLEDO

Kevin Culligan, O.C.D.
Edith Stein House of Studies
Chicago, Illinois

By his own account, John of the Cross was transformed in God through love, not in a peaceful hermitage in the spacious Segura mountains of Andalusia, but in a dark monastic prison cell in the Spanish imperial city of Toledo. Charged with disobedience by his Carmelite superiors for his involvement in Teresa of Avila's reform of the Order, John was sentenced to confinement in the monastery at Toledo from early December, 1577, until mid-August, 1578. These eight-and-a-half months, though filled with excruciating suffering, were the most decisive of John's life. For the Toledo imprisonment was, as John later expressed in poetry, the "dark night" that "united the Lover with his beloved, / transforming the beloved in her Lover" (N. poem. st. 5).[1]

The Toledo Imprisonment

The externals of John imprisonment in Toledo are well documented.[2] He was brought to Toledo from Avila where for the previous five years he had been confessor to the Carmelite nuns at the monastery of the Incarnation. Shortly after John's arrival in Toledo, the superiors formally read to him the decrees of the recent Carmelite General Chapter of Piacenza forbidding the expansion of the Teresian reform and asked him to renounce the reform. He refused on the grounds that the reform was approved by the Holy See and had the support of the King. He was then offered a position of leadership in the order if he would abandon the reform. When he refused again, he was sent to the monastery prison as a disobedient religious and placed under the watch of one of the other friars in the monastery.

John had been in the monastery prison less than two months when word arrived that another friar of the reform held prisoner in a different monastery had escaped. Fearing that John might also try to escape, the superiors removed him from the official monastery prison cell and placed him in what amounted to solitary confinement. He was sent to a small room on the top floor of monastery. The new cell was little more than a closet, about nine feet long and five feet wide. It was dark, without windows. The only light and air came through a small hole high on the wall. The only furnishings were a small bench to sit on and a board on the floor that served as his bed. He was allowed only two blankets to provide comfort and to protect against Toledo's cold winter nights. He was permitted no change of clothing. He was not allowed to say Mass. His only reading material was his breviary, which he read standing on the bench in his cell, holding the book up to the little light that came into the room during daytime.

John's food was mainly bread, water, and a few sardines brought to his cell twice a day. Regularly he was led to the monastery refectory to take his food on his knees in the midst of the community of some eighty friars as they ate at table. Following the meal, each of the friars disciplined John by striking his bared back and shoulders with a whip made of twigs. He was then returned to his cell to consider his disobedience before God and his own conscience. Every protection against escape was in place. The prisoner would know from the times he was permitted out of his cell that he was located so high above the ground and the river Tajo below that any attempt would be perilous; and with each day he was growing too weak even to attempt such a hazardous escape.

Around the first of May, John's situation improved somewhat when a new guard was assigned to watch him. The friar, Juan de Santa María, twenty-seven years old and eight years younger than John, was more sympathetic to his prisoner than the former jailer who seemed intent on enforcing strictly the punishments for recalcitrant friars. The young jailer arranged for fewer humiliating trips to the refectory. He provided his prisoner with a fresh change of undergarments, allowed him more exercise and greater freedom outside the cell, and gave him pen and ink for writing down his thoughts. Yet, despite these improvements, John was still in the same small cell that now became like an oven as the heat of summer intensified.

By August, John had decided his only hope for survival was to try to escape on his own. In the week following the feast of the Assumption, in the early hours of the morning, John climbed out of the window and let himself down to freedom by a rope he had made from his blankets. He found his way to the monastery of Teresa's daughters in Toledo who protected him and arranged for his convalescence in secrecy. Several days before his escape, John gave the crucifix he wore on his own tunic to Juan as a sign of gratitude for his kindness. For his negligence in allowing the prisoner's escape, Juan was deprived of his place in community and voice in chapter for a short period of time. Juan later testified that he was happy that John had escaped and that his sufferings were over. Apparently, if Juan had suspected that his prisoner was planning an escape, he made no effort to stop him.

John's interior life during his imprisonment is more difficult to ascertain. He kept no journal in Toledo, although he did compose poems there and shortly after his escape that enable us to imagine what was in his mind and heart during those long, lonely hours in a cramped cell. The prison imagery of his later writings also hints at the state of John's soul during these months. The rest—the thoughts, the feelings, the memories, the temptations, the inner conflicts, the agonies, and the ecstasies—we have to imagine for ourselves if we are to get some idea of the John's inner experience at Toledo and the decisive impact these months had upon him.

John obviously would never have chosen the external and internal deprivations of Toledo; yet, he eventually came to regard these painful diminishments, unwanted but accepted, as graces. Through them God taught him spiritual lessons he could learn nowhere else and prepared him for an experience of contemplation that transformed the rest of his life. In itself, prison does not foster the contemplative life, nor is it geared to disposing persons for transformation in God through love. Prison brings some persons to further crime, some to despair, others to suicide. Why was it different for John? Why were his eight-and-a-half months in Toledo a period of transformation? Imagining how John used his time in Toledo and his interior attitudes and dispositions there helps us see how an otherwise destructive experience became for him a graced moment.

Composing Poetry

To occupy his mind during the endless hours of inactivity in a dark cell, John composed verses inspired by biblical passages that he likely knew by heart. Reflecting over and over on the prologue of John's Gospel, he composed "Romances on the Gospel text "In principio erat Verbum'," over three hundred rhyming lines on the Trinity, Creation, the Incarnation, and the birth of the Word, "whom the gracious Mother / laid in a manger / among some animals / that were there at that time" [al cual la graciosa Madre / en un pesebre ponía, / entre unos animales / que a la sazón allí había]. (Romance on the Gospel, 9).

Inspired by the Old Testament Psalm 137, "By the waters of Babylon," John composed other verses that helped him cope with an intolerable situation. Also called a "Romance," these 62 rhymed lines are a meditation on a song from Israel's exile in Babylon. This biblical event inspired John to put into verse his own anguish of soul at being held captive, separated from Madre Teresa and his brothers and sisters in her reform, and being coerced to renounce a way of life he had come to hold dear. "I said: How can I sing, / in a strange land where I weep / for Zion, sing of the happiness / that I had there? / I would be forgetting her / if I rejoiced in a strange land" [Decid, como en tierra ajena, / donde por Sión lloraba, / cantaré yo la alegría / que en Sión se me quedaba? / Echaríala en olvido / si en la ajena me gozaba]. This divinely inspired psalm gave words to John's own resentment at those of his Carmelite brothers who were holding him captive and attempting to suppress the reform. The poem allowed him to sublimate his wrath into something approaching sacred song. "O Daughter of Babylon, / miserable and wretched! / Blessed is he / in whom I have trusted, / for he will punish you / as you have me; / and he will gather his little ones / and me, who wept because of you, / at the rock who is Christ / for whom I abandoned you" (Romance on Psalm 137).

A third poem, "Song of the soul that rejoices in knowing God through faith," expresses John's struggle to cope with the constant darkness of his cell and his continual physical thirst which grew worse in Toledo's oppressive summer heat. He rejoices in God as the inexhaustible source living waters, "*although it is night— aunque es de noche.*" Suffering from his meager diet, deprived of the Eucharist, and not permitted to offer mass, John hungers for union with the Source of eternal life. "This living spring that I long for, / I see in this bread of life, / *although it is night*" [Aquesta viva fuente que deseo, / en este pan de vida yo la veo, / *aunque es de noche*] (Song of the soul that rejoices st. 11).

The poem that most reveals John's interior life in Toledo is "The Spiritual Canticle." Inspired by the Song of Songs in the Old Testament, the "Canticle" eventually became one of John's major poems. He continued working on it for eight years after he left Toledo, adding nine new stanzas before its completion in 1586. But the first thirty-one stanzas, which John composed in his cell at Toledo, provide an open window into his soul during his long months of captivity.

John begins with an anguished cry of longing for Christ: "Where have you hidden, / Beloved, and left me moaning? / You fled like the stag / after wounding me; / I went out calling you, but you were gone" (st.1). John was thirty-five years old when he was brought to Toledo. To this point in his life, his continual search for God had led him from his pious youth into the Carmelite monastery in his hometown of Medina del Campo in 1563 when he was twenty-one. Four years later, his desire for God brought him to the verge of leaving the Carmelites for the Carthusians. Then Teresa of Avila pointed out to him "the great good that would be accomplished if in his desire to improve he were to remain in his own order and that much greater service would be rendered to the Lord."[3] Now, nine years after embracing Teresa's reform, he was in prison charged with disobedience to his religious superiors. God had surely wounded John's heart, for he longed for nothing but God; however, he now felt that God had abandoned him and left him alone in the dark. He begs "shepherds" to remind God: "I am sick, I suffer, and I die" (st. 2). Jesus alone can heal him and so he calls out to the "bridegroom" of his soul: "Now wholly surrender yourself! " (st. 6). And he prays further: "Why, since you wounded / this heart, don't you heal it? . . . Extinguish these miseries, / since no one else can stamp them out" (st. 9 & 10).

Though feeling abandoned by Jesus, John continues to long for union with him: "may my eyes behold you, / because you are their light, / and I would open them to you alone" (st.10). Confined to a dark room most of the day, he recalls stirring scenes from nature through which Jesus revealed himself to John in earlier times. Now he identifies his beloved Jesus with these beauties of nature, exclaiming: " My Beloved, the mountains, / and lonely wooded valleys, / strange islands, / and resounding rivers, / the whistling of love-stirring breezes, / the tranquil night / at the time of the rising dawn, / silent music, / sounding solitude, / the supper that refreshes and deepens love" (CA. st. 13/14; CB. st. 14/15).

Utterly abandoned, dying by inches, and longing for release from prison, John's love for Jesus was growing and his desire for union with

God was deepening. Now he realizes, however, that his cramped cell is to be the bridal suite and the board on the floor his marriage bed: "The bride has entered / the sweet garden of her desire, / and she rests in delight, / laying her neck / on the gentle arms of her Beloved" (CA. st.27; CB. St. 22). Toledo, despite all its hardships, has become the unlikely place of his loving encounter and transforming union with the Beloved he has sought all his life.

John celebrates this union in deeply moving erotic images: "Our bed is in flower . . ." (CA. st. 15; C. st. 24). "In the inner wine cellar / I drank of my beloved. . . . / There he gave me his breast; . . . and I gave myself to him, / keeping nothing back" (CA. st. 17 & 18; CB. st. 26 & 27). And John now realizes that this union with God alone is perhaps the entire purpose of his existence; to be lost in God is his greatest service to the church. "Now I occupy my soul / and all my energy in his service; / I no longer tend the herd, / nor have I any other work / now that my every act is love. If, then, I am no longer / seen or found on the common, you will say that I am lost; / that, stricken by love, / I lost myself, and was found" (CA. st.19 & 20; CB. st. 28 & 29).

Though John kept no prison journal, his "Spiritual Canticle" vividly tells the story of his soul during his confinement. His hours were spent longing for God, even though he keenly felt God had abandoned him. He nourished that longing by pouring out to God all his suffering, by recalling scenes from nature that reminded him of God's beauty, by imagining the intimacies of human love to enkindle his own desire for his Beloved, by accepting that the ideal place for the mutual surrender of himself and Christ was in the very place of his confinement. Though he longed for his freedom, John came to accept that if a prison cell is where his life were to end, then in his union with his beloved he had achieved the end for which he was created and that alone benefited the church.

One of John's most important discoveries in Toledo was that "the soul lives where she loves more than in the body she animates" (C.8.3; also, C.11.10). Day after day, his body suffered through the bitter cold of the Toledo winter and later the stifling heat of its summer, yet his soul was someplace else. John did not deny his suffering; but he did not center his attention on his pain, nor condemn the people and circumstances that caused it. Rather than replaying how badly he had been treated and rehearsing how he would get his revenge, thereby reinforcing negative emotions with equally negative thoughts, he spent his time filling his mind with the Word of God and his heart with desire for the God he felt had abandoned him. Interiorly, he lived where he loved, in God. There he not only found strength to survive, but also transformation of his life in God. And by spending his long monotonous hours in prison composing, memorizing, and finally writing these experiences down on paper, he both creatively dealt with an inhuman situation and left us a record of what persons can endure when they strive continually to live in God, whatever their circumstances.

Identification with the Suffering Christ

The poetry that emerged from John's cell did not, however, make his imprisonment a time of esthetic ecstasy. Undoubtedly there were moments of intense love which he expressed in "The Spiritual Canticle"; but there was also the agony of his physical pain and suffering. Begging creatures to tell the Beloved "I am sick, I suffer, and I die" may be elevated mystical language, but these words also accurately describe John's deteriorating physical condition as the months of his captivity dragged on. His meager diet led to loss of weight; the lack of daily exercise enervated his musculature, leaving him increasingly weak. Without regular bathing and change of clothing, vermin began infesting his body. His weakened physical condition made his doubts, temptations, and uncertainties more difficult to resist. He was wasting away to nothing. To cope, he turned his thoughts frequently to Jesus Crucified.

From what John later wrote in book 2, chapter 7, of *The Ascent of Mount Carmel*, we can easily imagine how he identified his own sufferings with Christ's. If John felt the sting of the whiplashes on his back in the Carmelite refectory, so too Jesus endured more painful scourging from the Roman soldiers at the pillar. If his fellow friars insulted John, so too did the religious leaders mock Jesus. If John felt abandoned by God, so too did Jesus. And if John should die in prison, as he feared he might, he would die knowing that his suffering and death would not be wasted, because he had united them with Jesus' life-giving death.

John understood that in his death Jesus "accomplished the most marvelous work of his whole life, surpassing all the works and deeds and miracles that he had ever performed on earth or in heaven," for it was at that moment that he reconciled and united "the human race with God through grace." John wrote later: "The Lord achieved this, as I say, at the moment in which he was most annihilated in all things: in his reputation before people, since in watching him die they mocked him instead of esteeming him; in his human nature, by dying; and in spiritual help and consolation from his Father, for he was forsaken by his Father at that time, annihilated and reduced to nothing, so as to pay the debt fully and bring people to union with God" (A.2.7.11).

Against the mystery of Jesus' sufferings and death, John now realized that the "great works" people do are "measured by the annihilation of themselves for God in the sensory and spiritual parts of their souls." He would later state: "When [spiritual persons] are reduced to nothing, the highest degree of humility, the spiritual union between their souls and God will be an accomplished fact. This union is the most noble and sublime state attainable in this life. The journey, then, does not consist in consolations, delights, and spiritual feelings, but in the living death of the cross, sensory and spiritual, exterior and interior" (A.2.7.11).

Before Toledo, John knew Jesus' words, "How narrow is the gate and how constricting is the way that leads to life, and few there are who find it" [Mt. 7:14]. He understood them as a call to detachment from any object that would deter him from traveling the road leading directly to union with God. But now in Toledo, he saw how all inclusive this detachment must be. It extends far beyond objects pleasing to the senses; it also includes spiritual objects such as one's own reputation, or understanding of God, or plans for serving God. John later called this total detachment "a supreme nakedness and emptiness of spirit." He believed it was necessary for spiritual persons because they are on a "venture in which God alone [sólo Dios] is sought and gained; thus only God ['sólo Dios'] ought to be sought and gained" (A.2.7.3).

Long before Toledo, John had also begun fashioning his own life as a response to Jesus' invitation, "If anyone wishes to follow my way, let him deny himself, take up his cross and follow me. For whoever would save his soul will lose it, but whoever loses it for me will gain it" [Mk. 8:34-35]. He knew for himself and taught others that following Christ and carrying the cross is the way to union with God. Now in the months of prison in Toledo, as he was dying by inches and struggling to identify his condition with the suffering and death of Jesus, he saw clearly, probably for the first time in his life, the full extent of the self-denial required to follow Jesus and gain one's soul. He came to see that more is required than simply being "content with a certain degree of virtue, perseverance in prayer, and mortification"; rather, following Christ and denying self means seeking "the distasteful in God rather than the delectable, leaning more toward suffering than toward consolation, more toward going without everything for God rather than toward possession, and toward dryness and affliction rather than toward sweet consolation." He now saw clearly the difference between seeking God in oneself and "seeking of self in God—something entirely contrary to love. Seeking oneself in God is the same as looking for the caresses and consolations of God. Seeking God in oneself entails not only the desire to do without these consolations for God's sake, but also the inclination to choose for love of Christ all that is most distasteful whether in God or in the world; and this is what loving God means" (A.2.7.5).

All his life, John had followed Jesus Christ as the "way" to union with God. Now he discovered that this "way" is "a death to our natural selves in the sensory and spiritual parts of the soul" (A.2.7.9). It demands total self-emptying of sense and spirit, just as Jesus emptied himself completely on Calvary. This was a lesson only Toledo could teach him. On his own, John could not possibly have devised a program of self-denial as effective as the one God prepared for him in Toledo. Without the prison experience John would never have understood the depth of self-emptying that following Christ demands. He would never have learned that self-emptying in sense and spirit in imitation of Jesus Crucified is the royal road for contemplatives who desire union with God through love and the transformation of their lives in Christ. For John, this was the grace of Toledo. It was a lesson he would never forget.

Lifting First Movements to God

Another means John undoubtedly used to cope interiorly with Toledo's deprivations was to lift his "first movements" to God. For John, first movements [*primeros movimientos*] were thoughts, desires, memories, sensations, temptations, "diabolical communications"— any mental experience which comes into consciousness and is present there before we decide how to respond to this experience. On a hot day, for instance, we are first moved by the desire for a refreshing glass of water long before we decide to pour ourselves a drink. Or when we are hurt by a cynical remark, we are first moved to retaliate long before we decide whether to answer back. First movements are morally indifferent until we decide how we are going to act upon them. If we decide not to act on them, they ordinarily pass out of consciousness, at least for the time being. As John would later note in *The Ascent of Mount Carmel,* even "diabolical communications," though disturbing, "can only arouse the first movements without being able to move the will any further if it is unwilling to be moved. The unrest caused by them will not last long, unless the individual's lack of courage and caution becomes the occasion for the unrest to continue" (A.2.11.6). In this vein, John years later counseled a scrupulous nun about her first movements: "In regard to thoughts and imaginings (whether they concern judgments, or other inordinate objects or representations, or any other motions *[movimientos])* that occur without being desired or accepted or deliberately adverted to: Do not confess them or pay attention to them or worry about them. It is better to forget them no matter how much they afflict the soul" (L.20).

Attending to first movements and deciding whether to act on them or to let go of them was, for John, an essential spiritual practice in disposing oneself for contemplation. For example, he offers this advice on handling the first movements of joy so that this emotion does not become an impediment to God's transformation of the person. "At the first movement of joy toward things, the spiritual person ought to curb it, remembering the principle we are here following: There is nothing worthy of a person's joy save the service of God and the procurement of his honor and glory in all things. One should seek this alone in the use of things, turning away from vanity and concern for one's own delight and consolation" (A.3.20.3). Following this general principal, John gives specific instructions for handling first movements of joy in one's own natural gifts of body and mind such as "beauty, grace, elegance, bodily constitution, . . . good intelligence, discretion and other talents" (A.3.21.1): "As soon as the heart feels drawn by vain joy in natural goods, it should recall how dangerous and pernicious it is to rejoice in anything other than the service of God." Invoking the Latin poet Ovid for reinforcement, he continues: "Take courage and use in time the remedy suggested by the poet for those beginning to grow attached to this joy: 'Hurry now in the beginning to apply the remedy, for when evils have had time to increase in the heart, medicine and remedies arrive to late'" (A.3.22.6).

The mental discipline of attending to first movements thus requires (1) awareness that these movements are occurring, (2) peaceful acknowledgment of these movements as present in our consciousness, no matter how disturbing they may be, and (3) deciding whether to act on these movements or to let them pass out of consciousness. As we develop the habit of acting only on those movements which procure the "honor and glory" of God (A.3.20.3) and letting go of those which do not, we gradually create the interior emptiness that best disposes us to receive the inflow of God's loving knowledge in contemplation that increasingly fills our consciousness and directs our lives. This gift of contemplation even transforms our first movements so that one in the state of divine union is, like the virgin Mary, "always moved by the Holy Spirit" (A.3. 2.10) and "does not even suffer the first movements contrary to God's will" (C.27.7).[4]

John undoubtedly had endless opportunities in Toledo to practice this essential mental discipline himself. We can imagine the questions, thoughts, memories, emotions, doubts, and temptations that came into his consciousness. "How is it possible that the God I have loved and served so faithfully all my life could abandon me? . . . Oh, to be in Castile again among the warmth of family and friends! . . . Where are Teresa and the other discalced friars? After all I've done for them, they leave me here to rot! . . . Oh, what I wouldn't give for the comfort of a loving woman . . . . If only I could have just one good meal . . . . Oh, to have some clean, warm clothing . . . . If ever I get out of here, I'll make these friars pay for the way they are treating me. Yet, what if they're right? This reform thing may really be just an illusion. Possibly it's even the work of the devil." These or similar movements must have arisen in his mind hour after hour, day after day during his long imprisonment. Recognizing them all as involuntary first movements and not rational choices, he struggled not to let his mind indulge them, thus preventing them from hardening into resentment, self-pity, guilt, cynicism, and revenge. He courageously let them pass through his consciousness unattended, lifting his mind instead to God in prayer, "lead me not into temptation, . . . deliver me from evil" (A.3 .44.4).

As John chose not to entertain this continuous flow of feelings, memories, thoughts, and emotions, he recognized that he was depriving himself of every natural satisfaction his mind could provide him. Yet he also believed this deliberate self-emptying was the only way the "living image of Christ crucified" (A.3.35.5) would grow in him and sustain him in his suffering. This experience undoubtedly led him to advise others about the value of "darkening the memory in regard to knowledge and discursive reflection" (A.3.3. chap.title). "The soul," he later wrote in *The Ascent of Mount Carmel,* "should remain closed . . . without cares or afflictions, for he who entered the room of his disciples bodily while the doors were closed and gave them peace, without their knowing how this was possible [Jn. 20:19-20], will enter the soul spiritually without its knowing how or using any effort of its own, once it has closed the doors of its intellect, memory, and will to all apprehensions. And he will fill them with peace, *descending on them,* as the prophet says, *like a river of peace [Is. 66:12].* In this peace he will remove all the misgivings, suspicions, disturbances, and darknesses that made the soul fear it had gone astray. The soul should persevere in prayer and should hope in the midst of nakedness and emptiness, for its blessings will not be long in corning" (A.3.3.6).

This self-emptying apparently did not negate John's logical thinking and practical judgement. At some point during his incarceration he realized that he was dying and that there was no hope of release. He had to decide either to allow himself to die or to attempt an escape. He must also have reasoned that to accept death passively was not God's will for him. His death would neither glorify God nor serve Teresa's reform. He chose to escape. And once he decided to escape, he had to figure out how. Escape required detailed planning. When should he try? How would he free himself from his cell? How would he get to the ground from the top floor of the monastery? Where would he go once he made it to the outside?

His careful planning paid off One night during the middle of August, while his guard was asleep, John pushed open the door of his cell that he had quietly loosened from its hinges. Taking only his poems, he went to the edge of the monastery roof and let himself down the side of the wall on a rope he had made from strands of his blankets. Once below, he unexpectedly found himself trapped within the garden of the

Conceptionist nuns whose convent walls adjoined the Carmelite monastery. He patiently searched for a way out of this enclosure until he found access to the street. Then he made his way through the dark Toledo streets to the reform convent of Carmelite nuns, who hid and protected him from the friars once they discovered their prisoner had disappeared.

John's escape suggests that the practice of elevating first movements of emotions, thoughts, feelings, and memories to God, rather than negating practical judgement, seems to enhance it. By not allowing himself to indulge the first movements of self-pity, resentment, and guilt, John freed his practical judgement to function more clearly and effectively. Furthermore, as John later taught, emptying consciousness of negative thoughts, distorted memories, and exaggerated emotions clears the way for the Holy Spirit to guide our practical judgement. John explained this when he described the mental operations of a person in the transformed state of divine union: "These souls . . . perform only fitting and reasonable works, and none that are not so. For God's spirit makes them know what must be known and ignore what must be ignored, remember what ought to be remembered—with or without forms—and forget what ought to be forgotten, and makes them love what they ought to love, and keeps them from loving what is not in God. Accordingly, all the first movements and operations of these faculties are divine. There is no reason to wonder about these movements and operations being divine, since they are transformed into divine being" (A.3.2.9).

Life after Toledo

The Carmelite nuns arranged for John's convalescence in Santa Cruz hospital under the protective care of their friend, Don Pedro Gonzales de Mendoza, the hospital administrator. After six weeks in Santa Cruz, which interestingly was located very near the monastery where he had been a prisoner for nearly nine months, John left Toledo and traveled south through LaMancha to Almodóvar del Campo where he rejoined his discalced brethren who were gathered in chapter. Assuming it would be dangerous for John to return to Castile, the chapter appointed him superior of El Calvario, a small community of friars near Beas de Segura in Andalusia, in the south of Spain. John took up his new office in November, 1578, nearly one year after he had been taken prisoner at the Incarnation in Avila. John would remain in Andalusia for the next ten years, and would return there to die in 1591 after three years in Segovia in Castile.

John's last thirteen years were intensely pastoral and creative. After El Calvario, he lived for varying periods of time in Baeza, Granada, Segovia, La Peñuela, and Ubeda. He held at various times the offices of local superior, seminary rector, vicar-provincial, and provincial councillor. As a religious superior, he was spiritual father to the growing number of discalced friars and nuns, as well as a spiritual guide for many clergy and laity outside the order. From this ministry arose his major spiritual writings, his prose commentaries on the poems "The Dark Night," "The Spiritual Canticle," and "The Living Flame of Love."

In 1588, John left Andalusia for Castile when he was elected to the general consulta of the newly formed province of Discalced Carmelites and made local superior of the monastery in Segovia. Following his three year term in Segovia, he returned again to Andalusia apparently to prepare for the missions in Mexico for which he had volunteered at the chapter held in Madrid in June, 1591. The several months following his return to Andalusia, however, suddenly and unexpectedly became a time of preparing to meet Jesus, the bridegroom of his soul, in death.

In the autumn of 1591, as he prepared to depart for Mexico in the desert monastery of La Peñuela, John contracted a leg inflection, which spread quickly throughout his entire body, leading to an unexpected and untimely death on December 14, 1591, in the monastery of Ubeda. Strangely, his deteriorating physical condition during the last months of his life was exacerbated by personal suffering not unlike that he had endured in Toledo thirteen years earlier. A fellow friar, Diego Evangelista, this time one of his own discalced brothers, had falsely accused John of improprieties in his ministry to the Carmelite nuns. Diego was determined, not to imprison John, but to drive him out of the order. John's response to this threat reveals that his transformation in Toledo thirteen years earlier still endured in his mind and heart. A letter he wrote at this time to one of his Carmelite sisters reflects his attitude: ". . . Do not let what is happening to me, daughter, cause you any grief, for it does not cause me any. . . . Men do not do these things, but God, who knows what is suitable for us and arranges things for our our good. Think nothing else but that God ordains all, and where there is no love, put love, and you will draw out love" (L.26).

Writings after Toledo

Once settled in Andalusia and encouraged by the positive response of those who listened to his prison poetry, John resumed work on the "Spiritual Canticle," the poem he began in the darkness of Toledo. A Carmelite nun's comments on her delight in God's beauty inspired him to add more stanzas. He then made a second redaction adding a new stanza and rearranging others. He also wrote a prose commentary to explain the mystical meaning of the poem's symbols and images. Thus, what began in Toledo as an anguished cry for the God he felt had abandoned him eventually became by the time of its completion in 1586 a love story between the soul and the Bridegroom—John and Christ—as well as a classic description of the entire spiritual journey to union with God through love.

A more concentrated poetic expression of John's transformation in Toledo is his "En Una Noche Oscura" [One Dark Night] which he wrote during his first year in Andalusia. It was eventually to become his best known poem and a classic of Spanish lyric poetry.[5] Unmistakably autobiographical, the opening stanzas detail almost literally John's escape from prison.

1. One dark night,
fired with love's urgent longings
—ah, the sheer grace!—
I went out unseen,
my house being now all stilled.

2. In darkness, and secure,
by the secret ladder, disguised,
—ah, the sheer grace!—
in darkness and concealment,
my house being now all stilled.

3. On that glad night
in secret, for no one saw me,
nor did I look at anything
with no other light or guide
than the one that burned in my heart.

More than a mere recounting of his escape, John's images of departure in darkness express the detachment in senses and spirit he arrived at in the prison that disposed him for transformation:

5. Oh guiding night!
O night more lovely than the dawn!
O night that has united
the Lover with his beloved,
transforming the beloved in her Lover.

The concluding stanzas of the poem reveal that John's transformation in Toledo was primarily an experience of self-transcendence, a total letting go of self in order to be filled with God.

8. I abandoned and forgot myself,
laying my face on my Beloved;
all things ceased; I went out from myself,
leaving my cares
forgotten among the lilies.

John used these poems and others he would write in Andalusia, including "The Living Flame of Love," in his ministry of spiritual guidance. He shared the poems with those he guided to stimulate dialog about their experience of God and their spiritual journey. Eventually they asked him to explain more in detail the poetic symbols and their applications to the spiritual life.

Responding to these requests, he wrote first *The Ascent of Mount Carmel* and *The Dark Night,* a commentary on the poem "One Dark Night" that explains his teaching on the "nakedness of spirit" required for union with God for "some of the persons of our holy order of the primitive observance of Mount Carmel, both friars and nuns. . . since they are the ones who asked me to write this work" (A.prol. 9). Later, in 1584, he composed for his close friend and colleague in the Teresian reform, Madre Ana de Jesús, the prioress of the Carmel in Granada, his commentary on the "The Spiritual Canticle" that "explains certain matters about prayer and its effects" (C. title). Finally he wrote the commentary on his poem, "The Living Flame of Love," for his spiritual daughter, the lay woman Doña Ana de Peñalosa, to explain the "very intimate and elevated union and transformation of the soul in God" (F. title). These poems and commentaries, containing the substance of John's spiritual doctrine as we know it today, detail the entire spiritual journey from its first stages to transformation in God.

These writings, the fruit of thirteen intense years in the ministry of spiritual guidance, bear the unmistakable imprint of Toledo upon John's creative imagination. "The soul," writes John, "through original sin is a captive in the mortal body, subject to passions and natural appetites; when liberated from this bondage and submission, it considers its escape, in which it is unnoticed, unimpeded, and unapprehended by its passions and appetites, a sheer grace" (A.1.15.1). An unmortified life, where one lives subject to one's natural appetites and passions, is a "wretched state of captivity" (A.1.15.1; A.3.16.6). To find "genuine freedom . . . [and] the enjoyment of union with its Beloved," (A.1.15.2) "the enamoured soul must leave its house. . . . It must go out at night when all the members of its house are asleep, that is, when the lower operations, passions, and appetites of its soul are put to sleep or quelled by means of this night" (N.2.14.1). The transition from the purgative way to the illuminative way, from "discursive meditation" to "loving contemplation," is like being "liberated from a cramped prison cell" (N.2.1.1; F.3.38). Still, "the intellect of its ordinary power, while in the prison of this body, is neither capable of nor prepared for the reception of the clear knowledge of God" (A.2.8.4). Therefore, persons must journey to union with God in faith, which is darkness for the natural intellect.

Even as faith grows deeper, persons still feel the painful effects of deeply-rooted disordered passions and appetites. In the "state of spiritual betrothal the soul is able to see her excellent qualities and ample riches and also that she does not possess and enjoy them as she would like because she still dwells in the body .... Her presence in the body makes her feel like a noble lord held in a prison. Such a prisoner is subject to a thousand miseries, while his dominions are confiscated and he is prevented from making use of his lordship and wealth; all he gets from his riches is a little food, and that very sparingly. . . . As a result the soul feels as though she were in the land of enemies and tyrannized among strangers and like one dead among the dead" (C.18.1-2).

The spiritual marriage, the perfect transformation of the soul in God through love, comes only after God has completely purified the soul in the dark night of spirit. John recommends "deep compassion for the soul God puts in this tempestuous and frightful night" (N.2.7.3). Because of the "passive" nature of this night, "their helplessness is even greater because of the little they can do in this situation. They resemble one who is imprisoned in a dark dungeon, bound hands and feet, and able neither to move nor see nor feel any favor from heaven or earth. They remain in this condition until their spirit is humbled, softened, and purified, until it becomes so delicate, simple, and refined that it can be one with the Spirit of God, according to the degree of union of love that God, in his mercy, desires to grant" (N.2.7.3).

Once united with God in spiritual marriage, the soul's strong and purified love for God, like a single strand of her hair fluttering about her neck, now takes God as *her* prisoner.

> O how worthy of utter admiration and joy! God is taken captive by a hair! The reason this captivity is so estimable is that God wished to stop and gaze at the fluttering of the hair. . . . For God, to gaze at is to love. If in his infinite mercy he had not gazed at us and loved us first—as St. John declares [1 Jn. 4:10,19]—and descended, the hair of our lowly love would not have taken him prisoner, for this love was not so lofty in its flight as to be able to capture this divine bird of heights. But because he came down to gaze at us and arouse the flight of our love by strengthening and giving it the courage for this [Dt.32:11], he himself as a result was captivated by the flight of the hair, that is, he was satisfied and pleased. . . . It is indeed incredible that a bird of lowly flight can capture the royal eagle of the heights if this eagle descends with the desire of being captured. . . . Consider the joy, happiness, and delight the soul finds in such a prisoner, she who for so long had been his prisoner. The power and the tenacity of love is great, for love captures and binds God himself. Happy is the loving soul, since she possesses God for her prisoner, and he is surrendered to all her desires. God is such that those who act with love and friendship toward him will make him do all they desire... (C.31.8–32.1).

Teachings after Toledo

But Toledo provided John with more than compelling metaphors to describe the human soul and its journey to union with God. In prison, John discovered what he believed to be the secret of "how to reach divine union quickly"(A.title)—total self-emptying expressed in desiring only God, imitating Jesus Christ in his passion and death, and lifting one's first movements to God in order to journey in perfect faith, hope, and love. He shared this discovery with others at every opportunity, not only in his poems and commentaries, but also in the private conferences, letters, counsels, and spiritual sayings that flowed forth from him after he left Toledo.

For example, in 1589 he counseled the prioress of the Carmelite monastery at Cordoba about new members to the community: "See to it that they preserve the spirit of poverty and contempt for all things, with the desire to be content with God alone. . . . For the poor in spirit are happier and more constant in the midst of want because they have placed their all in nothingness, and in all things they thus find freedom of heart" (L.16). He is no less insistent about imitating Jesus. John wrote out brief "Sayings of Light and Love" on small slips of paper and gave them out to encourage others on their spiritual journey. One of them contains this advice: "Crucified inwardly and outwardly with Christ, you will live in this life with fullness and satisfaction of soul, and possess your soul in patience [Lk. 21:19]" (S, 87). He gives this same counsel in a letter to one of his Carmelite brothers in 1590: ". . . If at any time someone, whether superior or anyone else, should try to persuade you of a lax teaching, even though it be confirmed by miracles, do not believe or embrace it; rather, greater penance and greater detachment from all things. And do not seek Christ without the cross" (L. 24). The contemplative journey, John kept insisting, "does not consists in consolations, delights, and spiritual feelings, but in the living death of the cross, sensory and spiritual, exterior and interior" (A.2.7.11).

Finally, John taught others a sure way to union with God and transformation in Christ that he discovered in Toledo. Years earlier as a theology student at the University of Salamanca, he learned that the theological virtues of faith, hope, and love are the "proximate means" to union with God in this life. In Toledo he realized that a practical method for deepening faith, hope, and love is to free the intellect, memory, and will from "apprehensions" or specific thoughts, memories, and emotions that might become an obstacle to receiving the general, nonspecific loving knowledge that God communicates to the soul in contemplation. He called this method lifting one's first movements to God.

Aware from his own experience that contemplative growth depends less upon profound thoughts about God or deep religious emotions and more upon emptying consciousness of these "apprehensions" to receive

God's self-communication, John systematically taught his readers in *The Ascent of Mount Carmel* how to lift their first conscious movements to God. For example, he gave this advice for purifying the memory in order to grow in the theological virtue of hope: "What souls must do in order to live in perfect and pure hope in God is this: As often as distinct ideas, forms, and images occur to them, they should immediately, without resting in them, turn to God with loving affection, in emptiness of everything rememberable. They should not think or look on these things for longer than is sufficient for the understanding and fulfillment of their obligations, if these refer to this. And then they should consider these ideas without becoming attached or seeking gratification in them, lest the effects of them be left in the soul. Thus people are not required to stop recalling and thinking about what they must do and know, for, if they are not attached to the possession of these thoughts, they will not be harmed" (A.3.15.1).

According to Eliseo de los Mártires, a Carmelite who knew him well during the Andalusia years, John also taught this method to his fellow friars as the best way of overcoming temptation and growing in other virtues. John said there are two ways to acquire virtues and avoid vices. The first is "to resist some vice, sin or temptation by means of the acts of virtue which conflict with this vice, sin or temptation and destroy it." For example, if I am conscious of being tempted to retaliate against a person who has harmed or insulted me, I resist by meditating on the passion of our Lord, who "when he was insulted, returned no insult" (1 Pet 2:23) or by considering the freedom acquired by self-conquest or by recalling that suffering can bring spiritual profit. Such reflections help me to accept the affront for God's honor and glory. This is an effective way of working with temptation and developing the virtue of patience, but very difficult.

John proposed a second approach by means of "loving anagogical movements and acts." He considered this anagogical or spiritual practice "easier, more profitable and more perfect." Eliseo reports that John taught this better way in the following manner:

> When we feel the first movement or attack of any vice, such as lust, wrath, impatience or a revengeful spirit when some wrong has been done to us, we should not resist it by making an act of the contrary virtue, in the way that has been described, but, as soon as we are conscious of it, we should meet it with an act or movement of anagogical love directed against this vice, and should raise our affection to union with God, for by this means the soul absents itself from its surroundings and is present with its God and becomes united with Him, and then the vice or the temptation and the enemy are defrauded of their intent, and have nowhere to strike; for the soul, being where it loves rather than where it lives, has met the temptation with Divine aid, and the enemy has found nowhere to strike and nothing whereon to lay hold, for the soul is no longer where the temptation or enemy would have struck and wounded it. And then, oh, marvelous thing! the soul, having forgotten this movement of vice, and being united and made one with its Beloved, no longer feels any movement of this vice wherewith the devil desired to tempt it, and was succeeding in doing so; in the first place, because, as has been said, it has escaped, and is no longer present, so that, if it may be put in this way, the devil is as it were tempting a dead body and doing battle with something that is not, feels not and is for the time being incapable of feeling temptation.[6]

These anagogical acts are relatively easy for the soul whose love of God is strong and who has no "concern about being praised or exalted or insulted or humbled or about whether men speak well of it or ill." However, beginners in the spiritual life, whose love is still weak and their virtue inconsistent, will not always succeed at first in overcoming temptations by this method. They should nonetheless be taught how to make these anagogical acts and encouraged to use them as often as possible. If the practice does not always prove effective, the first method of holy considerations and repeating phrases from Sacred Scripture should also be employed until the temptation has past. With time and effort, though, most persons committed to desiring God alone and following Christ in his passion and death will find the anagogical method as the easier and more effective way of dealing with temptation and practicing virtue.[7]

What John taught to his brother and sister Carmelites, he taught to the laity as well. This included the lifting of one's first movements to God. When Juana de Pedraza, a young lay woman in Granada, apparently complained that this method left her in the dark, without clear ideas of God or fervent religious feelings to sustain her, John responded:

> What is it you desire? What kind of life or method of procedure do you paint for yourself in this life? What do you think serving God involves other than avoiding evil, keeping his commandments, and being occupied with the things of God as best we can? When this is had, what need is there of other apprehensions or other lights and satisfactions from this source or that? In these there is hardly ever a lack of stumbling blocks and dangers for the soul, which by its understanding and appetites is deceived and charmed; and its own faculties cause it to err. And thus God does one a great favor when he darkens the faculties and impoverishes the soul in such a way that one cannot err with these. And if one does not err in this, what need is there in order to be right other than to walk along the level road of the law of God and of the Church, and live only in dark and true faith and certain hope and complete charity, expecting all our blessings in heaven, living here below like pilgrims, the poor, the exiled, orphans, the thirsty, without a road and without anything hoping for everything in heaven? (L.19)

For thirteen years, from 1578 when he left Toledo until his death in Ubeda in 1591, John taught the lesson he himself had learned during nearly nine months in prison—the self-emptying involved in living only for God, identifying with Christ's passion and death, and lifting one's first movements to God is the royal road to transformation in Jesus Christ. Consistently and unhesitatingly, he proclaimed the good news of "nakedness, poverty, selflessness, [and] spiritual purity (which are all the same)" (A.2.7.5) to clergy, religious, and laity, to every Christian who desired union with God. Such unequivocal insistence upon the one disposition necessary for the entire spiritual journey—"*nada, nada, nada, nada, nada, nada y aun en el monte nada*" [nothing, nothing . . . and even on the mountain nothing] (Sketch of Mt. Carmel)—surely results from John's own personal experience. The reassuring voice of that experience is un-mistakably present when he describes the rewards of a life built on the solid foundation of emptiness. "When individuals have finished purify-ing and voiding themselves of all forms and apprehensible images, they will abide in this pure and simple light [of God's self-communication] and be perfectly transformed into it. This light is never lacking to the soul, but because of creature forms and veils that weigh on it and cover it, the light is never infused. If individuals would eliminate these impediments and veils, and live in pure nakedness and poverty of spirit, . . . their soul in its simplicity and purity would then be immediately transformed in simple and pure Wisdom, the Son of God. As soon as natural things are driven out of the enamored soul, the divine are naturally and supernaturally in-fused since there can be no void in nature" (A.2,1 S .4).

Life as Imprisonment

John's advice to his fellow sixteenth-century Spaniards, arising as it did from the prison experience of Toledo, helps us today as we deal with the limitations in our own lives. Indeed, imprisonment is apt metaphor for life itself, for none of us can escape its restrictions. Our very presence in a flesh and blood body limits us. Our physical senses put us in contact with the world around us and through this world we come to know God and the transcendent world of spirit. At the same time, this body situates us in one place only, limiting us from being physically where we desire to be, with loved ones and even with God. "While we are at home in the body we are away from the Lord," observes St. Paul, ". . . and we would rather leave the body and go home to the Lord" [2 Cor 5:6-8].

In our younger years, when we were awakening to all that out bod-ies revealed to us about life, we seldom considered ourselves confined. But as we age, we become more aware of our imprisonment. Our bodies impose severe limitations on our spirit. Like St. Paul, we too begin to long for release from "this mortal body" [Rom 7:24] to be with God.

This is not a dualism that sets body in opposition to soul. Each is created for the other. They are inextricably united, and even after death temporarily separates them, they are destined to be reunited in a life beyond this world, our souls then still "flesh-bound when found at best, but uncumbered" as Gerard Manley Hopkins imagined in "The Caged Skylark."[8] John of the Cross himself, often accused of promoting an unhealthy antagonism between body and soul, described them as a "whole harmonious composite" [toda esta armonía] (N.2.11.4; C.16.5 & 10; F.3.7). Nonetheless, in this world our body undeniably limits the longings of our spirit, often leaving us feeling imprisoned. Sometimes we also feel imprisoned in our life's work or vocation. Our place in this world may be the result of a wise choice and be very fulfilling. It can also leave us feeling captive. "I love my husband and my children," a woman in her middle-adult years once shared with me, "and we have a lovely home. I have everything I could ever ask for in life, but I still feel trapped. There is so much more I would love to do with my life, but I just can't. I have to be here for them." My friend was not asking for release; she was simply stating a fact. As good as life gets, it's always limited. An older couple, their own family raised and enjoying the freedom of their retirement years, suddenly find themselves imprisoned when their recently divorced son requires their help in raising his three daughters. The grandparents make the sacrifice willingly, but cannot avoid feeling the new confinement.

Imprisonment takes many forms. There are people who are imprisoned in jobs they hate or in marriages that are dead. Some who grow up loving the spaciousness of the country, feel enslaved when they have to live in a city. For some city folks, living in the country is just as confining. And for those in real prisons, many on death row awaiting execution, imprisonment is not metaphor, but harsh daily reality.

In different ways, we experience life as imprisonment. Our situation may not be as severe as John's in Toledo or those in our country's prison system, but the limitations are inescapable. They need not, however, prevent our transformation in Christ. As John teaches us, these restrictions, rather than crushing our spiritual aspirations, can transform us.

His first lesson is simply, whatever our circumstances, to center the desires of our heart upon God alone (A.1.10.1). God is our life's goal, a goal that transcends this world. Nowhere on earth will we find ourselves completely satisfied or fulfilled, because we have been created with an infinite capacity for God, and God alone—solo Dios!—can satisfy these longings. Thus, life in this world means continually nourishing our longing for God, even when we feel God has abandoned us. At first, this appears to be excluding everything but God from our lives; paradoxically, however, we discover that this longing, as it deepens, becomes all-inclusive. We desire—and to some degree find—communion both with God and all God's creation. Nourishing this longing, John assures us, leads us to "the true fulfillment of the first commandment which, neither disdaining anything human nor excluding it from this love, states: *You shall love your God with your whole heart, and with your whole mind and with your whole soul, and with all your strength* [Dt. 6:5]" (N.2.11.4).

Secondly, John advises: "Let Christ crucified be enough for you" (S.92). Our sufferings in this life may never equal John's in Toledo, yet they are uniquely our own and usually all that we can handle. These may include perhaps the most intense suffering of all—our feelings of impotence to relieve injustice, violence, and poverty in our world. Joining our pain to Jesus' passion is the great work of our lives, more significant than any of our external accomplishments. For Jesus' death and resurrection is the source of new life for our world—the paschal mystery that reconciles the human family with God. Daily uniting our suffering with Jesus' allows us to participate in this glorious mystery, no matter how ordinary or meaningless the rest of our life may seem.

Finally, John encourages us to form the habit of lifting our first movements to God. "Bear fortitude in your heart against all things that move you to that which is not God" (S. 95). Our first natural reactions to the normal constrictions of life are often self-pity, resenting God, blaming others, and fantasies of escape. The practice of not indulging these sentiments as they move into consciousness, but choosing instead to lift our mind and heart to God in loving acceptance of the divine will, frees our soul for the guidance of the Holy Spirit. At first, this practice seems extraordinarily difficult to be aware of all our first movements at the same time that we are attending to daily responsibilities. But as we become particularly sensitive to our very first feelings of pleasantness or unpleasantness associated with thoughts, memories, and emotions as these emerge within us, we can quickly respond to these feelings, choosing to cultivate them or let them pass through consciousness, without being diverted from the task at hand.[9]

This mental discipline develops the radical self-emptying that John believed to be the heart of contemplative living. It frees the intellect, memory, and will for growth in faith, hope, and love, the virtues that most unite us with God in this life. Perhaps more importantly, this practice effectively dismantles our distorted self-image that has been formed by a life time of thoughts, memories, and emotions—"apprehensions" as John calls them—allowing the Holy Spirit to form us in the image of Christ. This interior discipline, along with our continual longing for God and identifying our suffering with those of Christ, insures that we are seeking "God in ourselves" rather than "ourselves in God." They make our imprisonment in this world, as they did John's in Toledo, the means of our transformation in God through love.

John of the Cross: Mystical Doctor

In 1618, twenty-seven years after his death, John's writings were first published in Spain. By 1630 these writings were also available in French and Italian. In 1675, John of the Cross was beatified and Pope Benedict XIII declared him a saint in Saint Peter's Basilica, Rome, on December 27, 1726. Two hundred years later, on August 24, 1926, Pius XI proclaimed Saint John of the Cross a doctor of the universal church.

Today, spiritual seekers everywhere now turn to him for enlightenment. He has become a sure guide not only for Christians who seek a deeper union with God, but also for all who desire transformation in Ultimate Wisdom. Through his life and writings John teaches us all the secret of the contemplative life—"to possess all, desire the possession of nothing"—a lesson he learned, not in a mountaintop hermitage, but in a dark prison cell.

Notes

1. English translations of John of the Cross's writings in this chapter are taken from Kieran Kavanaugh and Otilio Rodriguez, trans., *The Collected Works of Saint John of the* Cross, rev. ed. (Washington, DC: ICS Publications, 1991). Citations are given in the text following each quotation.

2. For details of John's life, especially his imprisonment in Toledo, I rely on Federico Ruiz et al., *God Speaks in the Night: The Life, Times, and Teaching of Saint John of the Cross,* trans. Kieran Kavanaugh (Washington, DC: ICS Publications, 1991), 157-88; and Kieran Kavanaugh's "General Introduction," in *Collected Works of Saint John,* 9-38.

3. St. Teresa of Avila, *The Book of Her Foundations,* 3,17, in Kieran Kavanaugh and Otilio Rodriguez, trans., *The Collected Works of St. Teresa of Avila,* vol. 3 (Washington, DC: ICS Publications, 1985), 112.

4. In *The Ascent of Mount Carmel,* John gives detailed counsel on how to handle the first movements of joy toward various objects (see A.3. 20.3–4; 21.2; 22.6; 24.4; 26.7; 28.6; 37.2). Though he is speaking here specifically of joy, his advice may be applied to other emotions like hope, sorrow, and fear, as well as to thoughts, memories, temptations, and, in fact, to whatever mental phenomena appear in our consciousness.

5. Gerald Brenan, St *John of the Cross: His Life and Poetry* (Cambridge [Eng.]: Cambridge University Press, 1973), xi.

6. "Spiritual Sayings Attributed to Saint John of the Cross," in E. Allison Peers, trans. and ed., *The Complete Works of Saint John of the Cross,* rev. ed., vol. 3 (London: Burns Oates & Washbourne Ltd., 1953), 289-90.

7. Ibid.

8. "The Caged Skylark," in John Pick, ed., *A Hopkins Reader* (New York: Oxford University Press, 1953), 15.

9. John's practice of lifting first movements to God is similar to other Christian spiritual practices such as "the practice of the presence of God" and "abandonment to divine providence." See, for example, Brother Lawrence of the Resurrection, *Writing*

and Conversations on the Practice of the Presence of God, ed. Conrad De Meester, trans. Salvatore Sciurba (Washington, DC: ICS Publications, 1994); and J. P. de Caussade, *Abandonment to Divine Providence,* ed. J. Ramiere (St. Louis: B. Herder Book Co, 1921). It is also similar to "mindfulness" practice in the Buddhist tradition. For the integration of Buddhist mindfulness practice and John's lifting first movements to God within Christian prayer, see Kevin Culligan, Mary Jo Meadow, and Daniel Chowning, *Purifying the Heart: Buddhist Insight Meditation for Christians* (New York: Crossroad, 1994), 77-83, 178-80.

DARK NIGHT:
EDUCATION FOR BEAUTY

Keith J. Egan, T.O.Carm.
Center for Spirituality
St. Mary's College
Notre Dame, Indiana

"Let us go forth to behold ourselves in your beauty."[1]

Hans Urs von Balthasar calls John of the Cross one of the two "most decidedly aesthetic theologians of Christian history," the other being Pseudo-Dionysius.[2] However, this essay is not an attempt to articulate a theory of aesthetics based on the writings of John of the Cross who was not a theoretician. John did not elaborate a doctrine of philosophical or theological aesthetics; in fact, he never defined beauty, but he would have known Thomas Aquinas's description of beauty: that which delights or pleases when it is seen.[3] John would also have been aware of the characteristics of beauty noted by Aquinas: radiance/light, order/harmony, and integrity/wholeness. Beauty is found perfectly in God, imperfectly and derivatively in creatures.[4] John of the Cross was a poet and a spiritual guide who, in the latter capacity, expounded his spiritual doctrine briefly and only when necessary. He did so to explain spiritual experience and to give specific advice about the journey to union with God through love.

This essay explores the relationship between beauty and the dark night in the writings of John of the Cross. Beauty is not usually associated with John's dark night, but the neglect of beauty in the writings of John of the Cross and in spirituality in general has deprived the religious quest of a most compelling element in both arenas. Since the role of the dark night in the reclamation of beauty is crucial to the thought of John of the Cross, this essay focuses on the connection between beauty and dark night in an effort to alert readers of John of the Cross how critical beauty is to an understanding of his message.

The Power of Beauty

Religion that turns exclusively to truth runs the risk of being lost in irrelevant abstractions or in dogmatism. When the good is the sole concern, the risk is love without rigor or an excessive preoccupation with ethical issues. To banish beauty from religion is to empty it of a powerful divine and human component essential to its wholeness. Of the three transcendentals—often cited together: goodness, truth, and beauty—beauty is the transcendental that most easily disappears because beauty is so expansive, elusive, and ultimately indefinable.[5] Beauty as a religious concern has its risks, for example, superficial romanticism and nebulous suppositions. But, the absence of a sensitivity to beauty, divine or creaturely, has left much of religion utterly boring for too many moderns. Beauty, however described, is compelling in an age when little compels, captivating when there are so few captivating moments, invites to commitment when commitment is so fragile, and refines one's sensitivities when refinement is not highly valued.

The litany of ugly moments in the twentieth century is endless: two World Wars, countless lesser wars, the Holocaust for which no adjective will do, the abuse of women at a time when media ironically idealize women as beautiful, rampant racism, and the ceaseless savagery in the once Yugoslavia and elsewhere. On and on goes this atrocious litany. Is there no beauty left to invoke? Will religion take no lead in reminding an age soaked in ugliness and superficial beauty that holiness is more than compliance to laws, that beauty is a divine attribute and a mark of all creation? Jessica Powers, much schooled in the wisdom of John of the Cross, reminds her readers of the power of Beauty and its expression in created beauty.

> God's beauty, too, surrender seeks
> and takes in the will's lull
> whatever lets itself be changed
> into the beautiful.[6]

I have long been interested in the connection between beauty and holiness,[7] but who has not been haunted by Augustine's passionate recognition of God as Beauty? "Late have I loved you, beauty so old and so new: late have I loved you."[8] John of the Cross, poet and artist, saint and doctor of the church, seems an ideal subject for an exploration of the role of beauty on the sometimes dark journey to God. His teaching, moreover, deserves to be known whole and untruncated. In the search for the meaning of the connection between beauty and dark night, this essay consults as often as possible John's own words. The intent is to send the reader to these texts and their contexts. In other words, this essay is a walk through John's texts. Such has been the intent of the Carmelite Forum's summer seminars—to send participants to the texts of Carmelite spirituality. Indeed, John of the Cross is more interesting and illuminating than his commentators.

John of the Cross and Beauty

Michel Florisoone, once a conservator at the Louvre in Paris, cites approvingly Crisógono de Jesús to the effect that John of the

Cross was obsessed with beauty.[9] The word obsession, with its intimation of compulsivity, is hardly an apt description of John of the Cross's attitude to beauty or to anything else. John sought throughout his life to be free from whatever hindered loving union with God. John's goal was "freedom of heart," "a liberated heart."[10] But, beauty is undeniably a common sanjuanist motif. Beauty and related concepts and symbols appear constantly in John's writings.[11]

John was a many-sided artist. Salvador Dali took inspiration from John's sketch of Christ Crucified, and critics have admired this sketch for its artistic originality. John also had the eye of an architect. He designed and built the aqueduct and cloister at Granada, and he worked with the young artist who sculpted and painted at the Carmelite foundation at Baeza.[12] John also liked to carve crucifixes and other images.[13] In his writings, he frequently turned to imagery taken from painting and carving,[14] and John of the Cross loved music and singing.[15] His sensitivity to the beauty of music is apparent in his commentary on the celebrated phrase "silent music":

> In that nocturnal tranquility and silence and in knowledge of the divine light the soul becomes aware of Wisdom's wonderful harmony and sequence in the variety of her creatures and works. Each of them is endowed with a certain likeness of God and in its own way gives voice to what God is in it. So creatures will be for the soul a harmonious symphony of sublime music surpassing all concerts and melodies of the world. . . . And thus there is in it the sweetness of music and the quietude of silence. Accordingly, she says that her Beloved is silent music because in him she knows and enjoys this symphony of spiritual music.[16]

The poetry of John of the Cross reveals his profound affection and appreciation for the beauty of nature. His poetry is a veritable thesaurus of nature's images, many of which come from the lush imagery in the Song of Songs or from his keen appreciation of creation.

For John, faith in Christ is greeted as "¡Oh cristalina fuente, O spring like crystal!"[17] John addresses nature tenderly:

> O woods and thickets,
> Planted by the hand of my Beloved!
> O green meadow,
> Coated, bright, with flowers,
> Tell me, has he passed by you? (CB.4)

This Spanish Carmelite knows as well as the English Jesuit Gerard Manley Hopkins that "the world is charged with the grandeur of God."[18] A story describes John and a fellow friar enjoying to the full the beauty of the farm at Santa Ana that belonged to the Carmelite college at Baeza some distance away.[19]

Without a doubt, John's keen affinity for beauty is most evident in the beauty of his poetry. Admirers around the world, but especially the poets of Spain, have esteemed the beauty of John's poetry. Jorge Guillén told an audience at Harvard University that "no Spanish poet inspires more unanimous admiration today than San Juan de la Cruz." Guillén added that John wrote verse that is "the highest pinnacle in Spanish poetry."[20] Dámaso Alonso, who may have done more than anyone else to spread word about the beauty of John's poetry, says, at the conclusion of a study of that poetry, that John's poems contain eminently the three characteristics of beauty articulated by Thomas Aquinas: wholeness, harmony, and clarity.[21] On March 8, 1993, John Paul II, declared John of the Cross patron of Spanish poets. In doing so, the pope spoke of John's poems as drawing readers to celestial Beauty, eternal Truth, and infinite Goodness.[22] Sensuous imagery, captivating symbols, and arresting rhythms evoke the beautiful and inspire in readers an awe for the lovely sounds and imagery in John of the Cross's poetry. If one had only John's poetry and knew nothing of his life, one would conclude that the composer of these poems had a perceptive eye and a sensitive ear for the beautiful wherever it was to be found. Read aloud, as it should be in Spanish, John's poetry is a festival of beautiful sounds.

Yet, the beauty of the poem "Dark Night" and the "terrible/horrible" content of John's commentaries on this poem reveal a paradox.[23] How do they go together? Why are the form of the poem and the content of the commentaries so disparate? There has been widespread acclaim for the beauty of this poem, "Noche oscura," which Jorge Guillén says "is perhaps the purest of the three great poems,"[24] and Gerald Brenan has called the "Dark Night" "the most perfect of San Juan's poems."[25] It is certainly John's best-known poem and symbol, but its beauty belies the pain and the suffering described in its two commentaries. Indeed, the poem opens with the memory of a once-upon-a-time journey: "One dark night,/fired with love's urgent longings/—ah, the sheer grace!—/I went out unseen,/ my house being all stilled."[26] But, the poem has nothing like the commentary's graphic description of the "constricted road . . . called a dark night" (N.prologue). John says that "the first purgation or night is bitter and terrible to the senses. But nothing can be compared to the second, for it is horrible and frightful to the spirit" (N.1.8.2). Those passing through the dark night of the spirit "resemble one who is imprisoned in a dark dungeon, bound hands and feet, and able neither to move nor to see any favor from heaven or earth" (N.2.7.3). "Both the sense and the spirit, as though under an immense and dark load, undergo such agony and pain that the soul would consider death a relief" (N.2.5.6). This dark contemplation brings about "a terrible anguish (like hanging in midair, unable to breathe)" (N.2.6.5).

Juan de la Cruz provides a clue to this paradox between a poem that celebrates a "night more lovely than the dawn"[27] and the poem's commentaries that highlight dryness, pain, and darkness. In the prologue to the *Dark Night,* John alerts his reader:

> Before embarking on an explanation of these stanzas, we
> should remember that the soul recites them when it has already

reached the state of perfection—that is, union with God through love—and has now passed through severe trials and conflicts by means of the spiritual exercise that leads one along the constricted way to eternal life, of which our Savior speaks in the Gospel [Mt. 7:14]. (N. prologue)

The poem, "Dark Night," beautifully constructed, celebrates the journey to union with God in rich, erotic symbolism inspired by the Song of Songs: "there he lay sleeping/and I caressing him" and "laying my face on my Beloved," and so on.[28] John composed the poem "Dark Night" apparently with the same "love flowing from abundant mystical understanding" with which he composed "The Spiritual Canticle" (CB. prologue 2). Yet, John's commentaries on the "Dark Night" reveal that a harsh journey precedes the love in which the poem was composed. For John, the journey to God is "the rough road of the cross" (N.1.6.7) that culminates when one is "filled with good and glory" (F.4.17). This is the journey from the old self to the new self, New Testament imagery that John finds congenial as a description of the transformation from self-centeredness to God-centeredness (N.2.2.1; 2.3.3.; etc.; see Eph 4:22–4; Col 3:9–10). The "Dark Night," composed by the new self in love with God, knows, through experience and interpretation, about the suffering of the old self during the night journey. A stanza from one of John's loveliest poems says it this way: "I know that nothing else is so beautiful,/and that the heavens and the earth drink there,/*although it is night*."[29]

An anecdote reveals John's attitude to the spiritual significance of beauty. When John was superior at El Calvario, he acted as an adviser to the Carmelite nuns at Beas who lived only a few miles from his friary. One day John questioned a young nun, Francisca of the Mother of God, about her prayer. Francisca replied that her prayer consisted "in looking at the beauty of God and rejoicing that he has it." This description of Francisca's prayer delighted John so much that he spent days talking about the beauty of God. As a consequence,

John composed the five stanzas of "The Spiritual Canticle" that begin with the lines "Let us rejoice, Beloved, and let us go forth to behold ourselves in your beauty."[30] John's commentary on the line "Let us go forth to behold ourselves in your beauty" may be one the most eloquent panegyrics about beauty in mystical literature. It deserves comparison with the less personal but widely known praise of Beauty in *The Divine Names* of Pseudo-Dionysius [31] and with Bernard of Clairvaux's lovely sermon on the verse from the Song of Songs, "Behold, how beautiful you are, my dearest, O how beautiful, your eyes are like doves!"[32] John's commentary on the lines, "Let us rejoice, Beloved," will be given below.[33]

Although Fray Juan de la Cruz had a unique and lifelong kinship with beauty, readers recall that he also has a reputation for not always being lyrical about creation.

> All the beauty of creatures compared to the infinite beauty of God is the height of ugliness. . . . So a person attached to the beauty of any creature is extremely ugly in God's sight. A soul so unsightly is incapable of transformation into the beauty that is God because ugliness does not attain to beauty.
>
> All the grace and the elegance of creatures compared to God's grace is utter coarseness and crudity. That is why a person captivated by this grace and elegance of creatures becomes highly coarse and crude in God's sight. Someone like this is incapable of the infinite grace and beauty of God because of the extreme difference between the coarse and the infinitely elegant. (A.1.4.4)

John's calls for renunciation appear to cast a pall on creation: "renounce and remain empty of any sensory satisfaction that is not purely for the honor and glory of God" (A.1.13.4). The beauty of creation appears to be mere fodder for mortification. Put poetically, John writes:

> Not for all of beauty
> will I ever lose myself,
> but for I-don't-know-what
> which is so gladly gained.[34]

Is the beauty about which John sings so eloquently only the Beauty who is a transcendent God or merely a kindred spiritual beauty that has nothing to do with material creation? First of all, John of the Cross radically affirms the transcendent, and he starkly differentiates transcendent Beauty from creaturely beauty. But, Urs von Balthasar argues that Pseudo-Dionysius and John of the Cross are able to exalt the vertical only because they keep a grasp on the horizontal.[35] For Pseudo-Dionysius and John, Beauty is the cause of beauty and, yet, beauty remains beauty despite the infinite distance between it and Beauty. John of the Cross is no Manichee nor a Gnostic. He affirms the goodness and sacramentality of creation. The person united with God in love knows from the depths of her heart the divine origin of creation and has a completely positive appreciation of it:

> By the "living beauty" of this grove, for which she asks
> the Bridegroom here, she intends to beg for the grace, wisdom
> and beauty that every earthly and heavenly creature not only
> has from God but also manifests in its wise, well ordered,
> gracious, and harmonious relationship to other creatures. (CB.39.11).

In his commentary on stanza 5 of "The Spiritual Canticle," which ends with the words: "[he] clothed them in beauty," John writes of a dialogue between creatures and the soul (the bride) in which creatures respond about the "testimony they in themselves give the soul of God's grandeur and excellence." John continues his commentary by adding:

> The substance of this stanza is: God created all things with
> remarkable ease and brevity, and in them he left some trace of
> who he is, not only in giving all things being from nothing, but

> even by endowing them with innumerable graces and qualities,
> making them beautiful in a wonderful order and unfailing
> dependence on one another. All of this he did through his own
> Wisdom, the Word, his only begotten Son by whom he created
> them. (CB.5.1)

John's teaching about the beauty of creation is in no way reluctant. Rather it is a hearty endorsement of this beauty with a realization that, through the Incarnation, the Father bestowed beauty on creation in abundance:

> And in this elevation of all things through the Incarnation of
> His Son and through the glory of his resurrection according
> to the flesh not only did the Father beautify creatures partially,
> but, we can say, he clothed them in beauty and dignity. (CB.5.4)

Not only does John say that the beauty of creation is the work of the Word, he teaches that one gets to know cataphatically something of the beauty of God through creatures: "The soul, wounded with love through a trace of the beauty of her Beloved, which she has known through creatures, and anxious to see the invisible beauty that caused this visible beauty, declares . . ." (CB.6.1).[36]

Yet, while the Spanish mystic affirms the beauty of creation, he also maintains the infinite distance between creation and the Creator, between the human and the divine. However, John's strictures about creatureliness target not creation itself but disordered attachments with which a person clings to things and other persons as if they were divine. These attachments block the gift of union with God. John employs the "expression 'night' to signify a deprival of the gratification of the soul's appetites in all things" (A.1.3.1). These gratifications prevent union with God. John says that "all objects living in the soul . . . must die in order that the soul enter divine union, and it must bear no desire for them but remain detached as though they were nonexistent to it, and it to them" (A.1.11.8).

John of the Cross, as spiritual guide, seeks to help his directees become disentangled from the mesh of misbegotten attachments. "Do not go about looking for the best of temporal things, but for the worst, and, for Christ, desire to enter into complete nakedness, emptiness, and poverty in everything in the world" (A.1.13.6).

The Ascent of Mount Carmel directs its readers away from worldly objects and even warns them against attachment to devotional objects and oratories (A.3.35–45; see also A.3.15.2; N.1.3.1). Yet, this mystic is no iconoclast. John of the Cross values religious art and architecture since they have the power to arouse devotion. But, he is not happy with sloppy work. "Some artisans so unskilled and unpolished in the art of carving should be forbidden to continue their craft" (A.3.38.2). John recognizes too the worth of beautiful language.

> Indeed, it is neither the Apostle's intention nor mine to condemn good style and rhetoric and effective delivery; these, rather, are most important to the preacher, as they are in all matters. Elegant style and delivery lift up and restore those things that have fallen into ruin, just as poor presentation spoils what is good. (A.3.45.5)

But, John of the Cross wants his readers to "seek the living image of Christ crucified within themselves" (A.35.5). He warns them against getting lost in an object or its artistry. Interior recollection is what John fosters. Good human art must take a backseat to God, but it remains good art and a reflection of its source. However, affection for even good things is imperfect until the heart is transformed in God—until the "eye of the soul" is illumined (F.3.71). Then the heart can love God and creatures as they are meant to be loved.

This radical doctrine, of course, did not mean that, in the meantime, one was not to love others as one's self nor God with all one's heart. John does mean that this human love remains imperfect until it is perfected by union with God. Yet, John does not want those on the journey to God to be disheartened by what he considers the Gospel imperative of love of God and love of neighbor. To those on the journey he says, "if anyone is seeking God, the Beloved is seeking that person much more" (F.3.28).

Dark Night

The process of mortification and the dark night of contemplation are the road to the restoration of one's ability to love God and to delight in God's beauty as well as to reclaim an ordered love for all creation. That dark journey makes it possible for one to know and love creation and others as they deserve to be loved. John of the Cross's eye is always on the best outcome possible: union with God through love. Above all else, he is single-minded. For him, the dark nights of active or human liberation and passive or divine liberation make possible union with God. When that process is completed, one is available for transformation in God, ready to love God and see beauty as one ought. George Tavard makes this very point this way: "At the acme of mystical exprience, the world of nature is reintegrated into divine beauty." [37]

The consummation of the journey to union with God in love is a story of restoration, integration, and fulfillment:

> The bride knows that now her will's desire is detached
> from all things and attached to her God in most intimate love;
> that the sensory part of her soul . . . is in harmony with the
> spirit, and its rebelliousness brought into subjection . . . that
> her soul is united and transformed with an abundance of
> heavenly riches and gifts . . . flowing with delights, to the
> glorious thrones of her Bridegroom. (CB.40.1)

Union with God through love brings one into the glory of God, and a key dimension of glory is beauty.[38] Here the person takes delight in God and in creation. For John of the Cross, a necessary aspect of this journey is the dark night. The luminosity of beauty is regained through the experience of darkness, a darkness that is always for the sake of light (N.2.9; A.2.3.4). Contemplation of God's beauty and of created beauty becomes possible through the purifying power of the dark night that is itself contemplation, a contemplation that is God's presence. "For contemplation is nothing else than a secret and peaceful and loving inflow of God" (N.1.10.6).[39] God's presence makes possible the redemption of beauty for the human community.

John of the Cross says that "the soul must ordinarily walk this path [dark night] to reach that sublime and joyous union with God." This is a gospel path described by our Savior: "for the gate is narrow and the road is hard that leads to life, and there are few who find it" (N. prologue; Mt 7:14; see also A.1.4.1). In *The Ascent of Mount Carmel*, John treats the active or human purification of the soul. It is a journey from selfish pre-occupations and disordered attachments to a life of virtue. This is the active dark night. In *The Dark Night* commentary, John describes the passive purification or liberation of the senses and the spirit. *The Dark Night* describes God's work of liberation that is achieved through the inflow of God, contemplation that is the liberating presence of God.

For John of the Cross, the human person is a unity, but with sensory and spiritual dimensions. Book 1 of *The Dark Night* is an account of God's liberation from the sense attachments of the heart. Book 2 describes the divine liberation of the spirit, which gives access to "the deepest center" of the human person (F.1.9). Many experience the dark night of the senses as described in book 1, says John, but "very few" pass through the dark night of the spirit. (N.1.8.1,2,4; 14.1).

After one has been initially converted and begins to follow Jesus Christ and is serious about one's commitment, there is joy and consolation through growth in virtue and in the practice of meditation, for example, "imagining Christ crucified or at the pillar or in some other scene; or God seated on a throne with resplendent majesty; or imagining and considering glory as a beautiful light" (A.2.12.3). However, meditation has the capacity to take one only so far on the journey to God. Human thoughts, no matter how beautiful, or human activities, no matter how intense, are unable to make one ready for full union with God. Human effort must give way to divine activity, meditation must cede to contemplation. "God must take over," says John (N.1.3.3.). The dark night is God's work. However, the pain of the dark night comes not from God's presence but from the resistance of human imperfection and insufficiency.

> There is nothing in contemplation or the divine inflow that of itself can give pain; contemplation rather bestows sweetness and delight....The cause for not experiencing these agreeable effects is the soul's weakness and imperfection at the time, its inadequate preparation, and the qualities it possesses that are contrary to this light. Because of these the soul has to suffer when the divine light shines upon it. (N.2.9.11)

The dark night of the senses and of the spirit is a purifying contemplation, which, John says, "is nothing else than a secret and peaceful and loving inflow of God, which, if not hampered, fires the soul in the spirit of love" (N.1.10.6). John adds elsewhere:

> This dark night is an inflow of God into the soul, which purges it of its habitual ignorances and imperfections, natural and spiritual, and which the contemplatives call infused contemplation or mystical theology. Through this contemplation, God teaches the soul secretly and instructs it in the perfection of love without its doing anything or understanding how this happens. (N.2.5.1)

Here God is the educator of the human person, teaching through the gift of dark contemplation, God's presence. This contemplation or inflow of God is the cause of the dark night because, in her imperfection, the human person is not empty enough for the fullness of God's presence and is too distracted by other preoccupations. God's loving presence is too much for human frailty. Because of human impoverishment, the inflow of God causes in the human person affliction, dryness, and pain (N.2.5.1–2, nn.1,3). This contemplation is a dark and purifying contemplation that liberates first the senses and then the spirit of all that makes union with God impossible. This purifying contemplation prepares the human person to enter into union with God in love where there occurs the vision of God's beauty and a proper, restored appreciation of the beauty of creation.

The dark night, a "journey toward union with God," begins with a departure from the desires for "worldly possessions" and is a journey of faith, which "is also like a dark night." In the end, the dark night is a journey into God for "God is also a dark night to the soul in this life" (A.1.2.1). These three nights are really only one night, John says, with three parts: early evening (twilight), midnight, and "very early dawn just before the break of day" (A.1.2.5). God thus draws one into union with God's self through the gift of contemplation, which darkens and dries up the imperfections that hinder union with God in love.

The dark night of the spirit, "that frightful night of contemplation" (N.2.1.1), without which there is no union with God, completes the work of the dark night of the senses (N.2.2.5). The subsequent union with God in the darkness of early morning restores the human person to wholeness/integrity, to a knowing and to a loving for which every human person was created. Chapters 1 and 2 of Genesis describe what God meant creation to be. Chapter 3 of Genesis is the story of the collapse of that plan. Redemption—walking again with God "in the garden at the time of the evening breeze" (Gn 3:8)—comes to the human community through the dying and rising of Jesus of Nazareth. John of the Cross describes the fullness of that redemption as the work of the dark night, which restores the human person's capacity to know the truth, to love the good, and to see the beautiful.

In the culmination of the dark night, there occur "substantial touches of divine union" through which "the soul is purified, quieted, strengthened, and made stable so she may receive permanently this divine union, which is the divine espousal between the soul and the Son of God" (N.2.24.3).[40]

Restoration of the Capacity to Behold the Beautiful

The Living Flame of Love. John of the Cross did not complete *The Ascent of Mount Carmel* or *The Dark Night.* For John's descriptions of union with God through love, one must turn to later stanzas of *The Spiritual Canticle* and the whole of *The Living Flame of Love* where the human person reposseses the capacities lost through sin and imperfection. *The Spiritual Canticle* is, indeed, lyrical about the encounter of the human person with God as Beauty, but we shall turn first to *The Living Flame of Love* where the Son of God "awakens" in the human soul so that it may "get a glimmer of him as he is" (F.4.7). This awakening is "the communication of God's excellence to the substance of the soul" (F.4.10). However, John is less explicit about beauty in the *Flame* than he is in the *Canticle.* The experience of God in *The Living Flame of Love* leaves John near speechless. This experience is "indescribable" and "beyond words" (F.3.8; 4.10), John says, and he brings the *Flame* to a close with these words:

> I do not desire to speak of this spiration, filled for the soul with good and glory and delicate love of God, for I am aware of being incapable of doing so; and were I to try, it might seem less than it is. It is a spiration that God produces in the soul, in which, by that awakening of lofty knowledge of the Godhead, he breathes the Holy Spirit in it in the same proportion as its knowledge and understanding of him, absorbing it most profoundly in the Holy Spirit, rousing its love with a divine exquisite quality and delicacy according to what it beholds in him. Since the breathing is filled with good and glory, the Holy Spirit, through this breathing, filled the soul with good and glory in which he enkindled it in love of himself, indescribably and

incomprehensibly, in the depths of God, to whom be honor and glory forever and ever. Amen. (F.4.17)

Faced with the ineffability of his encounter with God, John leaves only hints of this his deepest experience of spiritual marriage (F. prologue.3). His words "filled with good and glory" are an evocation of Isaiah's vision of God in the temple: "holy, holy, holy" and an allusion to the liturgical song the *Sanctus*.[41]

John speaks of the mystical experience of glory when "the soul in a sublime experience of glory feels and understands most distinctly all these things that the Holy Spirit, desiring to introduce it into glory, shows it in this gentle and tender blaze" (F.1.28). This is not the full experience of glory that comes only in the beatific vision, but consists of "sudden flashes of glory," for, like Moses, in this life one would die of full exposure to the glory of God (F.1.27). This experience of God's glory is a manifestation in part of God's beauty.[42]

Typically impatient to get on with his writing, John only briefly discusses the dark night in *The Living Flame of Love*. Yet, John sees the dark night as a "time or stage along the spiritual road" (F.1.25). For John, the dark night prepares for and becomes the loving contemplative union with God in which there are glimpses of the glory of God where, transformed in God, the person encounters God's beauty.

The Spiritual Canticle.   In the later sections of *The Spiritual Canticle* (st. 22–40) where John of the Cross describes spiritual marriage—union with God through love—John is more explicit about the encounter with Beauty and the restoration of the human capacity for seeing divine and human beauty. Here John is most explicit, lyrical, and bold about beauty. His commentary on the following line from stanza 36 of "The Spiritual Canticle," "Let us go forth to behold ourselves in your beauty," becomes a prayer addressed to Beauty:

> This means: Let us so act that by means of this loving activity we may attain to the vision of ourselves in your beauty

in eternal life. That is: That I be so transformed in your beauty
that we may be alike in beauty, and both behold ourselves in
your beauty, possessing then your very beauty; this, in such
a way that each looking at the other may see in the other their
own beauty, since both are your beauty alone, I being absorbed
in your beauty; hence, I shall see you in your beauty, and you
will see me in your beauty, and I shall see myself in you in
your beauty, and you will see yourself in me in your beauty;
that I may resemble you in your beauty, and you resemble me
in your beauty, and my beauty be your beauty and your beauty
my beauty; wherefore I shall be you in your beauty, and you
will be me in your beauty, because your very beauty will be
my beauty; and thus we shall behold each other in your beauty.
(CB.36.5)

John immediately puts this prayer into a Christological and ecclesial
context. Commenting on John 17:10, he says: "He declared this not
only for himself, the Head, but for his whole mystical body, the Church,
which on the day of her triumph, when she sees God face to face,
will participate in the very beauty of the Bridegroom" (CB.36.5). One
then repossesses what is of earth and what is of heaven: "The soul
cannot see herself in the beauty of God unless she is transformed into
the wisdom of God, in which she sees herself in possession of earthly
and heavenly things" (CB.36.8).

John's encounter with Beauty is no idle romantic leap. Suffering,
the dark night, and the cross are presupposed:

Oh! If we could but now fully understand how a soul
cannot reach the thicket and wisdom of the riches of God . . . without
entering the thicket of many kinds of suffering . . . in order to
enter this wisdom by the thicket of the cross! . . . The gate
entering into these riches of his wisdom is the cross. (CB.36.13)

John of the Cross's doctrine of the dark night is a metaphor for
the way of the cross as the way to glory. Entering into the dying and
rising of Christ is the journey from the darkness of self-centeredness

through active and passive liberation of the dark nights of sense and spirit to the union with God through love.

In this journey that is a dark night, God is the teacher, the educator who teaches through dark contemplation. "Through this contemplation, God teaches the soul secretly and instructs it in the perfection of love without its doing anything or understanding how this happens" (N.2.5.1). This is an education that takes place deep within the human spirit since "the Master who teaches the soul dwells within it substantially where neither the devil nor the natural senses nor the intellect can reach" (N.2.17.2). The dark night of the spirit teaches humility since "love is teaching them what God deserves" (N.2.19.3). It is "the Holy Spirit, the Teacher [who] leads the way and gives light" (A.2.29.1). The dark nights, which are contemplation (N.1. explanation.1; 2.13.10; 2.16.10; 2.25.2; passim), educate the human person for love and for beauty. This dark education/contemplation continues until death for the soul in union with God.

> This contemplation, in which the soul, by means of her transformation, has sublime knowledge in this life of the divine grove and its living beauty, is consequently called "night." Yet however sublime this knowledge may be, it is still a dark night when compared with the beatific knowledge she asks for here. In seeking clear contemplation, she asks that this enjoyment of the grove and its living beauty, as well as the other goods mentioned, take place now in the serene night; that is, in beatific and clear contemplation, the night of the dark contemplation of this earth changing into the contemplation of the clear and serene vision of God in heaven. (CB.39.13)

Conclusion

This essay has highlighted the connection between beauty and dark night in John of the Cross. No reader of John can miss the dark night, but many have bypassed beauty and beauty's relationship to dark night. The author's hope is that this essay will be a gentle reminder to attend more diligently to the connection between beauty and dark night in John's poetry and prose. Let me add, however, that this essay has touched only the surface of the beautiful in John's writings. Selections in this chapter from John of the Cross are nearly always from specific references to beauty. One must also take into account ideas and words like loveliness, delight(s), splendor, glory, and a host of other words, concepts, and symbols that evoke the beautiful throughout John's poetry and prose. One should also keep in mind that, seen from the perspective of one living in love with God, the dark night is a "night more lovely than the dawn." Even this night becomes beautiful from that vantage point.

John's passionate concern for beauty reminds us to take seriously Beauty as a name for God, a God with a compelling presence in the world. Vatican II's passing reference to "God's boundless beauty"[101] must not become a throwaway line.[43] Preachers, liturgists, religious educators, pastoral ministers, and theologians cannot afford to neglect the beauty of creation nor the ultimate source of that beauty. Hans Urs von Balthasar and others have signaled the need to give proper attention to beauty. Note that, in von Balthasar's exposition of a theological aesthetics, John of the Cross is a major resource.[44] Moreover, other signs of the times, like ecological sensitivity, require us to share from the Christian tradition its many resources for a retrieval of beauty. Christianity will not be all that it can be until it becomes more contemplative, better able to contemplate God's beauty, the beauty of creation, and the sacramental relationship between the two: "the shadow that the lamp of God's beauty casts over the soul will be another beauty according to the measure and property of God's beauty." (F.3.14).[45] Were Plato around in our day, the Athenian would be shocked that Christians pay so little attention to the religious significance of eros, desire, and beauty.

The recovery of beauty in Christian culture can have far-reaching effects for spirituality and, I would say, for the enhancement of

Prayer
to
St. Odilia

O God, Who in Your Kindness
did give us St. Odilia
Virgin and Martyr, as the
Protectress of the Order
of the Holy Cross and
the Patroness of the eyes
and afflicted, grant us
we humbly beseech You
to be protected, through her
intercession, from the darkness
of ignorance and sin and to
be cured from the blindness
of the eyes and other bodily
infirmities. Through Him,
Who is the Light and Life
of the World, Jesus Christ,
Your Son, Our Lord. Amen

Courtesy of
NATIONAL SHRINE OF ST. ODILIA
ONAMIA, MINNESOTA 56359

Christian ethics where beauty would act as a revelation of the good and a powerful attraction for this good. John of the Cross's work is one of many resources for laying the foundations of a theology of delight that would restore greater joy and celebration to the Christian life. The mystical tradition, with its fascination for the beauty of God, has much to offer an age looking for a way out of aimlessness. As Noel Dermot O'Donoghue has written, "there is no such thing as a mystic who is a bore."[46] But, portrayals of mysticism often are abstract, unrelated to ordinary life, and even boring. Attention to the theme of beauty in John of the Cross and other mystics can act as a corrective to a tendency to the dull that occurs too often in religion.

This essay has examined the connection between dark night or suffering and beauty.[47] But, there is another relationship that emerges from this study of beauty in John of the Cross. The connection between beauty and love is not articulated often enough in spirituality. John of the Cross's description of the journey to God ends with the human person living in union with God through love. Love is what life is all about for John: "When evening comes, you will be examined in love" (S.60).[48] It is in loving union with God that one fully encounters Beauty. The connection between love and beauty has deep roots in the Christian tradition. Gregory the Great thought that "the human person was created to contemplate the Creator so that he might always seek his beauty and dwell in the solemnity of his love."[49] "The good and the beautiful are lovable to all," says Thomas Aquinas, "hence, everyone loves the beautiful."[50]

Before this essay concludes, I must face the perennial issue that John of the Cross raises for every reader. In the context of this chapter, the problem is this: the full repossession of Beauty and beauty is delayed until one passes through the dark night of the spirit and reaches loving union with God. Indeed, John keeps an eschatological eye on the final goal. God is our destiny, insists John. All else falls into place when we love the Lord our God with all our heart, all our soul, all

our mind, and all our strength.[51] Is that elitism? Or shall we take
John at his word that Scripture is the source of his teachings and
his guide in all things "since the Holy Spirit speaks to us through
it" (A. prologue.2)? Is not his radical call to liberation from all that
is not God merely a mystic's reading of the Gospel imperative to
love God with the whole heart? John like other poets and prophets
does not try to say everything. He does not qualify every statement.
He says only as much as he seeks to communicate. He dares not
dilute his message. For him the full restoration of the human capacity
to love God and to see the beauty of God and creation comes only
through loving union and only completely in "beatific transformation"
(CB.39.14).

Taken on its own without qualifiers, John's single-minded vision
of human destiny is the Gospel message. However, the necessary task
of interpreting John's message requires that we note that his own
journey to God had recurring glimpses of divine and human beauty
not yet made full through union with God. Recall that he reports that
few pass through the dark night of the spirit. In this life these, few
come to the full repossession of the capacity for beauty. John of the
Cross's love of beauty, the beauty of his poetry, and his other artistic
gifts give us a context for interpretation. While he wants us to keep
our eyes always on God, to become free of disordered attachments,
to give ourselves wholly to the search for God, John of the Cross
is a realist who knows the depths of human weakness as well as
he knows the power of God's grace. He knows few can make
the whole journey to God in this life, but that is no reason not to
journey, not to enjoy the glimpses of beauty that break into one's
life as one does all that is in one. John remains a poet and prophet
who directs the "eye of the soul" (F.3.71) to Beauty as the destiny
of the human community created in the image and likeness of God.[52]

Notes

1. "Spiritual Canticle" (B) 36. Kieran Kavanaugh and Otilio Rodriquez trans.,*The Collected Works of St. John of the Cross,* rev. ed. (Washington, DC: ICS Publications, 1991); Juan de la Cruz, *Obras completas,* ed. Eulogio Pacho (Burgos: Editorial Monte Carmelo, 1990). The poetry of John of the Cross in this essay is in quotation marks; commentaries are in italics. The author is grateful for the sabbatical time awarded by Saint Mary's College and for the Senior Fellowship in the Lilly Fellows Program in the Humanities and the Arts at Valparaiso University, which made possible the research and writing of this essay whose first steps occurred in the author's workshop at the 1994 summer seminar of the Carmelite Forum, Saint Mary's College. My thanks to Dr. R. Corby Hovis who patiently solved some computer glitches during the composition of this essay.

2. Hans Urs von Balthasar, *The Glory of the Lord: A Theological Aesthetics,* vol. 1, *Seeing the Form,* trans. E. Leiva-Merikakis (San Francisco: Ignatius Press; New York: Crossroad, 1982), 125. Henceforth: *Seeing the Form*; see also von Balthasar, "St. John of the Cross," *The Glory of the Lord: A Theological Aesthetics,* vol.3, *Studies in Theological Style: Lay Styles* (San Francisco: Ignatius Press, 1986), 105–71. For sensitive and incisive reviews of Balthasar's project, see Louis Dupré, *Religion and Literature* 19 (1987): 67–81 and *Theological Studies* 49 (1991): 299–318.

3. *Summa Theologiae* I.5.4; I-II.27.1.

4. *Summa Theologiae* I.13.11. See Armand Maurer, *About Beauty: A Thomistic Interpretation* (Houston, TX: Center for Thomistic Studies, 1983), 115 and passim. For the philosophical and theological climate at the University of Salamanca when John of the Cross was a student there (1564–8) see *Juan de la Cruz: Espíritu de Llama,* ed. Otger Steggink (Rome and Kampen: Institutum Carmelitanum, 1991), 175–230, articles by Vincente Muñoz Delgado and Melquíades Andrés Martín.

5. Transcendental is used here as a universal characteristic of everything that exists. John of the Cross does not use the word *transcendental*, but he had to be aware of its scholastic use and its application to goodness, truth, and beauty. On beauty as a transcendental, see Maurer, index: transcendental. See also Umberto Eco, *The Aesthetics of Thomas Aquinas,* trans. Hugh Bredin (Cambridge, MA: Harvard University Press, 1988), chap. 2. For a critique of Balthasar's use of the term, see N. D. O'Donoghue, "Do We Get Beyond Plato? A Critical Appreciation of the Theological Aesthetics," *The Beauty of Christ: An Introduction to the Theology of Hans Urs von Balthasar,* ed. B. McGregor and T. Norris (Edinburgh: T&T Clark, 1994), 253–66.

6. "Beauty, Too, Seeks Surrender," *Selected Poetry of Jessica Powers,* ed. Regina Siegfried and Robert F. Morneau (Kansas City, MO: Sheed & Ward, 1989), 72.

7. See James A. Martin, *Beauty and Holiness: The Dialogue between Aesthetics and Religion* (Princeton, NJ: Princeton University Press, 1990); and Frank Burch Brown, *Religious Aesthetics: A Theological Study of Making and Meaning* (Princeton, NJ: Princeton University Press, 1989).

8. *Confessions*, trans. Henry Chadwick (New York: Oxford University Press, 1992) 10.xxvii.38.

9. Michel Florisoone, *Esthétique et Mystique; d'après Sainte Thérèse d'Avila et Saint Jean de la Croix* (Paris: Editions du Seuil, 1956), 161, citing Crisógono de Jesús, *San Juan de la Cruz; su obra científica y su obra literaria* II (Madrid and Avila, 1929), 56. I was unable to consult the latter book. See also José Camon Aznar, *Arte y Pensamiento en San Juan de la Cruz* (Madrid: Biblioteca de Autores Cristianos, 1972).

10. *Collected Works of St. John,* 751 (letter 16); 126 (A. 1.4.6).

11. Beauty (*hermosura*) appears 192 times; beautiful *(hermoso)* 40 times; to beautify (*hermosear*) 27 times in the writings of John of the Cross, including double versions of *Canticle* and *Flame* but not including variants. *Concordancias de las escritos de San Juan de la Cruz*, ed. J. L. Astigarraga, A. Borrell, F. J. Martín, and Martín de Lucas (Rome: Teresianum, 1990). See alphabetical entries for these words and also the *Tabla estadística*. The words cited in this note do not exhaust by far the place of beauty in the writings of John of the Cross.

12. *God Speaks in the Night: The Life, Times, and Teaching of St. John of the Cross*, trans. Kieran Kavanaugh (Washington, DC: ICS Publications, 1991), 146–9; 236–7; 210–1.

13. Crisógono de Jesús, *The Life of St. John of the Cross*, trans. Kathleen Pond (New York: Harper & Brothers), 131.

14. *Concordancias* 1432–3 (painting), 707, 749, 1777 (carving).

15. Richard P. Hardy, *Search for Nothing: The Life of John of the Cross* (New York: Crossroad, 1982), 14; Florisoone, 93.

16. *Spiritual Canticle* (B) 14/15.25; see *Concordancias,* 1237 (música).

17. *Collected Works of St. John,* 75; "Canticle" (A) 11; (B) 12. *Canticle* (B) 12.3.

18. "God's Grandeur," in *Poems and Prose of Gerard Manley Hopkins* (Baltimore, MD: Penguin, 1953), 27.

19. Crisógono, 165–7.

20. Jorge Guillén, "The Ineffable Language of Mysticism: San Juan de la Cruz," in *Language and Poetry: Some Poets of Spain* (Cambridge, MA: Harvard University Press, 1961), 79–80.

21. Dámaso Alonso, *La Poesia de San Juan de la Cruz*, 3d ed. (Madrid: Aquilar, 1958), 178. Only edition available to me.

22. *Acta Apostolicae Sedis* 85 (1993): 552–3. My thanks to Kevin Culligan for this reference.

23. *Ascent of Mount Carmel* comments on stanzas one and two of "Dark Night." *Dark Night* breaks off as it begins to comment on the third stanza of this poem. David Tracy's characterization of John's prose as lacking the disclosive and the dialectical quality of his poetry is too sweeping a statement. Even in John's prose there are, often enough, powerfully apt reflections of the poetic beauty of his poetry. See especially *The Spiritual Canticle* and *The Living Flame of Love*. David Tracy, *The Analogical*

Imagination: Christian Theology and the Culture of Pluralism (New York: Crossroad, 1981), 174.

24. Guillén, 82. John's other major poems are "The Spiritual Canticle" and "The Living Flame of Love."

25. Gerald Brenan, *St. John of the Cross: His Life and Poetry* (Cambridge, Eng.: Cambridge University Press, 1973), 103.

26. *Collected Works of St. John,* 50–1 and 358.

27. *Collected Works of St. John*, 51 and 359.

28. Ibid.

29. "Song of the soul that rejoices in knowing God through faith," *Collected Works*, 58–60.

30. "Canticle" (B), st. 36–40, *Collected Works of St. John*, 80. John had composed the first 31 stanzas of this poem while he was in prison at Toledo. *Collected Works of St. John*, 464.

31. *The Divine Names* 4.7–12,18–9; 5.3. *Pseudo-Dionysius. The Complete Works*, trans. Colm Luibheid (New York: Paulist Press, 1987).

32. *On the Song of Songs* II, *The Works of Bernard of Clairvaux*, vol. 3, trans. Kilian Walsh (Kalamazoo, MI: Cistercian Publications, 1976), sermon 45, 232–40; see also sermon 27.

33. See pp. 248.

34. "A gloss (with a spiritual meaning)," *Collected Works of St. John*, 71.

35. *Seeing the Form*, 125.

36. See H. Egan, "Christian Apophatic and Kataphatic Mysticisms," *Theological Studies* 39 (1978): 399–426.

37. George H. Tavard, *Poetry and Contemplation in St. John of the Cross* (Athens, OH: Ohio University, 1988), 125.

38. Breandán Leahy, "Theological Aesthetics," in *The Beauty of Christ*, 24.

39. The repeated mention of dark contemplation as the presence of God in this essay serves as an illustration of the argument made by Professor Bernard McGinn for considering mysticism principally under the theme of presence. Bernard McGinn, *The Foundations of Mysticism*, vol. 1 of *The Presence of God: A History of Western Christian Mysticism* (New York: Crossroad, 1991), xvii–xix.

40. John speaks here of spiritual marriage.

41. Keith J. Egan, "The Biblical Imagination of John of the Cross in *The Living Flame of Love*," in *Juan de la Cruz: Espíritu de Llama*, 518.

42. P. Deseille, "Gloire de Dieu," *Dictionnaire de Spiritualité* 6 (1967): 422.

43. *Constitution on the Sacred Liturgy*, n. 122.

44. *Laystyles*, 104–71 and passim in the various volumes of *The Glory of the Lord*.

45. Balthasar begins his study, *The Glory of the Lord*, with this quote. *Seeing the Form*, [8].

46. N. D. O'Donoghue, "The Mystical Imagination," *in Religious Imagination*, ed. James P. Mackey (Edinburgh: University Press, 1986), 197.

47. Suffering not connected with the dark night and the connection of this suffering with beauty must await examination at another time.

48. *Collected Works of St. John,* 90.

49. *Moralia* 8.18.34, cited by Bernard McGinn, *The Growth of Mysticism*, vol. 2 of *The Presence of God* (New York: Crossroad, 1994), 50.

50. *In Psalmos Davidis Expositio* 25.5, cited by Maurer 6:19, n. 1.

51. See Mark 12:30 and pars. See *Night* 2.11.4.

52. The author is aware that more work needs to be done on how best to appropriate John of the Cross's demands for complete detachment into the Christian spiritual life. The attempt to deal with the issue at the end of this essay is, at best, a provisional foray into the problem.

CONTEMPLATION IN "THE SPIRITUAL CANTICLE": THE PROGRAM OF SAINT JOHN OF THE CROSS

Ernest Larkin, O.Carm.
Kino Institute
Phoenix, Arizona

This chapter is the skeleton of a seminar, designed as a primer on Carmelite spirituality. The opening verses of John of the Cross's poem, "Spiritual Canticle," are used as the framework. The first fifteen stanzas of this poem allow us to formulate some basic programmatic themes of St. John of the Cross as well as call on St. Teresa of Avila for concrete applications in the area of contemplative prayer and human relationships.[1]

The Spiritual Canticle

The "Spiritual Canticle" is about divine union, "stanzas between the soul and the bridegroom." The first fifteen stanzas of the total forty of version B recapitulate the sweep of the journey in the scholastic categories or "ways" of purification, illumination, and union. John's didactic teaching is set in this developmental perspective, as is illustrated in the fifteen stanzas (CB.22.3).

267

The first five verses of the poem pertain to purification, specified in the commentary as "meditation and mortification;" verses 6–12 describe illumination or "the contemplative way," which analysis shows to be the state of contemplation and poverty of spirit or the wholesale renunciation of desires; the rest of the poem is about divine union under the symbols of spiritual betrothal and marriage, sampled in verses 13–5.[2]

In the first two ways or stages, there are both a positive and negative thrust: the move toward God in prayer and the dealing with obstacles through mortification and poverty of spirit. The code words, prayer and penance, sum up this dialectic. They are the two arms that reach up and embrace God and lead into the gratuitous crowning of the divine-human collaboration in the gift of mystical union with God and sacramental communion with all of creation.

John of the Cross's two-point program of prayer and penance might profitably be related to Bernard Lonergan's teaching on conversion. For Lonergan, the state of grace is the primordial gift of religious conversion defined as being in love with God and appropriated by ongoing self-transcendence on the several levels of consciousness.[3] The redeemed status of the child of God needs to be taken seriously and affirmed and owned through living out the transcendental imperatives: be attentive, be intelligent, be reasonable, and be loving. This process is intellectual and moral conversion and brings the religious conversion to completion.

John reduces the imperatives to prayer and penance. In their active or ascetical form, they are meditation and mortification; in their passive or mystical form, they are contemplation and poverty of spirit. In both forms, the basic double principle enunciated in ascetical language at the beginning of the *Ascent* (A.1.13.3–4) is being implemented. Here is the call to search out and make one's own the truth about Jesus Christ (st. 3) and to live by this knowledge through individual choices (mortification) or by the freedom of total renunciation (poverty of spirit) (st. 4). The beginner studies the life of Christ in order to put on the Lord Jesus Christ with the building blocks of one-by-one choices. The total renunciation envisioned in stanza 4 is the long-range goal, but it will be achieved only by contemplation. The challenge to act always in pure faith, hope, and love with no regard for one's own self-satisfaction (A.2–3) is a realistic possiblity only through the infused light and love of contemplation.

Poverty or nakedness of spirit, which goes by a rich series of names in John (see, e.g., F.3.34; A.2.7.5), is both the condition and fruit of contemplation. Human and divine elements work together in various combinations to achieve this state, which frees the person and maximizes the union with God in knowledge and love (CB.1.11).

The search for God is a life project, not just a prayer project; God is not found only in isolated acts of formal prayer and specific works of penance but in the total daily life of the person and the community. Thus the project of transformation embraces all the relationships of one's life. What is going on in human relationships is happening in one's prayer life and vice versa. This existential aspect is addressed in human community and ministry. There are thus four programmatic themes: prayer, penance, community, and ministry. These themes are summarized in this chapter, but they are also treated elsewhere in this volume at greater length.

Desire: Foundation for the Journey

The poem opens with a statement of intense desire for the beloved. The life situation of the author at the time of composition was the painful experience of the Toledo prison that mirrored interior desolation. This suffering was the prelude to the mystical exaltation that takes up the major part of the poem.

The desolation describes the interval between the two dark nights and the spiritual betrothal and marriage. The purified soul has entered the "deep caverns of feeling" but has not yet received the full communication of God in mystical union (F.3.l8). There is the experience of the infinite emptiness of the human spirit and the felt absence of the only Reality that can fill this cavity. The desire for God is at a fever pitch, the pain overwhelming.

Some degree of this desire for God is at the root of every spiritual journey. Experientially, the condition may be embryonic, only partially recognized, or, as in the present instance, the love of God may have been tenderly and resolutely cultivated. In both cases, the point of departure is the orientation to God celebrated in the famous words of St. Augustine: "You have made us for your self, O Lord, and our hearts are restless till they rest in you."[4]

The yearning for God lies dormant in many people, buried under the distractions and preoccupations of life. It needs to be brought into consciousness and fostered and nurtured by prayer and penance. Original sin, according to the Greek Orthodox theologian Alexander Schmeman, is precisely the blunting of this desire for God and the loss of true sacramental communion with creation.[5] Personal sin adds to this debility (Rom 5:12).

The sanjuanist project makes the desire for God the organizing principle of life. The desire becomes a single-hearted search for God, and there is no room for any deviation or compromise or any lesser goal that is not integrated with the desire for the pure honor and glory of God. We are dealing with a keen sense of God's transcendence and the will to fit one's life into God rather than fit God into one's life.

A new beginning starts the journey. A new burst of love for Christ gives the energy to rise above the pleasure principle, which to this point has been a large factor in the person's life. Personal pleasure is no longer the issue. The "new and better love" of the heavenly bridegroom (A.1.14.2), further strengthened by "longings of love," gives a new focus to life. This love is the human response to God's prior love (1Jn 4:10; Rom 5:5; Gal 4.9) and fuels the "urgent longings" ("Dark Night") that move the person to nakedness of spirit and transformation in Christ.[6]

This second conversion is more than the dramatic experience of "baptism in the Spirit" or the good resolutions in a cursillo or a retreat. It is the intention to pursue the total commitment of *The Ascent,* chapter 13. "Have a habitual desire to imitate Christ in all your deeds by bringing your life into conformity with his" (A.1.13.3). The real challenge is to implement this proposal by fidelity to ongoing graces. Fidelity is the project of the spiritual life.

The desire for God puts feeling and psychic energy at the service of the love of God. The desire itself is an act of loving faith, that is, an act of understanding and will in response to God's offer of God's very self. Faith engages the feelings but not in any one particular way; both positive and negative feelings are dealt with. Faith is the measure and the only point of contact, encounter, and reception of God. John expresses this truth by saying that faith is the only proximate means of union with God; all other modes of relating are at best remote means and need to be subsumed in faith (A.2.4.5).

The candidates for this journey, whether charismatics like those who flourished in sixteenth-century Spain (N.1.1.3) or nondemonstrative practioners of a "wintery" piety (Karl Rahner), are beginners who have not yet set their faces toward Jerusalem, persons who are under the false impression that they can serve both God and mammon. To both groups John offers a spirituality of substance (A.prologue. 8) in place of a fatally flawed consumerist approach (see A.3.19). Self-serving spiritualities cannot adequately dispose of egoism; they leave the "I" outside the full redemption of grace, and hence they cannot reach the nakedness of spirit that is needed for divine union.

Popular spirituality often betrays this deep truth of the Gospel. It often confuses attractive emotional experiences, such as personal fulfillment, excitement, adventure, and enthusiasm, with authentic spirituality. These are all human goods indeed, but only if they are pursued in their truth (A.3.20.2) with the "eye of love" that is faith. As personal satisfactions unconnected with the larger picture of the love of God, they are competitors and hazards and need to be renounced; in this sense, the cost of divine union is "not less than everything" (T. S. Eliot). The reward is the "hundredfold," the repossession of a fully human life organized around faith. Divine fullness and human emptiness are coextensive and mutually inclusive (C.7.2.7).

Beginners by definition are engaged in the balancing act of living by faith and "doing one's own thing" at one and the same time. They endeavor to sugarcoat their faith. This makes for ambivalence. Their choices are partly for God, partly for themselves. A new strategy is needed, the direct route of seeking only God's will, whatever the fallout. This way leads to contemplation, in which the faith motivation subsumes (i.e., ordering but not destroying) all other considerations. This radical stance leads one into the laborious and painful dark night of sense and spirit that is the only way to the summit of the "Mount of Perfection." Out of this process and concomitant with it, the new being in Christ emerges, whose entire personality orchestrates the praise and service of God and whose human life is filled with the presence of God.

Holiness in the Carmelite scheme is eminently incarnational. For all its emphasis on the transcendence of God, of getting beyond the merely human in order to live the divine life of the theological virtues, Carmelite spirituality embraces everything in creation, especially human values like persons and community and the earth itself, always from the perspective of their rootedness in God. John of the Cross goes to the heart of reality and finds there the living presence of God. This center holds everything together and makes the human and the earthy the sacrament of God. The mystical is the root of the sacramental.

The Process of Growth

The poem is a human love story; the bride (the soul) seeking and ultimately attaining her beloved (Christ) in the intimacy of the spiritual marriage. The imagery is pastoral as well as nuptial. The bride is the dove and the bridegroom the stag. In the opening verse, the stag, usually the wounded one in this mythology, inflicts the wound in the dove. Later, it becomes clear that the stag too is wounded and healed through the mutuality of their love (st. 13). Both parties thus participate in the same suffering and triumph, as theologians today point out.[7] What is the process of healing and perfecting in the rest of the stanzas? What must the bride do or suffer to possess her lost spouse? The answer is the saga of every love story.

One such love story can serve as an interpretive key to these stanzas. Some years ago, I discovered a grafitti message on the wall of a viaduct near a large university in Chicago. The message from Bob to Sandy speaks for itself and is recorded here without any editing or correction:

> Sandy,
> Time keep's passen away, my love; I need you to
> stop the pain. The day we diparted I felt it
> commin: I new I would go insane. The days are
> short and the nights are long because I need you
> to be close to me. It's your love and
> understanding girl that really set me free.
> WHERE ARE YOU?   BOB

Bob's distraught state is the mystic's in a minor key. In both cases, physical presence is desired. The question is what must Bob do to make this happen? Three things: he must seek out the beloved; he must endure the suffering; he must wait in hope for the love to return. The agenda of the God-seeker is no different.

The first task is the active search for God. We seek out God in our prayer, work, relationships, and human experiences. These human efforts enclose moments of encounter, but the encounter is distant and partial, since it is buried in complex human processing. *Lectio Divina* is a good example. The first three acts of reading, meditating, and praying are the search, and the encounter is the fourth step of contemplation. John specifies this outcome in meditation as "morsels of spirituality," dribs and drabs of insight and love received in faith. These are moments of contemplation.[8] The same process is present in the other activities of life. The mortification is the follow-up, acting out the truth in loving choices for God and rejecting what is not of God.

Our second task is to suffer the frustration and emptiness of human limits when God is no longer available through the imagination and euphoric feelings. The reality of God is too much for the human container. God is too large for human thoughts. This time of dry faith comes across as the experience of nothing. God is lost, and the seeker grieves and pines for the absent beloved. This is the salutary but painful experience of contemplation, which heals and purifies the desire for God.

Contemplation has different degrees of intensity. Sometimes it will be like the morsels of the first stage; at other times, it will be recognized for itself, at least by St. John of the Cross's three signs —loss of pleasures, inability to meditate discursively, and painful longing for God. In either case, the call is to be faithful to the practice of the Christian life, especially to prayer in spite of the aridity and to hope in spite of the anxiety and depression. One chooses what is right because it is right, whatever the self-doubt or troubled state of soul that looks in vain for human reassurance. This state is common among serious searchers after holiness. God is actually very active at this time forming the mind and heart of the believer in subtle ways. Only a great master of the spiritual life like John of the Cross could detect the hand of God in this experience.

Commentary on the Stanzas

Stanza 1 is the groan of desire, and stanzas 2 and 3 the expression of intent. Shepherds are enlisted to look for the beloved in the mountain heights (his natural habitat?) and convey the message that the bride is dying down below (st. 2). The bride asserts that she will go anywhere, take any means, brook any obstacle in the pursuit (st. 3). Stanzas 4 and 5 spell out the strategy of meditation.

The woods and thickets, forests and meadows, flowers and trees, all the beauties of nature are canvased for the presence of the beloved. These natural phenomena are easily expanded to the places where people find God in their lives: liturgy, family, social activism, pastoral ministry. Everything bears the stamp of the divine presence; everything can reveal the living God and be the occasion of love and praise.

But external indicators are only remote means of communication. Meditation and mortification uncover aspects of the truth or of the good or of beauty; they will not reveal Truth and Goodness and Beauty itself. The mind and imagination and feelings remain on the outside of things; they touch the rind that encloses the fruit (A.2.17.5). The inside is the divine presence itself, touched only by faith and the gift of contemplation, and this is the subject of stanzas 6–12.

Deep love will not settle for letters or pictures of the one loved. It wants physical presence. The seven verses play on this theme: "No more messengers" (st. 6). No more reports; they pale before the "I-don't-know-what" of contemplation (st. 7). The encounter now highlights the "otherness" of the other, giving a personal knowledge that is shrouded in darkness. Contemplation is always inexpressible, untranslatable, since it moves on a deeper plane than representations. In the present case, the dissonance between Creator and creature is overwhelming. More preparation of the receiving subject is needed before there is blissful congruence. Now there is only presence in absence.

Different forms of this purifying contemplative experience are a staple in the spiritual lives of holy people. In stanza 8, the beloved is out of reach, the heart having given itself away to the absent lover. There is only frustration and pain (st. 9). In the darkness, the bride emits a mournful cry to see what she senses to be present (st. 10).

Sight and eyes become the focus of this and the next two verses. The eyes are the windows of the soul; lovers yearn to look into each other's eyes. In a real sense, the eyes are the other person; they reveal the other (st. 11). So the bride asks to look into the eyes of the beloved, which eyes, his eyes, are already "imprinted deep within [her own] heart" (st. 12). His eyes are already part of her own being, a sign that transformation of one person into the other is already taking place. The realism of the union indicates not merely functional but ontological identification. The two actors in the drama are now one as eyes meet eyes, and the look causes the flight of the spirit, the ecstasy that Teresa connects with the sixth dwelling places (C.6.5.1). Henceforth, the soul will look out on the world with the eyes of God.

Stanzas 14 and 15 describe this experience. Union with God brings sacramental communion with the universe. The beloved is all the beauties of creation, including persons and community and personalist realities like "the supper that refreshes and deepens love" (st. 15). The Eucharist interprets beautifully this last metaphor.

Community, Creation, Ministry

The genius of Carmelite spirituality is interiority, not for its own sake, but as the source and center of human life. The experience of God founds authentic human community and motivates ministry. The three themes of prayer, community, and ministry along with penance as the essential condition for interior growth make up the program of "apostolic life" in the primitive church in Jerusalem (Acts 2:42–7; 4:32–5); this *vita apostolica* is the model for the religious life of Carmelites, especially from 1247 onward.

This model illustrates the unity of the love of God and love of persons of the New Testament, where God's love is described as descending from above and fanning out in horizontal relationships. Teresa and John maintain this perspective. Even the call to a life of undisturbed contemplation in solitude, which John justifies for the purified soul, is in service to the church and humanity (CB.29.2). Teresa points out that the expected fruit of prayer life is ministry both inside and outside the local community (C.7.4.6, 9, 12, 14–5). The life of contemplation, moreover, generates a prophetic stance, since union with God equips one to speak for God on behalf of deeply loved people in their concrete needs.

Prayer and community move on the same level of spiritual development. The embracing of the world in stanzas 14 and 15 is the living out of mystical union. Verses 4 and 5 represent an earlier spiritual stage in which reflection and reasoning make the connections with God. The contemplative gaze of stanzas 14 and 15 intuits God and the world together in one simple act and beyond duality, though without loss to the autonomy and distinction of God and creation.

The woods and thickets in the earlier stanzas are signs of God's beauty, which need to be connected by reflection with the One Signified. They become symbols of the Reality, when they are transparent of the divine presence and are seen in God in one intuitive act. The symbol contains and evokes the Reality. The mystic looks out on the world as it really is and experiences the *pan-en-theism* of the universe. God is in all and all is in God. Creation is the mirror of God. So my Beloved is the mountains, is my family, my world, my life. This is the prayer of the enamoured soul (S. 27).

The transition from sign to symbol is the movement from meditation to contemplation. It is the passage from the "sensible-spiritual love" to the "spiritual love" of *The Way of Perfection* (chaps. 4–7). The former is a two-sourced love, a combination of self-interest (e.g., natural attraction, blood relationship) and faith, with the two motivations only imperfectly integrated. The more perfect, single-sourced love called "spiritual love" comes out of a purified faith and love and goes to the deepest center of the other perceived in faith.

This is contemplative love. The distinction corresponds exactly to Teresa's teaching on "contentos" or sensible consolations that characterize active, self-directed prayer and "gustos" or spiritual delights, which are mystical graces in contemplative prayer (C.4.1.4). There is thus perfect correlation between what goes on in one's relation to God and in human relationships. In these descriptions, Teresa is putting into clear images the same teaching we have been expounding from John of the Cross. The correlation between prayer and life in the world allows us to transpose the teachings on either topic from one sector to another. There is profound unity in all the relationships of one's life.

The different levels of community and ministry also correspond to the growth in prayer. The same principles are at work, the same stages of development, the same conditions for progress, and the same outcomes. Community and ministry have their own dark nights: natural attraction gives way to purifying struggles to be faithful when the excitement dies out and impasse is reached; only gradually is there perfect integration of the human and divine in these areas. For the Carmelite mystics, the dynamo for human development and for building human community in all its phases is the inner life of grace. This gift is at the core of each person, and it touches the cosmic Christ at the heart of the universe. The Carmelite saints teach their disciples how to uncover this ultimate meaning of creation. Teresa and John witness to the primacy of the spiritual in human affairs, without denying the role of other approaches and disciplines for human advancement. Their perspective and their expertise is the divine presence at work in the world.

Conclusion

Contemplation is at the center of things. This teaching is the important legacy of the Carmelite tradition. Personal union with God is not only the ultimate goal of human existence, but the unifying center of a humanized world. The three ways of the spiritual life, expounded in the opening verses of the "Spiritual Canticle," are a construct that lays out the topography of the journey. They help us plot the course to the summit of Mount Carmel.

Notes

1. The material from St. Teresa draws on two previous studies by the present author, the first on "Centering Prayer in St. Teresa of Avila," *Carmelite Studies,* ed. John Sullivan, O.C.D. (Washington, DC: ICS Publication, 1984) 3:191–211, and the second on "Human Relationships in St. Teresa of Avila," *The Land of Carmel: Essays in Honor of Joachim Smet, O.Carm.,* ed. Paul Chandler and Keith J. Egan (Rome: Institutum Carmelitanum, 1991), 285–97.

2. These themes have been developed in my article, "The Prayer Journey of St. John of the Cross," in *Juan de la Cruz: Espiritu de Llama* ed. Otger Steggink, O.Carm. (Rome: Institutum Carmelitanum. 1991).

3. *Method in Theology* (New York: Herder & Herder, 1972), 104–112. For an excellent commentary see Vernon Gregson, *Lonergan. Spirituality, and the Meeting of Religions* (Lanham, MD: University Press of America, 1985), 16–21; 29-36; 38–51.

4. *Confessions,* trans. Henry Chadwick (Oxford: Oxford University Press, 1991), l.i.1. (p. 3).

5. *For the Life of the World* (Crestwood, NY: St. Vladimir Seminary, 1973), 16.

6. For texts on God's prior love for the person see Richard P. Hardy, "Embodied Love in John of the Cross," in *Carmelite Studies VI: St. John of the Cross,* ed. Steven Payne, O.C.D. (Washington, DC: ICS Publications, 1992), 141–161.

7. Elizabeth A. Johnson, CSJ, "Between the Times: Religious Life and the Postmodern Experience of God," *Review for Religious* 53 (1994): 6–28, esp. 20–4; Sandra Schneiders, IHM, "Contemporary Religious Life: Death or Transformation," in *Religious Life, the Challenge of Tomorrow,* ed. Cassian J. Yuhaus, CP (New York: Paulist, 1994), 9–34.

8. These moments are infused contemplation if one utilizes the distinctions of Karl Rahner's regarding mystical experiences. For Rahner, all contemplation, even the mysticism of everyday life, is infused. His point of view was developed by the present author in a seminar at the bicentennial of the Baltimore Carmel in 1990. The

presentation was recorded and published in audiocassette under the title, "Contemplation in Today's World," by Credence Cassettes (Kansas City, MO: National Catholic Reporter, 1990). Interpreting John with Rahner's viewpoints allows for variations in the passive dark night of the senses. For a different evaluation see James Arraz's audio-tape, "Are There Really Contemplatives Today?" (Chiloquin, OR: Inner Growth Books, 1988).

TRANSFORMATION IN WISDOM: THE SUBVERSIVE CHARACTER AND EDUCATIVE POWER OF SOPHIA IN CONTEMPLATION

Constance FitzGerald, O.C.D.
Carmelite Monastery
Baltimore, Maryland

Introduction

We need a spirituality for our time, an in-between time some have called it. Who is the God who will accompany us, if, as some suggest, there looms on the horizon for the inhabitants of this earth an era demanding a change of consciousness more radical than we can imagine?[1] Or what kind of spirituality will address our experience if, indeed, the tremendous emergence of the feminine in culture, visible in so many different ways, truly heralds the end of the fundamental masculine dominance of the "Western mind," as Richard Tarnas proposes.[2] Some suggest that it is at great transitions such as this, when there are such insoluble problems, such a radical breakdown of structures, and so many confusing questions, that a new religious tradition rises up.[3]

Must we begin again then or can we build a new conceptual house for faith by gathering up what Ray Hart calls "the debris" around us and using it to make something new?[4] More precisely, are the traditions and language of mysticism, muted and suspect in the public life for centuries and yet coming to life again in our time, capable of giving radical direction to our search for a meaningful God and a new way of living in the universe?[5] Can the mystical or contemplative tradition, specifically the teaching of a sixteenth-century *man*, John of the Cross, ground us in our passage from one age to another and deal with our questions about God, about the earth, and about the universe? The experience of the western mystics is, undoubtedly, confined in part by the language and culture of western civilization and particularly of their own specific time in history. But if we decode their contemplative teaching, will it point us into the future and push us to envision and even experience a new mysticism, truly new and appropriate to our time and yet in continuity with our past?[6]

If, as I continue to believe, mystics live on the frontiers of human consciousness and address us from the farthest edges of the human spirit, we should not be surprised to find in the mysticism of John of the Cross some extremely important and yet hitherto undecoded clues about a God image capable of supporting our crossing into a new era of life on our planet earth. This raises the specific question of whether the teaching of John of the Cross, which delineates with such clarity the critical, central function of "Divine Wisdom" in human transformation and communion with God, validates and even enlarges upon the extensive research and theological investigations of feminist thinkers and theologians regarding the feminine God gestalt, Sophia?

These questions and assumptions motivate this study of wisdom in John of the Cross, which will examine, first of all, the transformation of the person in Wisdom (Sophia), a transformation of human desire and consciousness that is in its unfolding a process of education for contemplation; second, the subversive and therefore emanciptory character of the experience of Sophia in contemplation; third, what this experience and process of transformation suggests regarding the feminine God image Sophia; fourth, what implications this has regarding education for contemplation.[7] Furthermore, because the members of the Carmelite Forum have been attempting to guide students in reading and interpreting the classic Carmelite texts, I will attempt to include in this interpretation of John of the Cross actual texts from his writings as an integral part of this essay in the hope that these texts will be educative rather than tedious and will not interrupt the flow of my thought. It is my desire that others will grasp and develop implications from this study of Divine Wisdom in John of the Cross, if indeed there are any implications of value to contemporary spirituality, which I am only able to hint at or may not even see.

I will frequently be using Sophia instead of Wisdom because feminists prefer the Greek *sophia,* which is *chokmah* in Hebrew and *sapientia* in Latin—all feminine grammatical gender. This in itself is not significant inasmuch as feminine grammatical gender cannot be equated with actual gender. Nevertheless, the biblical depiction of wisdom in pre-Christian Judaism is invariably female, suggesting to us a person rather than a concept or an attribute. Biblical wisdom is treated, not as an it, but as a summoning "I": sister, mother, spouse, female beloved, teacher, chef and hostess, preacher, judge, liberator, establisher of justice, and numerous other female roles.[8]

Influenced by feminist scholars, I have been working for a number of years with wisdom in John of the Cross. As I have searched and analyzed his many wisdom texts and tried to interface them with contemporary studies and the tradition of wisdom in Jewish theology and in the New Testament,[9] I have discovered considerable potential for spirituality today.

I now find myself asking if possibly this *is* the **time**, the **age**, for Sophia: God experienced in feminine categories from the ground up. Until now, the masculinity of the Western intellectual and spiritual tradition has been pervasive and fundamental as has been the mas-

culinity of the Western man's [*sic*] God.[10] Perhaps in a time when
this long dominant masculinity has become so apparent to us and when
the feminine principle is welling up with such powerful energy, Sophia
is a God image capable of moving with humanity into the next
evolutionary era when the universe will be experienced not as a
collection of objects for human use and mastery but rather as an
intimate, interconnected, and diverse communion of subjects.[11] If "the
evolutionary imperative for the masculine is to see through and
overcome its hubris and one-sidedness . . . [and] to choose [to
transcend itself and] enter into a fundamentally new relationship of
mutuality with the feminine in all its forms,"[12] then this embrace of
the feminine may well reveal Sophia-God.[13]

    This means the experience of Wisdom in transformation or
contemplation according to John of the Cross is so subversive it could
change the content of our theological discourse, as Elizabeth Johnson
suggests in her groundbreaking, scholarly study, *She Who Is*. Initially,
when I hinted at the subversive character of Sophia, it was because
I thought transformation in Wisdom radically changed desire, consciousness, and, ultimately, behavior, personal and societal. Now, I
realize the experience of Sophia may be subversive, above all, because
it affects how we understand the very nature of God, and our
understanding of God is what affects the character and quality of
our human living.

    For John of the Cross, the experience of contemplative union
reveals and supports an experience of God as Sophia. He moved in
the milieu of Sophia-Wisdom from the beginning of *The Ascent of
Mount Carmel* to the end of *The Living Flame of Love* and kept
the tradition of Sophia alive, waiting there for our discovery. When
the tradition of contemplation or mysticism was finally decisively
muffled by the condemnation of quietism in 1699, ending two centuries
of struggle and debate, so, perhaps, was the opportunity to develop
this strong experience of Sophia.[14] In fact, the marginalizing of the

language of mysticism has a symbolic affinity not only with the disparagement of Sophia but also with the marginalization of women and the neglect of the Spirit. Have no doubt that the muting of contemplation was/is directly related to the place of women in society, the role of conscience in religion and politics, the fear of direct inspiration by the Spirit, and the transformative and therefore seditious character of contemplative prayer.[15]

John of the Cross and Wisdom

To understand the contemporary significance of Sophia and attempt to interpret adequately the meaning of wisdom in John of the Cross, one has to have some knowledge of the complex background and extensive research related to wisdom. In the light of contemporary scholarship, particularly feminist studies, one has to examine not only possible influences on John from pre-Christian Judaism and the New Testament, but also from early Church writers and the mystical tradition as it developed through the centuries with particular emphasis on Christology and Trinitarian theology. One cannot make even a cursory study of these ancient and contemporary sources without coming up with questions that both challenge and confuse the religious imagination.

Mindful of this very complex backdrop and aware of the limitations of my own knowledge, I will attempt to contribute to contemporary studies of Wisdom or Sophia by concentrating on John of the Cross. When one begins to examine his major writings, one is awed by the extent and significance of the presence of Sophia who appears absolutely fundamental to John's understanding and description of contemplative experience. Although at times wisdom seems to be either an attribute or even a gift of God, Wisdom is basically a way of naming and symbolizing God's very self. Wisdom is primarily "Divine Wisdom," and Divine Wisdom is identified with Jesus Christ, the Word, the Son of God. Moreover, the entire process of human transformation is seen in terms of Wisdom, as evidenced, for example, by John's description of "the subject of [the] stanzas" of the poem, "The Spiritual Canticle," as "mystical Wisdom which comes through love" (C.prologue. 2).[16]

Pre-Christian Judaism

Many contemporary scholars believe that the development and biblical depiction of the figure of Sophia in Jewish wisdom theology was influenced by an extrabiblical figure of a female deity. While some endorse the Mesopotamian goddess, Ishtar, or the Canaanite goddess of love, Astarte, others prefer the Egyptian goddess Ma'at who represented law, order, and justice. More attractive to many scholars, however, is the theory that the figure of Jewish Sophia has been greatly influenced by the Hellenized form of the Egyptian goddess Isis. Personified Wisdom was the response of orthodox Judaism to the threat of the Isis cult, which was experienced as a temptation to the Jews to doubt and even turn from their traditional faith. While defending monotheism, Jewish wisdom theology was not afraid of the goddess but rather transferred the characterisitics of mighty Isis to the figure of personified Wisdom in a creative effort to counteract the influence of this popular deity. Using goddess language and imagery drawn from wider religious thought and worship, they presented Jewish worshippers with the most attractive possible alternative to the cult and philosophies prevalent in the ancient Near East at the time.[17] Divine Sophia is therefore, according to Fiorenza, Israel's saving and gracious God "in the language and gestalt of the goddess." With the exception of Yahweh, Sophia was, Elizabeth Johnson concludes, the most carefully limned God image in pre-Christian Judaism, far more common and extensive than Word, Spirit, Torah, or Shekinah.[18]

It would be helpful to bear this development in mind if we are threatened with talk about a Sophia-God. The Jews did not sacrifice their belief in a monotheistic God; they brought to the fore a feminine God/dess metaphor important for their age and used it to speak of the God of Israel![19]

Later, the writers of the New Testament took this very God image, this figure of personified Wisdom, and applied it to Jesus to show his continuity with the God of Israel in a manner that influenced the whole development of the doctrine of the Incarnation. The way this figure of Wisdom appeared in the literature of pre-Christian Judaism affected Christology, tradition, and John of the Cross. The problem here is, of course, the intervening tradition and what sources regarding Sophia-Wisdom from this cumulative tradition influenced John's education and study and ultimately his contemplative experience and writings.[20]

John of the Cross and Sophia in the Old Testament

While how much John or his contemporaries knew about the origins of personified Wisdom in Jewish thought and theology could be the subject of an historical study, an analysis of his major writings reveals the radical influence of the wisdom texts of the Old Testament in shaping not only his understanding of Sophia but also his expression of religious experience.[21] Particularly important in John's writings for defining who Sophia is and what she does are the books of Proverbs (chap. 8) and Wisdom (chaps. 7–9), and to some extent Sirach, to which he repeatedly returns throughout his three major works.[22] From these sources, the specific view of Wisdom we find in these texts arises. To summarize very briefly:

1. Sophia has a divine origin, that is, Sophia is the spotless mirror of the power of God, the image of God's goodness, the brightness of the eternal light.

2. Sophia has a unique role in creation. God creates through Sophia.

3. Sophia moves and recreates, more active than all active things. She touches, enlivens, penetrates, and energizes everywhere. The touch of Wisdom is important.

4. Sophia calls to all to come to her, to choose her.

5. Sophia dwells on the earth and delights to be with humankind in the world making them friends of God.

6. Sophia works gently, with order and harmony, taking account of created capacity and progressive development.

7. Sophia is secret; she dwells in secret and has an affinity for darkness.

8. Sophia eats at a common table with humankind in this world.   She says, "Come eat my bread and drink the wine I have mixed for you."

9. Sophia is loving, nurturing, and compassionate. Sophia is, in fact, a Lover: "My Beloved to Me . . ."

10. Sophia is loving knowledge of God, both the teacher and what is learned. Sophia is on the side of continual learning.

Out of his own distinctive configuration of Jewish wisdom literature, which one would expect research in John of the Cross's writings to refine and make more precise over time, emerge some of the most basic principles of his teaching. It fashions an understanding of *who Jesus is*, who God is and how this God functions in the dynamic of human purification and transformation. It suggests the place of Sophia in human suffering and hints at how the beloved of Sophia sees the world and functions in it. I want to tease apart this configuration in what follows though not necessarily in the order I have enumerated them.

Sophia Dwells on Earth and Calls to All to Desire Her and Come to Her

John begins *The Ascent of Mount Carmel* by describing the journey to God as a dark night and the completion or goal of that journey through the darkness as *union with Divine Wisdom*:

> When this third night (God's communication to the spirit . . .) has
> passed, a union with the bride, who is the Sophia of God, then
> follows. (A.1.2.4)[23]

In actuality, Divine Sophia figures prominently throughout the first
book of *The Ascent*. She takes her stand on the heights, along the
highways of this world, at the very crossroads of the human enterprise,
calling the children of this earth to the path of transformation and
communion. She highlights human desire and pities those whose
primary focus of desire and meaning is askew. She challenges those
who are unfree, consumed by the possessive desire for what can
never completely satisfy. She calls them "little ones" because they
become as small as that which they crave, while the lasting affection
and reassurance they unconsciously search for in their choices are
present and available in Sophia. Therefore, Sophia says, "desire me":

> O people, I cry to you, my voice is directed to all that live. Be
> attentive, little ones, to cunning and sagacity; and you ignorant, be
> careful. Listen, because I speak of great things. Riches and glory are
> mine, high riches and justice. The fruit you will find in me is better
> than gold and precious stones; and my generations . . . are better
> than choice silver. I walk along the ways of justice, in the midst of
> the paths of judgement, to enrich those who love me and fill their
> treasures completely. [Prv. 8.4–6; 18–21]. (A.1.4.8)

It is important to note at this point that at the beginning of *The Ascent*,
when John begins to set in place his core teaching on the education
of human desire, he uses specifically "Sophia" texts showing some
of the same connections between the Sophia of the Old Testament
and Sophia-Jesus in the New Testament that contemporary scholars
are indicating.[24]

The presence of Jewish Sophia with humankind (Prv 8:31; Wis
24:1–12) provides the context for one of John's most basic and yet
most misunderstood and difficult principles, one that appears to be

at odds with his mystical experience of the harmonious presence of Sophia in all of creation. At first reading, the text seems to insist that only God is worthy of our desire and that this earth, people, human ability, and human love are worthless, nothing. Yet, it must be carefully noted that it is *only in comparison with* Divine Wisdom that they pale into insignificance; *only when preferred* to Sophia do they become idols, addictive, and obsessive in character.[25]

> Oh, if people but knew what a treasure of divine light this blindness caused by our affections and [desires] deprives them of. . . . They must not rely on their sharp intellects or upon their gifts received from God as to believe that their attachments or [desires] will not blind, darken, and cause them to grow gradually worse . . . . Solomon [wise man] . . . although in the beginning he was truly restrained, *this rush after his desires*, and the failure to deny them gradually blinded and darkened his intellect so that finally *the powerful light of God's Wisdom was extinguished.* (A.1.8.6)

For John of the Cross, desire has a central and defining role in our lives. He assumes, first of all, that we are inescapably driven and motivated by our desires; secondly, if our desires are addictive and unfree, they weaken, weary, torment, blind, and demean us; and thirdly, the desire for Divine Wisdom (who is Jesus Christ) has to become greater than the desire for everyone and everything else that gives us pleasure.

> A love of pleasure, and attachment to it, usually fires the will toward the enjoyment of things that give pleasure. A more intense enkindling of another, better love (love of the soul's Bridegroom) is necessary for the vanquishing of the [desires] and the denial of this pleasure. (A.1.14.2)

What is indicated here is a decisive, preferential choice of the heart for God,[26] a conscious shift in one's focus of meaning, which ever so slowly redirects and claims desire. The love of Divine Wisdom as it grows and develops in life experience actually *educates human desire*, that is, effects a gradual transference of desire to Jesus Christ, Beloved Sophia! John writes with profound insight about the agony and ecstacy of the journey of human desire and explains for us what kind of affective education is carried on by Divine Sophia over a lifetime. Contemplation, which is the concern of this volume, comes by the very gradual adherence of our desire to God, which truly illuminates human perception and understanding. *We educate people to contemplation, therefore, by consciously guiding the complex education of human desire as it is being influenced and effected by Beloved Sophia in each one's life situation.*

For it is Divine Sophia, herself, who sets the stage by her presence and invitation for the long and difficult life-passage, first of all, from a possessive, confining, unfree desire for pleasure, safety, and reassurance to a desire and passion for God transcending that consuming concern for oneself and one's own interests, where human desire is transformed and fulfilled in the deep communion of love; and secondly, from a myopic, self-centered, isolated, nonnurturing presence to others and to reality to a Wisdom surpassing the knowledge we learn and accumulate through education and culture.

As in *The Ascent*, so at the very beginning of the commentary on *The Spiritual Canticle*, in the context of an Old Testament wisdom text, we see the underlining of the cost and significance of the self-transcendence required to pursue the desire for Divine Sophia:

> Sophia is bright and never fades and is easily seen by them that love her, and found by them that seek her. She goes out before them that covet her that she might first show herself to them. Those who awake early in the morning to seek her shall not labor, but will find her seated at the door of their house [Wis. 6:13–5]. *This passage indicates that when the soul has departed from the house of her own will and the bed of her own satisfaction, she will find outside Divine Wisdom, the Son of God, her Spouse.* (C.3.3)

Those who decide to commit their lives to God frequently fail to realize that this very decision will activate an uncomfortable self-knowledge. Nevertheless, there is reason for encouragement when one realizes that *in the painful self-searching* that a choice for Divine Wisdom stimulates, content is being put into our relationship with Beloved Sophia and our desire for God is growing.[27] The deepening presence of Holy Wisdom pervading one's whole life and environment gradually educates desire and in that process eventually fulfills it. In other words, Wisdom is not only the teacher, but also what is learned, not only the educator of desire, but also the love perception and fulfillment itself!

Sophia Moves, Touches, Recreates, Energizes, Gently, Always with Order

A fundamental dynamic of this transformation of desire is inspired by the first verse of the eighth chapter of the Book of Wisdom. Understanding this dynamic allays some of our anxiety about purification. Even though Divine Wisdom is always active, re-creating, touching, energizing powerfully from one end of the earth to the other, and the all-pervading effectiveness of Wisdom in the world is reiterated again and again, still Sophia touches gently, with order, and with careful respect for the human maturation process.[28] Moreover, if we understand the human spirit as the crowning point of earth's evolution at the present time, or if, aware of the incalculable limitations of our knowledge of the mystery of the evolving universe, we yet dare, as some do, to consider the human spirit as the cosmos come to full consciousness, then in the gentle, energizing touch of Divine Sophia resides an equal, correlating respect for the gradual, evolutionary process of the earth.

This means that Wisdom moves from within the person and teaches through the human processes of knowing and loving, so that step-by-step over a lifetime, in the experience of human relationships and human love, in the experience of the created universe, of one's task in this world, and even of one's deepest self, human desire gathers strength and passion and moves toward God. In other words, we gradually see the dedication of all our desire or affectivity by a hunger for God. Divine Sophia is so at home on the pathways of this world and so delights in dwelling with the children of earth that a person grows and is transformed, not by a leap over or denial of life, not by suppression of desire, but through the experience of the sensual and sexual, the physical and material, through life and life's loves, through what one cherishes and what gives one delight, security, and support.[29] Sophia is so subtle and so patient, *so indwelling human experience*, that only looking back can one say: Sophia, the fashioner of all, taught me everything I know (A.3.2.12; Wis 7:22).[30]

Within this epistomological framework we are able to understand the progressive character of the schema of the nights: active night of sense, passive night of sense, active night of spirit, and passive night of spirit. The dark night is in actuality a *gradual* purification and transformation of desire and consciousness with a corresponding *developing* experience of Divine Sophia who is loving knowledge.

Sophia Creates with Harmony and Order

Contrary to what many readers initially believe about the mystic's feelings for the world, relationships, and human love, the true mystic is enthralled by the diversity and beauty, the unfailing harmony and interconnectedness of the entire creation. All this is the work of Sophia ("the Word") by whom they were created. Everyone and every living thing are clothed with the image of Sophia as we see in "The Spiritual Canticle" poem where the lovesick bride questions the created world:

> O woods and thickets,
> planted by the hand of my Beloved!

> O green meadow,
> coated, bright, with flowers,
> tell me, has he passed by you?

Creatures then respond:

> Pouring out a thousand graces,
> he passed these groves in haste;
> And having looked at them,
> with his image alone,
> clothed them in beauty. (C.4–5)

The commentary explains:

> Only the hand of God, her Beloved, was able to create this diversity
> and grandeur. . . . This reflection on creatures, this observing that
> they are things made by the very hand of God, her Beloved, *strongly*
> *awakens the soul to love [God].* (C.4.3)

Far from being an obstacle, delight and immersion in the wonder
of the universe propels desire on its way toward God. The genuine
mystic has frequently been prophetic in transcending the hierarchical
dualism[31] of his/her time in contemplative "knowing." In every living
thing, therefore, the mystic sees a *trace* of God's passing through
which one can track down God's *image* or presence in the world:[32]

> God created all things with remarkable ease and brevity, and in
> them left some trace of Who [God] is, not only in giving all things
> being from nothing, but even by endowing them with innumerable
> graces and qualities, making them beautiful in a wonderful order
> and unfailing dependence on one another. *All of this [God] did*
> *through [God's] own Sophia, the Word, [the] only begotten Son by*
> *Whom [God] created them.* (C. 5.1)

And she says "he passed" because creatures are like a trace of
God's passing. Through them one can track down [God's] grandeur,
might, wisdom, and other divine attributes. (C.5.3)[33]

The *image* of Jesus-Sophia, developmental and transformative in
character, is central to John's theology. Whenever we encounter "image"
(i.e., trace, sketch, imprinting, mirror) in his writings, we can be
certain we are in the sphere of wisdom Christology.[34] John of the
Cross follows St. Paul in teaching that this image is Jesus-Sophia
and that it is in Jesus-Sophia, the Son, the splendor of God's glory,
that God "looked at" all creation, that is, created everything and made
all complete and whole by the imprinting of Sophia:

> and having looked at them,
> with his image alone,
> clothed them in beauty.

> St. Paul says: *the Son of God is the splendor of [God's] glory
> and the image of [God's] substance* [Heb. 1:3]. It should be known
> that only with this figure, [the] Son, did God look at all things, that
> is, [God] communicated to them their natural being and many
> natural graces and gifts, and made them complete and perfect, as is
> said in Genesis: *God looked at all things that [God] made, and they
> were very good* [Gn. 1:31]. To look and behold that they were very
> good was to make them very good in the Word, [God's] Son.
> (C.5.4)[35]

To look at and experience the beauty, gifts, and sacredness of the
earth, therefore, is to behold and experience Divine Sophia who, looking
back, marvelously energizes human desire:

> The soul, *wounded with love through a trace of the beauty of her
> Beloved, which she has known through creatures* and anxious to
> see that invisible beauty which caused this visible beauty, declares
> . . . who has the power to heal me?

> Since creatures gave the soul signs of her Beloved and showed
> within themselves traces of [her Beloved's] beauty and excellence,
> *love grew in her and, consequently, sorrow at [her Beloved's]*
> *absence. The more the soul knows of God the more the desire and*
> *anxiety to see [God] increase.* (C.6.1–2)

If this experience of the creative presence and image of Jesus-
Sophia in the world strongly awakens the person to love and causes
desire for God to grow, what can we say about the experience of
Sophia in *human* relationships?

> All who are free
> tell me a thousand graceful things of you;
> all wound me more
> and leave me dying
> of, ah, I-don't-know-what
> beyond their stammering. (C.7)

The commentary continues:

> In this stanza she asserts that she is wounded with love because of
> another higher knowledge she receives of the Beloved through rational
> creatures. . . . She also asserts she is not merely wounded, but is
> dying of love . . . due to an admirable immensity these creatures
> disclose to her, yet do not completely disclose. Because this
> immensity is indescribable she calls it an "I-don't-know-what."
> And because of it the soul is dying of love. (C.7.1)

Desire for Beloved Sophia is enkindled and gathers even more
passion and momentum by nothing so much as human friendship
and love, even when one is captivated by a powerful infatuation
and thus largely unconscious that the power and attraction experienced come from the image or trace of Sophia within the loved
one. John of the Cross's incarnational position, like Karl Rahner's,
insists that created mediations do not destroy the immediate re-

lationship of the graced person to God. Rather, they make it
possible and attest to its authenticity in everyday life.[36] This means
that human desire is moved toward Divine Sophia and gathers
strength through what/whom we cherish, and it is purified and
transformed through not only the joys and ecstacies but also the
sorrows, losses, and disappointments of human relationships. (C.7.1–
9; 8.1)

   While this stance found in *The Spiritual Canticle* (st. 3–7)
is not always easy to reconcile with the teaching on desire in book
1 of *The Ascent,* where all desires are potential idols, still for the
mystic the experience of this world is an experience of God!
Although every desire has the latent possibility of focusing on an
idol, love of God and human love are not in competition. The
totality of creation—ourselves, our relationships, our world—is a
milieu of prayer. Our very experience of creation puts content into
our relationship with Beloved Sophia. This is how our desire or
affectivity is educated. To express this another way, to experience
Divine Sophia in this manner sketches color and depth into one's
own slowly developing, inner image of Sophia-Christ.

   I will return to this later and to what it means to be a friend
and prophet of Sophia possessing the perspective and desire of
Divine Sophia in and for the world. It is sufficient to indicate
here that in the last part of both *The Spiritual Canticle* and *The
Living Flame,* one of the astounding graces of transformation in
wisdom, or union with the divine, is that one actually *experiences*
the harmony, mutuality, and diversity of all creation *moving in
God* in a unified, interdependent connectedness and enjoys this as
a mirror or image of Sophia-God. This is so true that the universe
itself and all it nurtures with life become for the person a harmonious symphony surpassing the most wonderful melodies one
has ever heard (C.14/15.10 & 25; 36.6–7; 39.11; F.4.4–7).

Sophia Delights to Be with the Children of the Earth and Makes Them Friends of God

Sophia is not, therefore, distant or removed from human affairs nor from this world. She is involved in and concerned with the lessons and significance of human experience. By the gates, at the approaches to the city she waits, her delight and concern with the children of the earth. Again and again we are assured of her undiscriminating delight:

> the Father of lights [Jas. 1:17] . . . is not closefisted but diffuses himself abundantly, as the sun does its rays, without being a respecter of persons [Acts 10:34], wherever there is room—always showing himself gladly along the highways and byways—does not hesitate or consider it of little import to find his delights with the children of the earth at a common table in the world [Prv.8:31]. (F.1.15)

This text is complex since it draws on the book of Proverbs for its strong wisdom content but does so in the context of the Letter of James and the Acts of the Apostles. Here Sophia's delight to be with humanity is associated with the doctrine of the indwelling of the Trinity and, in the process, Sophia's presence and delight are transferred to the Father, thereby masculinizing Sophia. The commentary continues:

> And it should not be held as incredible in a soul now examined, purged, and tried in the fire of tribulations, trials and many kinds of temptations, and found faithful in love, that the promise of the Son of God be fulfilled, the promise that the Most Blessed Trinity will come and dwell within anyone who loves him [Jn.14:23]. The Blessed Trinity inhabits the soul by divinely illuminating its intellect with the Wisdom of the Son, delighting its will in the Holy Spirit, and by absorbing it powerfully and mightily in the delightful embrace of the Father's sweetness. (F.1.15)

> And this is what happens, in an indescribable way, at the time this flame of love rises up within the soul. Since the soul is completely purged in its substance and faculties (memory, intellect, and will), the divine substance which, because of its purity, as the Wise Man says, *touches everywhere profoundly, subtly, and sublimely* [Wis.7:24], absorbs the soul in itself with its divine flame. *And in that immersion of the soul in Wisdom*, the Holy Spirit sets in motion the glorious flickerings of his flame. (F.1.17)

Sophia delights precisely in dwelling with the human person and rejoicing in her delight and happiness. John's central emphasis on a relationship of mutual indwelling is rooted in this truth:

> The Son of God finds delight in the soul in these her delights, and is sustained in her, that is, he dwells in her as in a place that pleases him. . . . This, I believe, is what he meant through what Solomon said in Proverbs: *My delights are with the children of this earth* [Prv. 8:31], *that is, when their delight is to be with me, Who am the Son of God.* (C.17.10)

Sophia desires human presence and companionship. From the very beginning of *The Ascent of Mount Carmel* through the concluding stanzas of *The Spiritual Canticle* to the end of *The Living Flame of Love*, these writings never swerve from this framework in which union with Divine Wisdom through a mutual likeness effected by the companionship of love is the promise and the goal. Sophia is so desirous of this mutual transfiguration that she is actually called *the spouse* of the soul. This central role of Wisdom is explicit in the book 1 of *The Ascent* in a text already quoted:

> When this third night . . . has passed, a union with the bride, Who is the Sophia of God, then follows. . . . Love is perfect when the transformation of the soul in God is achieved. (A.1.2.4)

And in one of the last stanzas of *The Spiritual Canticle* we hear the plea:

> Transform me into the beauty of Divine Sophia and make me
> resemble the one who is the Word, the Son of God. (C.36.7)

Jesus Christ Is Divine Wisdom: John of the Cross and the New Testament

It is clear that for John of the Cross, as for St. Paul and the writers of the Gospels of Matthew and John, Jesus Christ *is* Divine Wisdom (Sophia), the Word, the Son of God. In the unitive experience of Jesus-Sophia, the person is transformed, and in this Jesus, the entire creation is touched and gathered into the tender, unifying embrace of Sophia-God who pervades and connects the entire cosmos and every form of life in it.

John of the Cross appropriates not only some of the understandings of Sophia in the Old Testament, but he seems to be completely at home with the identification of Jesus with Divine Sophia that some of the writers of the New Testament make: *Jesus is Sophia incarnate.*[37] In Jesus, therefore, we find the incarnation of a feminine gestalt of God. To underpin his own cohesive Christology, John uses most of the significant wisdom texts of the New Testament currently being analyzed by contemporary scholars, and he does this in a context that frequently reveals his knowledge of their connection with the wisdom texts of the Old Testament. The tradition of personified Wisdom, which played a foundational role in the development of Christology in the early church, seems to have been singularly important to him since some of his most profound Christological assertions are couched in its terms. The recognition of the central, critical function of Wisdom is therefore basic to understanding John's Christology. Elizabeth Johnson clarifies precisely what this means when she writes:

Whoever espouses a wisdom Christology is asserting that Sophia
in all her fullness was in Jesus so that in his historicity he embodies
divine mystery in creative and saving involvement with the world.
In Augustine's words, "But she was sent in one way that she might
be with human beings; and she has been sent in another way that
she herself might be a human being." [38]

I have met numerous religious people in recent years who,
because of their own spiritual experience, feel a great affinity for the
writings of John of the Cross but do not want to deal with the dominant
place of Christ in his teaching. One cannot begin to explore the
transformative function of Sophia in John, however, without simultaneously probing *the role of Jesus Christ* in the process of Christian
transformation, or vice versa.[39] John appropriates as his own the words
of the Book of Wisdom together with those of Paul the Apostle to
accent the centrality and complete sufficiency of Jesus, Sophia incarnate:

If you desire me to answer with a word of comfort, [God
says] behold my Son, subject to me and to others out of love for
me, and you will see how much he answers. If you desire me to
declare some secret truths or events to you, fix your eyes on him,
and you will discern hidden in him the most secret mysteries, and
wisdom, and the wonders of God, as My Apostle proclaims: In
the Son of God are hidden all the treasures of wisdom and knowledge
of God [Col. 2:3]. These treasures of wisdom and knowledge will
be far more sublime, delightful, and advantageous than what you
want to know.[40] The Apostle, therefore, gloried, affirming that he
had acted as though he knew no other than Jesus Christ and him
crucified [1 Cor. 2:2]. And if you should seek other divine or
corporeal visions and revelations, behold him, become human, and
you will encounter more than you imagine, because the Apostle
also says: In Christ all the fullness of divinity dwells bodily [Col.
2:9]. (A.2.22.6) [41]

In investigating Sophia-Wisdom, one discovers just how cohesive and
all-pervasive John's wisdom Christology really is. Furthermore, it is

rooted in the whole Christological development beginning with the New Testament and early Church writers.[42]

To see the significance of John's understanding of Jesus as Sophia and his use of a wisdom Christology, we must examine briefly how and why the writers of the New Testament, particularly Paul, Matthew, and John, understood Jesus in wisdom categories and what this meant for them and for the tradition.[43] Elizabeth Johnson tells us that when the communities of first-century Christians started to reflect on the identity and "saving significance of Jesus of Nazareth and to his ultimate origin in God's gracious goodness," they turned to Jewish theology and Hellenistic culture for elements of interpretation. One of the very first they put to use was the Jewish figure of personified Wisdom, that female figure of the late Old Testament and intertestimental literature whose words, characteristics, and functions they quickly shifted to Jesus. They therefore interpreted Jesus within the framework of the tradition of personified Wisdom.[44]

Through the feminine Sophia-God image, New Testament writers linked the man Jesus to Yahweh of Israel, thereby showing the intrinsic continuity between their Yahwistic faith and Christianity and revealing how, in Jesus Christ, all that Yahweh is was present in their midst. Johnson writes:

> What Judaism said of Sophia, Christian hymn-makers and epistle writers now came to say of Jesus: he is the image of the invisible God (Col 1:15), the radiant light of God's glory (Heb 1:3); he is the firstborn of all creation (Col 1:15), the one thru whom all things were made (1 Cor 8:6). Likewise, the way in which Judaism characterized Sophia in her dealings with human beings, Christian gospel writers now came to portray Jesus: he calls out to the heavy burdened to come to him and find rest (Mt 11:28–30); he makes people friends of God and gifts those who love him with life (Jn 15:15; 17:2). As the trajectory of wisdom Christology passages in the New Testament shows, the identification of Jesus with Sophia was so closely made that Jesus is presented not only as a wisdom

teacher, not only as as a child and envoy of Sophia, but more significantly as Sophia herself: Biblical scholarship in recent decades has been lifting this tradition from the footnotes of scripture studies into more central consideration. Regarding NT Christology James Dunn concludes, "Jesus is the exhaustive embodiment of divine wisdom"; M. Jack Suggs argues that for Matthew, "Jesus is Sophia incarnate"; according to Raymond Brown's analysis, "in John, Jesus is personified Wisdom"; This early use of Wisdom categories had profound theological consequences. It enabled the fledgling Christian communities to attribute cosmic significance to the Crucified Jesus, relating him to the creation and governance of the world, and was an essential step in the development of incarnation Christology.[45]

The Role of Jesus in Our Lives

In John's anthropology, the human person is seen as an "infinite" capacity for God (F.3.19–22).[46] As long as the great "caverns" of the mind, heart, memory, and imagination are filled with human knowledge, loves, dreams, and memories that seem or promise to satisfy completely, the person is unable even to feel or imagine the depths of the capacity that is there. Only when one becomes aware of the emptiness of these caverns, in the face of the experience of the fragility and breakdown of what/whom we have staked our lives on, the limitation and failure of our life project and life love, and the shattering of our dreams and meanings, can the depths of thirst and hunger that exist in the human person, the infinite capacity, really be felt.

The mind is a deep cavern whose emptiness is a thirst for God. The mind thirsts, often unknowingly, for the waters of God's Wisdom to satisfy and complete human knowing. The will is a great cavern whose affective emptiness is a hunger for the ultimate, unconditional reassurance and fulfillment of love. The memory is a cavern, too, and its obsession with the past, its suffering over losses, and its confusion with and need to organize images become a deep void of yearning for the possession of God.

Few people understand that John is actually addressing this infinite capacity when he urges them at the end of the first book of *The Ascent* to have an ongoing desire to pattern their lives on Christ's:

> Have a habitual desire to imitate Christ in all your deeds by bringing your life into conformity with his. You must then study his life in order to know how to imitate him and behave in all things as he would behave. (A.1.13.3)[47]

This means only one thing: *desire to know* Jesus Christ. Human desire is educated by an immersion in the Jesus of the Gospels. However, if you channel your desire toward knowing Jesus Christ, this person who has become in his life, death, and resurrection the Sophia of God, the one you will learn to know is loving Sophia who will slowly and secretly redirect and claim your desire and subvert your life. Desire is educated, therefore, by the companionship, the friendship, of Jesus-Sophia. This dynamic underlies John's whole philosophy of prayer and indicates how a conscious decision of the heart for Christ takes place, how a shift in the focus of desire and meaning *begins* in our lives.

But often the human person is not satisfied with the day-to-day fidelity to this companionship, nor to its slow, unpretentious, mysterious development. Too many people educated in our culture live with a consuming desire for novelty, excitement, change, new pleasures, visions, and extraordinary experiences. We have only to reflect on the way Americans flocked to Medjugorje before the war in Bosnia or the way people in our country search for unusual spiritual experience at the sites of reported apparitions. But John, appropriating both St. Paul and the Book of Wisdom in a Christological passage quoted previously, affirms that we do not need unusual new revelations, visions, or secret truths. We have everything we desire in the Gospel and the unitive companionship of the human Jesus in whom dwells for us the nearness and fullness, the compassionate kindness, of Sophia-God embracing and energizing from within the totality of the human situation. Jesus-Sophia is the "sole Word" spoken by the "mouth of God."[48]

> Those who now desire to question God or receive some vision or revelation are guilty not only of foolish behavior but also of offending him by not fixing their eyes entirely on Christ and by living with the desire for some other novelty.
>
> God would answer as follows: If I have already told you all things in my Word, my Son, and if I have no other word, what answer or revelation can I now make that would surpass this? Fasten your eyes on him alone, because in him I have spoken and revealed all, and in him you shall discover even more that you ask for and desire. You are making an appeal for locutions and revelations that are incomplete, but if you turn your eyes to him you will find them complete. For he is my entire locution and response, vision and revelation, which I have already spoken, answered, manifested, and revealed to you, by giving him to you as a brother, companion, master, ransom, and reward. Since that day when I descended upon him with my Spirit on Mount Tabor proclaiming: "This is my beloved Son in whom I am well pleased, hear him" [Mt. 17:5], I have relinquished these methods of answering and teaching and presented them to him....Behold him well, for in him you will uncover all these revelations already made, and many more.
>
> . . . Thus we must be guided humanly and visibly in all by the law [Gospel] of Christ, who is human, and that of his Church and his ministers. . . . One should not believe anything coming in a supernatural way, and believe only the teaching of Christ who is human. (A.2.22.5, 7)

This long text is particularly enlightening since John places it within the context of Sirach 24, where Sophia speaks of herself:

> Wisdom praises herself and tells of her glory in the midst of the people. In the assembly of the Most High she opens her mouth,

and in the presence of his hosts she tells of her glory: *I came forth
from the mouth of the Most High*, and covered the earth like a mist
(Sir 24:1–3).

In accenting the complete sufficiency and unlimited potential of
Christ as Divine Sophia, John of the Cross validates new possibilities
for appropriating in our time the inexhaustible meaning of Jesus. If
Jesus is Sophia incarnate, then new possibilities for studying his life
do open before us. And what will we unlock if *in contemplative prayer*
we experience again the life, death, and resurrection—the meaning—
of Jesus in the light of Sophia, thereby transforming for our time
the symbol of Christ and reclaiming Christ and Christological doctrine
in a new way? [49]

Image of Jesus Christ and Growth in Wisdom

This walking with the historical Jesus is how Sophia becomes
a life-giving, indwelling image and one's primary focus of affective
and cognitive meaning. This image is unique for each person, as a
basis for relationship, direction, love, purification, and transformation.
In fact, a gradual transference of desire occurs as the presence of
loving Sophia takes shape within, influencing motivation and affecting
imagination.[50] While it is the intimacy of prayer which, above all, shapes
this image, nevertheless study, theological reflection, art, music, and
a myriad of other life experiences contribute to this Christic patterning.
We have already seen how in *The Spiritual Canticle* (st. 3–7) the
experience of oneself, others, and the whole creation slowly roughs
in and sketches color and depth into one's developing, inner image
of Jesus-Sophia.

A principle fundamental to John's wisdom Christology is operative here: love will never reach the fullness of its possibilities, human
desire will never stop yearning and aching, until the lovers are so
alike that one is transfigured in the love and goodness of the other.

This means an imprint of Jesus-Sophia transformative of the human person is, in a mysterious way, totally harmonious with human development, gradually etched within the human personality. As I know Jesus-Sophia, this knowledge subverts my life, shows me to myself as in a mirror, and redirects and purifies my desire.

If I look long enough at one who truly loves me, I become what I see in the other's eyes. I am transfigured. The image of the loved one, the eyes of the beloved are burnt into my heart and seen with my inner eye. This image is not impersonal! Rather, it is relational. We see this with remarkable clarity in "The Spiritual Canticle" poem:

> Reveal your presence,
> and may the vision of your beauty be my death;
> for the sickness of love
> is not cured
> except by *your very presence and image.*
>
> O spring like crystal!
> If only, on your silvered-over faces,
> you would suddenly form
> the eyes I have desired,
> which I bear sketched deep within my heart. (CB.11–12)

This is not difficult to understand when we reflect on how, when we love someone very much, we carry the image of that loved one within, where he/she is always present with us influencing motivation. John explains:

> The soul experiences within herself a certain sketch of love . . . and she desires the completion of the sketch of this image, the image of her Bridegroom, the Word, the Son of God, who, as St. Paul says, *is the splendor of [God's] glory and the image of [God's] substance,* [Heb. 1:3]; for this is the image . . . into which the soul desires to be transformed through love. (C.11.12) [51]

In wonderfully graphic imagery along the same line of wisdom symbolism, the commentary continues:

> [The person] feels that she is like wax in which an impression, though being made, is not yet complete. She knows, too, that she is like a sketch or the first draft of a drawing and calls out to the one who did this sketch to finish the painting and image. (C.12.1)

Because this is a fundamental experience, and not just a concept, it is important to understand the educative and transformative function of this wisdom image and its affective power over desire. Through this image the whole creative aspect of Old Testament Sophia is brought to human transformation. If it is not valued relative to spiritual growth, the tender, careful, nurturing creativity of Sophia will be thwarted and we will "damage or lose the sublime image that God [is] painting within [us]."[52]

At first, the developing image of Jesus-Sophia is a strength and consolation motivating one toward a generous, self-giving life influenced by the Jesus of the Gospels and sensitizing one to this Sophia presence in the world energizing and connecting all of reality—the likeness within recognizing and catching the reflection of the outer likeness.[53] In fact, the presence of this tracing in human relationships, throughout the beauty and wonder of the created universe, in human culture and in all that human creativity is able to achieve, causes desire for God to grow by leaps and bounds.

Dark Night and the Continuing Role of Secret Sophia

As the intimacy with Christ matures, however, this presence, within and without, begins to make deeper claims and there is a shift in the way Sophia operates within the depths of human personality.[54] Romance departs, and I see myself, my relationships, my community, and my world clearly in the mirror of loving Sophia.[55] This is almost more than one can endure. Now we experience Sophia as a teacher, that is, one who is always on the side of continual learning, even though everything we learn from Sophia is not comforting.[56]

In time, the presence of Sophia becomes afflictive. The image becomes too threatening. Jesus-Sophia subverts my own self-image, and this marks the first level of subversion. I cannot accept the claims of Sophia upon me nor can I accept Wisdom as a life vision in an unconditional commitment; this vision is too revolutionary and seditious. Sophia turns life upside-down, challenges my most deeply held beliefs and values, undermines what I have learned, claims whom and what I possess, and highlights the limitations and oppressive character of what I depend on most for satisfaction and assurance.

This brings us to the relationship between the presence of loving Wisdom and the dark night.[57] John says explicitly that dark night, infused contemplation, *is* the loving Wisdom of God.[58] *Dark Night = inflow of God = infused contemplation = loving Wisdom:*

> This dark night is an inflow of God into the soul, which purges it of its habitual ignorances and imperfections, natural and spiritual, and which contemplatives call infused contemplation or mystical theology. Through this contemplation, God teaches the soul secretly and instructs it in the perfection of love without its doing anything nor understanding how this happens.
>
> Insofar as infused contemplation is loving Wisdom of God, it produces two principal effects in the soul: it prepares the soul for union with God through love by purging and illumining it. Hence the same loving Wisdom that purges and illumines the blessed spirits, purges and illumines the souls here on earth. (N.2.5.1)

Why, if it is a divine light. . . does the soul call it a dark night? In answer to this, there are two reasons why this Divine Wisdom is not only night and darkness for the soul but also affliction and torment. First, because of the height of the Divine

> Wisdom that exceeds the abilities of the soul; and on this
> account the Wisdom is dark for the soul. Second, because of
> the soul's baseness and impurity; and on this account it is
> painful, afflictive, and also dark for the soul. (N.2.5.2)[59]

Contemplation = mystical theology = secret Wisdom = ray of darkness:

> Contemplation, consequently, by which the intellect has a higher
> knowledge of God, is called mystical theology, meaning the
> secret Wisdom of God. For this Wisdom is secret to the very
> intellect that receives it. St. Dionysius on this account refers
> to contemplation as a ray of darkness. The prophet Baruch
> declares of this wisdom: "There is no one who knows its way
> or can think of its paths" [Bar. 3:23]. To reach union with God
> the soul must obviously blind itself to all the paths along which
> it can travel. (A.2.8.6)[60]

It follows that if Jesus Christ *is* Divine Wisdom (Sophia), then *dark
contemplation is the presence of Jesus Christ as Wisdom* and dark
night is the time when the image of Jesus-Sophia takes on all the
marks of crucifixion: violence, suffering, isolation, failure, marginality,
rejection, abandonment, hopelessness, meaninglessness, death. The
image of the Crucified One,[61] reflective of a seemingly silent, incomprehensible God, functions in the dark night as *incomprehensible,
secret, hidden,* and yet *loving* Sophia. And this is the second level
of subversion: not only has my self-image been subverted, but now
too the image of Christ and of God. Therefore, when John says that
the dark night is an inflow of God, *this inflow of God is very precisely
in terms of secret Wisdom who is Jesus Crucified*, a secret, unitive,
loving knowledge indicative of more intimate relationship (N.1.10.6;
N.2.5.1–2; N.2.17). Dark night is not primarily *some thing*, an impersonal darkness like a difficult situation or distressful psychological
condition, but *someone*, a presence leaving an indelible imprint on the
human spirit and consequently on one's entire life.

This imprint is the touch of the hand of God marking, wounding, challenging, shaping, purifying, and transforming human personality.

> You have wounded me in order to cure me, O divine Hand, and you have put to death in me what made me lifeless, deprived me of God's life in which I now see myself live. You granted me this with the liberality of your generous grace, which you used in contacting me with the touch of the splendor of your glory and the figure of your substance, which is your only begotten Son, through whom, being your substance [Heb. 1:3], you touch mightily from one end to the other [Wis. 8:1]. And your only begotten Son, O merciful hand of the Father, is the delicate touch by which you touched me with the force of your cautery and wounded me. (F.2.16) [62]

In the mirror of *this* broken, ambiguous image of suffering Wisdom, we see the miseries and hypocrisies of our lives. [63] This Crucified image is living knowledge of human darkness, violence, limitation, oppression, and sinfulness that overpowers our shallow self-confidence and sense of direction, questions what we think we know about God, raises doubts about what we have accomplished, and undercuts our entire affective life. [64]

In fact, this Crucified presence subverts and contradicts our whole individualistic perception of reality, that is, the way we experience not only other people, not only the loved one and loved community, but also the victims and scapegoats of our society, and even other species, the earth itself, and the cosmos (N.2.8.4). This image of crucifixion is the language of God (Word) opening and teaching the human mind and heart, calling us in our confusion and emptiness to pass over into the perspective of loving Sophia by an identification or profound unitive relationship with Jesus Crucified.

At this point in life and prayer development, the images of the poor, the victimized, the oppressed, the exploited, and the suffering take on a clarity and significance that is overpowering. They are clearly a suffering extension of the inner imprinting of Jesus-Sophia, and they make a claim. They are the darkness of humanity; they are *our* darkness. In the image of Crucified Sophia, our violence is unveiled.[65] Just as personal darkness is exposed in the mirror of suffering Sophia, so is the collective darkness and violence of humanity. The "poor" are recognized and embraced to the degree that this identification with suffering Sophia has taken place in the inner darkness. This is a major internal connection Sophia effects with "the world." Having subverted our images of ourselves and of God, Sophia now subverts our relationship to the world and this is the third level of subversion. Here, *now*, in the dark night, the Crucifixion is recognized finally for what it is: the total, irrevocable unveiling of our cultural violence. Consciousness is the issue, but a love-consciousness born when this unitive relationship with Crucified Sophia takes hold in darkness and in deprivation of one's deepest affective resources, thereby redeeming or redirecting affectivity and transforming human desire. For so long, year after year, in meditation, in theological reflection, in liturgy, in suffering, during the dramatic liturgy of Good Friday, we have looked at the Crucified One, but only now do we realize *that Christ is looking back* with all the pain of the world in his eyes.

In other words, in the secret, painful, unitive relationship with dark Sophia, a new kind of *participatory love-knowledge* begins to take over human desire and consciousness and to express itself, not only in the gradual repudiation of all kinds of personal and sociocultural violence and oppression, but also in an entry, *albeit still dark and unfinished*, into the experience of mutuality, communion, connectedness, and kinship with the earth that marks transformed or mystical consciousness.[66] Richard Tarnas suggests that a "subtler understanding of human knowledge," a participatory way of knowing that moves beyond the hierarchical dualism[67] characteristic of the Cartesian-Kantian paradigm, has been emerging in philosophy for over a century. Common to all its thinkers—Goethe, Schiller, Schelling, Coleridge, Hegel, and

Rudolf Steiner—is an essential conviction that the relation of the human mind to the universe is ultimately not dualistic but *participatory.*[68]

> In its own depths the imagination directly contacts the creative process of nature, realizes the process within itself, and brings nature's reality to conscious expression.
> Then the world speaks its meaning through human consciousness. Then human language itself can be recognized as rooted in a deeper reality, as reflecting the universe's unfolding meaning. Through the human intellect, in all its personal individuality, contingency and struggle, the world's evolving thought-content achieves conscious articulation, . . . the world's truth achieves its existence when it comes to birth in the human mind. As the plant at a certain stage brings forth its blossom, so does the universe bring forth new stages of human knowledge. And as Hegel emphasized, the evolution of human knowledge is the evolution of the world's self-revelation.[69]

I quote at length because this view of an emerging, different epistemological perspective, a "participatory epistemology," to which I will return later in dealing with transformation or the awakening of God, is strikingly similar, not only to the experience of contemplative consciousness in John of the Cross and other mystics, but also to the new paradigm of connectedness and communion emerging in various other disciplines and numerous other writers. Without necessarily realizing the relationship to contemplative consciousness and transformation in Suffering Wisdom, some of these trailblazers in religious thinking challenge humanity to accept the limitation and death (dark night) that will usher in the next great epoch or evolutionary era when the long-alienated modern mind will break through to discover its intimate relationship with nature and the larger cosmos. Then the universe will be experienced, as Thomas Berry suggests, as an intimate, interconnected, and diverse communion of subjects rather than a collection of objects or victims existing only for human use or domination.[70]

Integral to and one with this rising participatory way of knowing and understanding life on earth is the tremendous emergence of the feminine in our culture rising out of the unitive energies at work in the universe and heralding the end of the fundamentally masculine dominance of the Western mind. It appears that we are truly at a highly critical stage of purification, closely associated with the emerging numinosity of Sophia, in which the masculine (in all of us) must voluntarily transcend itself in its own dark night of death, which will fit it to enter into a fundamentally new and reconciling relationship of mutuality with the feminine in all its forms.[71]

As we observe the twentieth-century's massive deterioration of so many structures, suggesting the necessary deconstruction or death prior to new birth, we see this participatory vision struggling to break through on so many levels and in so many disciplines. Experienced, first, in the bald exposure of so much violence and evil in our time and, second, in an increasing oneness with the suffering, this vision appears to be reflective of a deep and powerful process impelled by forces beyond the merely human. This is where the personal experience of dark Crucified Sophia intersects and resonates with the current state of the collective "soul" because the human spirit in the dark night does follow a numinous paradigmatic path unfolding from within on a trajectory that leads to transformation. This means the unitive relationship with Suffering Sophia can be so deep and, consequently, the solidarity with "the other" so profound that not only does the contemplative person in this dark night carry and bring to consciousness the collective longings and pain of humanity and the energies of the cosmos, but also brings *to them,* in her very being and desire, this participatory love-knowledge, which Jesus-Sophia gives and is.

This contribution of Sophia mysticism to a broader transformation must not be overlooked by those in other disciplines: namely, feminists, ecologists, creationists, geologians, scientists, philosophers, or theologians. Above all, it must not be overlooked by educators. Those who teach the next generation need to understand and believe in the transformative character of the contemplative process inasmuch as this process is integral not only to fully developed humanity, but also to the new form of human existence struggling to be born, therefore, to the continued evolutionary thrust of the earth and the universe. Teachers need to know how to educate for contemplation and transformation if the earth is to be nurtured, if the people are to be delivered from the scapegoating oppression of all kinds of violence, and if humanity is to fill its role in ushering in the next era of life on earth. This may be the *most* basic challenge of religion today: not sexual mores nor bioethics, nor commitment to justice, not dogmatic orthodoxy, not even option for the poor and oppressed nor solidarity with women, but education for a transformative contemplation, which would radically affect human motivation, consciousness, desire, and, ultimately, every other area of human life and endeavor. As if to verify this at the end of his extremely significant book, *Violence Unveiled*, Gil Bailie moves from contemporary versions of crucifixion, wrenching accounts of the Buchenwald death camp, and the rape and murder of a young girl on La Cruz during the massacre at El Mozote, El Salvador, to the Gospel (Mt 22:37–9):

> The Jesus of Matthew's Gospel did not say the greatest commandment was to *believe* in God and love humanity. He did not say that we should be nice to one another because that's the way God would like us to behave. He said the first and most essential thing is to *love God* with a paramount love. It is the most hackneyed notion in the world, but once or twice in a lifetime its dulling familiarity vanishes, and one feels for a moment the unfathomable significance and centrality of Jesus' suggestion for breaking the grip of sin and death: *to love God*. Partly due to humanists' romantic idea of basic benevolence and partly to the rationalistic "where-there's-a-will-there's-a-way" spirit of the Enlightenment, the modern world came to believe it could fulfill the requirements of the second commandment without having to bother with the first. We moderns came to believe

that, in effect, that, by itself, the second commandment was a civilizing
force sufficient to the task at hand. The creaking and groaning, indeed,
the shouting and shooting, that we now hear all around us is coming
from the collapse of that assumption.[72]

This makes it critical to realize that the dark night is the time
in contemplative prayer development to seek, not the consolation and
escape of other images, experiences, practices, relationships, or spiritual
experiences, but "the living image of Christ Crucified within" (A.3.35.5)
and stand open to this purifying, transforming image of suffering
Sophia, *which is actually experienced as "no image" or "nothing"*
but which nonetheless acknowledges, reflects, and even accepts our
personal and societal darkness, violence, disgrace, failure, injustice,
and selfishness. This soul experience is not easy to grasp because
to all appearances Christ recedes from consciousness and loses significance, God is beyond reach, belief is threatened, and atheism is
logical. This experience has nothing to do with imagining or "seeing"
the Crucified Christ (A.2.12.3–6), but with staying in the hidden, dark
mystery of Suffering Sophia with an incredibly simple faith-attentive-
ness that does not even perceive or feel the participatory love-
knowledge secret Sophia-Jesus is (A.2.14.8).[73]

It is only in the context of this dark experience that we are
able to make any sense out of the difficult and complex directives,
found in the second and third books of *The Ascent*, to cease clinging
to images and to reject visions and revelations:

> When individuals have finished purifying and voiding themselves
> of all forms and apprehensible images, they will abide in this pure
> and simple light, and be perfectly transformed into it. . . . If
> individuals would eliminate these impediments and veils and live in
> pure nakedness and poverty of spirit, . . . their *soul in its simplicity
> and purity would then be immediately transformed into simple and
> pure Sophia, the Son of God.* (A.2.15.4)

Since these imaginative apprehensions, visions, and other forms and species are presented through some image or particular idea, individuals should neither feed upon nor encumber themselves with them. . . . The reason is that in being apprehended these forms are always represented, as we said, in some limited mode or manner. But God's Wisdom, to which the intellect must be united, has neither mode nor manner, neither does it have limits nor does it pertain to distinct and particular knowledge, because it is totally pure and simple. That the two extremes, *the soul and the Divine Wisdom*, may be united, they will have to come to accord *by means of a certain likeness*. As a result the soul must also be pure and simple, unlimited and unattached to any particular knowledge, and unmodified by the boundaries of form, species, and image. *Since God cannot be encompassed by any image, form or particular knowledge,* in order to be united with [God] the soul should not be limited by any particular form or knowledge. (A.2.16.6–7)[74]

By and large, most of us are ill-equipped to understand the contemplative process of identification with the Crucified Sophia whereby our desire and consciousness are being transformed. The image of secret Sophia teaching, nurturing, and purifying, unlike clearly defined images of the past, blocks out or makes ineffective other images life-giving until now. When, therefore, in book 2 of *The Dark Night* we read that a person is no longer able to pray or communicate as before, that, in fact, one feels abandoned and rejected, we learn that *in experience* darkness eclipses other images in one's life as sources of satisfaction and ultimate assurance: the loved one, the beloved community, images of oneself as successful and loved, but above all, lifelong images of God and Christ.

This teaching is important today for two very different reasons. First, we must not decide to do away with human images by sheer will power, most of all the image of Jesus Christ, until contemplative development undermines them. Second, lacking the tools of contemplative interpretation and hindered by the marginalization of Divine Sophia and ignorance of how her secret touch marks one's life, contemplatives at this stage, instead of understanding this positive unveiling of darkness, begin to feel alienated from Jesus Christ.[75] In an effort to understand their experience and rescue their God from oblivion, it is not uncommon for them to speak of their God experience in terms of God present in others or of a kind of "cosmic" power or presence. This "vague presence" is actually understandable when one considers the secret Mystery that Crucified Sophia really is in the dark night. Not only the awareness of our own darkness and deficiency, therefore, but the dark beginning of a whole new consciousness of God without the clearly defined parameters of the past characterizes "the union of love" that is being activated. This is the blackest time of night when the last delicate shading of the image of Christ, crucified and abandoned, is being sketched within the human heart and flesh in total darkness and silence. As *The Spiritual Canticle* expresses it:

> The soul cannot see herself in the beauty of God unless she is transformed into the Sophia of God . . . [and made to resemble the one who is the Word, the Son of God]. . . . [But] the gate entering into these riches of Sophia is the cross. (C.36.7–8 & 13)

Deeper Level of Night

When the invisible, silent God of an abandoned Jesus seems to draw us into lonely introspection where prayer and relationships as we have known them are painful or gone; when loss, failure, and hopelessness loom large; when all supports drop from one's consciousness and life's deepest meanings and symbol systems are empty and stale; when our inherited language and images no longer reveal the divine, then a dark Wisdom is operative, nurturing the human person with love and confirming values little prized in our society.[76]

Book 2 of *The Dark Night* throws a stark light on the experience by showing *the whole person* deprived totally in her or his imaginative powers, intellectual intuitions, and human sensibilities, that is, in all one's human powers:

> God divests the faculties, affections, and senses, both spiritual and sensory, interior and exterior. God leaves the intellect in darkness, the will in aridity, the memory in emptiness, and the affections in supreme affliction, bitterness, and anguish by depriving the soul of the feeling and satisfaction it previously enjoyed from spiritual blessings. For this privation is one of the conditions required that *the spiritual form, [the image] which is the union of love,* may be introduced into the spirit and united with it. The Lord works all this in the soul by means of a pure and dark contemplation. (N.2.3.3)

As long as one cannot receive and hold the imprinting of the image, or "spiritual form," there is suffering. If one keeps a death grip on one's affective life and fulfillment as it has been experienced in the past and clings tenaciously to one's previous experience of life and perception of Christ/God, one is unable to *completely* "hold" the contradictory presence of Crucified Sophia (N.2.8.2 & 9.1). One's habitual way of understanding, long in use and characteristic of conventional wisdom,[77] has to go, wrenched from us either by the circumstances of life or finally in death. Likewise, one's habitual way of feeling and experiencing love has to go so that one can *experience the transforming touches* of divine love (N.2.9.3–4). Finally, one's habitual way of harboring memories has to be refined with the effect that the memory will feel alien to all familiar things, a stranger to one's own life, as it were (N.2.9.5–6).

Such a drastic subversion of the human powers can only be understood when we remember what was said earlier in the context of John's anthropology. As long as the great "caverns" of the mind, heart, will, memory, and imagination are filled with human knowledge, loves, dreams, and memories that seem to

satisfy completely, the person will never realize the depths of the
capacity that is there. It is only when we actually *feel* their
emptiness and darkness, that we thirst and hunger and yearn for
these caverns to be filled with God.

> When these caverns of the faculties are not emptied, purged, and
> cleansed of every affection for creatures, they do not feel the vast
> emptiness of their deep [infinite] capacity. (F.3.18)

The powers of the human person—John calls them intellect, memory,
and will—are central to his anthropology. The purification process is
centered on them in the darker experiences of night with an almost
frightening specificity about this experience of the self.

But what, precisely, can it mean to say *the intellect* is emptied
and left in darkness? Perhaps we are warned that the time does come
when our philosophy of life, our theology, our carefully constructed
meanings fall apart before our eyes. All we have accumulated intellectually that has given us "God," "faith," and security loses its
significance. Nothing makes any sense. The mind, while *full* on one
level of a lifetime of knowledge, is in total darkness on another, the
level of meaning. We feel as if we have been duped and succumb
to silence, afraid to shock others by the depth of our cynicism and
unbelief (N.2.9.3; 5.3–5; A.2.4 & 8).

To understand this symbolic, intuitive language of dark contemplation is very difficult (N.2.17). Suffering Sophia, called by John
"living knowledge," is so potent, so contradictory, so immanent and
yet so transcendent that this presence really obscures what has been
learned in life and consequently darkens and confuses our understanding.

> When this divine light of contemplation strikes a soul not yet
> entirely illumined, it causes spiritual darkness, for it not only
> surpasses the act of natural understanding but it also deprives the
> soul of this act and darkens it. (N.2.5.3)

A dark Wisdom is operative here, confirming values little prized by the masculine mind of Western society. Divine Sophia defies the supremacy of linear logic and rational analysis; she rejects the pyramid of hierarchical dualism by resisting our dichotomies (e.g., between self and others, matter and spirit, body and soul, passion/desire and reason, feeling and thinking, masculine and feminine, humanity and the earth, success and failure, sacred and profane) and withstanding the compartmentalized, objective mind-set to which we have been educated and out of which much of our society lives and operates. In a word, Wisdom undermines the need to control life (F.3.38–9).

Our minds stumble, also, over the concept of emptiness in *the memory* because we know human memory is *full* of experience. But now the imagination can no longer connect life's memories to create meaning and hope. We can speak of emptiness in the memory, not because one remembers nothing, but because all the memory holds, which once provided motivation and security, which engendered trust and promise for the future, seems now an illusion and a mockery. Memories do not mean what one thought they did. The memory is indeed empty, possessing nothing but the scattered remains of cherished experiences and the crushing remembrance of personal failure and defeat.

> Persons feel so unclean and wretched that it seems God is against them and they are against God. . . . [There is a] a deep immersion of the mind in the knowledge and feeling of one's miseries and evils; it brings all these miseries into relief so that the soul sees clearly that of itself it will never possess anything else. . . . The soul at the sight of its miseries feels that it is melting away and being undone by a cruel spiritual death. (N.2.5.5 & 6.1)[78]

Doubts, imaginings, and fears tear the person to pieces and fill one's affections and energies with indescribable anguish and lethargy.

This kind of clarity about one's miseries generates the over-whelming feeling of being rejected and abandoned not only by one's friends but particularly by God. In fact, abandonment and the betrayal of trust are the hallmark of this dark experience. However it happens, what or whom one cherishes most in life is cut off, taken away. The worst thing about this "purification of *the will*" is that the loved one, the very focus of one's love and desire, becomes the cause of one's agony.[79] There is nothing so destructive of affirmation and worth as the feeling of being rejected by one who has loved you and on whom you have counted with complete assurance (N.2.10.2). It leaves one unable to grasp anything affectively. The seeming destruction of mutuality, with its deep frustration of desire, leaves one without any strength of purpose, bereft of motivation, and prone to bitterness. A transcendence in which one is not at home and against which one rebels is forced upon the person.

Alternative Vision: Faith, Hope, and Love

We face a challenge in this night to throw into gear the kind of radical faith, hope, and love that can endure the death-dealing "touch of God's hand," the imprint which is emptying out our isolated self-sufficiency, on the one hand, and our unfree dependence and fear of transformation and change, on the other. Activated by Sophia's dark presence, the *theological* virtues are our only option, presenting a very uncomfortable alternative vision. Because initially we do not *feel* faith, hope, and love, maintaining this basic *contemplative posture* in our prayer and life is extremely difficult. It must overcome an anger, fear, and rebellion that want to refuse these theological *gifts* rather than be left with "nothing." Yet the only way the deprivation of the dark night will open into a radical change of consciousness and affectivity is by the *acceptance* of this contemplative posture or vision whereby one actually passes over to the love perspective of Divine Wisdom (A.2.6.6; N.2.21.11–12).

This seems so contradictory, however, because *faith* causes darkness in our very power to understand. Now, in this dark period, it is at cross-purposes with our ability to make logical sense out of life, death, or eternity. In fact, as Denys Turner suggests in *The Darkness of God: Negativity in Christian Mysticism,* we are actually dispossessed intellectually by faith of any power to construct a meaningful world or a meaningful God.[80] When Jesus Christ recedes from consciousness, it is faith that moves us into the Mystery that is unimaginable, incomprehensible, and uncontrollable. While we do not set out to empty the mind, imagination, or memory, prayer development and life exacts this of us, and then faith becomes an opening into a realm of significance far beyond human understanding.[81]

> Faith darkens and empties the intellect of all its natural understanding and thereby prepares it for union with Divine Wisdom, [who is the Word, the Son of God]. (N.2.21.11)

The hopelessness and emptiness of the dark night is precisely the condition that makes *hope* in the strictly theological sense possible. Hope comes into play when we are really radically at the end, unable to find any further resources to connect the memories, feelings, images, and experiences of life in a meaningful pattern, an independent identity of one's own, or a promising future. Then hope, transvaluing the past and forfeiting the struggle to press meaning out of loss, becomes a free, trustful commitment to the impossible, which cannot be built out of what one possesses.[82]

> Hope empties and withdraws the memory from all creature possessions, for as St. Paul says, hope is for what is not possessed [Rom. 8:24]. It withdraws the memory from what can be possessed and fixes it on that for which it hopes. Hence, only hope in God prepares the memory perfectly for union with God. (N.2.21.11)

Estrangement and abandonment administer the final test of love. Theological *love* prevents us from forcing the loved one into the constraints of our needs and so takes the beloved as he or she is. In the face of seeming rejection and affective loss, theological love will not in the end surrender to hate or violence nor forfeit belief in one's own worth and lovability. Overcoming the will to die, this love lives honestly with the pain of its own woundedness and longing. It continues to serve others, often with great effectiveness, in spite of intense affective deprivation and loss. This is a profound dispossession of the self, which frees the will from its own *possessive* desire and readies the person for transformation, as John explains:

> Charity. . . . empties and annihilates the affections and appetites of the will of whatever is not God and centers them on God alone. Thus charity prepares the will and unites it with God through love. (N.2.21.11)

The contemplative posture of faith, hope, and love slowly repatterns or transforms desire and consciousness and prepares the human person for the participatory love-knowledge Divine Wisdom is and gives (N.2.21.12). However, even though secret Wisdom is the beginning of a new, more symbolic and integrated way of knowing and valuing, a deeper mutuality and connectedness that subverts our usual understanding of life and reality and expected experiences of satisfaction, nevertheless, Sophia is imperceptible, hidden from our view as a focus of meaning and motivation. She functions, on the one hand, when the image of Christ who has accompanied us thus far recedes from consciousness and cannot be recaptured for motivation and meaning. On the other hand, the subversive dynamic of beloved Sophia is set in motion when human suffering, loss, and emptiness have reached such a pitch of consciousness, are such a reflection of Jesus silenced, rejected, abused, dismissed, and abandoned, that the capacity of the human person is hollowed out for deeper knowing, deeper mutuality, a Wisdom presence and vision in the world (N.2.17).

Then the image of Jesus-Sophia dying, the image of all that is dying within and without, reaches completion.

> [This is] the real imitation [imprinting] of the perfect life of the Son of God . . . [through which God] will bring her to the high perfection of union with the Son of God, her spouse, and transformation in him through love. (C.1.10)[83]

Ever so slowly, Divine Sophia actually shows herself in the soul and in the world transforming and completing human knowing and loving, fulfilling human desire.

> When this . . . night (God's communication to the spirit, which usually occurs in extreme darkness of soul) has passed, a union with the bride, *who is the Sophia of God*, then follows and love is . . . . perfect when the transformation of the soul in God is achieved. (A.1.2.4)

> Loving knowledge [Divine Wisdom] is given in the beginning thru interior purgation and suffering, after in the delight of love. (F.3.34)

> First, we can understand that *the very loving light and Sophia into which the soul will be transformed* is that which in the beginning purges and prepares it, just as the fire which transforms the wood by incorporating it into itself is that which was first preparing it for this transformation. (N.2.10.3)

Transformation and Images of Fruition

What does it mean to be united with and transformed in Sophia? What does the person see and know as a result? And how will a person who becomes such a friend and companion, the Beloved of Sophia, live and function in the world? While the text does not speak specifically of the image of the risen Jesus to indicate the completion of the image of Christ, the symbols of fruition it uses to describe the experience of transformation do indicate the reality of passing from death to life, from old to new, from present to future. Two of these, *the touch of God* and *the awakening of God*, help us to probe these questions about transformation in wisdom.

The Touch of Sophia-God

First of all, in an experience of loving communion and total mutuality,[84] the person is touched and marked with an "image of fruition" that now heals and affirms rather than wounds and oppresses (F.3.81). With this symbol of the touch of God, a distinctly wisdom image found in *The Living Flame*,[85] we see the mysterious evolution from the imprinting of dying Crucified Sophia to the image or all-pervading presence of a Sophia-God who gently touches the totality of a person's life with acceptance and gathers up the scattered fragments of alienation, loneliness, longing, loss, and failure into a meaningful whole. Life is no longer seen in painful, confusing, segmented parts.

> You have wounded me [with your touch] in order to cure me, O divine Hand, and you have put to death in me what made me lifeless, deprived me of God's life in which I now see myself live. . . . [You] touch [with] the splendor of your glory and the figure of your substance [Heb. 1:3], which is your only begotten Son, through whom, being your substance, you touch mightily from one end to the other [Wis. 8:1]. And your only begotten Son, O merciful hand of the Father, is the delicate touch by which you touched me with the force of your cautery and wounded me. . . . [Now] then, [through] the delicate touch, the Word, the Son of God, . . . you subtly penetrate the substance of my soul and, lightly touching it all, absorb it entirely in yourself in divine ways of delights and sweetnesses. (F.2.16-17)[86]

> O sweet cautery,
> O delightful wound!

> O gentle hand! O delicate touch
> that tastes of eternal life
> and pays every debt!
> In killing you changed death to life. (F.2)

John indicates that now the *glorious* image of Sophia-Jesus has been sketched within: a touch of affirmation, a seal of divinity on a person's life and being (F.2.8). This touch is gentle, adjusting to human readiness, for although Wisdom reaches from one end of the universe to the other, pervading everything, she shows herself in order to exalt and affirm those she loves (Wis 8:1) and this is a continuing and deepening subversion of the self-image, this time on the side of exaltation. Ultimately, Sophia-Beloved is the presence of a God who not only delights to be with us but whose only desire is to exalt us, delight us, affirm us, and make us an equal.

> Since God's purpose in granting these communications is *to exalt the soul,* God does not weary and restrict it, but enlarges and delights it; God does not blacken and convert it to ashes, . . . but brightens and enriches it. (F.2.3)

> If anything pleases [God], it is the exaltation of the soul. Since there is no way by which [God] can exalt her more than by making her equal to [the Divine], God is pleased only with her love. . . . Since the soul in this state possesses perfect love, she is called the bride of the Son of God, which signifies equality with him. In this equality of friendship the possessions of both are held in common. (C.28.1)[87]

While there is a time to see our miseries and hypocrisies in the mirror of secret, suffering Wisdom and to recognize our suffering lives as a reflection of Jesus rejected, abused, and dismissed, the time does come to see one's own beauty in the mirror of the glorified Jesus-Sophia and to experience oneself so loved, so cherished, so affirmed—"a union of love"—that one realizes God deals with one now as with "a Queen," that is, an equal.[88] Over and over again, John accents the exaltation, affirmation, delight, sweetness, and equality of love:

> Let us rejoice, Beloved,
> and let us go forth to behold
> ourselves in your beauty,
> to the mountain and to the hill,
> to where the pure water flows,
> and further, deep into the thicket. (C.36)[89]

The person is only able to see herself in the mirror of God's beauty because she has been transformed in Divine Sophia, has received the imprint of the *total* life of Jesus Christ in whom she experiences herself in possession of everything worthwhile on earth and in heaven (C.36.8). As in the dark night, Sophia is full of subversive, creative power, the source of newness and radical self-valuation.[90]

> When you looked at me
> your eyes imprinted your grace in me;
> for this you loved me ardently;
> and thus my eyes deserved
> to adore what they beheld in you.
>
> Do not despise me;
> for if, before, you found me dark,
> now truly you can look at me
> since you have looked
> and left in me grace and beauty. (C.32–3)

> By this look of love God made her gracious and pleasing to himself. And. . . . from this grace and value she received from him, she merited his love and *a value within herself.*(C.32.2)

A value, an appreciation, within herself! If anything marks transformation in Sophia, it is self-acceptance and self-appreciation. In the latter part of both *The Spiritual Canticle* and *The Living Flame of Love,* one can trace a thrilling affirmation of the gifts of the person that undercuts any temptation to false humility.[91] When a person is transformed in Divine Sophia, therefore, her view of herself is radically altered. She moves from self-doubt, loneliness, powerlessness, inferiority, and subordination to see the completed inner image and to claim her own inner truth, her own inner voice, that is, to claim Wisdom: the creative power to bring into being new ways of thinking, new ideas and priorities, new visions, new ways of living and being together with others on the earth in cooperation and mutuality.[92] In other words,

> the experience is not only within her but overflows and becomes manifest outside of her, and those capable of recognizing it are aware of her experience. . . . This causes awe and respect in others. (C.17.7)

She moves, as well, from domination, control, anxiety, competition, and exploitation to receive Wisdom in mindless, playful joy, and delight. For the transformed person there is, therefore, not only validation of the inmost self but a fundamental revision of previously held beliefs and a radical questioning of deeply entrenched societal systems.

But the glorious presence or imprinting of Divine Sophia effects even more. When Sophia-Beloved transforms and exalts a person, every wound of the past, every hurt and bitterness, becomes a wound of love. In fact, the person becomes "completely healthy in love" (F.2.7).[93] Can we even imagine all our wounds, sufferings, obsessions, and sins being energized for love, becoming a power for love? The force and weight of our mistakes and failures flipped over to reveal sheer love? Can we imagine feeling a love commensurate with all our life sufferings and losses? The healing promised here is indescribable, and it is theological in character rather than simply psychological. This is the other side of the dark night revealing the Resurrected One whose wounds shine brightly forever as wounds of love, and this is the image the tranformed person bears sketched within. In the mirror of this Sophia-Jesus risen from the dead, every wound is seen to be and therefore given back a wound of love, given back, in fact, as a capacity to see and an empowerment to touch tenderly the mysterious imprinting of divinty present in every person. Furthermore, these wounds of love have been in the making for a very long time. Here the text sings of the person so healed:

> The soul feels its ardor strengthen and increase and its love become so refined in this ardor that seemingly there are seas of loving fire within it, reaching to the heights and depths of the earthly and heavenly spheres, inbuing all with love. It seems to it that the entire universe is a sea of love in which it is engulfed, for conscious of the living point or center of love within itself, it is unable to catch sight of the boundaries of this love. . . . For the soul is converted into an immense fire of love which emanates from the enkindled point at the heart of the [human] spirit. (F.2.10–1)

What must be understood here is that the contemplative person "no longer goes about in search of her own gain" or self-filfillment, nor does she occupy herself with matters foreign to God's concerns since now she has traded her former self-centered manner of dealing with life for a love and service of the Beloved One, which embraces the universe. All the powers of the person move in love (C.28.2–3 & 8).

> Now I occupy my soul
> and all my energy in his service;
> I no longer tend the herd,
> nor have I any other work
> now that my every act is love. (C.28)

As Teilhard de Chardin has also insisted in *The Divine Milieu,* nothing in the universe is a more powerful energy than love. This is what Sophia-God makes use of to bring creation to completion (C.27.8). These acts of love are so precious that they are more valuable for the world than any acts that could be done without this love (F.1.3). Furthermore, this love overflows of necessity and is therefore effective in the service of the world (C.36.4). And few of us would dispute the need for this kind of effective love as a resource for humanity today.

The Awakening of Sophia-God

We have here such a radical change of desire and consciousness that John, in the final stanza of his last major poem, "The Living Flame of Love," writes about *the awakening of God,* a second image of fruition. It is the symbol of the dark night itself that gives the clue and direction for one of the most dynamic and all-embracing images of the transforming presence of the risen Christ, Divine Sophia. After the silence and suffering of a long dark night, secret Wisdom awakens:

> How gently and lovingly
> you wake in my heart,
> where in secret you dwell alone;
> and in your sweet breathing,
> filled with good and glory,
> how tenderly you swell my heart with love.
> (F.4)

The awakening of God in the fourth stanza of *The Living Flame* is one of the most significant wisdom sections in John's writings. It is an ode to the fullness of the presence of Divine Sophia in a life and therefore in the world. It shows how profound was John's conscious dependence on the Book of Wisdom for an understanding of *who* the glorified Jesus is for us, how progressively subversive Wisdom really is, and who the friend of Wisdom becomes in the world. We read again the description of Sophia influencing John here:

> Wisdom is more mobile than any motion; because of her pureness she pervades and penetrates all things. For she is a breath of the power of God and a pure emanation of the glory of the Almighty. . . . For she is a reflection of eternal light, a spotless mirror of the working of God, and an image of God's goodness. Although she is but one, she can do all things; and while remaining in herself, she renews all things; in every generation she passes into holy souls and makes them friends of God and prophets. . . . She reaches mightily from one end of the earth to the other and orders all things well. (Wis 7:24–8; 8:1; F.4.6)

The awakening of God within the human heart is, obviously, human awakening to what is. However, since such a fundamental transformation of knowledge, such a radical conversion of perspective and desire, such a drastic expansion of imagination are experienced, it is perceived as God's waking up (seeing) and gently breathing love from the very core of a person to every thought, emotion, desire, and action.

> For since it is the soul that is renewed and moved by God so that it might [have] supernatural sight, and since that divine life and the being and harmony of every creature in that life, with its movements in God, is revealed to it with such newness, it seems to the soul that it is God who moves. . . . *For Wisdom is more moveable than all moveable things* [Wis. 7:24]. And this is not because she moves but because she is the principle and root of all movement. *Remaining in herself the same . . . she renews all things* [Wis. 7:27]. Thus . . . Wisdom is more active than all active things. We then ought to say that in this movement it is the soul that is moved and awakened from the sleep of natural vision to supernatual vision [i.e., God's vision]. . . . And [thus] the soul sees what God is in [God's very self] and what God is in . . . creatures in only one view. . . . God effects this awakening and view given to the soul

[by] remov[ing] some of the many veils and curtains hanging in front of it so that it might get a glimmer of [God] as [God] is. And then that countenance of God, full of graces, becomes partially and vaguely discernible, for not all the veils are removed. (F.4.6–7)

The person then "knows" with a deeper kind of participatory love-knowledge, for when Divine Sophia, the Beloved, the Word "awakens" and "moves" in this way, altering permanently and radically one's vision of reality, then absolutely everyone and everything in the universe is experienced as indissolubly and harmoniously interconnected and part of an energizing Mystery that binds everything together. In the lover of Divine Sophia we see a remarkable instance of the earth, the cosmos, becoming truly conscious of itself as it really is, every species connected to every other, seeing itself for the first time, as it were, in the eyes of the person transformed in Sophia. For such a person, the face of the awakening God is filled with the gifts and graces of all creatures, the entire creation. The grace, the beauty, of every form and species of life is seen in the inner mirror of Wisdom and is, therefore, known in a new way and valued for itself in God.

To see a "trace" of God's passing in the beauty of creatures and the wonder of the earth is one way of knowing and experiencing God. We learn to love God through this experience: finding God in all things! To see and possess the beauty of the created universe and everyone and everything in it *in God* is quite another vision.[94] Some of John's most frequently quoted lines of poetry express this vision:

> My Beloved, the mountains,
> and lonely wooded valleys,
> strange islands,
> and resounding rivers,
> the whistling of love-stirring breezes,
> the tranquil night
> at the time of the rising dawn,
> silent music,

> sounding solitude,
> the supper that refreshes and deepens love.
> (C.14–5)

These mountains—my Beloved is this to me! These valleys—my Beloved is this to me! Strange islands and resounding rivers that drown our dark desires and fill everything with peace—God is this to me! The Beloved becomes everything, and yet everything becomes the "Beloved" one, the Sophia of God, and therefore integrally part of the beloved friend of Wisdom who now experiences herself connected to every other form of life on the earth (C.14/15.4–9; 24.6).[95] In this unearned, gratuitous awakening of consciousness, the participatory love-driven knowledge initially experienced secretly and painfully in the dark night now explodes into an undeniable, conscious insight and passionate love for "the world." This identification with the entire cosmic order and the discovery of the earth as a living organism is the mystical basis for an intimate and compassionate human presence to other humans, to the earth, and to all living things.

First of all, then, the capacity for hearing the cry of the poor and suffering of the earth breaks open into a nearly incomprehensible desire to "enter all the afflictions and sorrows of the world" (C.36.11) in order to enter even more deeply into the Divine Wisdom in which all are rooted and connected. Because it brings together delight and suffering, happiness and death, *The Spiritual Canticle* 36.11–3 is a mysterious text, difficult to interpret, showing a distinctly different experience from the identification with "the poor" in *The Dark Night*. Since the experiences described in these texts are never disembodied, no matter how lofty they seem to be, one has to think that the person transformed in Divine Wisdom is to the rational mind a confusing and wonderful paradox, propelled *to run* with joy into the thicket of the poor and suffering, seeing there *already* the resurrected face of Beloved Sophia.[96]

And, in exchange, it will be a singular comfort and happiness for her to enter all the afflictions and trials of the world, and everything that might be a means to this, however difficult and painful, even the anguish and agony of death, all in order to see herself further within her God. (C.36.11)

Suffering is the means of her penetrating further, deep into the thicket of this delectable Wisdom of God. The purest suffering brings with it the purest and most intimate knowing, and consequently the purest and highest joy, because it is a knowing from further within. (C.36.12)

Oh! If we could but now fully understand how a soul cannot reach the thicket and wisdom of the riches of God, which are of many kinds, without entering the thicket of many kinds of suffering, finding in this her delight and consolation; and how a soul with an authentic desire for *Divine Wisdom wants suffering first in order to enter this Wisdom by the thicket of the cross.* Accordingly, St. Paul admonished the Ephesians not to grow weak in their tribulations and be strong and rooted in charity in order to comprehend with all the saints what is the breadth and height and depth, and to know also the supereminent charity of the knowledge of Christ, in order to be filled with the fullness of God [Eph. 3:13, 17–19]. *The gate entering into these riches of [God's] Wisdom is the cross*, which is narrow, and few desire to enter by it, but many desire the delights obtained from entering there. (C.36.13)

One suspects the beloved of Sophia has a whole new slant on suffering and identification with the poor and marginalized. Sophia is so related to the world, to the people, that the friend of Sophia will experience herself immersed in and connected to the suffering with the compassion of Sophia. She will value life and health everywhere; value food for bodies as well as education and love for mind and soul; value justice and affirmation and equality. This means that in the transformed person, Sophia's compassionate presence will be productive and deeply subversive.

Second, and related to the first, the capacity for listening to what the earth is telling us opens up. The text speaks, in fact, of an immense, powerful voice that sounds in the soul: the voice of creation in all the magnitude of its struggles and wonders.

> What a person knows and experiences of God in this awakening is entirely beyond words. Since this awakening is the communication of God's excellence to the substance of the soul, . . . an immense, powerful voice sounds in it, the voice of a multitude of excellences, . . . infinite in number. The soul is established in them . . . [and it sees God whose] countenance [is] filled with the graces of all creatures, awesome in power and glory, and with the voice of a multitude of excellences. (F.4.10–1)[97]

In actuality, compassionate presence and subversive identification with the marginal experienced in the dark night take on broader and even more effective cosmic significance here. In other words, Sophia awakens not only in a person's individual self, not only in one's sisters and brothers, not only in the poor and marginalized, but Spirit-Sophia awakens simultaneously in all of matter to be enjoyed in the immensity of all that is. The person transformed in Sophia experiences the sacred community of the earth, the entire earth with all its energies and diversity and all its species, awakening and coming to life—all a part of each, and all a part of her—each possessing a value and a wisdom of its own, all moving in a wonderful harmony and each giving voice to what Creator-Sophia is in it.

> In the nocturnal tranquillity and silence and in that knowledge of the divine light the soul becomes aware of Wisdom's wonderful harmony and sequence in the variety of her creatures and works. Each of them is endowed with a certain likeness of God and in its own way gives voice to what God is in it. So creatures will be for the soul a harmonious symphony of sublime music surpassing all concerts and melodies of the world. (C.14/15.25)

To know oneself, the human, one with the immensity of all that is, is an ecstatic experience in which to rest and rejoice, and even to suffer. Because historically until very recently we have been deprived of the language of contemplation or mysticism in ordinary life and religious education, American spirituality is not at home with words like resting, tasting, ecstacy, being, delight, joy, and Lover/Beloved, nor are Americans, therefore, at home with "the languages of the multitude of beings" inhabiting the earth in such a highly differentiated unity.[98] Our culture has had far too much to do with achieving mastery over the earth, other earth species and one another, to be mindful that there is a contemplative time for resting and delighting in the exquisite harmony of all that is and for understanding and communicating in the nonhuman languages of mountain, river, tree, wolf, stars. The person transformed in Beloved Sophia hears the new, more symbolic languages needed to enter into the subjective depths of things.

We need this experience, enhancing self-appreciation and yet relativizing self-importance, if we are to move toward an understanding of the connectedness of the cosmos that will save existing life on earth. Divine Sophia, the glorified Christ, shows us the unbreakable connection between creator and creatures, between "heaven" and earth, and between one another, for Sophia pervades, connects, and energizes the entire cosmos. It is not that Sophia-Jesus reconnects us to the earth and to one another. Rather, in the experience of awakening, one *sees and knows* it is a delusion to perceive ourselves as separate from the earth, from one another, and from all other species of life, superior and unaccountable to the earth and to other forms of life. The vision of Divine Sophia enables contemplative people to be keepers of the earth and of beauty because they experience the connectedness of it all in *the* Beauty.

John of the Cross could not have expressed this experience as twentieth-century writers like Thomas Berry, Brian Swimme, Elizabeth Johnson, and Sallie McFague do:

> Even as a species we are not separate and isolated, but in all our
> uniqueness . . . "[w]e belong, from the cells of our bodies to the
> finest creations of our minds, to the intricate, constantly changing
> cosmos." [99]

Nevertheless, within the framework of a Sophia-God, this sixteenth-century mystic does describe this experience of the reality of the universe in a way we are only beginning to comprehend and express.

> This is the third gift the Beloved will bestow on the soul.
> Since many plants and animals are nurtured in it, the "grove"
> refers to God, for God nurtures and gives being to all creatures
> rooted and living in God. Through this gift God shows himself to
> her and reveals himself as Creator.
> By the "living beauty" of this grove, for which she asks the
> Bridegroom here, she intends to beg for the grace, wisdom, and
> beauty which every earthly and heavenly creature not only has
> from God but also manifests in its wise, well-ordered, gracious,
> and harmonious relationship to other creatures. Thus we find this
> accord among the lower creatures and among the higher, and we
> find it as well in the relationship between the higher and lower.
> The knowledge of this harmony fascinates and delights the soul.
> (C.39.11)

Implications

The Mystic Vision. In actuality, John had a vision of kinship with the earth whose evolutionary truth and meaning he could not have begun to fathom with his sixteenth-century cosmology and worldview.[100] Yet it welled up from the ageless roots of his being, from the Source of all life, from the Wisdom of the Universe itself and all the collective energies of the cosmos, all the reserves of life in the earth coalesced and reached for consciousness in this sixteenth-century mystic. His wisdom vision was far ahead of his time—in a sense, ahead of himself. Yet he looked over the edges of human consciousness and dwelt there. And his life, dedicated to the companionship of Sophia-Jesus, not only endured the darkness of a dying time, but actually called forth the *unitive* energies of the cosmos and gave them sanctuary within himself. The universe spoke its meaning in him.[101]

If indeed matter, alive with energy stretching back through galactic ages to the big bang, does somehow evolve to spirit, as Teilhard de Chardin insisted some years ago and others are suggesting now, if the human spirit is the cosmos come to consciousness, then the mystic transformed in Divine Sophia is the human spirit itself at the fullest consciousness possible to the human species at any one time in history.[102] This means that transformation in Divine Sophia is not something completely new and extraordinary added to the universe from outside by a God distant from the cosmos; rather, this transformation is the most advanced evolutionary possibility and expression, the cutting edge of evolution, the full flowering of the earth and of the cosmic energies within the human. As such, the mystic is a prophecy and a promise. And the wisdom language of the mystic is a code to be broken by us for our time and situation when the survival of life on the earth hangs on humanity's total, unwavering appropriation of a new vision of the cosmos and even a new vision of God.

In John's writings, we gain some idea of the frontiers to which Sophia brings us. Sophia is a key for understanding the place of the mystic at the forefront of the earth's evolutionary process, the cosmos coming to full consciousness. If, as Thomas Berry and Brian Swimme believe, the next stage in the development of the universe will require above everything else the insight of shamanic powers, then Sophia may be the God we need to make us mystics.[103]

The Prophet of Sophia and Contemplative Transformation. Transformation in Loving Sophia actually changes the mind, the imagination, the memory, the heart, the desires, and the will through a painful process of death, thereby advancing human knowing and loving with a vision of the universe that places Sophia in intimate, dynamic, energizing, life-giving relationship to the whole evolutionary process. Therefore, the mystic's human powers, the "deep caverns of feeling," united with and transfigured in Sophia, take on the Divine Energy at the heart of the universe (C.26.5–9; 28.3–5).

The person no longer knows and understands with the vigor of her own natural light but with the divine light. This is, in effect, the transformation of the mind through a new kind of loving knowledge: Sophia. The memory, too, is changed in this union by an experience of ultimate assurance. Obsession with the past gives way to a new possession and sense of belongingness, and this conversion of memory releases creativity. The human capacity to love is also changed by the experience of God's love, as has been said above. The mystic is transformed by love and therefore loves with the love God has for us. The imprinting ("I live now not I but Christ lives in me") is so complete that the mind is God's mind, the will is God's will, the memory is the eternal memory of God, and its delight and desire are God's delight and desire (F.2.34). The person becomes, therefore, "like the shadow of God" in the world: in other words, the prophet of Sophia (F.3.78).

These are realities almost impossible to comprehend or even believe in with our postmodern consciousness, but what is significant is that for the friend and prophet of Divine Sophia the conventional way of knowing and loving is gone (C.26.13–7). The process of contemplative transformation is, moreover, not only an irreversible maturation but also a very radical reeducation of human desire and consciousness. This is why Sophia-Wisdom is so subversive and, perhaps, why her presence and power have been so confined and muted in the history of Christianity.

Those who have become friends and intimates of Wisdom, the shadow of God in the world, whose consciousness, imaginations, hearts, and desires are radically expanded by the awakening of God, by the drink of Loving Sophia, truly touch the interiority of everything living and understand the community of which we are all a part. These prophets embody the desire of Sophia-Christ for the world. They threaten the security of our way. They stand, as it were, on the side of the creative Wisdom of God actively calling us to re-creation and continual learning, to sensitivity, to beauty and wonder, to responsibility for one another and for the earth, to participative living and teaching, to connectedness and community, to justice in coherence with the harmony and order of everything on earth, over against selfish detachment, isolated individualism, self-concerned competition, domination, and oppression of others.

Participatory Love-Knowledge. It should be clear now why the Wisdom of the mystic can be called a *participatory* way of knowing and loving that moves beyond the paradigm of hierarchichal dualism that has been, in the past, part of the philosophical underpinning for our lives. There is a thrilling intersection between the love-knowledge of the contemplative and the participatory epistemology Richard Tarnas believes has been slowly surfacing in philosophy. The experience of the person transformed in Sophia validates the emerging conviction that the relation of the human mind to the cosmos is ultimately not dualistic but participatory. This throws additional light on Tarnas's previously quoted words:

> In its own depths the imagination directly contacts the creative process of nature [the universe], realizes the process within itself, and brings nature's reality [of the cosmos] to conscious expression.

> Then the world speaks its meaning through human consciousness. Then human language itself can be recognized as rooted in a deeper reality, as reflecting the universe's unfolding meaning. Through the human intellect, in all its personal individuality, contingency and struggle, the world's evolving thought-content achieves conscious articulation, . . . the world's truth achieves its existence when it

comes to birth in the human mind. As the plant at a certain stage brings forth its blossom, so does the universe bring forth new stages of human knowledge. And as Hegel emphasized, the evolution of human knowledge is the evolution of the world's self-revelation.[104]

This understanding is strikingly similar to the new paradigm proposed by Thomas Berry, Danah Zohar (*The Quantum Self*), feminist thinkers, and many others. While we do witness the breakdown of numerous structures—cultural, philosophical, scientific, religious, moral, artistic, social, political, atomic, ecological—we see, also, this new participatory world view breaking through on so many levels.[105]

Sophia-God Image. In this worldview presently crying out for paradigmatic significance, Sophia may well be a God image that corresponds and resonates with the current state of the evolving collective psyche of the earth. It seems to me that Sophia is one, clear, significant God gestalt, retrieved from the tradition and emerging out of a long, dark night of broken God symbols.[106] Spiritual directors find that people, both women and men, are actually experiencing Sophia and her emancipatory and transformative potential in their prayer, theologically confusing as this may sometimes seem to them. We may see Jesus more and more taking on the marks of Sophia, and this is probably what will save Jesus for some people. This is where *the tradition of Wisdom* in mysticism, so long muted and marginalized but embodied with such prophetic power in John of the Cross's writings, will reassure us and enable theology to speak anew about Jesus Christ.[107] The mysticism of John of the Cross supports a Sophia-God image, and a Sophia-God image, before everything else, subverts the way we understand God. It has the potential, therefore, to transform not only our consciousness and desire but most of all to change radically our theological discourse.

Feminist Consciousness and New Relationship of Mutuality. Just as there was a correlation in the past between the muting of contemplation, the suppression of Sophia, the exploitation of the earth, and the marginalization of women, so now is the emergence of feminist consciousness in so many cultures and disciplines directly connected to both the Sophia-God image and the participatory or contemplative way of knowing and understanding human life, as was already indicated in relation to the dark night. The emergence of women's voices and influence is part of an enormous epochal shift taking place in human consciousness and rising out of the unitive energies at work in the universe. As far back as the sixteenth century, a mystic like John, educated by lifelong companionship with Divine Sophia, experienced the movement of this marginalized feminine toward reconciliation and mutuality. Even the major symbolism of his poetry, lover/beloved, is testimony to this experienced mutuality and as such is prophetic for our time, for who is Lover, who beloved, who masculine, who feminine?[108]

It is not by accident, therefore, that Sophia-God, bearing the marks of the feminine, comes to the forefront at a time when many believe the dominant and pervasive masculinity of the Western intellectual and spiritual tradition is dying. Actually, the mystical language of John was a promise of this and a validation for us now of its rightness and inevitability.

Feminists have long been conscious of the darkness of this dying time as they have struggled to find meaning in the experience of impasse in their God images, in their churches and theology, in their institutional lives, and in their social and political lives. Richard Tarnas, however, emphasizes that the crisis of modern man [sic] is essentially not a feminine but a masculine crisis whose transforming resolution is actually occurring within the tremendous emergence of the feminine in our culture and in the struggles surrounding it. The dominance of the masculine (in all of us) is not only dying (dark night) but, touched by the increasing numinosity of Holy Sophia, is truly at a highly critical stage of awakening and is slowly entering, as Tarnas writes, into a fundamentally new relationship of mutuality with the feminine in all its forms. The feminine then becomes not that which must be controlled, denied and exploited, but rather fully acknowledged, respected, and responded to for itself. It is recognized not as the objectified "other," but rather source, goal, and immanent presence.[109]

In the concluding paragraphs of *The Passion of the Western Mind*, Tarnas responds to the question often asked: "Is this not just a passing fad, the last gasp of the Enlightenment?" Why have we become so aware of the pervasive masculinity of our culture and spiritual tradition only now when for almost every previous generation it was nearly invisible?

> I believe this is occurring now because, as Hegel suggested, a civilization cannot become conscious of itself, cannot recognize its own significance, until it is so mature that it is approaching its own death. Today we are experiencing something that looks very much like the death of modern man. . . . Perhaps, the end of "man" himself is at hand. But man is not a goal. Man is something that must be overcome—and fulfilled in the embrace of the feminine. . . . And their synthesis leads to something beyond itself: It brings an unexpected opening to a larger reality that cannot be grasped before it arrives, because this new reality is itself a creative act.[110]

Perhaps now, when the dominance and effects of the isolated masculine have become so apparent, and when the feminine is welling up with such powerful energy, Sophia is a God-presence capable of moving with humanity into the next epoch of life on earth. When we have passed through this night, says the mystic, we will be united with and transfigured in Divine Sophia, she who is the Word, the Christ. In this union, the evolutionary imperative of the earth, which is before us now, will come to full consciousness in the human spirit. We need a Sophia-God for this, a God who, while touching and embracing tenderly both man and woman, truly transcends patriarchy and is able, therefore, to sustain this cultural death and new synthesis and give life and meaning to them.

Conclusion

It is no wonder that now, when the human species' manipulation of the earth and the long oppression and neglect of the feminine truly threaten the survival of life on earth, when we are conscious of so many insoluble problems coming to a head in our age, when so much is breaking apart in violence and hatred, we may finally be ready and open to the experience of Sophia-God, that is, to the mystical experience and to a kind of love-knowledge as yet uncommon in human consciousness today.

At a time when philosophy is shifting radically and theology is searching for a meaningful God, when the age of technology, with all its magnificent achievements, has yet exploited the earth as an object for domination, and when a new participative epistemology is beginning to operate, a mystic like John provides some of the most precious materials for the new conceptual house of faith we are trying o build for ourselves. He "knew" that "all thinking must begin with [belief in that] cosmic genetical relatedness" that the mystic transformed in the mirror of Sophia experiences.[111]

I believe we have held up John of the Cross as if he were the end of the process of transformation. The wisdom of this mystic is more like a beginning in that his insight and experience point toward and even usher in an age yet unborn. He had the magnificent contemplative experience of mutuality and connectedness, of being part of and kin to all creation in Beloved Sophia who secretly deconstructed the pyramid of hierarchical dualism that philosophically supported his life.[112] Now, at the end of the twentieth century, there is a significance to his experience that only we can name and understand this way, as his insight, once so prophetic and almost unimaginable, actually takes shape in postmodern consciousness.

Most importantly, this means John's vision is not just a goal to be repeated, but rather one example of lifelong companionship with Sophia. His vision is only one segment of a sequence of irreversible transformations in space and time into which we need to enter on our own, thereby creating another segment, our own piece,[113] in the evolution of cosmic consciousness. We must be ready to surrender to the process of transformation ahead of us; eager, or at least willing, to appropriate the patterns of Beloved Sophia and move with the earth toward greater variety, intensity, and depth of expression and to more intimate bonding with woman, with man, with every species of life that exists.

One thing is certain: in this movement of transformation, the mystical intuition does not allow the suppression of Divine Sophia's personal engagement in the developmental process of the earth. Furthermore, since Spirit-Sophia is the unceasing, dynamic flow of divine power that sustains and pervades and embraces the universe, bringing forth life and energy at every moment, the prophet of Sophia cannot transcend the human nor the cosmos, and contemplation is more starkly necessary than ever before.

We are faced with a question repeatedly raised through the centuries by the contemplative tradition and repeatedly muted, suppressed, or ignored by the churches and society: is it time for a public contemplation, public education for contemplative prayer, that is, the integration into public life and education of a societal understanding of the contemplative process of transformation,[114] rather than a contemplative life largely hidden in the cloisters, hermitages, and ashrams of the world, muted by those who fear, however unconsciously, not only Divine Sophia but the evolutionary power of mystical transformation? And what would we have to do to achieve this if we believed it? What would educators in our schools and colleges do? What would business leaders meeting to discuss how to break the cycle of violence and bolster the economic vitality of our cities do? What agenda would politicians pursue? What would women's groups do? Where would Church leaders put their energies? What would each one of us do if we believed in the enormous power of contemplative transformation, transformation in Beloved Sophia?

Notes

1. For example, Brian Swimme, a mathematical cosmologist, and Thomas Berry, a historian of cultures, suggest that we stand between two great eras: "the Cenozoic era," which began 67 million years ago and is now in its terminal phase due to a distorted aspect of the myth of progress, and "the Ecozoic era," whose central commitment believes "that the universe is a communion of subjects rather than a collection of objects," (*The Universe Story* [San Francisco: Harper, 1992], 241–3). Cultural theorist, René Girard, according to Gil Bailie, writes in terms of "the disintegration of conventional culture, a process that is irreversible and one that constitutes humanity's moment of truth . . . . Coming to grips with the depths of the crisis (the greatest anthropological challenge in history precipitating a major epochal shift) is a daunting task, but it is also one that is full of promise, and the price to be paid for shrinking from it is too horrendous to seriously contemplate" (*Violence Unveiled* [New York: Crossroad, 1995], 5,13).

2. Richard Tarnas, *The Passion of the Western Mind* (New York: Harmony Books, 1991), 441. Tarnas sees the masculine dominance as beginning "four millenia ago with the great patriarchal nomadic conquests in Greece and the Levant over ancient matriarchal cultures, and [being] visible in the West's patriarchal religion from Judaism, its rationalist philosophy from Greece, its objectivist science from modern Europe."

3. Swimme and Berry, *255*.

4. Ray L. Hart, *Unfinished Man and the Imagination* (New York: Seabury Press, 1968), 26–36.

5. We need to understand the history that makes us the inheritors of a long period of what historian, Joseph Chinnici, calls "muted mysticism." When the sixteenth- and seventeenth-century debates over the role of mystical prayer in the context of the early modern church and state finally culminated in the condemnation of quietism in 1699, the language of mysticism and the whole tradition of contemplative prayer were muffled and privatized. In these debates carried on in Spain, England, France, and Italy, as political and social as they were religious, some questioned the advisability of mystical prayer for the common, unlearned people, particularly women. They feared the influence of interior inspiration on the obedience of the people and the effect of trust in experience and personal discernment on the order of the prevailing system, civil and ecclesiastical. "Feared

by authority in both church and state, confined by 'reason' to the cell of the 'irrational,' and removed from the marketplace by the forces of capitalism, mysticism after 1700 lost its place in the communal consciousness. Now cloistered, contemplative prayer ceased to be available to all, and the hightest reaches of holiness eluded the aspirations of the baptized. Now privatized, contemplation lost its connection with political and social change; its practioners became irrelevant. It is this history, also, which we inherit, and the mutation of our true mystical tradition accounts in large measure for the contemporary groping for a stable spiritual center" (Joseph Chinnici, "The Politics of Mysticism: Church, State, and the Carmelite Tradition," delivered during the Bicentennial Symposium of Baltimore Carmel: *Contemplation and American Culture*, Baltimore, 1990).

     6. I am conscious of how "the master narratives" of Western culture and theology are, as Elisabeth Schüssler Fiorenza believes, "always implicated in and collude with the production and maintenance of systems of knowledge that either foster exploitation and oppression or contribute to a praxis and vision of liberation." Furthermore, I am specifically aware of how some interpretations of John of the Cross's works have contributed to oppression and isolation, and I have no wish to surrender to what Fiorenza calls "a hermeneutics of undiscriminating acceptance of . . . tradition" in this study (*Jesus: Miriam's Child, Sophia's Prophet* [New York: Continuum, 1994], 5, 12). However, I do continue to ask if the tradition of mysticism as we find it in John of the Cross (and other mystics) can function for the liberation and transformation of people?

     7. These areas may prove to be important in the emergence in spirituality of a new cosmic experiential gestalt.

     8. See Elisabeth Schüssler Fiorenza, *In Memory of Her* (New York: Crossroad, 1983), 133; and *Jesus: Miriam's Child*, 135–9. In the latter treatment, Schüssler Fiorenza has an interesting development of the gender question. See also Elizabeth A. Johnson, *She Who Is* (New York: Crossroad, 1992), 87, whose lucid theological writing on Sophia has inspired and influenced my own work with Sophia in John of the Cross. See also Johnson's "Redeeming the Name of Christ," in *Freeing Theology*, ed. Catherine LaCugna (San Francisco: Harper, 1993); and Roland E. Murphy, *The Tree of Life: An Exploration of Wisdom Biblical Literature* (New York: Doubleday, 1990), 133–49, for a treatment of "Lady Wisdom." The endnotes and bibliographies in the works cited above provide evidence of the very extensive research available on Sophia.

     9. I have decided, with some hesitation, to use "New Testament" in this essay even though some scholars today propose "Christian Testament" or "Second Testament" as possibilities. Because I realize New Testament is considered by some scholars to be offensive to Jews, I considered this change. However, my concern is that those who read this for spirituality and prayer may be unfamiliar with this discussion.

10. Tarnas, 441–5. When I am using or building on Tarnas's thought, I use his capitalization of "Western."

11. Swimme and Berry, 243.

12. Tarnas, 444.

13. I realize the danger of this language since God is for John of the Cross and for us incomprehensible, beyond all our images and forms. Nevertheless, even the mystics express their ineffable experiences in images and the human person and theology will always symbolize God in some specific anthropomorphic image or images, which in turn affect human self-understanding.

14. Augustine Baker, *Sancta Sophia or Directions for the Prayer of Contemplation* (Doway: John Patte & Thomas Fievet, 1657), introductory letters and preface give some feel for this debate. This volume is in the archives of the Carmelite Monastery, Baltimore.

15. Although I have realized for a long time the relationship between the cloistering of contemplation, the role of women, and the seditious character of contemplative prayer, nevertheless Joseph Chinnici has added new historical dimensions to this understanding.

16. Most references to John of the Cross are inserted in text. Although I have made some changes in the text for inclusivity, most quotations are from Kieran Kavanaugh and Otilio Rodriguez, trans., *The Collected Works of St. John of the Cross*, rev. ed. (Washington, DC: ICS Publications, 1991). Italics in quotations are mine.

17. For further clarification and development, investigate Johnson, *She Who Is*, 92–3; and James Dunn, *Christology in the Making* (Philadelphia: Westminster Press, 1980), 170f. I draw closely on these writings. See Johnson above and "Jesus, the Wisdom of God: A Biblical Basis for Non-Androcentric Christology," *Ephemerides Theologicae Lovaniensis* (December 1985): 269–71, and Schüssler Fiorenza, *Jesus: Miriam's Child*, 135–6, for a comparison of texts regarding Isis and Sophia.

18. Johnson, *She Who Is*, 87; "Jesus, the Wisdom of God," 264.

19. Sandra Schneiders, "Feminist Spirituality," *The New Dictionary of Catholic Spirituality,* ed. Michael Downey (Collegeville, MN: Liturgical Press, 1993), 397–9, has a concise, lucid treatment of "The Rediscovery of the Goddess."

20. While I see it as a deficiency in this study, the limits of this essay prevent me from dealing with any adequacy with the presence of Sophia-Wisdom in the development of spirituality from the time of the early Church up to sixteenth-century Spain, but future study in this area is important for a more comprehensive understanding of John's use of Divine Wisdom.

21. I am using Old Testament for the first testament of the Christian Bible, especially since the Book of Wisdom is not part of the *Jewish Scriptures*, the Jewish Bible as it is used today among Jews. For a good explanation, see Sandra M. Schneiders, *The Revelatory Text* (San Francisco: Harper, 1991), 6. Besides, "Old" need not mean superseded but rather revered, venerable, and valuable.

22. Not only Proverbs, chap. 8 and Wisdom, chaps. 7–9, but also Wisdom 6:13–5; 8:1 & 31; 18:14–5; Baruch 3:23 & 31; Ecclesiasticus 51:25 & 29; Song of Songs; Psalm 76:19–20; Job 37:16; Genesis 1:31 are used by John of the Cross in a wisdom context.

23. There is an notable gender change in this passage in the 1991 translation of *The Collected Works of St. John of the Cross* where Kieran Kavanaugh equates *bride* rather than bridegroom with Divine Wisdom.

24. See, e.g., *Ascent* 1.7.3–4 in connection with *Ascent* 1.4.8, and 13.3–4.

25. "All creatures of heaven and earth are nothing when compared to God" or "all the being of creatures compared to the infinite being of God is nothing and . . . therefore, anyone attached to creatures is nothing in the sight of God" (A.1.4.3–4). *Ascent* 1.4 is a pivotal chapter on this subject, but *Ascent* 1.6–12 delineates the destructive effects of addictive desire which weaken, weary, torment, blind, and defile.

26. A key text for understanding and interpreting John is indicated here, one to which I will return later: "Have a habitual desire to imitate Christ in all your deeds by bringing your life into conformity with his. You must then study his life in order to know how to imitate him" (A.1.13.3).

27. In other words, the experience of one's self, painful as this can be, is an experience of God or stimulates the desire for God: "The soul has made known the manner of preparing oneself to begin this journey: to pursue delights and satisfactions no longer, and to overcome temptations and difficulties through fortitude. *This is the practice of self-knowledge, the first requirement for advancing to the knowledge of God*," (C.4.1) that is, the initial step on the path to contemplation. See Karl Rahner, "Experience of Self and Experience of God," in *Theological Investigations,* vol. 13 (New York: Crossroad, 1983), 122–32. Rahner's work, here and elsewhere, shows a striking familiarity with John of the Cross and Teresa of Avila. Elizabeth Johnson also deals with the self in relation to Rahner in *She Who Is*, 65–7.

28. See *Ascent* 2.17.1–5 for this important dynamic and its relationship to wisdom. This is a very important text in interpreting John of the Cross because he gives here his epistomology, or the way he understands the whole process of acquiring knowledge.

29. See my earlier work on the Dark Night: Constance FitzGerald, "Impasse and Dark Night," in *Living With Apocalypse*, ed. Tilden Edwards (San Francisco: Harper & Row, 1984), 97; and Michael Buckley, "Atheism and Contemplation" in *Theological Studies* 40 (1979): 696, which I cite there.

30. Wisdom 7:13–22.

31. Elizabeth Johnson, *Women, Earth, and Creator Spirit* (New York: Paulist Press, 1993), 10–1, explains "hierarchical dualism" as the dominant form of western rationality, a major taproot connecting the exploitation of the earth and the treatment of women. "This is a pattern of thought and action that (1) divides reality into

two separate spheres, and (2) assigns a higher value to one of them. In terms of the three basic relations that shape an ecological ethic, this results in a view in which humanity is detached from and more important than nature; man is separate from and more valuable than woman; God is disconnected from the world, utterly . . . transcendent over it. . . . . Hierarchical dualism delivers a two tiered vision of reality that privileges the elite half of a pair and subordinates the other, which is thought to have no intrinsic value of its own but exists only to be of use to the higher." See pp. 10–22.

32. See *The Spiritual Canticle*, st. 4–6 with the corresponding commentary.

33. The influence of Sophia as she appears in Proverbs 8:22–30 is apparent in this section of *The Spiritual Canticle*: "The Lord begot me. . . . When [God] established the earth I was there." See also Wisdom 7:24–7.

34. For a contemporary treatment of image of God, see Elizabeth Johnson, *She Who Is*, 69–75.

35. Hebrews 1:2 is significant here: "In this the final age [God] has spoken to us thru [the] Son whom [God] has made heir of all things and thru whom [God] first created the universe."

36. Harvey Egan, *What Are They Saying about Mysticism?* (New York: Paulist Press, 1982), 106.

37. See, e.g., Dunn, 177–209; Johnson, "Jesus, the Wisdom of God," 276–89.

38. "Redeeming the Name," 127.

39. To witness a feminist theologian underlining the importance of Jesus for personal spirituality, see Sandra M. Schneiders, "The Resurrection of Jesus and Christian Spirituality," in *Christian Resources of Hope*, ed. Maureen Junker-Kenny (Dublin: Columba Press, 1995), 81–114.

40. In Canticle 37.4 John comments again on this same text.

41. Compare with Wisdom 7:26 and Colossians 2:2–3, & 9; see also *Flame* 3.17.

42. Feminist writers suggest this is not necessarily positive for feminist emancipation. See, for example, Schüssler Fiorenza, *Jesus: Miriam's Child*, 131–62.

43. This study limps, as was said before, as long as we do not understand the precise theological trajectory of wisdom Christology to which John was heir.

44. "Jesus, The Wisdom of God," 261.

45. Ibid. See also James Dunn, *Christology*, 164–6 and all that of chaps. 6 and 7 for an excellent treatment that includes the scriptural texts.

46. While an *infinite* human capacity for God can be questioned, John explains in *Flame* 3.22 that "the capacity of these caverns [intellect, memory, will] is deep because the object of this capacity, namely God, is profound and infinite. Thus in a *certain fashion their capacity is infinite, their thirst is infinite, their hunger is also deep and infinite, and their languishing and suffering are infinite death.*"

47. This is a fundamental text regarding affective purification. It interprets all that precedes it in book 1 of *The Ascent*.

48. See *Ascent* 2.22.3. Although in this part of the text Sophia is subsumed in the Word, the Logos, nevertheless by using "the mouth of God" symbolism, an allusion to Sirach 24, it distinctly shows the connection made between the two.

49. See Fiorenza, *Jesus: Miriam's Child*, 162.

50. In *Canticle* 12, John develops at length this inner image as a faith experience, which has intellectual, volitional, and emotional components. There is a sketch of faith in the mind giving meaning to a person's life (C.12.6), a sketch of love in the will effecting commitment to the beloved, and a sketch of hope in the memory producing trust and a sense of belongingness (C.12.7).

51. There is such an interplay of wisdom symbolism here: crystal, face, sketch, mirror, eyes, seeing, knowing and being known, being carried away by the beauty one beholds, and, therefore, being changed and made beautiful like the beauty one sees.

52. In *Flame* 3.41–5, John castigates those spiritual directors who do not understand the secret, loving wisdom of contemplative prayer, that is, "the sublime anointings and shadings of the Holy Spirit," and therefore damage or destroy by poor direction the image God is painting within the human person. "Who will succeed," he says, "in repairing that delicate painting of the Holy Spirit once it is marred by a coarse hand?" Without an understanding of the essential role of the developing pattern of Jesus-Sophia in a person's spiritual growth, one can "lose the sublime image that God [is] painting within."

53. We can note an intersection here with John M. Staudemaier's interpretation of the dynamic of the Second Week of the Exercises of St. Ignatius, which "inculcates a form of personal intimacy with Jesus that opens out to intimacy with the larger world, an intimacy of affective engagement that leads to action in the world." See "To Fall in Love with the World" in *Studies in the Spirituality of Jesuits* (May 1994): 1–28.

54. This section on the dark night was first published in part in "Ignatian Prayer," *The Way Supplement* 82 (Spring 1995), as "Desolation as Dark Night: The Transformative Influence of Wisdom in John of the Cross," 96–108. I intended the title to have been "The Transformative Influence of Wisdom in the Dark Night" since I do not deal with Ignatian desolation there, and never intended to do so.

55. Teresa of Avila writes about this kind of experience in *The Book of Her Life*. See, e.g., Kieran Kavanaugh and Otilio Rodriguez, trans. *The Collected Works of St. Teresa of Avila*, vol. 1 (Washington, DC: ICS Publications, 1976), chap. 40.10, 280–1.

56. See *Ascent* 2.17 and note 28, to understand John's teaching on knowledge and Sophia's role in this process.

57. When I wrote "Impasse and Dark Night" in *Living with Apocalypse*, later reprinted in *Women's Spirituality*, ed. Joanne Wolski Conn (New York: Paulist

Press, 1984 and 1996), I did not directly address the significance of Jesus-Sophia in the dark night. This Christological way of experiencing the dark night is a necessary complement to the impasse experience, just as the impasse experience I describe is a part of my development here.

58. See *Dark Night* 2.5.1–2; 2.17; *Ascent* 2.8.6 to study in context the equivalencies that John sets up.

59. Another relevant text is *Dark Night* 1.10.6 where infused contemplation is, according to Kieran Kavanaugh, mentioned for the first time and equated with "dark and secret contemplation" and "secret and peaceful and loving inflow of God." "Such persons should not mind if the operations of their faculties are being lost to them; they should desire rather that this be done quickly so they may be no obstacle to the operation of the infused contemplation God is bestowing, so they may receive it with more peaceful plenitude and make room in the spirit for the enkindling and burning of the love that this dark and secret contemplation bears and communicates to the soul. For contemplation is nothing else than a secret and peaceful and loving inflow of God, which, if not hampered, fires the soul in the spirit of love."

60. See also *Dark Night* 2.17 for an extensive and very beautiful treatment of secret mystical Wisdom and dark contemplation.

61. In *Ascent* 2.7.8–9, we note how Christ Crucified is seen as the pattern or mirror of the dark night. The whole context of this chapter is important because it shows Jesus dying as the unitive image.

62. See also *Flame* 2.17 and Wisdom 7:24 and 8.

63. *Dark Night* 2.5.5: "This divine and dark light causes deep immersion of the mind in the knowledge and feeling of one's own miseries and evils; it brings all these miseries into relief so that the soul sees clearly that of itself it will never possess anything else."

64. This is what I have called the purification of desire in "Impasse and Dark Night." This purification takes place in one's life situation and therefore is mediated through one's central human relationships and life project.

65. This is the powerful title of Gil Bailie's groundbreaking work mentioned at the beginning of this study.

66. As I have suggested in "Impasse and Dark Night," 97, "transfiguration does not happen at the end of the road; it is in the making now. If we could see the underside of this death, we would realize it is already resurrection." Furthermore, as Sandra Schneiders suggests in "Feminist Spirituality," 400: For feminist spirituality groping to claim and understand Sophia, the personal is always political; personal transformation is the only possible basis for societal transformation. In this context, it is important to note that the presence of loving Wisdom in John of the Cross is not an esoteric, condescending, or world-transcending presence, but an affirmation of and solidarity with the human, with the body, with the earth, in all its fragility and poverty. Sophia is at home on the streets of the

world. Where Sophia is, we hear the call: "Come all who are burdened. . . . Come, eat and drink you who have no money. . . . Come all who are thirsty."
    67. Description given in note 31 above.
    68. Tarnas, 433–45. I draw on his thought in the following section.
    69. Ibid., 434-5.
    70. Among these trailblazers in religious thinking is Thomas Berry, *The Dream of the Earth* (San Francisco: Sierra Club Books, 1988); see also Swimme and Berry, 243: "Existence itself is derived from and sustained by this intimacy of each being with every other being."
    71. Tarnas, 444.
    72. Bailie, 272.
    73. John says in *Ascent* 2.12.3: "The soul will have to empty itself of these images and leave this sense in darkness if it is to reach divine union. For these images, just as the corporeal objects of the exterior senses, cannot be an adequate, proximate means to God." In *The Collected Works of St. John*, 186, Kavanaugh adds a note: "Having in mind . . . a contemplative simplification of prayer, John stresses communion in living faith more than discursive reflection. These passages do not advise one to turn away from Jesus Christ but insist on the simple gaze of faith and personal communion rather than on imaginative representation. John's teaching is in harmony with St. Teresa of Avila's. Strongly asserting that one must never turn from the humanity of Christ, she nonetheless admits that it is common for contemplative souls to be unable to engage in discursive thought about the mysteries of Christ's life. Communing with the Person, however, 'dwelling on his mysteries with a simple gaze,' is another matter and 'will not impede the most sublime prayer' (*Interior Castle* 6.7.6–7, 11–2; *The Way of Perfection* 34.11)."
    74. In this context, Ascent 2.8 (chapter heading) and 4–5 are instructive also: "No creature or knowledge comprehensible to the intellect can serve it as a proximate means for divine union with God. . . . Everything the intellect can understand, the will enjoy, the imagination picture is most unlike and disproportionate to God. . . . The intellect will be unable through its ideas to understand anything like God, the will unable to experience a delight and sweetness resembling God, and the memory unable to place in the imagination remembrances and images representing him." See also *Ascent* 2.9.4: "Union with God in this life, and direct communication with [God], demands that we be united with the darkness in which, as Solomon said [1 Kgs. 8:12], God promised to dwell."
    75. This experience may be further complicated by contemporary developments and questions in Christology, particularly those regarding the divinity of Jesus.
    76. I first began developing the interpretation of "the dark night of the spirit" set forth in this section in "A Discipleship of Equals: Voices from Tradition— Teresa of Avila and John of the Cross" in *A Discipleship of Equals: Toward a Christian Feminist Spirituality*, ed. Francis A. Eigo (Villanova: Villanova University Press, 1988), 63–97. I have included it in *The Way* article and here because the Villanova volume has been unavailable almost from the time of its publication.

77. That Jesus as the Sophia of God subverts conventional wisdom is persuasively suggested by Marcus J. Borg, *Jesus, a New Vision* (San Francisco: Harper, 1987), chap. 6: "Jesus as Sage: Challenge to Conventional Wisdom," and *Meeting Jesus Again for the First Time* (San Francisco: Harper, 1994), 84–8, 106, 134.

78. See also *Dark Night* 2.10.2 and *Flame* 1.22 & 23. No. 23 is on the will.

79. See *Dark Night* 2.7 on "straits of the will"; *Dark Night* 2.9.3 & 7; *Ascent* 3.16; 35.5; *Flame* 1.23.

80. Denys Turner, *The Darkness of God: Negativity in Christian Mysticism* (Cambridge: Cambridge University Press, 1995), 246.

81. For a description of faith see *Ascent* 2.3; 4.1–3; 8 & 9; *Dark Night* 2.16.8–12.

82. Karl Rahner has helped me interpret John's thought on hope and on the theological virtues. See "On the Theology of Hope," *Theological Investigations,* vol. 10 (New York: Herder & Herder, 1973), 242–53, and "Theology of Death," *Theological Investigations* vol. 13 (New York: Crossroad, 1983), 169–86.

83. Elizabeth Johnson reminds us of a long-standing tradition of interpretation concerning martyrs, a tradition which Vatican II continues: "Martyrdom 'transforms' a disciple into an intense image of Christ, *imago Christi,* for the martyr 'perfects that image even to the shedding of blood' " (*She Who Is,* 74; *Lumen Gentium,* 42).

84. See, e.g., *Flame* 3.79.

85. The "touch of divinity" is found also in *The Ascent* (e.g., A.2.26.5–10; 2.32) and *The Dark Night*.

86. See *Flame* 3.81. Touch is also an important symbol of desire in *The Spiritual Canticle*. Here in *Flame*, the Word, the Son of God, is a touch of the divine hand. Note the comparison at the end of *Flame* 2.17 between the touch or tracing within and the withdrawal from the touch or trace of creatures. This is to accent the touch of Sophia-Jesus "compared with" all other touches and is an allusion to *Ascent* 1.4.

87. See *Canticle* 39.6: ". . . equals and companions of God."

88. *Flame* 4.13 brings together the Wisdom image of Christ or Word with the experience of equality: "There *the face of the Word,* full of graces, . . . *shines on the queen,* which is the soul, and clothes it in such fashion that, transformed in these attributes of the heavenly king, it is aware of having become a queen." See also *Canticle* 30.6.

89. See commentary Canticle 36.5 on this stanza for equality emphasis and extravagant expression of mutuality. See also *Canticle* 32.6; 24.5; 38.3–6. This equality is taken to even greater lengths when God becomes the person's slave and prisoner, subject to her desires (*Canticle* 27.1; 32.1).

90. Susan Cady, Marian Ronan, Hal Taussig, *Sophia: The Future of Feminist Spirituality* (San Francisco: Harper & Row, 1986), 84, suggests that "by identifying

with the one who took a playful part in creation, women can imagine new and larger arenas in which their creativity can flourish" in the world.

91. There are many texts that could be cited. See, e.g., *Canticle* 30.2–3; 14/15.29; 33.6–9; 16.1 & 8–9; 32.2; 36.5; 24.2–4; 17.5–7.

92. See Cady, Ronan, and Taussig, 84.

93. Examine *Flame* 2.7–8 to see what "completely healthy" in love means.

94. This vision is familiar to the mystics. See, e.g., St. Teresa's experience in *The Book of Her Life,* 40.9–10, *Collected Works*, 1:280–1: "Once while in prayer I was shown quickly, without my seeing any form—but it was a totally clear representation—how all things are seen in God and how [God] holds them all in himself. . . . Let us say . . . that the Divinity is like a very clear diamond, much greater than all the world; or like a mirror, as I said referring to the soul in that other vision, except that it is a mirror in so sublime a way that I wouldn't know how to exaggerate this. And we could say that everything we do is visible in this diamond since it is of such a kind that it contains all things within itself; there is nothing that escapes its magnitude. It was a frightening experience for me to see in so short a time so many things joined together in this diamond."

95. Dichotomies are reconciled and cease to exist when the self is no longer defined by opposition and separation but by relationship and connectedness.

96. I am reminded of an impressive report made some years ago by representatives of the Leadership Conference of Women Religious after atttending a conference with religious of Latin America. The LCWR representatives were deeply moved by the joy, the sense of resurrection, that emanated from the religious of Central America who lived and worked with the poor and oppressed and in many cases lived under death sentences because of their ministry.

97. See also *Canticle* 39.8–9 & 11; 14/15.4 & 9–11 for more on this voice.

98. Here John of the Cross's teaching intersects with Brian Swimme's and Thomas Berry's thinking in *The Universe Story,* 258. They suggest we need an earth-centered language, one enjoyed, until now, only by the mystics and poets: "Beyond any spoken or written language are the languages of the multitude of beings, each of which has its own language given to it generally, in the world of the living, by genetic coding. Yet each individual being has extensive creativity in the use of language. Humans are becoming more sensitive to the nonhuman languages of the surrounding world. We are learning mountain language. . . . This capacity for understanding and communicating in these languages, until now enjoyed only by our poets and mystics, is of immense significance since so much of life is lived in association with the other beings of the universe. . . . A more symbolic language is needed to enter into the subjective depth of things."

99. Elizabeth Johnson, *Women, Earth, and Creator Spirit* (New York: Paulist Press, 1993), 32, with note: Sallie McFague, *Models of God: Theology for an Ecological, Nuclear Age* (Philadelphia: Fortress, 1987), 7–8. Johnson proposes a model of kinship "that traces an organic connection between human beings and the earth."

100. According to Kieran Kavanaugh, *Collected Works of St. John*, 709, John seemed to have accepted the Copernican theory. The University of Salamanca, where John studied, was the first to accept and teach the Copernican system, but by the time the first edition of John's works appeared, Copernicus's work was on the Index of Forbidden Books.

101. Tarnas, 435.

102. For one careful analysis of the evolution of human consciousness, see Johnson, *Women, Earth*, 37–8. I have drawn on her development, aware that recent discoveries in outer space raise questions about the beginning of the universe as well as the evolution of human life and consciousness. Another theory may in time replace the one Johnson describes. Furthermore, other species may evolve with a greater consciousness than our own. Then the cosmos may come to even fuller consciousness in them.

103. See Swimme and Berry, 238.

104. Tarnas, 434–5.

105. Tarnas clarifies that this participatory epistemology is not a "regression to naive participation mystique but . . . the dialectical synthesis of the long evolution from the primordial undifferentiated consciousness through the dualistic alienation. It incorporates the postmodern understanding of knowledge but goes beyond it" (434–5).

106. Tarnas writes with incisive clarity about the progression in history from one paradigm to another, about the birth and death of paradigms and why one paradigm is perceived at one time as a liberation and then at another as a constriction and prison: "For the birth of every new paradigm is also a conception in a new conceptual matrix, which begins the process of gestation, growth, crisis, and revolution all over again. Each paradigm is a stage in an unfolding evolutionary sequence, and when the paradigm has fulfilled its purpose, when it has been developed and exploited to its fullest extent, then it loses its numinosity, it ceases to be libidinally charged, it becomes felt as oppressive, limiting, opaque, something to be overcome—while the new paradigm that is emerging is felt as a liberating birth into a new, luminously intelligible universe. . . . As the inner gestalt changes in the cultural mind, new empirical evidence just happens to appear, pertinent writings from the past suddenly are unearthed, appropriate epistemological jus-tifications are formulated, supportive sociological changes coincidentally take place . . . new psychological predispositions and metaphysical assumptions emerge from the collective mind, from within many individual minds simultaneously" (438–9).

107. See Tarnas, 438, and Johnson, "Redeeming the Name," 116: "Is the Christological tradition hopelessly patriarchal or are there marginalized impulses that can be released to shape a Christology of healing and liberation? With critical analysis and alternative possibilities in view, theology then speaks anew about Jesus the Christ." Moreover, John of the Cross is not the only one in the tradition who was prophetic for a future time concerning wisdom. He stands in a long line of

church writers and mystics. See, for example, Sophia Barbara Moore's treatment of wisdom and Louis de Montfort in "Wisdom, A Hidden Treasure," *Christian Spirituality Bulletin* 3 (Spring 1995): 18–23.

108. Sandra Schneiders writing in *Women and the Word: The Gender of God in the New Testament and the Spirituality of Women* (New York: Paulist Press, 1986) on the Song of Songs, which influenced John so profoundly, says: "As Phyllis Trible has explained, this celebration of human sexual love is completely devoid of patriarchal overtones. In fact scholars continue to be unable to distinguish precisely between the discourse of the woman and the man. . . . Although the androcentric imagination of commentators has always assumed that the male lover is God and the female Israel, the Church, or the soul, there is nothing in the Canticle itself to suggest this. God might just as plausibly be represented by the woman as by the man" (34f). Schneiders's essay provides a powerful underpinning for this entire study.

109. Tarnas, 444 with 435, 442.

110. Ibid., 445.

111. Brian Swimme cited by Sallie McFague, "Imaging a Theology of Nature: The World as God's Body," in *Liberating Life: Contemporary Approaches to Ecological Theology,* ed. Charles Birch, (Maryknoll, NY: Orbis Books, 1990), 225.

112. See Johnson, *Women, Earth,* 28, 60, 63. John could only write with the philosophical assumptions and language of sixteenth-century Spain. Nevertheless, his experience, I believe, surpassed in significant ways the philosophical paradigms of his time. So we struggle with his language, even while we resonate with the experience described.

113. While I am conscious of having done a new critical reading of John of the Cross in retrieving wisdom, I believe that there is another creative step in interpretation that must be taken in contemporary spirituality.

114. The desire for this pervades our society. See, e.g., Michael Crichton, *Travel* (New York: Ballantine Books, 1988) for the account of an unusual lifelong search for contemplative experience. Crichton concludes his book: "We need the insights of the mystic every bit as much as we need the insight of the scientist" (375).

CONTRIBUTORS

Donald W. Buggert, O.Carm., is chair of the department of systematic theology at the Washington Theological Union where he joined the faculty in 1969. He received his S.T.D. in systematic theology at the Catholic University of America. His writings have concentrated on the hermeneutical retrieval through contemporary systematic theology of the Carmelite mystical and prophetic tradition. His articles include "Liberation Theology: Praxis and Contemplation" in *Carmelus* (1987), "Jesus in Carmelite Spirituality" in *The Land of Carmel* (1991), and "St. Jesus orJesus Savior?" in *New Theology Review* (1998).

Kevin Culligan, O.C.D., is a member of the Edith Stein House of Studies affiliated with the Catholic Theological Union at Chicago. During the 1999-2000 academic year, he was writer-in-residence at Saint Mary's College, Notre Dame, Indiana. A licensed psychologist, he began the spiritual direction sequence in the Pastoral Counseling Program at Loyola College, Baltimore. He edited *Spiritual Direction: Contemporary Readings* (1983) and coauthored *Purifying the Heart: Buddhist Insight Meditation for Christians* with Daniel Chowning and Mary Jo Meadow (1994).

Keith J. Egan, T.O.Carm., holds the Joyce McMahon Hank Aquinas Chair in Catholic Theology at Saint Mary's College, Notre Dame, Indiana, and is adjunct professor of theology at Notre Dame University. He is the founder and program director of the Center for Spirituality at St. Mary's

College. He has coedited and contributed to *The Land of Carmel: Essays in Honor of Joachim Smet* (1991) and *Master of the Sacred Page: Essays in Honor of Roland Murphy* (1997). He is also coauthor with Lawrence Cunningham of *Christian Spirituality: Themes from the Tradition* (1996).

Constance FitzGerald, O.C.D., is a member of the community of Carmelite nuns, Baltimore, Maryland, where she has served as prioress andformation directress. She has lectured and written widely on Carmelite spirituality, specializing in the contemporary interpretation of classic Carmelite texts. Her frequently quoted essay, "Impasse and Dark Night," first appeared in *Living with Apocalypse: Spiritual Resource for Social Compassion*, edited by Tilden Edwards (1984). In 1990, she edited *The Carmelite Adventure*, documents related to the first foundation of Carmelite nuns in the United States.

Kieran Kavanaugh, O.C.D., is the American translator of the works of both Saint Teresa of Avila and Saint John of the Cross. His translation of Teresa's *Life,* her spiritual autobiography, was a Book-of-the-Month Clubselection in 1995. He has taught spiritual theology in his order's college of theology and at the Catholic University of America. He has contributed to the *New Catholic Encyclopedia* and other dictionaries and journals. Currently, he is translating St. Teresa's letters, which will complete *The Collected Works of St. Teresa of Avila.*

Ernest Larkin, O.Carm., has spent nearly all his more than fifty years as a Carmelite priest in educational work. In the 1950s, he taught at Whitefriars Hall in Washington, DC, then the major seminary of his community. After teaching throughout the 1960s at the Catholic University of America, he moved to Phoenix, Arizona, where he helped found the Kino Institute. Since 1981, he has been active in promoting Carmelite spirituality in retreats, workshops, and writing. He is the author of *Silent Presence: Discernment as Process and Problem* (1981) and *Christ Within Us* (1984).

Bernard McGinn is the Naomi Shenstone Donnelley Professor of Historical Theology and the History of Christianity at the University of Chicago Divinity School. His numerous writings include books on the history of Christian mysticism, Meister Eckhart, and apocalyptic spirituality. He is the author of the four-volume work in progress, *The Presence of God: A History of Western Christian Mysticism.* He is also a coeditor and contributor to *Christian Spirituality* (1986, 1988) and *The Encyclopedia of Apocalypticsim* (1998).

Vilma Seelaus, O.C.D., is prioress and former formation directress at the Carmelite Monastery, Barrington, Rhode Island. As lecturer and author, she has published in books and spiritual journals here and abroad. She has a special interest in the intersection between psychology and spirituality, as well as world religions and the Carmelite tradition. Her popular audiocasette programs include *Prayer and Human Liberation in Teresa's Interior Castle* (1986), *Teresa's Way of Peacemaking in a Nuclear Age* (1987), and *Live from Your Center: Teresa and the Momentum of Prayer* (1992).

John Welch, O.Carm., is President of the Carmelite Institute in Washington, DC. He received his Ph.D. from Notre Dame University and is now professor at the Washington Theological Union where he specializes in Carmelite spirituality and human development. An award-winning author, he has written *Spiritual Pilgrims: Carl Jung and Teresa of Avila* (1982), *When Gods Die: An Introduction to John of the Cross* (1990), and *The Carmelite Way: An Ancient Path for Today's Pilgrim* (1996).

The Institute of Carmelite Studies promotes research and publication in the field of Carmelite spirituality. Its members are Discalced Carmelites, part of a Roman Catholic community—friars, nuns, and laity—who are heirs to the teaching and way of life of Teresa of Jesus and John of the Cross, men and women dedicated to contemplation and to ministry in the church and the world. Information concerning their way of life is available through local diocesan Vocation offices, or from the Vocation Director's office, 166 Foster Street, Brighton, MA 02135 or 5355 South University Avenue, Chicago, IL 60615.